UNDERSTANDING AND EVALUATING RESEARCH IN APPLIED AND CLINICAL SETTINGS

WAGGONER LIBRARY
DISCARD

UNDERSTANDING AND EVALUATING RESEARCH IN APPLIED AND CLINICAL SETTINGS

George A. Morgan
Jeffrey A. Gliner
Colorado State University

Robert J. Harmon
University of Colorado School of Medicine

In Collaboration With

Helena Chmura Kraemer
Stanford University

Nancy L. Leech
*University of Colorado at Denver
and Health Sciences Center*

Jerry J. Vaske
Colorado State University

WAGGONER LIBRARY
TREVECCA NAZARENE UNIVERSITY

 LAWRENCE ERLBAUM ASSOCIATES, PUBLISHERS
2006   Mahwah, New Jersey   London

Copyright © 2006 by Lawrence Erlbaum Associates, Inc.
All rights reserved. No part of this book may be reproduced in any form, by photostat, microform, retrieval system, or any other means, without the prior written permission of the publisher.

Lawrence Erlbaum Associates, Inc., Publishers
10 Industrial Avenue
Mahwah, New Jersey 07430
www.erlbaum.com

Cover design by Tomai Maridou

Library of Congress Cataloging-in-Publication Data

Morgan, George A. (George Arthur), 1936–
    Understanding and evaluating research in applied and clinical settings /
George A. Morgan, Jeffrey A. Gliner, Robert J. Harmon; in collaboration
with Helena Chmura Kraemer . . . [et. al.].
        p. cm.
    Based on the textbook Research methods in applied settings / Jeffrey A. Gliner and
George A. Morgan. 2000.
    Includes bibliographical references and index.
    ISBN 0-8058-5331-6 (cloth : alk. paper)
    ISBN 0-8058-5332-4 (paper : alk. paper)
    1. Social sciences—Research—Methodology. 2. Psychology—Research—Methodology.
3. Social sciences—Statistical methods. 4. Psychometrics. I. Gliner, Jeffrey A.
II. Harmon, Robert John, 1946– III. Gliner, Jeffrey A. Research methods in applied settings.
IV. Title.

H62.M645 2005
300′.72—dc22   2005046282
                                                                    CIP

Books published by Lawrence Erlbaum Associates are printed on acid-free paper, and their bindings are chosen for strength and durability.

Printed in the United States of America
10 9 8 7 6 5 4 3 2 1

Contents

Preface   ix

Acknowledgments   xiii

I. INTRODUCTORY CHAPTERS

1 Framework and Sample Studies   3

2 Definition, Purposes, and Dimensions of Research   9

3 A Tale of Two Paradigms: Quantitative and Qualitative   14

4 Ethical Problems and Principles in Human Research   18

5 Ethical Issues Related to Publishing and Reviewing   24

II. VARIABLES AND THEIR MEASUREMENT

6 Research Problems and Variables   31

7 Measurement and Descriptive Statistics   36

8 Measurement Reliability   44

9   Measurement Validity   50

10 Data Collection Techniques   59

III. RESEARCH APPROACHES, QUESTIONS, AND DESIGNS

11 Quantitative Research Approaches   69

12 Research Questions and Hypotheses   76

13 Quasi-Experimental Designs   81

14 Randomized Experimental Designs   89

15 Single-Subject Designs   95

16 General Design Classifications   103

IV. INTRODUCTION TO THE EVALUATION OF METHODS AND DESIGN

17 Internal Validity   113

18 Sampling and Population External Validity   122

19 Evaluating the Validity of a Research Study:
        An Introduction   129

V. INTRODUCTION TO INFERENTIAL STATISTICS AND THEIR INTERPRETATION

20 Introduction to Inferential Statistics and
        Hypothesis Testing   143

21 Problems With Null Hypothesis Significance
        Testing (NHST)   152

22 Using Effect Sizes and Confidence Intervals
        to Interpret the Results of a Statistical Test   159

VI. SELECTION AND INTERPRETATION
OF SPECIFIC STATISTICS

23 Selection of Inferential Statistics: An Overview   173

24 Single-Factor Between-Groups Designs: Analysis
and Interpretation   180

25 Single-Factor Repeated-Measures Designs: Analysis
and Interpretation   188

26 Basic Associational Designs: Analysis and Interpretation   195

27 The Chi-Square Test and Accompanying Effect
Size Indices   201

28 Between-Groups Factorial Designs: Analysis
and Interpretation   208

29 Pretest–Posttest Comparison Group Designs:
Analysis and Interpretation   215

30 Use and Interpretation of Multiple Regression   223

31 Logistic Regression and Discriminant Analysis:
Use and Interpretation   229

32 Selection and Use of Inferential Statistics: A Summary   236

33 Interpretation of Alpha, Factor Analysis,
and Principal Components Analysis   246

VII. APPLICATION CHAPTERS

34 Levels of Evidence for Evidence-Based Practice   257

35 Meta-Analysis: Formulation and Interpretation   265

36 Effect Sizes and Clinical Significance   272

VIII.   EVALUATION OF RESEARCH VALIDITY

37   Framework for a Comprehensive Evaluation
of the Research Validity of a Study   285

38   Evaluations of Four Sample Articles   310

Appendix A: Research Validity Evaluation Form   322

Appendix B: Completed Research Validity Evaluation Form   329

Appendix C: Comparative Numerical Evaluations
of the Four Sample Studies   337

Appendix D: Confusing Terms   339

References   344

Author Index   351

Subject Index   357

Preface

In this book, we provide an integrated approach to quantitative research methods, data analysis, and article evaluation for consumers of research, especially those involved in practical or clinical applications. The recent emphasis on evidenced-based practice often leaves practitioners faced with the prospect of having to evaluate journal articles as part of staying abreast within the profession. Few clinicians have had extensive course work in research design and data analysis, and for those who have, it was often many years previous and unrelated to clinical research.

This book is updated and expanded from 33 relatively short articles that were originally published as a series, "Clinicians' Guide to Research Methods and Statistics" for the *Journal of the American Academy of Child and Adolescent Psychiatry*. That series was, in turn, based on a textbook, *Research Methods in Applied Settings: An Integrated Approach to Design and Analysis* (Gliner & Morgan, 2000, ISBN 0-8058–2992-X) published by Lawrence Erlbaum Associates, Inc. (www.erlbaum.com).

Our training and backgrounds are in developmental psychology, experimental psychology, and child psychiatry, respectively. For more than 25 years, we have done research and taught research-related courses in applied departments including psychology, education, occupational therapy, human development and family studies, and psychiatry. Thus, we feel that we have a good grasp of the types of research problems faced by clinicians and researchers in diverse applied areas. These are the type of practitioners that should find this book most helpful.

This book is designed to be user-friendly as well as sophisticated. We have tried to be consistent and clear in terminology and to organize the material so that the various chapters fit together logically. We realize that our attempt to use a consistent framework and terminology are in some places (e.g., research approaches and measurement) nontraditional. However, we think that the framework and consistency pay off in terms of understanding and evaluating research methods and data analysis.

As you can see from the contents, there are 38 chapters divided into eight parts: Introductory Chapters; Variables and Their Measurement; Research Approaches, Questions, and Designs; Introduction to the Evaluation of Methods and Designs; Introduction to Inferential Statistics and Their Interpretation; Selection and Interpretation of Specific Statistics; Application Chapters; and Evaluation of Research Validity.

Our approach is to relate statistics to research design so one can understand why a particular statistical test was used and how to interpret the results. The discussion of data analysis (statistics) is based on preceding chapters about research design. We show how the research approach and design help determine the appropriate statistical analysis.

Our book is neither intended to be an in-depth approach to research design and data analysis, such as Kazdin (2003), nor to be a text on how to conduct research; there already are numerous books in these areas. Instead, we have tried to make the approach conceptual and relatively brief, so that the consumer does not need to read a long chapter to understand why a particular statistic or research design was applied in a particular situation. Each chapter, except for the last two, is quite short and covers a circumscribed topic.

Although we have organized the chapters in a logical order, we also wanted the chapters to "stand alone" as much as possible. This required some repetition, or at least brief redefinition of terms at various points in the text. Thus, the reader should have some flexibility to skip chapters or read them in a different order.

Another strength of this book is the inclusion within the data analysis chapters of what we call "usable statistical information." We explain why statistical significance testing, especially *null hypothesis significance testing* (NHST), is often misleading and does not provide the information that is of most use to the clinician. A statistically significant finding is often misinterpreted as indicating the strength of the outcome or relationship. *Effects sizes* do describe the strength of relationships between variables. Therefore, we provide information on effect sizes to accompany particular statistical tests. Several different effect sizes, their relative strengths and weaknesses, and how they should be interpreted are described.

Part VII includes three application chapters that should be helpful to the clinician. Effect size computation and understanding are the foundations for research synthesis and *meta-analysis*, which we describe in chapter 35. Practitioners frequently use meta-analysis to provide evidence for therapeutic interventions (practice); *evidence-based practice* is discussed in chapter 34. In chapter 36, we discuss clinical significance and strengths and weaknesses of a number of relevant indices such as odds-ratios, risk reduction, and number needed to treat. We also discuss a relatively new effect size, AUC or the probability of a better outcome, which has advantages for helping to interpret clinical or practical significance. We have found that this clinical index based on a 2 by 2 contingency table is less potentially misleading than odds ratios, and it is easier to explain than traditional effect size measures such as *d* or *r* so it may facilitate communication between the practitioner and the lay person.

The book emphasizes becoming a good consumer of research by analyzing and evaluating examples of research articles. At several points we present an integrated framework for the analysis and evaluation of research studies, using eight rating scales to evaluate *research validity* (i.e., the validity of a whole study). Chapter 37, "A Framework for a Comprehensive Evaluation of the Research Validity of a Study," is especially helpful as a step-by-step guide with accompanying figures and tables to facilitate the review process. A number of other diagrams and tables that summarize various topics and show how concepts fit together are presented throughout our book.

There are four appendixes: (a) a blank article evaluation form that may be copied to use in evaluating articles, (b) a completed evaluation form to provide a detailed example of how we use the evaluation framework and form, (c) a side-by-side comparison of the proposed numerical evaluation of four sample studies, and (d) a listing of terms that are either synonymous or are used to mean similar things, perhaps in different disciplines. For example, *intervention* and *treatment* are similar terms.

This final appendix should be especially helpful to practitioners and students from various disciplines who may have taken a research and/or statistics course that used somewhat different terminology than we do here. Realizing this inconsistency across and even within disciples, we developed appendix D. The first part of this appendix provides sets of terms that are partly the same, but have different meanings and need to be distinguished. For example, *research validity* (chapter 19) is not the same as *measurement validity* (chapter 9). The second part of appendix D provides a list of terms, organized by chapter, that are essentially synonyms.

Although the book is based primarily on the quantitative research paradigm, one chapter deals in some depth with how the *qualitative or naturalist/constructivist paradigm* differs from the *quantitative or positivist paradigm*. In a number of chapters we point out the value of qualitative research, which should lead quantitative researchers to be more flexible and take into account the criticisms by qualitative researchers. Also, we point out what we think are the weaknesses of the qualitative paradigm.

   Another feature of this book is that it includes many examples taken mostly from applied or clinical journals. These examples should provide context and help facilitate the understanding of concepts because they were published in journals whose subscribers are interested in practical application. We introduce four of these studies in chapter 1 along with our framework for classifying types of research or *research approaches*. These examples are used in several later chapters and are evaluated comprehensively in our last two chapters.

Acknowledgments

This book is based on the Gliner and Morgan (2000) textbook, *Research Methods in Applied Settings* (ISBN 0-8058-2992-X), also published by Lawrence Erlbaum Associates, Inc. (www.erlbaum.com). We acknowledge the use of several tables, figures, and some text from that book. Chapters 22, 32, and 33 reprint some materials, including text, tables, and figures, from Leech, Barrett, and Morgan (2005) *SPSS for Intermediate Statistics* (ISBN 0-8058-4790-1) also published by Lawrence Erlbaum Associates, so we thank our colleagues, Nancy Leech and Karen Barrett, for use of those materials.

We also appreciate and acknowledge that Lippincott, Williams, and Wilkins (LWW), publisher of the *Journal of the American Academy of Child and Adolescent Psychiatry* (JAACAP), granted permission to republish edited versions of the 33 articles in the "Clinician's Guide to Research Methods and Statistics." Special thanks to Cordelia Slaughter of LWW for facilitating this permission and providing us with electronic copies of the articles to use as the starting point for the book. We also appreciate the encouragement and editorial assistance of Mina Dulcan, editor of JAACAP, who initially commissioned the Clinician's Guide series and encouraged us to find a source to republish these columns.

Next we acknowledge the help of our colleagues and collaborators, Helena Chmura Kraemer, Nancy Leech, and Jerry Vaske, who provided feedback on parts of this text and were coauthors on one or more of the original columns. We especially appreciate the critiques and advice of Helen Kraemer, professor of biostatistics at the Stanford University Medical School, who served as statistical consultant for the Clinician's Guide series in the JAACAP. We appreciate the advice and feedback of these collaborators, but we, the authors, take responsibility for the content of the book and any errors that might be identified.

We would like to thank several reviewers: Maura MacPhee, Mina Dulcan, Kenneth Solberg, Karen Atler, Brian Isaacson, and Marty Drell for their helpful reviews. Several colleagues, Robert Fetsch, Gail Gliner, Ray Yang, Mark Kretovics, and Gene Gloeckner also provided helpful reviews of certain chapters. Students in our classes have provided useful suggestions for improving the manuscript at several points in its development.

Our word processor, Catherine Lamana, was especially helpful in producing the final manuscript. Nancy Plummer was essential to the development of the manuscript for the JAACAP Clinician's Guide series, and Don Quick's technical help was critical.

Finally, we want to thank our spouses, Hildy, Gail, and Darlene, for their support during the writing of this book and over the years.

—*GAM, JAG, RJH*

Part I

INTRODUCTORY CHAPTERS

Chapter 1

Framework and Sample Studies

In this chapter, we describe our overall framework for quantitative research designs and then describe briefly several studies that are used in later chapters as examples, especially for demonstrating how to evaluate a research study. For this purpose, we have selected some of our own studies as well as those of other researchers, in part to show that all studies, including our own, have weaknesses as well as strengths.

RESEARCH TYPES AND APPROACHES

In this book, all quantitative research is divided into three main types that we call experimental, non-experimental, and descriptive. The first two types of research each have two approaches as follows:

Experimental Research

1. *Randomized experimental* approach (random assignment of participants to groups with an active or manipulated independent variable[1]).
2. *Quasi-experimental* approach (an active independent variable but without random assignment of participants to groups).

---

[1]A *variable* is a characteristic of a person or situation that has two or more values (it varies) in a study. An *active independent variable* is one such as a treatment, workshop, or other intervention that is given to one group of participants and withheld or given in another form to another group. An *attribute independent variable* is one that is not given or withheld in the study. It is a measure of a characteristic of the person or his/her situation.

Nonexperimental Research

3. *Comparative* (in which a few groups, based on an attribute independent variable, are compared; e.g., males are compared to females).

4. *Associational* (sometimes called correlational, in which two or more usually continuous variables are related or associated for the same group of participants). Again the independent variable is an attribute rather than active.

Descriptive Research

5. *Descriptive approach* (answers descriptive questions using only descriptive, not inferential, statistics).

Complex studies often use more than one of these approaches; for example, "survey" studies may have descriptive as well as comparative and associational research questions. Of the hundreds of studies that we have evaluated, all fit into one or more of these five categories based on the research questions and data analysis. Chapter 11 presents this categorization scheme in more detail.

There are several reasons to categorize research or, more accurately, research questions, into one of the five approaches. First, we feel that questions of *cause and effect* can be answered best with well-controlled randomized experiments and to a lesser extent with the quasi-experimental approach. Neither the comparative nor the associational approach is well suited to deal with cause and effect, but we realize that some complex statistics such as cross-lag panel correlations and structural equation modeling may provide some evidence for causality from nonexperimental studies. Furthermore, most *meta-analyses* (see chap. 35) separate studies by research approach. For example, experimental and nonexperimental studies often are not combined but instead make up separate meta-analyses. Some of these meta-analyses, composed completely of nonexperimental or observational studies, may be weak on *internal validity* (see chap. 17). However, they may be strong in *external validity* (chap. 18) and provide important information for clinical practice.

Our classification of research approaches and Fig. 1.1 should help the reader follow the research process from purpose through question/hypothesis to data analysis. For example, the experimental, quasi-experimental, and comparative approaches typically use what we call *difference inferential statistics* such as the *t* test or analysis of variance, whereas the associational approach uses *associational inferential statistics* such as correlation and multiple regression. As discussed later, all parametric inferential statistics are relational (special cases of canonical correlation), but we think that it is helpful educationally to make the preceding distinction, which is consistent with most basic statistics books.

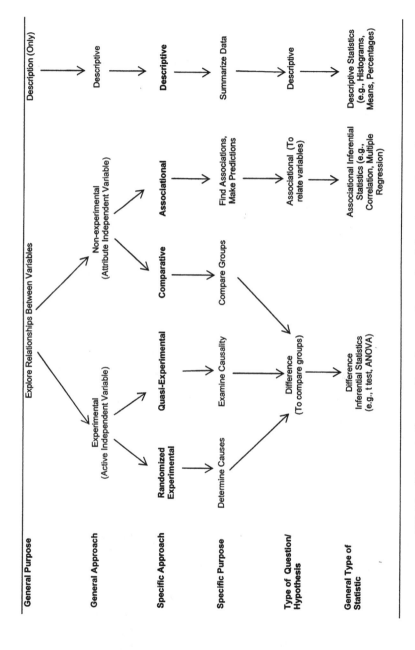

FIG. 1.1.   Schematic diagram of how the general type of statistic and research question correspond to the purpose and approach of the study.

SAMPLE STUDIES

In chapter 19, we provide an introduction to the research validity evaluation framework that we recommend. This framework is based on an earlier one by Cook and Campbell (1979) and several more recent updates, including our own (Gliner & Morgan, 2000). The study we use to illustrate how to do this brief overview evaluation is one by Gliner and Sample (1996). A brief description of that study is as follows.

Study 1, a Randomized Experiment. The purpose of the Gliner and Sample (1996) study was to increase quality of life for persons with developmental disabilities who were employed in sheltered work or supported employment, using an intervention of community life options. The key independent variables were the intervention (vs. no intervention), the type of employment (sheltered vs. supported), and change over time (pretest and four follow-ups at 6-month intervals). The Quality of Life Index (QLI) had three subscales so there were three outcome/dependent measures. The approach was randomized experimental because participants were randomly assigned to either the community life option or their present situation. The QLI had been used in several published studies that had reported good reliability coefficients (see chap. 8). The published studies also provided evidence in support of the measurement validity (see chap. 9) of the QLI with similar types of clients. The study attempted to achieve high internal validity (see chap. 17) by randomly assigning participants to the groups. The study also attempted to achieve high external ecological (see chap. 18) validity by carrying out the conditions in the actual community setting. However, obtaining good overall research validity on all dimensions could not be accomplished.

In chapter 37 we provide a comprehensive research validity evaluation framework, and in chapter 38 we evaluate Gliner and Sample (1996) and three more studies, including another one of ours, to show how a range of studies, experimental and nonexperimental, can be evaluated. Brief descriptions of these other studies are.

Study 2, a Quasi-Experiment. This study, titled "Using Short-Term Group Counseling with Visually Impaired Adolescents" (Johnson & Johnson, 1991), used the quasi-experimental approach because there was an active independent variable (group counseling) but the participants could not be randomly assigned to the two groups (counseling or no counseling). The groups are considered nonequivalent even though the researchers attempted to match the groups on age, IQ, race, and sex. There was potentially another independent variable (change over time) because there were pretests and posttests on the three dependent or outcome variables: self-concept, attitudes toward blindness, and locus of control. Three hypotheses stated that group counseling would produce more improvement in each of the three dependent variables.

Study 3, Nonexperimental, Using the Comparative Approach. DiLorenzo, Hapler, and Picone (2004) compared older (60–85 years old) and younger (29–59 years old) persons with multiple sclerosis on physical functioning, mental health, and quality of life. The independent variable, age, is an attribute that for this study had two levels, older and younger. The duration of illness was another independent variable. There were many dependent or outcome variables that fell into the three broad categories of physical functioning, mental health, and quality of life. The approach was basically comparative (older vs. younger).

Study 4, Nonexperimental, Using the Associational Approach. Redding, Harmon, and Morgan (1990) examined the relationship between maternal depression and infants' mastery behavior in a nonclinical sample of 1- and 2-year-olds and their mothers. The attribute independent or predictor variable was the degree of self-reported maternal depression. The three dependent outcome variables were infant competence at the mastery tasks (puzzles), their persistence at the more challenging tasks, and task pleasure, all observed in a laboratory playroom. Puzzles of varying difficulty were presented one at a time to the infants. The approach was associational because the independent variable maternal depression had many ordered levels.

The Mastery Motivation Program of Research. Another series of studies, related to the Redding et al. (1990) study, which we use as examples in the next chapter and several others, has to do with mastery motivation in young children (see Morgan, Harmon, & Maslin-Cole, 1990). For this research, we developed a new standardized behavioral testing procedure and an adult report questionnaire to assess the motivation of young children to master challenging tasks. The procedures were designed to be useful for normally developing children and also for children who are at risk for developmental problems. The "individualized method" of presenting behavioral tasks was designed to compare the motivation of children with different ability levels by varying the difficulty of the task in accordance with the child's ability level. Each child was given tasks that were moderately difficult for him or her. Each child's motivation was assessed with one task, from each of several graded sets of similar tasks (e.g., puzzles), that was found to be challenging, but not too difficult or too easy, for that individual child. Evidence for good interobserver reliability was obtained for the two key measures: persistence at challenging tasks and pleasure after completing a part of the task. The validity of these mastery task measures has been supported in several ways.

First, groups of children (such as those who are at risk or handicapped) who had been predicted to score lower on mastery motivation measures than appropriate comparison groups did, in general, score lower. Second, there were significant relationships between persistence at tasks and several other measures expected to reflect aspects of the concept of mastery motivation, for example, ratings of persistence during mental tests, engrossment during free play, and mother and teacher ratings of motivation (see MacTurk & Morgan, 1995).

The other assessment method, the Dimensions of Mastery Questionnaire (DMQ), was designed to provide a quicker and less labor-intensive assessment of young children's functioning than that gained from lengthier behavioral testing. Mothers, fathers, and teachers can complete the DMQ to rate children they know well. The DMQ has been used by a number of investigators, and data from more than 30 samples were reported (Morgan et al., 1993). Studies with previous versions of the DMQ (see Morgan et al., 1993; Morgan, Busch-Rossnagel, Barrett, & Harmon, 2005) provide support for its validity by the ability to differentiate low- and high-risk populations on mastery-related behavior and by relationships between maternal ratings, teacher ratings, and child behavioral measures. For example, the DMQ competence scale was found in two studies to be significantly related to the Bayley Mental Developmental Index.

In the next chapter we provide a definition of research, describe its dimensions, and discuss several purposes, using the mastery motivation example.

Chapter 2

Definition, Purposes, and Dimensions of Research

What is research? Smith (1981) suggested that a synonym for research is *disciplined inquiry* which

> must be conducted and reported so that its logical argument can be carefully examined; it does not depend on surface plausibility or the eloquence, status, or authority of its author; error is avoided; evidential test and verification are valued; the dispassionate search for truth is valued over ideology. Every piece of research or evaluation, whether naturalistic, experimental, survey, or historical, must meet these standards to be considered disciplined. (p. 585)

Smith's definition of disciplined inquiry points out the systematic nature of research. Regardless of the particular research paradigm, there must be underlying guidelines of how the research is to be carried out. The research must be disseminated (i.e., published in a journal or presented at a professional meeting), with a detailed description of the methods used. Unless the research is reported, others cannot utilize or examine it to determine whether they would come to the same conclusion. Smith's definition also refers to the fact that the research must stand on its own merit, not the status of the researcher or the eloquence of the writing.

PURPOSES OF RESEARCH

Research has two general purposes: (a) increasing knowledge within the discipline and (b) increasing knowledge within oneself as a professional consumer of research in order to evaluate and understand new developments within the discipline (Ottenbacher, 1986). Increasing knowledge within the discipline can serve several subpurposes:

1. To create methods to assess important concepts/phenomena.
2. To describe relevant phenomena and their relationships.
3. To provide evidence for the efficacy of a therapeutic technique or other change.
4. To provide support for the theoretical base of the discipline.

For many clinicians, the ability to understand research in one's discipline may be even more important than making research contributions to the profession. Dissemination of new knowledge occurs through an exceptionally large number of professional journals, workshops, and continuing education courses, as well as popular literature such as newspapers. Today's professional cannot simply rely on the statements of a workshop instructor or newspaper to determine what should be included in an intervention. Even journal articles need to be scrutinized for weak designs, inappropriate data analyses, or incorrect interpretation of these analyses. Current professionals must have the research and reasoning skills to be able to make sound decisions and support them. In addition, research skills can make professionals in therapeutic sciences better providers because they know how to assess their own clients and note whether improvement has occurred.

RESEARCH DIMENSIONS AND DICHOTOMIES

Theoretical Versus Applied

Most clinical science disciplines perform research with some application in mind. The goal of the research is directed toward some specific, practical use, such as treatment, learning enhancement, or evaluation. Some theoretical research also is performed, as mentioned earlier, but most of the research projects that we will examine are on the applied end of this dimension.

Laboratory Versus Field

A second dimension for examining research is the setting. The term field takes on many different meanings. Field could be a clinic, school, or home setting. Laboratory implies a structured setting that is not where the subjects or participants usually live, work, or obtain therapy. In the behavioral sciences, a laboratory often refers to a room with a video camera and microphones (i.e., a somewhat unnatural setting). Clinical disciplines perform research in both laboratory and field settings. Laboratory settings provide better control over extraneous variables, but field settings provide a more ecologically valid environment.

Self-Report Versus Researcher Observation

In some studies the participants report to the researcher (in writing or orally) about their attitudes, intentions, or behavior. In other studies the researcher directly observes and records the behavior of the participant. Sometimes instruments such as heart rate monitors are used by researchers to "observe" the participants' physiological functioning. Self-reports may be influenced by biases such as the halo effect, or participants may have forgotten or have not thought about the topic. Many researchers prefer observed behavioral data. However, sensitive, well-trained interviewers may be able to establish rapport with participants to alleviate some of the biases inherent in self-reports.

Quantitative Versus Qualitative Research

We believe that this topic is more appropriately thought of as three related dimensions. The first dimension deals with philosophical or paradigm differences in the approach to research. The second dimension, which is what many persons mean when referring to this dichotomy, deals with the type of data and data collection method. The third dimension refers to the type of data analysis. We think that, in distinguishing between qualitative and quantitative research, the first dimension (i.e., the philosophical dichotomy we have called positivistic versus constructivist) is the most important.

Positivist Versus Constructivist Paradigms.   The term *positivist* is not an accurate label for most quantitative social scientists, but it is commonly used by qualitative/constructivist writers and it helps us separate the philosophical or paradigm distinction from the data collection and analysis issues. Likewise, constructivist is not the most common identifier for what is often called the naturalist or qualitative paradigm, but we prefer it for reasons discussed in the next chapter. For now, note that a study could be theoretically positivistic, but the data could be subjective or qualitative. In fact, this combination is quite common. On the other hand, a researcher may embrace the constructivist paradigm, but some of the supporting data may be quantitative. Thus, the type of data and even data analyses are not necessarily the same as the research paradigm. However, qualitative data, methods, and analyses often go with the constructivist paradigm, and quantitative data, methods, and analyses are usually used with the positivist paradigm. The approach of this book is within the framework of the so-called positivist paradigm, but the constructivist paradigm provides us with useful reminders that human participants are complex and different from other animals and inanimate objects. Thus, as investigators of human behavior, we should not be overly dependent on the philosophy and methods of natural science.

Quantitative Versus Qualitative Data and Data Collection. Quantitative data are said to be "objective," which indicates that the behaviors are easily classified or quantified by the researcher. Some examples are demographic variables, such as age and gender, scores on tests, and time to recovery. The data are usually gathered with some sort of instrument (e.g., test, physiological device, questionnaire) that can be scored reliably with relatively little training.

Qualitative data are more difficult to describe. They are said to be "subjective," which indicates that they are hard to classify or score. Some examples are perceptions of pain, feelings about work, and attitudes toward therapy. Usually these data are gathered from interviews, observations, or documents such as biographies. Quantitative/positivist researchers also gather these types of data but usually translate such perceptions, feelings, and attitudes into numbers using, for example, rating scales. Qualitative/constructivist researchers, on the other hand, usually do not try to quantify such perceptions, instead categorizing them. We believe that the approach of this book is useful for dealing with both qualitative/subjective data and quantitative/objective data.

It is important to point out that researchers within both the quantitative/positivist paradigm and the qualitative/constructivist paradigm use interview and observational methods and both are interested in objective as well as subjective data. However, constructivist researchers prefer more open-ended interviews, observations, and documents such as diaries. Positivist researchers prefer more structured interviews (or questionnaires), observations, and documents such as clinic records.

Quantitative Versus Qualitative Data Analysis. In later chapters we discuss when to use the most common inferential statistics, show how they are related to the approaches and designs, and review how to interpret the results. Qualitative data analysis involves various methods for coding, categorizing, and assigning meaning to the data, which are usually words or images. This book does not deal with qualitative data analysis techniques, such as content analysis, but they have been addressed by some researchers within the positivist paradigm. Constructivist researchers rarely use inferential statistics but sometimes use descriptive statistics.

EXAMPLES AND RELATIONSHIPS
AMONG THE FOUR DICHOTOMIES

In terms of increasing knowledge in the field, the mastery motivation program of research, described in chapter 1, is an example of the development of data collection methods using both self-reports (questionnaire) and observations (behavioral tasks). The paradigm was clearly positivist/quantitative, but the data (infants' motivation to master) were subjective. The data were coded as task-directed or not, and then quantified as the duration of task-directed behavior (labeled as *persistence at tasks*). The research was mostly theoretical, attempting to test some of Robert White's (1963) notions about competence/effectance motivation, but also there were potential applications for early intervention. Testing of children was performed in a laboratory playroom, but some of the questionnaires and observations were done in the field/home.

The Gliner and Sample (1996) study was actually a multimethod study using both quantitative data collection methods (the Quality of Life Index, QLI) and quantitative data analysis but also three qualitative/constructivist case studies. The QLI was a self-report measure, but the Gliner and Sample study also used ratings of the quality of life made by recreational therapists who had observed the participants during the intervention.

Certain ends of the four dimensions or dichotomies described above tend, in practice, to go together. Qualitative research is almost always conducted in the field. On the other hand, theoretically oriented research tends to be done in the laboratory, using researcher observations. However, there is not a necessary association among any of these four dimensions. In the next chapter, we discuss the quantitative and qualitative paradigms in more depth.

Chapter 3

A Tale of Two Paradigms:
Quantitative and Qualitative

There is confusion in the social and health sciences about the difference between quantitative and qualitative approaches to research. Much of the confusion, as indicated in the last chapter, comes from equating these paradigms with the way data are collected. Investigators often associate "subjective" methods of data collection, such as open-ended interviews, with the qualitative approach and "objective" methods of data collection with the quantitative approach. The type of data collection is not adequate to distinguish between the two paradigms.

PARADIGMS

What is a paradigm? The term, coined by Kuhn (1970), refers to the beliefs shared by members of a specific scientific community. It is not strictly a methodology but more of a philosophy that guides how the research is to be conducted. A paradigm determines the type of questions that will be asked and how they will be answered.

There currently are two major paradigms within the social and health sciences. One paradigm, often referred to as the quantitative paradigm, has been the dominant one and is usually associated with the so-called "scientific method." Qualitative theorists (e.g., Lincoln & Guba, 1985) use the term *logical positivist* to identify the dominant paradigm. Even though the term is not totally appropriate, we use *positivist* when referring to the quantitative paradigm, in part to distinguish it from quantitative data collection and analysis. The other paradigm, referred to by Lincoln and Guba (1985) as *naturalistic* or *constructivist*, is usually associated with a qualitative approach to research (see also Phillips & Burbules, 2000).

Lincoln and Guba (1985) stated five axioms or issues, from their point of view as qualitative researchers, that separate the two paradigms. Since that time, they have modified their position somewhat, but it is instructive to examine these original five issues in some detail to gain a clearer picture of the differences between the two paradigms.

Issue 1: The Nature of Reality

Is there one reality or are there multiple realities? This issue is the most divisive because seemingly there are either many realities (constructivist) or one (positivist); both positions cannot exist at the same time. We think that part of the issue comes from the lack of an agreed-on definition of reality. Phillips (1992) pointed out that there is confusion because different people and different cultures have different views about what is real (which seems undeniable). In addition, there is the issue of whether or not we can know which view is correct, or even whether there is a correct view. Because we might not be able to reach agreement, it does not follow that there is more than one "reality."

Quantitative researchers, recognizing that participants have different perspectives or points of view, report those as variability. In addition, quantitative studies often examine factors that are related to and perhaps cause different perceptions. That a person states a belief does not necessarily mean that it is "real," even for that person. Sometimes people lie or are confused about their beliefs. It seems to us that it is important to acknowledge that people have different perceptions, but it is best to investigate *why* perceptions seem to be different and to be cautious about assuming that what one says is what one really believes.

Issue 2: The Relationship of Knower to Known

Can investigators and participants be in a study without influencing each other? "Double-blind" studies acknowledge this issue by having both the participants and the researcher be unaware of the conditions of the study (i.e., who was in the experimental groups and who was in the control group). However, only naive investigators would argue that their observations are not influenced by attributes of who is observed. The issue for the positivist is to determine how much of the outcome might be due to these effects. For the constructivists, how much difference does it make if the observer is a participant as compared to a "silent" observer? We think that issue two separates the approaches on a relative rather than absolute basis.

The positivist is usually more confident that bias can be overcome, but both paradigms need to be sensitive to this issue.

Issue 3: The Possibility of Generalization

Can the results of an individual study be generalized to other populations, settings, treatment variables, and measurement variables? Lincoln and Guba (1985) were correct that few studies using a positivist approach have employed proper sampling techniques. Usually, participants are not randomly sampled from a target population. Instead, participants are usually obtained from a "convenience" sample, often found at the investigator's clinic.

The constructivist professes to make no claims for generalizing the results beyond what was found in the study, but many qualitative studies seem to make conclusions beyond the specifics of their findings. Meta-analyses allow quantitative investigators to combine studies to make better generalizations. This issue seems to separate the two approaches on a relative rather than absolute basis. Researchers from both approaches should be cautious about generalizing their results.

Issue 4: The Possibility of Causal Linkages

Can we identify causes? Regarding this philosophical issue, positivists believe that under the proper experimental conditions, one can conclude that the independent variable "caused" the change (effect) in the dependent variable. These proper conditions include the random assignment of participants to groups. However, few positivists are willing to make more than a probability statement about causes.

Constructivists rule out the concept of causality on many grounds, but perhaps the most salient is their position that most events have multiple causes. We agree with this position as would most quantitative researchers. Lincoln and Guba (1985) took a much stronger stance on the issue of causality, suggesting that it is impossible to separate cause and effect. Instead, they introduced the concept of mutual simultaneous shaping. They argued that "everything influences everything else. . . . Many elements are implicated in any given action, and each element interacts with all of the others in ways that change them all" (pp. 151–152).

There is no way to resolve differences between the two paradigms on issue four. Lincoln and Guba (1985) were certainly correct in pointing out that much behavior is both cause and effect, that there is mutual simultaneous shaping of behavior, and that causes and effects are difficult, if not impossible, to distinguish. Also, it is true that journalists, the public, and even researchers are too loose in using words like "cause," "impact," and "determinant." In fact, one of the key points that we want to make in this book is that such words should be used with caution and then probably only after performing a study with a tight, randomized experimental design.

Issue 5: The Role of Values in Inquiry

Can researchers be unbiased? It is important for all researchers to recognize that research is not value-free. One might ask the positivist, "Who selected the research problem, variables, sample, or particular treatment?" Of course, the investigator selected all aspects of the study. Therefore, the constructivists are correct in assuming that research is not value-free. A part of a constructivist research report is to state the biases of the investigator, or to "come clean."

That the investigator may have a bias, however, does not necessarily mean that nothing can be done about that bias or that the outcome will be in the direction of the investigator's hypotheses. There are probably far more studies that fail to find significant differences between treatment and control groups than those that find significant differences. Furthermore, replication attempts by other researchers help to ensure that something other than the investigator's bias is influencing the results.

Issue 5 appears to separate the two paradigms on a relative basis. The degree of subjectivity in most constructivist studies, in which the investigator is the "instrument," seems to us far greater than that in the positivist approach. However, this difference is not all-or-nothing. Researchers in both paradigms should acknowledge that there will be subjectivity and bias; however, they should do what they can to minimize the potential effects of biases.

These issues lead to the following question: In the social and health sciences, is the purpose of research to predict and discover causes? The answer to this question provides a distinction between the two paradigms in how research should be carried out. We believe that if the purpose of the study is to identify causes and predict behavior, then a methodology for carrying out this research developed from the traditional scientific methods should be undertaken. Alternatively, if the purpose of research is a full description of the participants' "voices," then a methodology based on constructivism seems to be well adapted to the problem.

Chapter 4

Ethical Problems and Principles in Human Research

HISTORICAL OVERVIEW

Although there have been ethical problems regarding the treatment of human subjects throughout history, it is common to begin with the Nazi "research" atrocities of 1933–1945. Nazi research atrocities refer to experiments conducted by respected German doctors on concentration camp inmates that led to their mutilation or death. Surprisingly, before 1933 Germany had advanced moral and legal regulations concerning consent and special protections for vulnerable subjects. As a result of the trial of 23 of these doctors, the Nuremberg code was prescribed by an international court in 1947 (see Shuster, 1997). Although it is tempting to think that these deeds could be blamed on prison guards, or rogue scientists, the evidence indicates otherwise (e.g., Pross, 1992).

Examples of ethical problems in American research are not uncommon. Mentally impaired children from the Willowbrook State School in New York were given live hepatitis A virus. Some say that their parents were not adequately informed and were even coerced into volunteering their children for the study. A second example was the Tuskegee study of the natural course of syphilis, which took place between 1932 and 1972. The study involved more than 400 impoverished African American men in Alabama who were studied but not treated, even though antibiotics were available and commonly used to treat syphilis for more than 25 years of the study. In the African American community, the long-term effects of this study include mistrust and suspicion of medical research and of doctors in general.

In 1974 the Department of Health, Education and Welfare published regulations on the protection of human subjects. They mandated that there be institutional review boards (IRBs) at each research institution accepting federal funding to determine whether subjects were placed at risk and, if so, whether the risks were so outweighed by the benefits and importance of the knowledge to be gained that the subjects should be allowed to accept these risks.

PRINCIPLES AND POLICIES RELATED TO HUMAN RESEARCH PARTICIPANTS

The Belmont Report: Principles and Norms

In a report called the Belmont Report (National Commission, 1978), the National Commission for the Protection of Human Subjects of Biomedical and Behavioral Research identified three ethical principles and guidelines for the protection of human subjects.

Respect for Persons. This principle incorporates two ethical convictions. First, participants should be treated as autonomous agents, which means that the individual is capable of deliberating and making individual decisions and choices. Second, persons with diminished autonomy, such as children, the mentally retarded, and persons with emotional disorders, are entitled to protection.

Beneficence. Researchers should not harm participants, and good outcomes should be maximized for the participants as well as for science and humanity. This principle requires maximizing the potential benefits and minimizing the risks.

Justice. Research should not be exploitative, and there should be a fair distribution of risks and benefits. For example, those who bear most of the risks should benefit the most from the research. Participants should not be selected merely on the basis of convenience.

Voluntary Informed Consent

Informed consent is the procedure by which persons choose whether or not they wish to participate in a study. Consent is an ongoing process and may be withdrawn at any time during the study. The Belmont Report discusses three aspects of informed consent.

Information.   The information provided to participants should include the research procedure, purpose, risks, and anticipated benefits, including what a reasonable volunteer would want to know before giving consent. The information must be in language that the participants can understand, and efforts should be made to check that it is understood, especially when risks are involved.

Comprehension.   The participants should have the legal capacity and the ability to understand the information and risks involved so that they can make an informed decision. Some participants (e.g., children) are not legally qualified to make decisions of consent for themselves, so others must make the decision for them. This is usually the parent or guardian, but the child also must assent to the procedure. Comprehension also may be impaired in mentally retarded or emotionally disabled persons. To the extent possible, these persons should be allowed to assent or not, but a third party (e.g., the legal guardian) should be chosen to act in their best interest.

Voluntariness.   The third aspect of informed consent means that the participant freely, without threat or undue inducement, has decided to participate in the study. There should not be any element of deceit, constraint, or coercion. Persons in authority can elicit unjustifiable obedience from children and even from well-educated adults. Also voluntariness is reduced when the research offers financial or other inducements that the potential participants would find hard to refuse. Sieber (1992) listed a number of aspects of the consent process that should be considered. Rapport should be achieved, not only because participants are more likely to cooperate, but because it can strengthen the ecological validity of the study. It is important that the researcher not rush through this aspect of the study or give the impression that consent is unnecessary. Developing trust and understanding personal and cultural situations is important, especially for community-based research done in cultures that are different from the researcher's. The research also should be relevant to the concerns of the research population and explained in those terms.

The issue of who should provide the consent is easy when the potential participant is an adult who has the capacity to consent. The issue is less clear with children. We should not automatically assume that parental or guardian consent is sufficient, although in most cases it should be. In some situations there may be a conflict of interest. For example, poor parents offered large payment for their children's participation might not have the interest of the child foremost. How is consent obtained? IRBs require a formal signed consent form, except in certain situations specified in the federal regulations. A signed consent form may be omitted when adult subjects who have the legal capacity to consent can easily refuse by discontinuing a phone call with an interviewer or by not returning the survey that was received in the mail. It is important, however, that the interviewer or questionnaire cover letter describe the purpose of the research and any risks involved and state that participation is voluntary. Returning the survey or answering the questions is the subject's way of implying consent.

Privacy

Much of behavioral research involves asking participants to reveal some aspects of their behavior or attitudes. *Privacy* refers to participants' concern about controlling access to information about themselves (Sieber, 1992). Voluntary informed consent involves the participant agreeing to reveal certain aspects that may have been private previously. If participants feel that privacy is being invaded or confidentiality will not be maintained, answers that they provide may be distorted and, therefore, give misleading or false information. The essence of privacy is that the participant is free to choose the extent to which his or her attitudes, beliefs, and behaviors are to be shared with or withheld from others. There is always the potential for a conflict between the right of privacy and the goal of the research.

If the data are anonymous, the participant may be more willing to share. It is important to make a distinction between confidentiality and anonymity. *Anonymity* means that the person's name and other identifiers, such as a Social Security number, are not known and cannot be deduced by the researcher or others. In many studies the data cannot be anonymous because the researcher sees the participants face to face or must know their identity to match information about them from different sources. In all cases it is important that the data remain *confidential.* That is, there is an agreement that private information will remain private to the researcher, and the participant will not be identifiable in the reports or in conversations with persons outside of the research team.

Sensitive researchers will be very careful not to invade the privacy of participants, and IRBs are typically alert to this issue. This implies that fully informed voluntary consent will be obtained ahead of time and that the researcher will assure confidentiality of the data. The participants can then decide whether or not to participate. Participants who view the research as an invasion of privacy may feel some subtle pressure to participate but then distort answers. Thus, to be sensitive to the participant's concerns and to obtain the best data, it is important to consider whether participants view the research as an invasion of privacy. To learn about the privacy interests of your research population, you should ask persons who are members of the population whether they might find your questions an invasion of privacy.

Assessment of Risks and Benefits

Probably the most important concern about research ethics is that the individuals not be harmed by serving as participants in the study. *Risk* refers both to the probability of harm and to the magnitude and type of harm. There are many possible harms and benefits that need to be taken into account. Psychological and physical pain or injuries are the most often discussed, but other risks, such as legal, economic, or social (e.g., embarrassment, stigmatization, or invasion of one's privacy), should be considered.

Although it is rare to attempt to quantify the risks and benefits of a particular research study, there should be a systematic assessment of these factors. The Belmont Report states that the assessment of whether the research is justifiable should reflect at least five considerations:

1. Brutal or inhumane treatment is never justified.
2. Risks should be reduced to those that are necessary and consideration given to alternative procedures that would reduce risks.
3. When research involves risks of serious harm, review committees should be very careful that the benefits justify those risks. For example, in medical research, an unproven treatment may promise significant benefits even though there are risks of serious side effects.
4. When vulnerable populations are involved, the appropriateness of using them should be demonstrated.
5. Relevant risks and benefits must be fairly explained in the informed consent procedure and form.

In addition to minimizing the risks, it is important for researchers to maximize the benefits. This may be relatively easy to do in community-based and medical research where some clear benefit to the individual participants is envisioned. However, beforehand such benefits are only anticipated or predicted, or else there is no need for the study.

It is less easy to achieve benefits for the participants in survey research and certain kinds of laboratory experiments. Nevertheless, researchers must think about the issue of maximizing benefits and do this in a realistic manner, which avoids false promises or grandiose claims about benefits to science and society. Benefits to participants could include an informative debriefing, workbooks or materials, a chance to share concerns or interests with the researcher, and, in some cases, the effects of the experimental treatment. Benefits to the community could include improved relationships with a university, more understanding about the problems under study, materials such as books, special training, and the prestige of being associated with the program and university.

If participants have a good research experience (e.g., they are treated with respect and provided with results to validate their contribution), this increases the likelihood of future participation. Conversely, bad experiences predispose subjects to not participate in another study, resulting in their not benefiting from a new treatment. This would be a travesty and is perhaps the most significant risk of "benign" social research.

Chapter 5

Ethical Issues Related to Publishing and Reviewing

There are certain ethical principles that researchers should keep in mind when writing papers and reviewing the work of others. These ethical principles are no less real than those involving the protection of human subjects. The requirements for manuscripts submitted to biomedical journals (International Committee of Medical Journal Editors, 1997) and the American Psychological Association (2001) publication manual provide advice and discussion to supplement most of the issues raised in this chapter.

DISSEMINATION OF RESULTS

The research process is not complete until the results are disseminated to the public and to interested researchers. Although oral presentations and publications in semipopular magazines have their place, publishing in refereed journals is key to the progress of science. Considerable detail should be provided about the procedures and data analyses so that the researcher's work is available for scrutiny by the scholarly community. Refereed publications also are used to evaluate performance of the researcher, and they are an important aspect of tenure and promotion at a university. Because there is considerable pressure, especially for young faculty, to produce refereed publications, a number of potential ethical problems arise.

Plagiarism.   *Plagiarism* is presenting a portion of the work of another person without quotation or proper citation. Paraphrasing, which involves summarizing and rearranging sentences, is acceptable if credit is given in the text. Plagiarism refers not just to words but also to the data and ideas of another person. Because literature reviews and textbooks are based heavily on the work of others, there is tension between providing appropriate credit to others and overusing quotations or impeding the flow of the text with citations.

Multiple Publications. Duplicate publication distorts the knowledge base and wastes scarce journal resources. However, pressures on authors to have a large number of publications and limitations by editors on space often lead to multiple publications from one study. Authors should not submit to a journal a manuscript that has already been published in substantially the same form. However, manuscripts previously published as an abstract/summary or in a limited-circulation document can be published in full later. There is always an issue about how similar the current manuscript is to the original and the similarity of the audience. It is not uncommon, but perhaps ethically questionable, for researchers to rewrite a research paper for another journal with a different audience. Journal articles are sometimes revised for publication as a chapter in a book. This is acceptable as long as the original source is cited, and permission to adapt or reprint is obtained from the copyright holder. Problems of duplicate publication also may arise if the material is first published on the Internet or through the mass media. Articles must not be submitted to more than one journal at a time. Only after rejection or withdrawal of the manuscript is it appropriate to submit the same article to another journal.

It is common, but in some ways undesirable, for several substantively different articles to be published from the same study. However, for very large studies, multiple publications are unavoidable and may be necessary. The ethical issue is appropriate division into important pieces versus slicing into "just publishable units."

Authorship. There has been considerable discussion in recent years about who should be listed as an author and even whether the whole concept of authorship should be scrapped in favor of some other system. For example, Rennie, Yank, and Emanuel (1997) proposed that instead of authors, each article should provide a list of contributors, indicating their specific contribution(s) (e.g., designed the statistical analyses, conceptualized the design, wrote the results and discussion). Part of the reason for this proposal was to identify responsibility or accountability for parts of the article.

A general, but not universally agreed-on policy is that authorship is reserved for those who make a substantial *professional* contribution to the study and that order of authorship be determined by the importance of the contribution. Substantial professional contributions may include formulating the problem or hypothesis, structuring the experimental design, planning and organizing the statistical analysis, interpreting the results, or writing a major portion of the paper. Lesser contributions, which may be acknowledged, include supporting functions such as designing the apparatus, conducting the statistical analysis, collecting or entering data, and recruiting participants. Note that these latter contributions are often those of student volunteers or paid assistants, who may think that they deserve authorship.

Two types of problems result when determining authorship. On the one hand, there are "guest" authors, who have not made a significant professional contribution to the project but are given authorship as a favor or as a "right" due to their status in a department or laboratory, or because their names on an article increase the probability of acceptance. On the other hand, there are "ghost" authors who did make a significant professional contribution but are not included as authors. Sometimes persons in power simply take advantage of less powerful or departed colleagues or students, who become "ghost" authors. A different version of the "ghost" and "guest" author issue sometimes occurs with industry-sponsored research. The actual author is paid by the drug company to write the paper but is not listed as an author, and instead "prestigious" academics, who did not write the paper, are given authorship to add luster to it.

However, the issues are not always clear. Often difficulties arise when a person loses interest or leaves the area after playing an important part in the initial aspects of the study. Perhaps the person even wrote what turns out to be an early draft of the final paper. The issue is what kind of credit should be given to such a person when an article is rejected, reanalyzed, and fully rewritten without the assistance of the initial contributor.

A good practice is for the collaborators to meet at the beginning of the project and agree on who should be authors and the order of authorship. It is also necessary for these authors to keep in contact and to renegotiate authorship if circumstances change. Each person's contribution should be documented and updated as necessary.

Finally, there are two other issues related to authorship. First, consent should always be obtained before someone is included as an author. Some editors even say one should obtain permission before including persons in an acknowledgment, especially if it is implied that the acknowledged person agrees with the conclusions. Second, all authors should review the manuscript before it is submitted because their names as authors imply that they take responsibility for the article. However, with multiple-authored articles it is probably unrealistic to assume that all authors are knowledgeable and should be responsible for all aspects of the paper.

REVIEWS AND REVIEWERS

Most grant proposals and proposed journal articles are reviewed by peers who must be careful not to use the ideas of the original authors until they are published and then give credit. Editors and reviewers must not quote proposals they have reviewed unless given explicit permission by the author.

The process of reviewing requires a good deal of trust and integrity by the reviewers for the process to work fairly and not be exploitative. Problems related to fairness of reviews are relatively common, and most funding agencies and journals have specific policies to deal with them. Usually reviewers' identities are not revealed to the authors, on the assumption that this will make reviews more candid and negative reviews less open to reprisal. On the other hand, others have argued that reviews might be more responsible and balanced if the identity of the reviewer was known. In fact, in small fields, applicants can often guess the identity of the reviewer.

Masked, formerly called *blind*, review occurs when the author's identity is not given to the reviewer. This type of review is common for manuscripts, but it is unusual for grant proposals. The argument for anonymous or masked review is that it gives a better chance to a new scholar because the work is judged solely on its merits rather than on the status of the authors. Again, in small fields, it may not be possible to disguise the manuscripts of well-known researchers.

Once an article or book is published, a different kind of review takes place, not just in published book reviews but also in literature reviews and meta-analyses, in which the reviewers exclude studies judged not to be of high quality. Or the reviewer may decide to weight studies in terms of their merit, so some count more than others. Although these practices are a necessary part of the scientific process, they provide the opportunity for potential abuse and, at the least, hurt feelings.

CONFLICTS OF INTEREST

Although scholars do their research for a variety of reasons (e.g., curiosity and altruism), fame, tenure, and monetary gain are also motivators for doing research. A problem occurs when there is a real or apparent conflict between personal gain and obligations to the scientific community. One type of conflict is related to competition among scholars. This could lead to reviewers treating their competitors unfairly or withholding information from their colleagues. Because originality and priority are so important, there is often an inherent conflict of interest that may restrict collaboration and cooperation. On the other hand, it is usually considered a conflict of interest to review grants or papers from close colleagues or persons from the same institution because of potential loyalty. In addition, if research on the value of a product is funded by the producer of that product, the funding should be acknowledged in the notes of the article. Another type of potential conflict of interest exists for clinicians because of the large amounts of money pharmaceutical companies spend each year on gifts, meals, travel subsidies, and symposia. Wazana (2000) concluded that physician–industry interactions appear to affect prescribing behavior, indicating a conflict with best practice for the patient.

Conflicts of interest are not the same as scientific misconduct, but the latter can result from unacknowledged conflicts, which need to be recognized and disclosed. Conflicts of interest are inevitable and not inherently bad, but not disclosing them and not managing actual conflicts are problems. Even the appearance of conflicts should be disclosed.

MISCONDUCT AND THE STRUCTURE OF SCIENCE

In a controversial article, Woodward and Goodstein (1996), professors of philosophy and physics, made the argument that "many plausible-sounding rules for defining ethical conduct might be destructive to the aims of scientific inquiry" (p. 479). They asked how fraud could be reduced without losing the positive effects of competition and reward. Woodward and Goodstein (1996) said that "an implicit code of conduct that encourages scientists to be a bit dogmatic and permits a certain measure of exaggeration . . . and that does not require an exhaustive discussion of its deficiencies may be perfectly sensible" (p. 485). They argue that part of the responsibility of scientists is to provide the best possible case for their ideas. It is up to others to point out defects and limitations. They state that this is, in fact, what most scientists do. There are, of course, real limits here, and *exaggeration* is probably not the best word. Advocacy is appropriate, but any factual misstatement is unethical. The point here is that what may seem like simple, obvious rules about misconduct are often less clear in the specific case.

How is the researcher to know what is acceptable advocacy and what crosses the line? Peer judgment is required to decide whether a researcher's procedures for selecting particular participants or selectively discarding data are appropriate or involve scientific misconduct. Junior researchers can learn about the complexities of appropriate behavior in their field best by observing and discussing issues with senior scholars/mentors in their field. However, you should be careful whom you emulate because not all senior researchers are good role models. We hope that this chapter has conveyed not only the complexity of the issues presented but also some suggestions for action.

Part II

VARIABLES AND THEIR MEASUREMENT

Chapter 6

Research Problems and Variables

RESEARCH PROBLEMS

The research process begins with a problem. What is a research problem? Kerlinger (1986) described a problem as "an interrogative sentence or statement that asks: 'What relation exists between two or more variables?'" (p. 16). Kerlinger suggested that prior to the problem statement, "the scientist usually experiences an obstacle to understanding, a vague unrest about observed and unobserved phenomena, a curiosity as to 'why something is as it is'" (p. 11). For example, Harmon, Morgan, and Glicken (1984) investigated the problem of whether the motivation to master new skills or challenging tasks could be measured in infants and, if so, what factors seemed to influence the amount of such mastery motivation. The general problem might have been stated as, can infants mastery motivation be measured reliably and validly and what variables are related to an infant's mastery motivation? The problem for the Gliner and Sample (1996) study was to find out if the quality of life for persons with developmental disabilities could be improved using a community life intervention.

VARIABLES

A variable must be able to vary or have different values. For example, gender is a variable because it has two values, female or male. Age is a variable that has a large number of potential values. However, sometimes, as in the DiLorenzo et al. (2004) study, age can be divided into a few levels such as younger and older. Type of treatment/intervention is a variable if there is more than one treatment or a treatment and a control group. Mastery motivation is a variable like age that can have many ordered levels. However, if we are studying only girls or only 12-month-olds, gender and age are not variables; they are constants. Thus, we can define the term *variable* as a characteristic of the participants or situation that has different values *in the study.*

Operational Definitions of Variables

An operational definition describes or defines a variable in terms of the operations used to produce it or techniques used to measure it. Demographic variables like age or ethnic group are usually measured by checking official records or simply by asking the participant to choose the appropriate category from among those listed. Treatments are described so the reader knows what the researcher meant by, for example, cognitive therapy. Likewise, abstract concepts like mastery motivation need to be defined operationally by spelling out in some detail how they were measured. To do this, the investigator may provide sample questions, append the instrument, or provide a reference to a published article where more information can be found.

In the two sample experimental studies (Gliner & Sample, 1996; Johnson & Johnson, 1991) there are fairly extensive descriptions of how the intervention was accomplished. In the Redding et al. (1990) study, they refer to published articles using the Beck Depression Inventory and ones using mastery tasks in order to provide the reader with more details about the instruments and their reliability and validity.

Independent Variables

Active Independent Variables. One class of independent variables is referred to as *active independent variables* (Kerlinger, 1986). A frequent goal of research is to investigate the effect of a particular intervention. When studying an active independent variable, an intervention/treatment is given to a group of participants (experimental) but not to another (control group), within a specified period of time during the study. Thus, a pretest and posttest should be possible. When the investigator has control over the independent variable, that is, can decide which group will receive the intervention and which group will not receive the intervention, then the active independent variable is considered to be manipulated. However, there are many situations that evaluate the impact of an intervention, perhaps comparing two different treatments taking place in two different clinics, where the investigator is not able to assign one group to the intervention condition and the other to the control condition. In this situation, the independent variable is still active, but not manipulated.

In the Gliner and Sample (1996) study and in the Johnson and Johnson (1991) study, the interventions (community life and group therapy, respectively) were both active independent variables, and both variables were considered to be manipulated because the researcher decided which participants received the intervention and which did not.

Attribute Independent Variables.   Unlike some researchers, we do not restrict the term *independent variable* to those variables that are active. We define an independent variable more broadly to include any predictors, antecedents, or presumed causes or influences under investigation in the study. Attributes of the participants would fit within this definition. Type of disability (or level of disability) may be the major focus of a study and qualify as an independent variable because it is a presumed influence on behavior and can have different values. For example, cerebral palsy is different from Down syndrome, which is different from spina bifida, yet all are types of disability. However, disabilities are usually present when we begin a study, and a pretest is not possible, so disability is not an active variable. Such research where an apparent intervention is studied after the fact is sometimes called *ex post facto.* We consider such independent variables to be attributes.

A variable that could not be manipulated is called an *attribute independent variable* because it is an attribute of the person (e.g., gender, age, and ethnic group) or the person's usual environment (e.g., child abuse). For ethical and practical reasons, many aspects of the environment (e.g., child abuse) cannot be manipulated or given and are thus attribute variables. This distinction between active and attribute independent variables is important for determining what can be said about cause and effect. In our sample studies, age (under 60 vs. 60 and older) was an attribute independent variable in the DiLorenzo et al. (2004) study, whereas the degree of maternal depression was an attribute independent variable in the Redding et al. (1990) study.

Dependent Variables

The dependent variable is the outcome or criterion. It is assumed to measure or assess the effect of the independent variable. Dependent variables are scores from a test, ratings on questionnaires, or readings from instruments (e.g., electrocardiogram). It is common for a study to have several dependent variables (e.g., performance and satisfaction). In the DiLorenzo et al. (2004) study, there were many dependent variables such as various aspects of physical and mental health as well as quality of life. The Redding et al. (1990) study had three main dependent variables: performance on the mastery task, pleasure after solving a task, and performance on the harder tasks.

Extraneous Variables

These are variables that are not of interest in a particular study but could influence the dependent variable. Environmental factors (e.g., temperature or distractions), time of day, other attributes of the participants, and characteristics of the investigator or therapist are some possible extraneous variables that need to be controlled by methods such as holding them constant, randomization, statistics, or matching.

Levels of a Variable

The word *level* is commonly used to describe the values of an independent variable. This does not necessarily imply that the values are ordered from low to high. Suppose an investigator was interested primarily in comparing two different treatments and a third no-treatment control group. The study could be conceptualized as having one independent variable, treatment type, with three levels, the two treatment conditions and the control condition.

Other Considerations About Variables

Many studies such as Gliner and Sample (1996) have independent variables that have a few levels (the intervention or no intervention) and dependent variables that have many ordered levels (the degree of quality of life). However, in the associational/correlational approach, both independent and dependent variables usually have many ordered levels (such as degree of maternal depression and infant task performance). In later chapters we discuss different combinations of independent and dependent variables and how they are analyzed.

   Some variables (e.g., mastery motivation or quality of life) could be either the dependent variable or independent variable (or even an extraneous variable), depending on the study. Such variables are usually a changeable characteristic of the participant (such as an attitude or personality characteristic); if used as independent variables, they are attribute independent variables. *Individual* participants do not have to vary on a characteristic or variable—it is the group that must have more than one value (e.g., some men and some women). However, in some studies participants may change over time. In these studies, there are repeated measures of the same variable (e.g., a pretest and a posttest on math knowledge).

Groups or Sets of Variables

In analyzing research articles, it is sometimes difficult to distinguish between variables and the levels of variables. In complex studies researchers have many variables, so they often group them into what might be called sets of similar variables. For example, the variables age, gender, education, and marital status could be grouped together and be referred to collectively as *demographics*. Similarly, SAT verbal and quantitative scores could be called *scholastic aptitude scores*. Confusion arises if one mistakenly assumes that the sets or groups of variables (demographics and SAT scores) are the variables and the actual variables (age, gender, SAT verbal, etc.) are the levels.

How can one avoid this confusion? Thoughtful reading is the key, but remember that a variable has to have at least two levels. Thus, if something varies from low to high (e.g., age or SAT verbal) in this study it has to be a variable, not a level. If treated as a single value (e.g., female), it is either a level or a constant (i.e., not a variable in this study). This distinction is critical for deciding what statistics to use.

The Mastery Motivation Problem Revisited

Let us now identify the variables used in the studies on mastery motivation reported by Harmon et al. (1984). The article discussed a comparison of three groups of infants: abused, neglected, and low risk. This attribute independent variable, perhaps called risk type, had three levels. Another attribute independent variable, gestational status, had two levels, preterm and full term, that were compared. Intervention and nonintervention groups were also compared; they formed an active independent variable called intervention type. The dependent variables were several aspects of mastery motivation (task persistence and causality pleasure). Note that mastery motivation is not a single variable but rather a set of two variables, each varying from low to high. Age would not be a variable if all the infants were 12 months gestational age. Thus, the problem might be stated more specifically as, "What is the relationship of risk type, gestational status, and intervention type to mastery motivation?"

Chapter 7

Measurement and Descriptive Statistics

MEASUREMENT

According to Stevens (1951), "In its broadest sense measurement is the as-signment of numerals to objects or events according to rules" (p. 1). The process of research begins with a problem about the relationship between two or more variables. Measurement is introduced when these variables are translated into labels (categories) or numbers. Stevens went on to describe a hierarchy of four scales or levels of measurement that he labeled *nominal, ordinal, interval,* and *ratio.* Since the 1950s, these four levels have been discussed in most statistics and research methods textbooks and used to describe the level of measurement necessary to compute certain statistics. In general, the mean, standard deviation, and parametric statistics such as the *t* test that use them are said to depend on having at least *interval* level measurement of the variables. However, we have found the distinction between the traditional *ordinal* and *internal* levels somewhat confusing to apply, and other researchers have argued that this traditional distinction is not necessary to use parametric statistics if the data are approximately normally distributed (Gaito, 1980, 1986; Velleman & Wilkinson, 1993).

More useful for statistical purposes is a division into *dichotomous* or binary (a variable having only two values or levels), *nominal* (a categorical variable with three or more values that are not ordered), *ordinal* (a variable with three or more values that are ordered, but not normally distributed), and *normally distributed* (an ordered variable with a distribution that is approximately normal [bell-shaped] in the population sampled). This measurement classification, similar to one proposed by Helena Kraemer (personal communication, March 16, 1999), is shown in Table 7.1.

TABLE 7.1
Traditional Measurement Terms and Our Recommended Terms

Traditional Term	Traditional Definition	Our Term	Our Definition
Nominal	Two or more *unordered* categories	Nominal	Three or more *unordered* categories
—	—	Dichotomous	Two categories, either ordered or unordered
Ordinal	*Ordered* levels, in which the difference in magnitude between levels is not equal	Ordinal	Three or more *ordered* levels, but the frequency distribution of the scores is *not* normally distributed
Interval and Ratio	Interval: *ordered* levels, in which the difference between levels is equal, but there is no true zero	Approximately normal	Many (at least 5) *ordered* levels or scores, with the frequency distribution of the scores being approximately normally distributed
	Ratio: *ordered* levels; the difference between levels is equal, and there is a true zero		

Dichotomous Variables. Dichotomous variables are in many ways similar to nominal variables, and in many cases the same statistics are recommended for both. However, we contend that dichotomous variables are a special case. For example, the mean would be meaningless for a three or more category nominal variable (e.g., ethnic group). However, it does have meaning when there are only two categories. For example, if the average gender was 1.55 (with males = 1 and females = 2), then 55% of the participants were females. Furthermore, for multiple regression, dichotomous variables, called *dummy variables*, can be used as independent variables along with normally distributed variables.

Nominal Variables. If numerals are assigned to each category, they stand only for the name of the category, but have no implied order. For example, behavioral therapy might be assigned the numeral 1, cognitive therapy might be coded as 2, and psychoanalytic therapy might be coded as 3. This does not imply that one type of therapy is higher than another or that cognitive therapy is in the middle. The same reasoning applies to many other categories such as ethnic group, type of disability, and diagnosis. In each of these cases, the categories are distinct and nonoverlapping, but not ordered; thus each category in the variable is different from the others, but there is no necessary order to the categories. This means that one must not treat numbers used for identifying the categories as if they were numbers that could be used in a formula. "Average type of therapy" makes no sense, but if one asks a computer to compute an average, it will provide meaningless information.

Unfortunately, the literature is full of confusing terms to describe the measurement aspects of variables. *Categorical* and *discrete* are terms sometimes used interchangeably with nominal, but we think that nominal is better because it is possible to have ordered, discrete categories.

Qualitative or constructivist researchers rely heavily on nominal scales and on the process of developing appropriate codes or categories for behaviors, words, and so on. Although using qualitative/nominal variables dramatically reduces the types of statistics that can be used, it does not eliminate the use of statistics to summarize data and make inferences.

Ordinal Variables (Not Normally Distributed).   In ordinal scales there are not only mutually exclusive categories, as in nominal scales, but the three or more values are ordered from low to high in much the same way that one would rank the order in which horses finished a race (i.e., win, place, show, . . . , last). Thus, in an ordinal scale, one knows which participant is highest or most preferred on a dimension but the values are not equally spaced or normally distributed.

Normally Distributed Variables.   These variables not only have mutually exclusive categories that are ordered from low to high, but also the responses or scores are normally distributed (see following section). *Interval scale, continuous, dimensional,* and *quantitative* are terms that are seen in the literature for variables that range from low to high, many of which are assumed to be normally distributed. To use many common statistics (e.g., mean and standard deviation) appropriately, the variables (or their errors) should be at least approximately normally distributed in the population.

NORMAL CURVE

Figure 7.1 is an example of a normal curve. The normal curve is important because many of the variables that we examine in research are distributed in the form of the normal curve. Examples of variables that in the population fit a normal curve are height, weight, and psychological variables, such as IQ and many personality measures. For each of these examples, most people would fall toward the middle of the curve, with fewer people at each extreme.

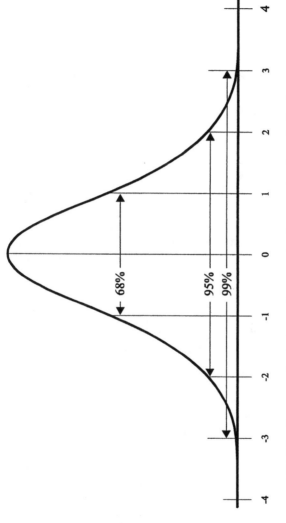

FIG. 7.1. Frequency distribution and areas under the normal and standardized curve.

39

The normal curve is derived theoretically and has the following properties.

1. The normal curve is unimodal. It has one "hump," and this hump is in the middle of the distribution.
2. The mean, median, and mode are equal.
3. The curve is symmetric; that is, it is not skewed.
4. The range is infinite. This means that the extremes of the curve approach but never touch the x axis.
5. The curve is neither too peaked nor too flat, and its tails are neither too short nor too long (has no kurtosis). Its proportions are like those in Fig. 7.1.

For our purposes, the important part of the normal curve is the area under the curve. Figure 7.1 demonstrates that one standard deviation from either side of the mean yields a total area of 68% and two standard deviations from the mean yield an area of 95%. The normal curve can be changed to a standard normal curve by converting raw scores to z scores, with a mean equal to 0 and a standard deviation equal to 1. The z scores are in standard deviation units and can be seen on the horizontal axis in Fig. 7.1. If the curve is converted to a standard normal curve it can be thought of as having a total area under the curve as 1.0 or 100%. The percentages of area can be interpreted as probabilities. Therefore, portions of this curve could be expressed as fractions of 1.0.

For example, if we assume that 5 feet 10 inches is the average height of men in the United States, then the probability that a man will be 5 feet 10 inches or taller is .5. The probability that a man will be over 6 feet 5 inches, or under 5 feet 3 inches, is considerably smaller. It is important to be able to conceptualize area under the normal curve in the form of probabilities because statistical convention sets acceptable probability levels for rejecting the null hypothesis at .05 or .01. As we show later, when events or outcomes happen very infrequently, that is, only five times in 100 or one time in 100 (way out in the left or right tail of the curve), we wonder whether they belong to that distribution or perhaps to a different distribution.

DESCRIPTIVE STATISTICS

We use descriptive statistics to summarize the variables from our sample in terms of frequency (Note: We might use the term "shape" here instead of frequency), central tendency, and variability. Inferential statistics, on the other hand, are used to make inferences from the sample to the population. We discuss inferential statistics starting with chapter 20.

Frequency Distributions. Relative frequency distributions indicate the percentage of participants in each category, whether those be ordered or unordered categories. There are several choices for a diagram of a frequency distribution; two of them are bar charts and box-and-whisker plots (Fig. 7.2). The *bar chart* is a good choice with dichotomous and nominal data. The box-and-whisker plot is useful for ordinal and normal data, but it should not be used with nominal data. The *box-and-whisker plot* is a graphical representation of the distribution of scores and is helpful in distinguishing between ordinal and normally distributed data (see Tukey, 1977).

Central Tendency. The three main measures of the center of a distribution are mean, median, and mode. The *mean* or arithmetic average takes into account all of the available information in computing the central tendency of a frequency distribution; thus, it is the statistic of choice if the data are normally distributed. The *median* or middle score is the appropriate measure of central tendency for ordinal-level data because if the distribution is skewed, the mean will be misleading. For example, the median income of 100 middle-class workers and a millionaire is substantially lower than and reflects the central tendency of the group better than the average income. For normally distributed data, the median is the same as the mean.

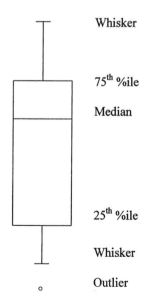

FIG. 7.2. Box-and-whisker plot.

The *mode*, or most common response category, can be used with any kind of data but generally provides you with the least precise information about central tendency. The mode is apparent from the relative frequency plot and is most useful for dichotomous and nominal data.

Variability.   Measures of variability tell us about the spread of the scores. If all of the scores in a distribution are the same, there is no variability. If they are all different and widely spaced apart, the variability is high. The *standard deviation* is the most common measure of variability, but it is appropriate only when one has normally distributed data. For nominal/categorical data, the measure of spread is the number of possible response categories. For ordinal data, the *interquartile range*, depicted in the box plot by the distance between the top and bottom of the box, is the best measure of variability (see Fig. 7.2). For normally distributed data, almost all responses are included between the bottom of the lower whisker and the top of the upper one. However, if the responses are not normally distributed, the whiskers will be unequal lengths and there may be outliers outside the whiskers.

For example, assume that Fig. 7.2 represents scores on a test or personality inventory given to a community sample. Half of the people have scores that are somewhere above the median but none are extremely high. Those below the middle are more spread out, including one (an outlier) who is abnormally low. Half the sample has scores between the top and bottom of the box. However, instead of the median being in the middle of the box, as in a normal distribution, it is above the middle. The whiskers are unequal lengths, and the low scorer is shown as an outlier. The presence of outliers is a warning sign of nonnormality or errors in the data.

CONCLUSIONS ABOUT MEASUREMENT AND THE USE OF STATISTICS

Table 7.2 summarizes much of the preceding information about the appropriate use of various kinds of descriptive statistics, given nominal, dichotomous, ordinal, or normal data. Statistics based on means and standard deviation are valid for normally distributed (normal) data. Typically, these data are used in the most powerful tests called parametric statistics (see chap. 23). However, if the data are ordered but grossly nonnormal (i.e., ordinal), means and standard deviations may not give meaningful answers. Then the median and a nonparametric test would be preferred. Nonparametric tests have less power than parametric tests (they are less able to reject the null hypothesis when it should be rejected), but the sacrifice in power for nonparametric tests based on ranks usually is relatively minor. If the data are nominal (unordered), one would have to use the mode or counts. In this case, there would be a major sacrifice in power. It would be misleading

TABLE 7.2
Selection of Appropriate Descriptive Statistics and Plots

	Nominal	Dichotomous	Ordinal	Normal
Frequency distribution	Yes[a]	Yes	Yes	OK[b]
Bar chart	Yes	Yes	Yes	OK
Histogram	No[c]	No	OK	Yes
Frequency polygon	No	No	OK	Yes
Box-and-whiskers plot	No	No	Yes	Yes
Central tendency				
Mean	No	OK	Of ranks, OK	Yes
Median	No	OK = Mode	Yes	OK
Mode	Yes	Yes	OK	OK
Variability				
Range	No	Always 1	Yes	Yes
Standard deviation	No	No	Of ranks, OK	Yes
Interquartile range	No	No	OK	OK
How many categories	Yes	Always 2	OK	Not if truly continuous
Shape				
Skewness	No	No	Yes	Yes

[a]*Yes* means a good choice with this level of measurement.
[b]*OK* means OK to use, but not the best choice at this level of measurement.
[c]*No* means not appropriate at this level of measurement.

to use tests that assume the dependent variable is ordinal or normally distributed when the dependent variable is, in fact, nominal.

Chapter 8

Measurement Reliability

Measurement reliability and measurement validity are two parts of overall research validity, the quality of the whole study. What is reliability? Reliability refers to consistency of scores on a particular instrument. It is incorrect to state that a test is reliable. Instead, we are interested in the scores from the test, taking into account the sample that took the test. For example, there may be strong evidence for reliability for adults, but scores of depressed adolescents on this test may be highly inconsistent. When we use tests or other instruments to measure outcomes, we need to make sure that they provide us with consistent data. If our outcome measure is not reliable, then we cannot accurately assess the results of our study.

An example illustrates the importance of measurement reliability and how it can be assessed. A researcher is interested in determining whether quality of life for depressed adolescents can be increased through an experimental exercise program. Both the experimental and control groups receive the pretest that measures quality of life (QL); then after the 6-month intervention period, they receive the same instrument on the posttest. The researcher hopes that the posttest scores from the experimental group are higher than those of the control group. The issue here is whether the QL inventory will measure quality of life consistently (reliably) in this study with this group of participants.

Most of our discussion of measurement reliability for this chapter is based on classical test theory. (Two other theories of measurement that assess reliability in a different manner are generalizability theory and item response theory, mentioned briefly later.) Any score from an individual on a particular instrument is an observed score. If Jones scores 49 on the pretest, then her observed score is 49. If we were to give Jones the QL a second time, her observed score probably will be different, maybe 53, or 43. If we give the QL a third time, the score probably will be different from either of the previous scores. How will we know whether the change from pretest to posttest is due to the intervention (systematic variation) or to something else?

According to classical test theory, an observed score is made up of a true score and error. If we could subtract the true score from the observed score, we could determine how much of the score is due to error. We never actually know the amount of the observed score that is due to the true score and the amount that is due to error. To minimize error, we should choose a test with strong evidence of reliability. The higher the reliability of scores on an instrument, the closer the true scores will be to observed scores for that instrument.

Conceptually, reliability is consistency. However, when evaluating instruments it is important to be able to express evidence of reliability in numerical form. The correlation coefficient, often used to evaluate reliability, is usually expressed as the letter r and indicates the strength of a relation. The values of r range between -1 and $+1$. A value of 0 indicates no relation between two variables or scores, whereas values close to -1 or $+1$ indicate very strong relationships between two variables. A strong positive relationship indicates that people who score high on one test also score high on a second test. To say that a measurement is reliable, one would expect a coefficient between $+.7$ and $+1.0$. Others have suggested even stricter criteria. For example, reliability coefficients of .8 are acceptable for research, but .9 is necessary for measures that will be used to make decisions about individuals, for example, instruments such as IQ tests and those for personnel decisions. However, it is common to see published journal articles in which one or a few reliability coefficients are below .7, usually .6 or greater. Although correlations of $-.7$ to -1.0 indicate a strong (negative) correlation, they are totally unacceptable as evidence for reliability. Such a high negative correlation would indicate that persons who initially score high on the measure later score low and visa versa. A negative reliability coefficient indicates a computational error or terrible inconsistency.

METHODS TO ASSESS RELIABILITY

Test–Retest Reliability

Sometimes referred to as a coefficient of stability, test–retest reliability is the most common method to assess reliability over time. To demonstrate evidence of reliability, when a test is given more than once, a person's scores should be very similar. To obtain evidence of test–retest reliability, a researcher would find another sample of persons similar to the target population and administer the QL twice to this new sample. Then the researcher would determine the reliability coefficient (correlation) based on the scores of the two administrations.

Certain considerations must be taken into account:

- Test–retest reliability is not established during a study. It must be established when little related to the substance of the instrument should be happening between the two administrations. This is especially important regarding experiments with children, where developmental changes between the two administrations of the instrument could alter test–retest reliability. With standardized instruments, evidence for test–retest reliability usually has been obtained, although not necessarily with the population of interest.
- The sample used to establish evidence of the reliability of the instrument should be similar to the sample used in the study.
- The length of time used to establish evidence of test–retest reliability is usually short, but for use in experiments it should be similar to the length of the intervention to be used in the study. Note that as the length of time increases between administrations, the reliability usually decreases.

Parallel Forms Reliability

One of the problems of using the same instrument for the pretest and the posttest of a study is that participants may use knowledge gained on the pretest. In this situation, often referred to as *testing* or *carryover effects*, it is impossible to determine whether the change in scores is due to the intervention or to knowledge obtained from the pretest. One way of avoiding the carryover problem is to create a design without a pretest (e.g., the posttest-only control group design; see chap. 14 about randomized experiments). However, that design can be used only if the investigator can randomly assign participants to groups. In applied settings, where quasi-experimental designs are more likely, the investigator will need a pretest.

Some standardized tests have a second or parallel form that could be used as a posttest in place of the instrument used for the pretest. Parallel forms reliability (coefficient of equivalence) involves establishing the relationship between the two forms of the same test. This method involves having a sample of participants take both forms of the same instrument, usually with very little time elapsed between administrations. Then, a correlation coefficient is computed for the two sets of scores, which should be at least .80 for parallel forms reliability.

Internal Consistency Reliability

Often, the researcher wants to know that the several items within an instrument are consistent. The investigator can use the results of a single administration to determine internal consistency. The most common method of determining internal consistency is the Cronbach alpha (α), often referred to as a measure of interitem reliability (see chap. 33 for more discussion of Cronbach's alpha). Alpha can be used only when one has data from several items that are combined to make a composite score.

Measures of interitem reliability, especially the Cronbach α, are common in research articles because it takes only one administration of the instrument, often done during the study. Researchers sometimes assume that because the Cronbach alpha is high (e.g., .90), the test is measuring only one construct. Unfortunately, even though the item correlations may be relatively high, they could be measuring more than one factor or dimension. Another problem with interpreting the Cronbach α is that the coefficient is directly related to the number of items that make up the composite score; that is, the more items, the higher is α, other things being equal. Thus, an α of >.9 based on a large number of items (say, 30) does not necessarily indicate that there are high interitem correlations or that there is a single underlying dimension. Thus, reliability is not adequately assessed with the Cronbach α alone.

Interrater (Interobserver) Reliability

When observation is the instrument, interrater reliability must be established among the judges. Although there are numerous ways to determine this form of reliability, the common theme is that two or more judges (observers) score certain episodes of behavior, and then some method of assessing agreement is performed.

Percentage Agreement Methods. These methods involve having two or more raters, prior to the study, observe a sample of behaviors that will be similar to what would be observed in the study. Suppose that rater A observes 8 occurrences of a particular behavior and rater B observes 10 occurrences of the same behavior. Sometimes a percentage (80) is then computed by dividing the smaller number of observations by the larger number of observations of the specific behavior. One of the problems with this method is that although both observers may agree that a behavior was elicited a particular number of times, it is possible that the 8 instances observed by one judge were not the same instances observed by the second judge. If so, the percentage agreement would be inflated. Instead, with a point-by-point basis of establishing interrater reliability, each instance of a behavior would be rated as an agreement or disagreement between judges. The point-by-point method would be facilitated if the behavior is on videotape, which could be stopped and replayed. To calculate percentage agreement in the point-by-point method, the number of agreements between the two judges would be divided by the total number of responses (agreements plus disagreements). Unfortunately, this method ignores chance agreements when only a few categories are used.

Intraclass Correlation Coefficients.   Often, observational studies use more than two observers. Intraclass correlation coefficients (ICCs) allow the researcher to calculate a reliability coefficient in these studies. One criterion that must be satisfied in order to use the ICC is that the behavior to be rated must be normally distributed. ICCs are computed with repeated-measures analysis of variance. ICCs also can be used for test–retest reliability and internal consistency reliability. An advantage of ICCs is that if the judges are selected randomly from a larger group of potential raters, the researcher can generalize the interrater reliability beyond the specific judges who took part in the reliability study.

Kappa.   A method of calculating ICCs when the data are nominal is Cohen's κ statistic, which can be computed with two or more raters. The κ also corrects for chance agreements. For an excellent review of ICC type methods, including κ, see Bartko and Carpenter (1976).

Generalizability Theory, Item Response Theory, and Reliability

The methods that we have discussed to assess reliability are based on classical test theory. A major problem with classical test theory is that measurement error is considered to be a single entity, which does not give the researcher the information necessary to improve the instrument. *Generalizability theory*, an extension of classical test theory, allows the investigator to estimate more precisely the different components of measurement error. In its simplest form, this theory partitions the variance that makes up an obtained score into variance components, such as variance that is attributable to the participants, to the judges (observers), and to items. *Item response theory* allows the researcher to separate test characteristics from participant characteristics. This differs from both classical test theory and generalizability theory by providing information about reliability as a function of ability, rather than averaging overall ability levels. Nunnally and Bernstein (1994) and Strube (2000) provide more complete discussions of these topics.

SUMMARY ON RELIABILITY METHODS

We have discussed different methods of assessing reliability. If one uses a standardized instrument, reliability indices should have been obtained and published in an instrument manual, often referred to in the original journal publication. The method section of a research article also should provide evidence about the reliability of the instrument. Although all methods to assess reliability give some measure of consistency, they are not the same. To say that an instrument is reliable has relatively little meaning because each statement about reliability should specify the type(s) of reliability, the strength of the reliability coefficient(s), and the types of participants used. Before using an instrument, an investigator should evaluate the types of evidence and their strength in support of reliability. Measurement reliability is a necessary but not sufficient prerequisite for measurement validity, the topic of the next chapter.

Chapter 9

Measurement Validity

Validity is concerned with establishing evidence for the use of a particular measure or instrument in a particular setting with a particular population for a specific purpose. In this chapter we discuss what we call *measurement validity*; others might use terms such as *test validity, score validity,* or just *validity*. We use the modifier *measurement* to distinguish it from internal, external, and overall research validity (discussed in chaps. 17–19) and to point out that it is the measures or scores that provide evidence for validity. It is inappropriate to say that a test is "valid" or "invalid."

Thus, when we address the issue of measurement validity with respect to a particular test, we are addressing the issue of the evidence for the validity of the scores on that test for a particular purpose, and not the validity of the test or instrument per se. A given test might be used for a number of purposes. For example, specialty area scores on the graduate record examination might be used to predict first-year success in graduate school. However, they also could be used as a method to assess current status or achievement in a particular undergraduate major. Although the same test is used in both instances, the purpose of the test is different, and thus the evidence in support of each purpose could be quite different.

As stated in the last chapter, reliability or consistency is necessary for measurement validity. However, an instrument may produce consistent data (provide evidence for reliability), but the data may not be valid. For example, one could construct a device for measuring weight. Suppose that we know an object weighs 12 pounds, but the device consistently records 13 pounds. The device would be producing reliable data, but it would not provide valid evidence for assessing weight because it does not accurately measure what it is supposed to measure.

In research articles, there is usually more evidence for the reliability of the instrument than for the validity of the instrument because evidence for validity is more difficult to obtain. To establish validity, one ideally needs a "gold standard" or "criterion" related to the particular purpose of the measure. To obtain such a criterion is often not an easy matter, so other types of evidence to support the validity of a measure are necessary.

In this chapter, we discuss five broad types of evidence to support the validity of a test or measure. These five types of evidence for validity are: (a) content, (b) responses, (c) internal structure, (d) relations to other variables, and (e) the consequences of testing. Note that the five types of evidence are *not* separate types of validity and that any one type of evidence is insufficient. Validation should integrate all the pertinent evidence from as many of the five types of evidence as possible. Preferably validation should include some evidence in addition to content evidence, which is probably the most common and easiest to obtain. Note that the current Standards for Educational and Psychological testing (Standards) (AERA, APA, & NCME, 1999) are different from earlier versions of the Standards and most previous discussions of this concept. Goodwin and Leech (2003) published a useful summary of the changes with recommendations for teaching measurement courses.

From 1966 until 1999, the Standards included the so-called "trinity" view of validity, which categorized validity into three types: content validity, criterion-related validity (including concurrent and predictive methods), and construct validity. However, the 1985 Standards warned that the use of the labels (content, criterion, and construct) should not lead to the implication that there were three distinct types of validity. Increasingly, validity has been conceptualized as a unitary concept; many types of evidence may be gathered, but there are not many kinds of validity. During the 1980s and 1990s, the process of accumulating evidence in support of validity began to be emphasized.

The current Standards (AERA, APA, & NCME, 1999) described validity as "the degree to which evidence and theory support the interpretations of test scores" (p. 9). The Standards went on to say that "the process of validation involves accumulating evidence to provide a sound scientific basis for the proposed score interpretations. It is the interpretations . . . that are evaluated, not the test itself" (p. 9).

We next discuss the five types of evidence, not types of validity, already mentioned and how they differ from the previous types, which may be more familiar to some readers.

Evidence Based on the Content of the Measure

Content evidence refers to whether the content that makes up the instrument is representative of the concept that one is attempting to measure. Does the instrument accurately represent the major aspects of the concept and not include material that is irrelevant to it? This type of evidence is important for almost all measures and is based on a logical analysis of the content of the measure. It is similar to content validity from the earlier Standards.

There is no statistic that demonstrates content validity. Instead, the process of establishing content validity usually starts with a definition of the concept that the investigator is attempting to measure. A second step is a literature search to see how this concept is represented in the literature. Next, items are generated that might measure this concept. Gradually, this list of items is reduced to form the test or measure.

One of the main methods of reducing items is to form a panel of experts to review the items for representativeness of the concept. Because this type of evidence depends on the logical, but subjective, agreement of a few experts, we consider it necessary but not sufficient evidence. The experts review the measure for clarity and fit with the construct to be measured. Goodwin and Leech (2003) indicated that the experts are often asked to review the measure for possible bias (gender, culture, age, etc.). It is also important to examine whether an unfair advantage can be given to certain subgroups because the test measures either more (*construct-irrelevant components*) or less (*construct underrepresentation*) than intended.

Evidence Based on Response Processes

Goodwin and Leech (2003) pointed out that in the 1985 edition of the Standards, evidence based on response processes was included under construct-related validity. The extent to which the types of participant responses match the intended construct is studied. For example, with self-report measures of constructs we need evidence that respondents are not just giving socially desirable answers. This sort of evidence can be gathered by observing examinees as they perform tasks and by questioning participants to identify their reasons for providing certain answers.

In addition to examining the responses of the participants, this type of evidence for validity could include an examination of the responses of observers, raters, or judges to determine whether they are using the appropriate criteria. This type of response process evidence is the extent to which raters are influenced by irrelevant factors in making their judgments.

Evidence Based on Internal Structure

This type of evidence, like that based on response processes, was placed in the "trinity" conception under construct validity. Evidence from several types of analysis, including factor analysis and differential item functioning (DIF), can be useful here. The Standards (AERA, APA, & NCME, 1993) said:

> Analyses of the internal structure of a test can indicate the degree to which the relationships among test items and test components conform to the construct on which the proposed test score interpretations are based. The conceptual framework for a test may imply a single dimension of behavior, or it may posit several components that are each expected to be homogeneous, but that are also distinct from each other. For example, a measure of discomfort on a health survey might assess both physical and emotional health. The extent to which item interrelationships bear out the presumptions of the framework would be relevant to validity. (p. 13)

Factor analysis can provide this type of evidence when a construct is complex and several aspects (or factors) of it are measured. If the clustering of items supports the theory-based grouping of items, factorial evidence is provided. Note that a high Cronbach's alpha is sometimes incorrectly assumed to provide evidence that a measure contains only one dimension or construct.

Evidence Based on Relations to Other Variables

This category of evidence is the most extensive, including the old categories of criterion-related validity and much of what was included under construct validity. Constructs are hypothetical concepts that cannot be observed directly. Intelligence, depression, mastery motivation, and anxiety are all constructs. Although we cannot observe a construct directly, most of us agree that these constructs can be inferred from observable behaviors. For example, we cannot directly observe anxiety, but under certain circumstances we may observe anxious behaviors, such as sweating or pacing, that are specific to a particular context, such as immediately before an important examination. In addition, we often infer a construct from self-reports on an inventory or from an interview. Such self-reports can be useful, but it is prudent to be cautious about accepting them as solid evidence for validity. It is common to create instruments to measure particular constructs (e.g., an inventory that measures state anxiety or a test that measures intelligence).

The construct that the instrument is measuring should be guided by an underlying theory. Often, especially in applied disciplines, there is little underlying theory to support the construct. Cronbach (1990) pointed out that sometimes a test is used for a long time before a theory is developed around it.

Test–Criterion Relationships.　This refers to correlating the instrument to some form of measurable external or outside criterion. A common example involves instruments that are intended to select participants for admission to a school or occupation. Two types of evidence for criterion validity are called *predictive* and *concurrent.*

Predictive Evidence.　When we try to determine how someone will do in the future on the basis of their performance on a particular instrument, we are usually referring to predictive evidence. Tests such as the Scholastic Aptitude Test (SAT) and the Graduate Record Examination (GRE) are examples of instruments that are used to predict future performance. If the SAT provided good predictive evidence, then students who score high on this test would perform better in college than those who do not score high. The criterion in this case would be some measure of how well the students perform in college, usually grades during their first year.

A problem with predictive evidence is that often not all of the participants who were evaluated on the original instrument can be evaluated on the criterion variable. This is especially the case in selection studies. For example, we may have SAT scores for a wide range of high school students. However, not all of these students will be admitted to college. Therefore, our criterion variable of first semester college GPA will not only have fewer participants than our predictor variable, but will represent a more homogeneous group (only those admitted to college). Therefore, the range of scores of those who could participate in the study on both the predictor and criterion variables is restricted, leading to a lower correlation coefficient and therefore less confidence in our predictive evidence.

A second drawback with predictive evidence is that the researcher must wait until those who were tested initially can be measured on the criterion. Sometimes this wait could take years. Therefore, a second type of criterion evidence was developed.

Concurrent Evidence.　Similar to predictive evidence, concurrent evidence also examines the relationship between an instrument and an outside criterion. For example, suppose that we want to see whether the SAT taken in high school is a good predictor of freshman grades in college. However, we do not wish to wait until the high school students finish their freshman year. To determine concurrent evidence, we could take current freshmen and have them take the SAT and see whether it correlates with their grades (present grades because they are now freshmen). If there is a high correlation, we can have some confidence in using the instrument as a predictor for success in college. However, concurrent evidence is not the same as predictive evidence, and one may not wish to place as much confidence in this procedure. In the preceding example, we must make the assumption that there is no change in SAT scores between high school and college because the target for the SAT is high school students. If there are large changes, the evidence for validity should be questioned. Concurrent evidence is appropriate when a test is proposed as a substitute for a more expensive criterion measure. The test developer hopes that the less expensive or time-consuming measure will provide very similar information and, thus, a high correlation with the criterion (Cronbach, 1990).

The major drawback to criterion validity is the problem of identifying and then being able to measure a suitable criterion. For example, admission to medical school programs in the United States is difficult because of the large number of applicants for the limited number of positions. To select successful applicants, criteria such as grades and achievement tests often are used. Students (especially those who are not admitted) might complain that high grades do not make a person a good physician. Could one create an admission test that would predict becoming a good physician? Consider the problems of defining and measuring the criterion of what makes a good physician. The difficulty of identifying good, measurable criteria for many complex concepts was one of the key reasons for developing other methods to provide evidence for validity.

Convergent and Discriminant Evidence. Convergent evidence is determined by obtaining relatively high correlations between a scale and other measures that theory suggests would be positively related. Discriminant evidence is provided by obtaining relatively low relationships between a scale and measures that the theory suggests should not be related. Discriminant evidence also can be obtained by comparing groups that should differ on a scale and finding that they do, in fact, differ.

The Standards (AERA, APA, & NCME, 1999) provide a good example of convergent and discriminant evidence based on relationships among variables.

> Scores on a multiple-choice test of reading comprehension might be expected to relate closely (convergent evidence) to other measures of reading comprehension based on other methods, such as essay responses; conversely, test scores might be expected to relate less closely (discriminant evidence) to measures of other skills, such as logical reasoning. (p. 14)

Validity Generalization. The other main type of evidence discussed under the category of evidence based on relationships to other variables is validity generalization. The Standards describe this type of evidence as raising the important issue in educational and employment settings of the degree to which criterion-related evidence of validity can be generalized to a new situation. Unfortunately, in the past, relationships of a test with similar criteria often varied substantially from one situation to the next. Thus, as in meta-analysis, "statistical summaries of past validation studies in similar situations may be useful in estimating test-criterion relationships in a new situation. This practice is referred to as the study of validity generalization" (AERA, APA, & NCME, 1999, p. 15).

Evidence Based on Consequences of Testing

Goodwin and Leech (2003) stated that this type of evidence for validity, which was new to the 1999 Standards, includes both positive and negative anticipated and unanticipated consequences of measurement. The Standards (AERA, APA, & NCME, 1999) stated that

> tests are commonly administered in the expectation that some benefit will be realized from the intended use of the scores. A few of the many possible benefits are selection of efficacious treatments for therapy, placement of workers in suitable jobs, prevention of unqualified individuals from entering a profession, or improvement of classroom instructional practices. A fundamental purpose of validation is to indicate whether these specific benefits are likely to be realized. (p. 16)

Measurement Validity—An Example

Several types of evidence were provided by Morgan et al. (1993) for the Dimensions of Mastery Questionnaire (DMQ), which was designed to measure five aspects of mastery motivation. *Factor analysis* supported the grouping of items into these five appropriate clusters, providing some evidence based on internal structure. Overall DMQ scores were related to infant persistence at behavioral tasks, providing *convergent evidence*, and maternal ratings of normally developing infants were higher than maternal ratings of at-risk and delayed infants, providing some *discriminant evidence*. If infants were correctly identified as being at risk for later mastery problems *and* obtained appropriate early intervention, the consequences of using this questionnaire for such a purpose would be positive. Notice that three different types of validity evidence were used to support the DMQ. It is unrealistic for any instrument or test to expect validity evidence from all possible methods, but, as mentioned earlier, it is highly desirable to have more than one type of evidence.

Evaluation of Measurement Validity

Our suggestions about how to evaluate the strength of the support for measurement validity depends on the type of evidence. Evaluation of evidence based on content, response process, internal structure, and consequences of testing is subjective and depends on logical judgments by the researcher and/or other experts.

Evaluation of evidence based on relationships (often correlations) with other variables also requires a judgment because there are no well established rules or even guidelines. Our suggestion is to use Cohen's (1988) guidelines for interpreting effect sizes, which are measures of the strength of a relationship. In chapter 22, we describe several measures of effect size and how to interpret them. For evaluating statistical evidence for validity, the correlation coefficient (r) is the most common statistic (correlation is described in chap. 26). Cohen suggested that generally, in the applied behavioral sciences, $r = .5$ could be considered a large effect, and in this context we would consider $r = .5$ or greater to be strong support for measurement validity. In general, an acceptable level of support would be provided by $r \geq .3$, and some weak support might result from $r \geq .1$, assuming that such an r was statistically significant (see also the chap. 37 discussion of measurement validity). However, for concurrent, criterion evidence, if the criterion and test being validated are two similar measures of the same concept (e.g., IQ), the correlation would be expected to be very high, perhaps .8 or .9. On the other hand, for convergent evidence, the measures should not be that highly correlated because they should be measures of different concepts. If the measures were very highly related, one might ask whether they were instead really measuring the same concept.

SUMMARY

Table 9.1 summarizes much of the preceding material, including the main types of evidence and a summary of what evidence would support the validity of the measure. An instrument is not valid or invalid; however, there may be various degrees of support for its use with particular populations for particular purposes. The strength of the evidence for the measurement validity of the measures is extremely important for research in applied settings because without measures that have strong evidence for validity the results of

TABLE 9.1
Evidence for Measurement Validity

Type of Evidence	Support for Validity Depends on
Evidence based on content—all aspects of the construct are represented in appropriate proportions	Good agreement by experts about the content and that it represents the concept to be assessed
Evidence based on response processes—participants' responses match the intended construct	Evidence that participants and raters are not influenced by irrelevant factors like social desirability
Evidence based on internal structure—relationships among items on the test consistent with the conceptual framework	Meaningful factor structure consistent with the conceptual organization of the construct(s)
Evidence based on relations to other variables	
Criterion-concurrent—test and criterion are measured at the same time	The effect size of the relationship[a]
Criterion-predictive—test predicts some criterion in the future	The effect size of the relationship[a]
Convergent—based on theory, variables predicted to be related are related	The effect size of the relationship[a]
Discriminant—variables predicted not to be related are not related	The effect size of the relationship[a,b]
Validity generalization—results using the measure generalize to other settings	Supportive meta-analytic studies
Evidence based on consequences—conducting the test produces benefits for the participants	Evidence that positive consequences outweigh unexpected negative ones in terms of the outcomes of therapy, job placement, etc.

[a]The strength or level of support for validity (weak, medium, strong) could be based on Cohen's (1988) effect size guidelines, with the qualifications noted in the text.

[b]Depending on the data, the appropriate strength of association statistic will vary.

the study can be very misleading. Validation is an ongoing, never fully achieved, process based on integration of all the evidence from as many sources as possible.

Chapter 10

Data Collection Techniques

In this chapter we provide a context for many of the types of data collection techniques used with human participants. We do not discuss methods for psychiatric assessment of diagnostic status, but we provide some information about developing or evaluating a questionnaire, test, or other data collection technique.

Research approaches or designs are approximately orthogonal to (independent of) the techniques of data collection, and thus, in theory, any type of data collection technique could be used with any approach to research. However, some types of data collection are more commonly used with the experimental approaches. Others are more common with comparative or associational (survey) approaches, and still others are more common in qualitative research.

Table 10.1 gives an approximation of how common each of several data collection techniques is within each of these three major groupings of research approaches. Note that we have ordered the data collection techniques along a dimension from observer/researcher report to self-report measures. The observer report end includes observations and physiological recordings that are probably less influenced by the participants' desire to conform, but they are affected by any biases the observer may have. Of course, if the participants realize that they are being observed, they may not behave naturally.

At the other end of this dimension are measures based on self-reports of the participants, such as interviews and questionnaires. In these cases, responses are certainly filtered through the participants' eyes and are probably heavily influenced by factors such as social desirability. Concern about

59

TABLE 10.1
Data Collection Techniques Used by Research Approaches

| | Research Approach | | |
| | Quantitative Research | | |
Data Collection Techniques	Experimental and Quasi-Experimental	Comparative, Associational, and Descriptive Approaches	Qualitative Research
Researcher report measures			
Physiological recordings	++	+	–
Coded observations	++	++	+
Narrative observations	–	+	++
Participant observations	–	+	++
Other measures			
Standardized tests	+	++	–
Archival measures/documents	–	+	++
Content analysis	–	+	++
Self-report measures			
Summated attitude scales	+	++	–
Standardized personality scales	+	++	–
Questionnaires (surveys)	+	++	+
Interviews	+	++	++
Focus groups	–	+	++

Note. Symbols indicate likelihood of use (++ = quite likely, + = possibly, – = not likely).

faulty memories or socially desirable responses lead researchers, especially those who use experiments, to be suspicious about the validity of self-reports. On the other hand, observer reports are not necessarily valid measures. For example, qualitative researchers point out that cultural biases may lead observers to misinterpret their observations. In general, it is advisable to select instruments that have been used in other studies if they have been shown to be reliable and valid with the planned types of participants and for purposes similar to that for the planned study.

TYPES OF DATA COLLECTION TECHNIQUES

Direct Observation

Many researchers prefer systematic, direct observation of behavior as the most accurate and desirable method of recording the behavior of participants. Using direct observation, the investigator observes and records the behaviors of the participants rather than relying on self-reports or those from parents, teachers, or other informants. Observational techniques vary on several dimensions.

Naturalness of the Setting.   The setting for the observations can vary from natural environments (such as a school or home) through more controlled settings (such as a laboratory playroom) to highly artificial settings (such as a physiological laboratory). Qualitative researchers do observations almost exclusively in natural settings. Quantitative researchers use the whole range of settings, but some prefer laboratory settings.

Degree of Observer Participation.   This dimension varies from situations in which the observer is a participant to situations in which the observer is entirely unobtrusive. Most observations, however, are done in situations in which the participants know that that observer is observing them and have agreed to it. Such observers attempt to be unobtrusive, perhaps by observing from behind a one-way mirror.

Amount of Detail.   This dimension goes from global summary information (such as overall ratings based on the whole session) to moment-by-moment records of the observed behaviors. Obviously, the latter provides more detail, but it requires considerable preparation and training of observers.

Standardized Versus Investigator-Developed Instruments

Standardized instruments cover topics of broad interest to a number of investigators. They usually are published, are reviewed in a *Mental Measurements Yearbook* (1938–present), and have a manual that includes norms for making comparisons with broader samples and information about reliability and validity.

Investigator-developed measures are ones developed by a researcher for use in one or a few studies. Such instruments also should be carefully developed, and the report of the study should provide evidence of reliability and validity. However, there usually is no separate manual for others to buy or use.

The next several sections utilize the distinction between standardized and investigator-developed tests. Some tests, personality measures, and attitude measures are developed by investigators for use in a specific study, but there are many standardized measures available. There are standardized questionnaires and interviews, for example, those for diagnostic classification, but most are developed by an investigator for use in a particular study.

Standardized Tests

Although the term *test* is often used quite broadly to include personality and attitude measures, we define the term more narrowly to mean a set of problems with right or wrong answers. The score is based on the number of correct answers. In standardized tests, the scores are usually translated into some kind of normed score that can be used to compare the participants with others and are referred to as *norm-referenced tests*. For example, IQ tests were usually normed so that 100 was the mean and 15 was the standard deviation.

Achievement Tests.   These are designed to measure knowledge gained from educational programs. There should be reliability and validity evidence for the type of participants to be studied. Thus, if one studies a particular ethnic group, or children with developmental delays, and there exists an appropriate standardized test, it should be used. In addition to saving time and effort, the results can be compared with those of others using the same instrument.

When standardized tests are not appropriate for your population or for the objectives of your study, it is better to construct your own test or renorm the standardized one rather than use an inappropriately standardized one. If one develops their own test, evidence for reliability and validity should be determined before using it.

Aptitude Tests.   In the past, these were often called intelligence tests, but this term is less used now because of controversy about the definition of intelligence and to what extent it is inherited. Aptitude tests are intended to measure general performance or problem-solving ability. These tests attempt to measure the participant's ability to solve problems and apply knowledge in a variety of situations.

In a quasi-experiment or a study designed to compare groups that differ in diagnostic classification (e.g., ADHD), it is often important to control for group differences in aptitude. This might be done by matching on IQ or statistically (e.g., using analysis of covariance with IQ as the covariate).

The most widely used individual aptitude tests are the Stanford–Binet and the Wechsler tests. The Stanford–Binet test produces an intelligence quotient (IQ), which is derived by dividing the obtained mental age by the child's actual or chronological age. A trained psychometrician must give these tests to one person at a time, which is expensive in both time and money. Group aptitude tests, on the other hand, may be more practical for use in research in which group averages are to be used.

Standardized Personality Inventories

Personality inventories present a series of statements describing behaviors. Participants are asked to indicate whether the statement is characteristic of their behavior, by checking *yes* or *no* or by indicating how typical it is of them. Usually there are a number of statements for each characteristic measured by the instrument. Some standardized inventories measure characteristics of persons that might not strictly be considered personality. For example, inventories measure temperament (e.g., Child Temperament Inventory), behavior problems (e.g., Child Behavior Checklist), or motivation (e.g., Dimensions of Mastery Questionnaire). Notice that these instruments have various labels, that is, *questionnaire, inventory,* and *checklist.* They are said to be standardized because they have been administered to a wide variety of respondents, and a manual provides information about norm groups and about the reliability and validity of the measures.

These "paper-and-pencil" inventories are relatively inexpensive to administer and objective to score. However, the validity of a personality inventory depends not only on respondents' ability to read and understand the items but also on their understanding of themselves and their willingness to give frank and honest answers. Although good personality inventories can provide useful information for research, there is clearly the possibility that they may be superficial or biased, unless strong evidence is provided for construct validity.

Another type of personality assessment is the projective technique. These measures require an extensively trained tester, and therefore they are expensive. Projective techniques ask the participant to respond to unstructured stimuli (e.g., ink blots or ambiguous pictures). It is assumed that respondents will project their personality into their interpretation of the stimulus, but, again, one should check for evidence of reliability and validity.

Summated (Likert) Attitude Scales

Likert initially developed this method as a way of measuring attitudes about particular groups, institutions, or concepts. Researchers often develop their own scales for measuring attitudes or values, but there also are a number of standardized scales to measure attitudes such as social responsibility. The term *Likert scale* is used in two ways: for the summated scale that is discussed next, and for the individual items or rating scales from which the summated scale is computed. Likert items are statements related to a particular topic about which the participants are asked to indicate whether they strongly agree, agree, are undecided, disagree, or strongly disagree. The summated Likert scale is constructed by developing a number of statements about the topic, usually some of which are clearly favorable and some of which are unfavorable. To compute the summated scale score, each type of answer is given a numerical value or weight, usually 1 for strongly disagree, up to 5 for strongly agree. When computing the summated scale, the weights of the negatively worded or unfavorable items are reversed so that strongly disagree is given a weight of 5 and strongly agree is 1.

Summated attitude scales, like all other data collection tools, need to be checked for reliability and validity. Internal consistency reliability would be supported if the various individual items correlate with each other, indicating that they belong together in assessing this attitude. Validity could be assessed by determining whether this summated scale can differentiate between groups thought to differ on this attitude or by correlations with other measures that are theoretically related to this attitude.

Questionnaires and Interviews

These two broad techniques are sometimes called *survey research methods*, but we think that term is misleading because questionnaires and interviews are used in many studies that would not meet the definition of survey research. In *survey research* a sample of participants is drawn (usually using one of the probability sampling methods) from a larger population. The intent of surveys is to make inferences describing the whole population. Thus the sampling method and return rate are very important considerations. Salant and Dillman (1994) provided an excellent source for persons who want to develop and conduct their own questionnaire or structured interview.

Questionnaires are any group of written questions to which participants are asked to respond in writing, often by checking or circling responses. *Interviews* are a series of questions presented orally by an interviewer and are usually responded to orally by the participant. Both questionnaires and interviews can be highly structured, but it is common for interviews to be more open-ended, allowing the participant to provide detailed answers, and providing the interviewer the opportunity to build new questions on previous answers.

Open-ended questions do not provide choices for the participants to select; rather, they must formulate an answer in their own words. This type of question requires the least effort to write, but it can be difficult to code and is demanding for participants, especially if responses have to be written or concern issues that the person has not considered.

Closed-ended items ask participants to chose among discrete categories and select which one best reflects their opinion or situation. Questions with ordered choices are common on questionnaires and are often similar to the individual items in a personality inventory or a summated attitude scale.

These questions may in fact be single Likert-type items, which the respondent is asked to rate from strongly disagree to strongly agree.

Two main types of interviews are telephone and face to face. *Telephone interviews* are almost always structured and usually brief, whereas *face-to-face interviews* can vary from what amounts to a highly structured, oral questionnaire with closed-ended answers to in-depth interviews, preferred by qualitative researchers. *In-depth interviews* are usually tape-recorded and transcribed so that the participant's comments can be coded later. All types of interviews are relatively expensive because of their one-to-one nature.

SUMMARY

We have provided an overview of techniques used to assess variables in the applied behavioral sciences. Most of the methods are used by both quantitative/positivist and qualitative/constructivist researchers but to different extents. Qualitative researchers prefer more open-ended, less structured data collection techniques than do quantitative researchers. Direct observation of participants is common in experimental and qualitative research; it is less common in so-called survey research, which tends to use self-report questionnaires. It is important that investigators use instruments that provide reliable and valid data for the population and purpose for which they will be used. Standardized instruments have manuals that provide norms and indexes of reliability and validity. However, if the populations and purposes on which these data are based are different from those of the researcher, it may be necessary to develop your own instrument and provide new evidence of reliability and validity.

Part III

RESEARCH APPROACHES, QUESTIONS, AND DESIGNS

Chapter 11

Quantitative Research Approaches

In this chapter, we describe our conceptual framework for the five quantitative research approaches: randomized experimental, quasi-experimental, comparative, associational, and descriptive. The research literature is inconsistent, but we think that it is important to make logical, consistent, and conceptually important distinctions among different approaches to research. We believe that this framework and labeling are helpful because the terminology (a) is more appropriate, (b) is more logically consistent, (c) helps make the leap from approaches and designs to selection of appropriate statistics, (d) provides appropriate guidance about inferring cause and effect, (e) separates approaches and data collection techniques, which are conceptually orthogonal, and (f) deals well with complex studies because the approaches relate to research questions or hypotheses and not necessarily to whole studies.

Remember from chapter 6 on variables that we distinguish between active and attribute independent variables. An *active independent variable* is a variable such as a treatment, workshop, or other intervention that is given to one group and withheld from another group of participants, within a specified period of time *during the study*. Or one level of the independent variable, perhaps a new therapy, is given to one group of participants and another level of the independent variable, perhaps a traditional therapy, is given to another group of participants. A second type of independent variable is called an *attribute independent variable* because it is a measure of a characteristic of the person or his or her situation. Ethnicity and type of disability are considered to be attribute variables because a subject cannot be assigned to an ethnicity or disability group. However, if determined by the institutional review board to be ethical, some "state" characteristics of participants, such as anxiety, can be manipulated. If some participants are assigned to an anxiety-reduction condition and others to a control condition, anxiety would be considered an active variable in that study. Usually anxiety is measured, not manipulated, and is considered to be an attribute variable.

Figure 11.1 indicates that the general purpose of all five approaches, except descriptive, is to explore relationships (in the broad sense) between or among variables. We point this out to be consistent with the notion that all common parametric statistics are relational and with the typical phrasing of research questions and hypotheses as investigating the relationship between two or more variables. Note that these approaches really apply to a research question, not necessarily to an entire study, which may have several research questions and use more than one approach. Figure 11.1 also indicates the specific purpose, type of research question, and general type of statistic used in each of the five approaches.

Research Approaches With an Active Independent Variable

Randomized Experimental Approach.   This approach provides the best evidence about cause and effect. For a research approach to be called randomized experimental, two criteria must be met. First, the independent variable must be active (i.e., be a variable that is given, such as a treatment). Second, the researcher must randomly assign participants to groups or conditions. As you can see from Table 11.1, this latter criterion is what differentiates experiments from quasi-experiments. Chapters 13–15 provide more discussion of specific randomized and quasi-experimental designs.

Quasi-Experimental Research Approach.   Researchers do not agree on the definition of a quasi-experiment. Our definition is implied in Table 11.1: There must be an active/manipulated independent variable, but the participants are not randomly assigned to the groups. Much applied research involves groups that are already intact, such as clinic participants, where it is not possible to change those assignments and divide the participants randomly into experimental and control groups. Such research is considered to be quasi-experimental and the designs are called *nonequivalent comparison group designs.*

We divide the quasi-experimental approach into strong, moderate, and weak designs. In the strong quasi-experimental designs, participants are already in similar intact groups, but the treatment (rather than the participants) is randomly assigned to these groups. In a moderate-strength quasi-experimental design, the participants again are in intact groups, but the investigator is not able to randomly assign the treatment to certain groups. Instead, the investigator takes advantage of a situation where it is known

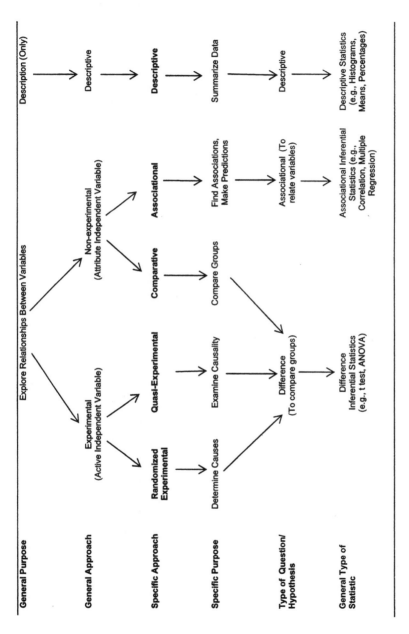

FIG. 11.1. Schematic diagram showing how the general type of statistic and hypothesis or question used in a study corresponds to the purposes and the approach.

TABLE 11.1
A Comparison of the Five Basic Quantitative Research Approaches

Criteria	Randomized Experimental	Quasi-Experimental	Comparative	Associational	Descriptive
Random assignment of participants to groups by the Investigator	Yes	No	No	No (only one group)	No groups
Independent variable is active	Yes	Yes	No (attribute)	No (attribute)	No independent variable
Independent variable is controlled *by the Investigator*[a]	Always	Sometimes	No	No	No
Independent variable has only a few levels/categories[b]	Usually	Usually	Usually	Typically 5+ ordered levels	No independent variable
Associations between variables or comparison of groups	Yes (comparison)	Yes (comparison)	Yes (comparison)	Yes (association)	No

[a]Although this is a desired quality of randomized experimental and quasi-experimental designs, it is not sufficient for distinguishing between the randomized experimental and quasi-experimental approaches.

[b]This distinction is made for educational purposes and is only "usually" true. In the associational approach, the independent variable usually is *assumed to be continuous*; i.e., it *has many ordered levels*/categories. We consider the approach to be associational if the independent variable has five or more *ordered* categories. Except for this difference and a difference in the statistics typically used with them, the comparative and associational approaches are the same. Note there are associational statistics that can be used when there are a few nominal levels of the independent variable.

that one setting (e.g., clinic) will receive the intervention and another (one hopes) similar setting will not receive the intervention. In weak quasi-experimental designs, the participants have assigned themselves to the groups by volunteering to be in the treatment or control group. In the weak quasi-experimental approach, the groups are likely to be very different and thus pose a serious threat to internal validity. Quasi-experiments, especially moderate and weak ones, do not provide good evidence about the cause of changes in the dependent variable.

Research Approaches That Have Attribute Independent Variables

Table 11.1 shows that in most ways the associational and comparative approaches are similar. Both are called nonexperimental approaches, as shown in Fig. 11.1. The distinction between them, which is implied but not stated in most research textbooks, is in terms of the number of levels of the independent variable. This distinction between comparative and associational approaches is made only for educational purposes. In the associational approach, the independent variable is assumed to be continuous rather than have a few levels or categories. Neither approach provides evidence for determining cause and effect.

It is common for *survey research* to include both comparative and associational as well as descriptive research questions, and therefore to use all three approaches. It is also common for experimental studies to include attribute independent variables such as gender and thus to use both experimental and comparative approaches. The approaches are tied to types of independent variables and research questions, not necessarily to whole studies.

Comparative Research Approach. Table 11.1 shows that, like randomized experiments and quasi-experiments, the comparative approach, which includes approaches sometimes called *causal comparative* or *ex post facto*, usually has a few levels (usually two to four) or categories for the independent variable and makes comparisons between groups. Studies that use the comparative approach compare groups based on a few levels of an attribute independent variable. For example, the DiLorenzo et al. (2004) study compared persons with multiple sclerosis (MS) who were younger than 60 with those 60 or older—that is, two levels or groups of age.

The randomized experimental, quasi-experimental, and comparative approaches tend to use the same types of inferential statistics, often a *t* test or analysis of variance. Figure 11.1 illustrates this point.

Associational Research Approach.   In this approach, the independent variable is often continuous or has a number of ordered categories, usually five or more. To show the similarity of the associational and comparative approaches, suppose that the investigator is interested in the relationship between IQ and self-concept in children. If IQ, the independent variable, had been divided into three groups (low, average, and high), the research approach would have been comparative. The associational approach would treat the independent variable, IQ, as continuous. In other words, all participants would be in a single group measured on two continuous, hopefully normally distributed, variables: IQ and self-concept. Likewise, the DiLorenzo et al. (2004) study would have used the associational approach if it had used actual age in years as the independent variable, instead of splitting age into younger and older groups.

Correlation and multiple regression are statistical methods commonly used with the associational approach. We prefer to label this approach *associational* rather *correlational*, as some books do, because the approach is more than, and should not be confused with, a specific statistic.

Although technically for correlation there is no independent variable, it is common for researchers to conceptualize their design so that one variable is presumed to be the independent or predictor variable and one is the dependent/outcome variable for a particular research question. This is important not only when doing regression statistics but because researchers almost always have some direction of "effect" in mind even if their statistics do not demonstrate cause.

In both the comparative and associational approaches, some things (e.g., analysis of covariance or partial correlation) can be done to strengthen the validity of the design but neither approach is inherently stronger. Although a high correlation does not prove cause and effect, neither does a highly significant t test, if the approach is comparative (or quasi-experimental).

Descriptive Research Approach

Most research books use a broader definition for descriptive research or do not seem to have a clear definition, using "descriptive" almost as a synonym for exploratory, or sometimes correlational, research. We think it is clearer and less confusing to restrict the term *descriptive research* to questions and studies that use only descriptive statistics, such as averages, percentages, histograms, and frequency distributions, which are not tested for statistical significance. This approach is different from the other four in that only one variable is considered at a time so that no comparisons or associations are determined. The descriptive approach does not meet any of the criteria listed in Table 11.1 for differentiating approaches. Although most research studies include some descriptive questions (at least to describe the sample), few stop there. In fact, it is rare these days for published quantitative research to be purely descriptive, in our sense; researchers almost always study several variables and their relationships. However, political polls and consumer surveys may be interested only in describing how voters as a group react to issues or what products a group of consumers will buy. Exploratory studies of a new topic may describe only what people say or feel about that topic. Furthermore, qualitative/naturalistic research may be primarily descriptive.

Approaches Versus Data Collection Techniques

We think that it is inappropriate to mix data collection methods with approaches. Hendricks, Marvel, and Barrington (1990) pointed out that this confusion/oversimplification exists in many psychology texts. We agree with them that data collection techniques, such as surveys and observations, are conceptually orthogonal to what we call approaches. Observation and questionnaires can be used, even if they usually are not, with any of the five approaches.

Chapter 12

Research Questions and Hypotheses

THREE TYPES OF BASIC HYPOTHESES OR RESEARCH QUESTIONS

A *hypothesis* is a predictive statement about the relationship between two or more variables. *Research questions* are similar to hypotheses, but they are in question format. Research questions can be further divided into three basic types: *difference questions, associational questions,* and *descriptive questions.* For difference and associational questions, *basic* means that there is one independent and one dependent variable. For descriptive questions, *basic* means that there is one variable.

Both difference and associational questions have the exploration of relationships between variables as a general purpose (see Fig. 11.1). This commonality across both types of questions is in agreement with the statement by statisticians that most common parametric inferential statistics are relational, and it is consistent with the notion that the distinction between the comparative and associational approaches is somewhat arbitrary. However, we believe that the distinction is educationally useful. Remember that difference and associational questions differ in specific purpose and the kinds of statistics they usually use to answer the question (see Fig. 11.1 again).

For difference questions, one compares groups or levels derived from the independent variable in terms of their scores on the dependent variable. This type of question typically is used with the randomized experimental, quasi-experimental, and comparative approaches. For an associational question, one associates or relates the independent and dependent

TABLE 12.1
Examples of Three Kinds of Basic Research Questions

1. *Basic difference (group comparison) questions*
   For this type of hypothesis or research questions, the levels or categories of the independent variable (e.g., anxiety) are used to split the participants into groups (e.g., high
   and low), which are then compared to see if they differ in respect to the average scores
   on the dependent variable (e.g., test performance).
   > *Example of a difference research question:* Do persons with low and high anxiety differ on
   > average test scores? In other words, will the average performance of the high anxiety
   > persons be different from the average performance for low anxiety persons?

2. *Basic associational (relational) questions*
   For this type of hypothesis or question, the scores on the independent variable (e.g.,
   anxiety) are associated with or related to scores on the dependent variable (e.g., performance).
   > *Example of an associational hypothesis:* There will be a negative association (correlation)
   > between anxiety scores and test performance. In other words, we hypothesized that
   > those persons who are high on anxiety tend to have low performance, those with low
   > anxiety tend to have high performance, and those in the middle on the one variable
   > tend to be in the middle on the other variable.

3. *Basic descriptive questions*
   For this type of question, scores on a single variable are described in terms of their
   central tendency, variability, or percentages.
   > *Example:* What percent will have scores between 70 and 80?

variables. Our descriptive questions are not answered with inferential statistics; they merely describe or summarize data.

There are a number of acceptable ways to state research hypotheses/
questions. An example of each of these types of questions is given in Table
12.1. We think it is advisable to use the research *question* format rather than
a hypothesis unless one has a clear directional prediction.

DIFFERENCE VERSUS ASSOCIATIONAL STATISTICS

We think it is educationally useful, although not commonly explicit in statistics books, to divide inferential statistics into two types corresponding to
difference and associational hypotheses/questions. As shown in Fig. 11.1,
difference inferential statistics are usually (but not always) used for the randomized experimental, quasi-experimental, and comparative approaches,
which test for differences between groups (e.g., using analysis of variance,
also called ANOVA). *Associational inferential statistics* test for associations or
relationships between variables and usually use some type of correlation or
multiple regression analysis. We realize that this dichotomy of using one
type of data analysis procedure to test for differences (where there are a few
levels of the independent variable) and another type of data analysis proce-

dure to test for associations (where there is a continuous independent variable) is somewhat artificial. Both continuous and categorical independent variables can be used in a general linear model (regression) approach to data analysis. However, the practical implication is that most researchers adhere to the above dichotomy in data analysis. We utilize this contrast between difference and associational inferential statistics in chapters 23 and 32 when discussing the selection of an appropriate statistic.

SIX TYPES OF RESEARCH QUESTIONS: THREE BASIC AND THREE COMPLEX

Many studies are more complex than implied by the preceding examples. In fact, most studies have more than one hypothesis or research question and may utilize more than one of the research approaches. It is common to find a study with one active independent variable (e.g., treatment) and one or more attribute-independent variables (e.g., gender). This type of study combines the randomized experimental approach (if the participants were randomly assigned to groups) and the comparative approach and asks two difference questions. We show later that there are actually three questions. This *set* of three questions can be considered a *complex difference question* because the study has two independent variables that can be analyzed together. They could both be active or both attribute; it would still be a study with a complex difference question. Likewise, *complex associational questions* are used in studies with more than one independent variable considered together.

Table 12.2 expands our overview of research questions to include both basic and complex questions of each of the three types: descriptive, difference, and associational. The table also includes examples of the types of statistics commonly included under each of the six types of questions.

The descriptive questions (1 and 2) are answered with descriptive statistics. Questions 3 to 6 are answered with inferential statistics, ones that make inferences about population means or associations based on data from the sample used in the study. Note that some complex descriptive statistics (e.g., a cross-tabulation table) could be tested for significance with inferential statistics; if they were so tested, they would no longer be considered descriptive. We think that most qualitative/constructivist researchers ask complex descriptive questions because they consider more than one variable/concept at a time, but they seldom use inferential/hypothesis testing statistics. Furthermore, complex descriptive statistics are used to check reliability and to reduce the number of variables (e.g., with factor analysis), as indicated by Table 12.2.

TABLE 12.2
Summary of Six Types of Research Questions

Type of Research Question— Number of Variables	Example Statistics
1. Basic descriptive questions—one variable	Mean, standard deviation, frequency distribution
2. Complex descriptive questions—two or more variables, but no use of inferential statistics	Box plots, cross-tabulation tables, factor analysis, measures of reliability
3. Basic/single-factor difference questions— one independent and one dependent variable. Independent variable usually has a few levels (ordered or not)	*t* test, one-way ANOVA
4. Complex/multifactor difference questions—usually two or a few independent variables and one dependent variable	Factorial ANOVA
5. Basic associational questions—one independent variable and one dependent variable. Usually at least five *ordered* levels for both variables. Often they are continuous	Correlation tested for significance
6. Complex/multivariate associational questions—two or more independent variables and one dependent variable. Usually five or more ordered levels for all variables, but some or all can be dichotomous variables	Multiple regression, logistic regression

Note. Many studies have more than one dependent variable. It is common to treat each one separately (i.e., to do several *t* tests, ANOVAs, correlations, or multiple regressions). However, there are complex statistics (e.g., MANOVA and canonical correlation) used to treat several dependent variables together in one analysis.

EXAMPLES OF COMPLEX DIFFERENCE AND ASSOCIATIONAL QUESTIONS

Complex Difference (and Interaction) Questions. When you have two categorical independent variables considered together, you have three research questions or hypotheses. As we discuss in later chapters, there are advantages of considering two or three independent variables at a time. An example of a set of three questions answered by one two-way (factorial) ANOVA is as follows:

- Is there a difference on average achievement scores between children having high anxiety and children having low anxiety?

- Is there a difference on average achievement scores between male and female children?
- Is there a difference on average achievement scores due to the interaction between the variables of anxiety and gender?

Note that the first question states the levels or categories of the first independent variable; that is, it states the groups that are to be compared (high-vs. low-anxiety children). The second question does the same for the second independent variable; that is, it states the levels (male and female) to be compared. However, in the third (interaction) question, it is asked whether the first variable itself (anxiety) interacts with the second variable (gender). The answer to this third question (whether there is a statistically significant interaction) is the key to understanding and interpreting the analysis, as we show in chapter 28.

Complex Associational Questions.   In the associational approach, when two or more independent variables are considered together, rather than separately, you get a new kind of question. Chapters 30 and 31 provide discussions of three complex associational statistics (multiple regression, logistic regression, and discriminant analysis) used to answer this type of research question. An example is as follows:

- What is the best combination of anxiety, gender, father's education, and motivation to predict achievement?

CONCLUSION

It is appropriate to phrase any difference or associational research question as simply a *relationship* between the independent variable(s) and the dependent variable. However, we think that phrasing the research questions/hypotheses, as shown in Table 12.1 and in the two sections just provided, helps match the question to the appropriate statistical analysis. What is not desirable, unless there is a well-controlled, randomized experiment, is to phrase the hypotheses/questions as "What is the effect of the independent variable on the dependent variable?" This phrasing is common in statistics books, but it may lead one to infer causation when that is inappropriate.

Chapter 13

Quasi-Experimental Designs

In earlier chapters, we introduced two types of independent variables, active and attribute. The randomized experimental and quasi-experimental approaches both have an active independent variable, which has two or more values, called levels. The dependent variable is the outcome measure or criterion of the study.

In both randomized and quasi-experimental approaches, the active independent variable has at least one level that is some type of intervention given to participants in the experimental group during the study. Usually there is also a comparison or control group, which is the other level of the independent variable. There can be more than two levels or groups (e.g., two or more different interventions plus one or more comparison groups), but for simplicity our examples will be limited to no more than two groups.

As discussed in chapter 11, the key difference between quasi-experiments and randomized experiments is whether the participants are assigned randomly to the groups or levels of the independent variable. In *quasi-experiments* random assignment of the participants is not done; thus, the groups are always considered to be nonequivalent, and there are alternative interpretations of the results that make definitive conclusions about cause and effect difficult. For example, if some children diagnosed with attention deficit hyperactivity disorder were treated with stimulants and others were not, later differences between the groups could be due to many factors. Unless children were randomly assigned to receive the medication or not, the groups could be different because families who volunteer (or agree) to have their children medicated may be different, in important ways, from those who do not. Or perhaps the more disruptive kids were given stimulants. Thus, later problem behaviors (or positive outcomes) could be due to initial differences between the groups.

In this chapter, we discuss specific quasi-experimental research designs. A specific research design helps us visualize the independent variables of the study, the levels within these independent variables, and when measurement of the dependent variable will take place. Examining these specific research designs helps determine the *internal validity* of the study, the strength of the design, and the extent to which one can validly infer that the treatment caused the outcome. We point out some threats to internal validity. These threats are discussed in more detail in chapter 17.

POOR QUASI-EXPERIMENTAL DESIGNS

Results from these designs (sometimes called *preexperimental*) are hard to interpret; they should not be used if it is possible to use one of the better quasi-experimental or randomized designs. Unfortunately, these poor designs are relatively common in clinical practice.

One-Group Posttest-Only Design

An example of this design, sometimes referred to as the *one-shot case study*, would be some evaluations of a new treatment. The investigator introduces the treatment and uses some outcome measure to determine the patient's response to the treatment. The design is diagramed as follows:

$$E: \quad X \quad O$$

This diagram and those that follow indicate a time sequence. First, all participants are in one group, the experimental group (E). Then the treatment (X) and, finally, a posttest (O) take place. The problem with the design is that it does not satisfy even the minimum condition for a research problem, which is the investigation of a relationship or comparison. Note that the intervention is not a variable because there is only one level. Does the one-group posttest-only design have any value? If nothing else, it provides a pilot test of the feasibility and cost of the treatment and the outcome measure. It can help get the "bugs" out of a procedure. The investigator could compare the results to data from an earlier group that had not received the treatment, but then the design would no longer be a one-group posttest-only design.

One-Group Pretest–Posttest Design

This design is diagramed as follows:

$$\text{E: } O_1 \ X \ O_2$$

For this design, an observation in the form of a pretest (O_1) is given first, then the intervention is given to all participants, and finally a second observation (O_2) or posttest is recorded.

The problem with this design is that the comparison is not with a second group, a control group. Instead, the comparison is between the pretest and the posttest within the same group. Because there is no comparison group, the design is susceptible to most of Cook and Campbell's (1979) threats to internal validity. An example of this type of design might be a study of the effects of therapy on pre- and posttest measures of motor performance on one group of children with physical disabilities. The *history* threat means that environmental events are a possible problem in this design. The lack of a control group prevents the investigator from knowing, for example, whether other activities happening in the children's school at the same time as the intervention might be contributing to any changes in motor performance. *Maturation* is also a possible threat to internal validity because the children are getting older and may be better coordinated and stronger even without the intervention. *Carryover effects* are a possible problem in this and all pretest designs because taking the pretest could influence the posttest. This design could be useful if previous research had convincingly demonstrated that without treatment the problem behavior would not decrease. In this situation, a successful intervention would be credible.

Posttest-Only Design With Nonequivalent Groups

This design is diagramed as follows:

$$
\begin{array}{lll}
\text{NR} & \text{E:} & X \quad O \\
\text{NR} & \text{C:} & {\sim}X \quad O
\end{array}
$$

This design has two (or more) groups, an experimental or intervention group and a comparison group (C) that does not receive ($\sim$X) the treatment. Because there is nonrandom assignment (NR) to groups and no pretest, it is impossible to determine the similarity of the groups prior to the treatment. Thus, this design is weak on equivalence of the groups on participant characteristics, especially if the participants volunteered to be in one group or the other, and any difference in outcomes could be due to differences between the groups or to a combination of the results of these differences and the treatment.

BETTER QUASI-EXPERIMENTAL DESIGNS

Pretest–Posttest Nonequivalent-Groups Designs

These designs are diagramed as follows:

$$\text{NR} \quad \text{E:} \quad O_1 \quad X \quad O_2$$
$$\text{NR} \quad \text{C:} \quad O_1 \quad {\sim}X \quad O_2$$

As with all quasi-experiments, there is not random assignment of the participants to the groups in this design. First, measurements are taken on the groups prior to an intervention. Then one group receives a new treatment, which the other group does not receive; often the comparison group receives the usual or traditional treatment. At the end of the intervention period, both groups are measured again to determine whether there are differences between the two groups. The design is considered to be nonequivalent because even if the two groups have the same mean score on the pretest, there may be characteristics that have not been measured that may interact with the treatment to cause differences between the two groups that are not due strictly to the intervention. We classify the pretest–posttest nonequivalent comparison group design into *three strengths* that look alike when diagramed but vary in similarity of the groups on participant characteristics and how much control the investigator has over the independent variable.

Weak Pretest–Posttest Quasi-Experimental Designs. This design occurs when trying to evaluate situations in which participation is voluntary; that is, participants self-select into groups. The participants may have chosen to be in a particular group in order to receive or avoid a particular treatment. Thus, the groups are likely to be different in a number of ways. A design of this type is common when trying to evaluate therapeutic workshops. People who want to attend the workshop volunteer to be in that group. A comparison group often is composed of people who choose not to attend the workshop or of a sample of people who were not invited to attend. Regardless, at least one group has volunteered; therefore, any posttest difference between the group that received the intervention and the group that did not receive the intervention must be tempered by this potential bias.

An obvious improvement in this design when using volunteers is to compose the comparison group of those participants who volunteered to be in the study but were not selected, perhaps due to restriction on numbers. This improvement depends whether there are enough volunteers so that an adequately sized group can be excluded from the treatment for comparison and whether it is ethical to do so. The ethical issue can be dealt with by a design sometimes called a *wait-list comparison group design*. In this design, volunteers who were not accepted for the initial treatment group are tested at the start of the study and at the time of the posttest for the experimental group. Then they receive the treatment.

Moderate-Strength Pretest–Posttest Quasi-Experimental Designs. This design also involves little direct control by the investigator over the independent variable. The moderate-strength quasi-experimental design usually has more similarity of groups prior to the intervention than in the weak design because participants do not assign (self-select) themselves to groups, but are in these groups due to other factors, which are not related to their preference for the intervention. For example, students might be assigned arbitrarily to sections of a class or people may choose their clinic because it is nearest their home. In both cases they are members of "intact" groups prior to a study. In a study of a new versus an established treatment, the researcher might know that one clinic was going to be using the new intervention and another similar clinic was not. The relative strength of this design rests on two questions. First, why did one clinic use the new treatment and why did the other clinic not use it? Second, are patients in the clinic that received the intervention different from patients in the clinic that did not? If there is no reason to suspect bias relative to the dependent variable for either question, then the design is almost as strong as the type discussed next.

Strong Pretest–Posttest Quasi-Experimental Designs. This design might be used in a study when several intact clinics or groups are available and the researcher has control over the active independent variable. The patients have already chosen one of the clinics, and thus the investigator cannot randomly assign participants to groups. However, in the strong quasi-experimental approach, the investigator can randomly assign the new treatment condition to half the intact clinics and the usual treatment to other. The strength of this quasi-experimental design is that it is quite similar to a randomized experimental design except that treatments instead of participants have been randomly assigned to groups or conditions. In some intact situations, which particular clinic patients end up attending may be haphazard; in those cases, the strong quasi-experimental design is almost equivalent to a randomized experimental design. Furthermore, even if the intact groups vary in important ways, such as socioeconomic status and ethnic composition, if there are a large number of groups (clinics) available to participate in the study, random assignment of the treatment to half the

TABLE 13.1
Issues That Determine the Strength of Quasi-Experimental Designs

Strength of Design	Random Assignment of Treatments to Intact Groups	Participant Characteristics Likely to Be Similar
Poor (or pre)	No	No, because no comparison group or no pretest
Weak	No	Not likely, because participants self-assign to groups
Moderate	No	Maybe
Strong	Yes	Maybe

groups is equivalent to random assignment of participants. In that case, this design is called a *cluster random assignment design*. However, these designs are widely regarded as lacking statistical precision.

Table 13.1 summarizes the two issues that determine the strength of the pretest–posttest nonequivalent groups design discussed in this section. These designs vary, as shown, on whether the *treatments* are randomly assigned to the groups or not and on the likelihood that the groups are similar in terms of attributes or characteristics of the participants. In none of the quasi-experimental designs are the *individual participants* randomly assigned to the groups, so the groups are always considered nonequivalent, but the participant characteristics may be similar if there was no bias in how the participants were assigned (got into) the groups.

Time-Series Designs

Time-series designs are different from the more traditional designs discussed in the previous section because they have multiple measurement (time) periods rather than just the pre and post periods. The two most common types are single-group time-series designs and multiple-group time-series designs (see Cook & Campbell, 1979). Within each type, the treatment can be temporary or continuous. The logic behind any time-series design involves convincing others that a baseline (i.e., several pretests) is stable prior to an intervention so that one can conclude that the change in the dependent variable is due to the intervention and not other environmental events or maturation. It is common in time-series designs to have multiple measures before and after the intervention, but there must be multiple (at least three) pretests to establish a baseline. Although the data generated from time-series designs always must be statistically analyzed, one of the hallmarks of time-series designs is the visual display of the data, which are often quite convincing.

Single-Group Time-Series Design. If the treatment is temporary, this design is diagramed as follows:

$$\text{E:} \quad O_1 O_2 O_3 O_4 \quad X \quad O_5 O_6 O_7 O_8$$

An example of this single-group time-series design could involve a clinic that was interested in the effects of a one-time intervention on attendance at therapy. Attendance would be taken weekly prior to the intervention, which as just diagramed is given after four baseline measures. In the diagram, the intervention is temporary, and attendance is recorded weekly for 4 weeks after the intervention. One would expect that if the intervention was successful, there would be an immediate increase relative to the preceding baseline periods, and the effects might or might not be long-lasting.

Multiple-Group Time-Series Designs. Multiple-group time-series designs are similar to those already mentioned, but the design is made stronger by adding a control group that receives the same number of measurement periods but does not receive the intervention. The multiple-group time-series design with temporary treatment is diagramed as follows:

$$\text{NR} \quad \text{E:} \quad O_1 O_2 O_3 O_4 \quad X \quad O_5 O_6 O_7 O_8$$
$$\text{NR} \quad \text{C:} \quad O_1 O_2 O_3 O_4 \quad {\sim}X \quad O_5 O_6 O_7 O_8$$

This type of design can be demonstrated by extending our therapy example from the single-group time-series design. Suppose that the researcher established a comparison group by examining attendance among clients at the clinic who did not receive the intervention. Or, a more common occurrence would be to examine attendance of clients at a similar clinic that did not offer the intervention.

Time-Series Designs With Continuous Treatment. The preceding diagrams showed the design with a temporary, one-time treatment. An example of a *single-group time-series design with continuous treatment* would be a school implementing a new reading curriculum. Pretest measures of the old curriculum might utilize the standardized reading scores from several previous semesters. The same measures could be used for several semesters after the onset of the intervention. The new curriculum is not a temporary intervention like a workshop, but takes place continually until replaced. This design is especially popular when there are records with many repeated measures that can be used for observations and when it is not possible or practical to implement a control group.

The single-group time-series design with continuous treatments could be extended to the *multiple-group time-series design with multiple treatments* by adding a comparison group, perhaps from a similar school district. This comparison group would have the same pretest and posttest measures, but would continue to receive the traditional curriculum.

CONCLUSION

Time-series designs (especially single-group time-series designs) have become important designs in educational and clinical settings, where it is often not practical to introduce a control group. The key advantage of such a time-series design, in contrast to the one-group pretest–posttest poor quasi-experimental design, is the repeated observations or records, which provide a degree of assurance that changes are not caused by other environmental events or maturation. In situations where multiple pretest observations are not possible, but a comparison group is available, the pretest–posttest nonequivalent group design can be used. The strength of such designs depends on the similarity of the experimental and comparison groups before the intervention. Random or unbiased assignment of the treatment to the intact groups should be done whenever possible.

Another type of quasi-experimental design, single-subject designs, is discussed in chapter 15. Randomized experimental designs are discussed in chapter 14.

Randomized Experimental Designs

In the last chapter, we discussed quasi-experimental designs and some of their weaknesses. Remember that quasi- and randomized experimental designs both have an active independent variable, but in randomized designs the participants are randomly assigned to the experimental and control groups. Random assignment of participants to groups should eliminate bias on all characteristics before the independent variable is introduced. This elimination of bias is one necessary condition for the results to provide convincing evidence that the independent variable caused differences between the groups on the dependent variable. For cause to be demonstrated, other biases in environmental and experience variables occurring during the study also must be eliminated.

Four types of randomized experimental designs are discussed. For each we describe and diagram the design, give an example, and present some of the advantages and disadvantages. The diagrams and discussion are limited to two groups, but remember that more than two groups may be used with any of these designs. The experimental group receives the intervention, and the "control" group(s) receives the standard (traditional) treatment, a placebo, and/or another (comparison) treatment. For ethical reasons, it is unusual and not desirable for the control group to receive no treatment at all, but it is difficult to decide which type of control group is appropriate. We label all such options the *control treatment*.

POSTTEST-ONLY CONTROL GROUP DESIGN

The posttest-only control group design can be shown as follows:

$$R \quad E: \quad X \quad O$$
$$R \quad C: \quad \sim X \quad O$$

The sequential operations of the design are to randomly (R) assign participants to either an experimental (E) or control (C) group. Then the experimental group receives the intended intervention (X) and the control group ($\sim X$) does not. At the end of the intervention period, both groups are measured (O), using some form of instrumentation related to the study (dependent variable).

An example of the posttest-only control group design is a study in which children who are at risk for some disorder are randomly assigned to receive an intervention or a control treatment. The intervention group receives a 15-week treatment using a new therapy or medication and the control group receives the traditional treatment. At the end of the 15-week session, both groups are tested on a self-concept scale.

The key point for the posttest-only control group design is the random assignment of participants to groups. If participants are assigned randomly to either one or the other group, the two groups should not be biased on *any* variable prior to the intervention. Therefore, if there are differences on the dependent measure following the intervention, it can be assumed that the differences are due to the intervention and not due to differences in participant characteristics.

PRETEST–POSTTEST CONTROL GROUP DESIGN

The pretest–posttest control group design can be shown as follows:

$$R \quad E: \quad O_1 \quad X \quad O_2$$
$$R \quad C: \quad O_1 \quad \sim X \quad O_2$$

The sequential operations of the pretest–posttest control group design are as follows: First, participants are randomly assigned to groups. Then each group is measured (O_1) on the dependent variable (pretest). After the intervention period, both groups are measured (O_2) again on the dependent variable (posttest).

The pretest–posttest control group design is a common randomized experimental design, because any time a treatment is compared to a control group across two time periods, usually pretest and posttest, this is the design that is used. It is a randomized experiment because the participants are randomly assigned to groups prior to the initial measurement (pretest) period. Reasons for using this design compared with the posttest-only control group design are to check for equivalence of groups before the intervention and to describe the population from which both groups are drawn. Another advantage of this design is that posttest scores could be adjusted statistically through analysis of covariance based on pretest score differences between the treatment and control groups. On the other hand, the problem is that if a pretest is used, it could bias the participants as to what to expect in the study, and practice on the pretest could influence the posttest (i.e., there could be carryover effects). Also, if the dependent variable is invasive (e.g., spinal tap), one would not want to use it as a pretest. The investigator must weigh the advantages of gaining pretest information about the groups with the disadvantage of possibly biasing the posttest.

In both the posttest-only and the pretest–posttest design, random assignment is intended to assure that experimental versus control group differences are not due to differences in the initial characteristics of the two groups. Random assignment does mean that the groups will not differ substantially on the average, but this assurance is adequate only if the sample is large. In small-sample clinical research, it is not uncommon to find some large differences in important characteristics even when the participants were randomly assigned to groups (Kraemer, Jacob, Jeffery, & Agras, 1979). One design that may help with this problem is the randomized design with matching described in the next section.

RANDOMIZED EXPERIMENTAL DESIGN WITH MATCHING

In this design, participants are matched on some characteristic prior to the introduction of any of the conditions of the study. The characteristic that is used for the match must be related to the dependent variable; otherwise, matching is a waste of time and results in a loss of statistical power. If the matching variable is highly related to the outcome, power will increase, making this design useful for clinical studies where only a small sample of participants is available (Kraemer et al., 1979). The design can be used with or without a pretest; in the following, we discuss and diagram only the variant without a pretest.

The sequential operations of the experimental design with matching are as follows:

$$M \quad R \quad E: \quad X \quad O$$
$$M \quad R \quad C: \quad {\sim}X \quad O$$

First, the investigator measures all of the participants on some characteristic, such as intelligence, that previous evidence indicates is related to the dependent or outcome variable. Next, if the independent variable has two levels, the investigator divides all of the participants into pairs matched (M) on their scores on the intelligence test. The idea is to have pairs that are as close as possible on the variable of intelligence. Then it is determined randomly which member of the pair is assigned to the intervention group and which to the control group. The key to the randomized experimental design with matching is to make it as if the two participants are identical (at least as far as the characteristics of interest). Therefore, it is as though one participant is receiving both conditions of the study, even though there are actually two different participants in each pair. Although it is important for the scores for each pair to be close on the matching variable, it is also important that there be a wide spread among all the scores within the sample on the matching variable. A wide spread in scores is important because for this design to be successful each of the pairs must be different from the other pairs. If all of the scores on the matching variable are quite similar, there is no point in matching.

WITHIN-SUBJECTS RANDOMIZED EXPERIMENTAL (OR CROSSOVER) DESIGN

In the simplest case, this design has two levels and can be shown as follows:

		Condition 1	Test	Condition 2	Test
R	Order 1	X	O_1	~X	O_2
R	Order 2	~X	O_1	X	O_2

The participants are randomly assigned to order 1, which receives the experimental condition first and then the control condition, or order 2, which receives the control condition and then the experimental. The approach is considered randomized experimental if the participants are assigned randomly to order 1 or order 2. If not, the approach is quasi-experimental. This type of design is frequently used in studies in which participants are asked to evaluate diets, exercise, and similar events assumed from previous research not to have carryover effects. The strength of this design is that participants act as their own control which reduces error variance. This design can have problems if there are carryover effects from the experimental condition. Furthermore, one must be extremely cautious with this design when comparing a new treatment with a traditional treatment. The problem, often referred to as *asymmetrical transfer effects*, occurs when the impact of one order (perhaps the traditional treatment before the new treatment) is greater than the impact of the other order (new treatment before the traditional treatment).

SUMMARY

Table 14.1 is a summary schematic diagram of the main types of experimental designs discussed in this chapter and chapter 13. Many possible variants of these designs are discussed in Shadish, Cook, and Campbell (2002). We

TABLE 14.1
Summary of Specific Designs
for Experiments and Quasi-Experiments

	Assign.	*Grp.*	*Pre.*	*I.V.*	*Post.*
Poor quasi-experimental designs					
One-group posttest-only design	NR	E:		X	O
One-group pretest–posttest design	NR	E:	O	X	O
Posttest-only design with nonequiva-	NR	E:		X	O
lent groups	NR	C:		~X	O
Quasi-experimental designs					
Pretest–posttest nonequivalent	NR	E:	O	X	O
Comparison-group designs	NR	C:	O	~X	O
Single-group time-series designs	NR	E:	OOO	X	OOO
With temporary treatment					
With continuous treatment	NR	E:	OOO	XOXO	XOXO
Multiple-group time-series designs	NR	E:	OOO	X	OOO
With temporary treatment	NR	C:	OOO	~X	OOO
With continuous treatment	NR	E:	OOO	XOXO	XOXO
	NR	C:	OOO	O O	O O
Randomized experimental designs					
Posttest-only control-group design	R	E:		X	O
	R	C:		~X	O
Pretest–posttest control-group design	R	E:	O	X	O
	R	C:	O	~X	O
Randomized experimental design	M R	E:		X	O
with matching	M R	C:		~X	O

		Order		Post 1		Post 2
Within-subjects or crossover design	R	E_1	X	O	~X	O
	R	E_2	~X	O	X	O

Note. Assign. = assignment of subjects to groups (NR = nonrandom, R = random, M R = matched then randomly assigned). Grp. = group or condition (E: = experimental, C: = control or comparision). Pre = pretest (O = an observation or measurement; a blank means there was no pretest for that group). I.V. = active idependent variable (X = intervention, ~X = control, comparison or other treatment). Post = postttest (O = a posttest observation or measure).

divide Table 14.1 into three sections: poor quasi-experimental designs, quasi-experimental designs, and randomized experimental designs.

Random assignment of participants to groups is what differentiates randomized experiments from quasi-experiments. We have discussed the strengths and weaknesses of each design. Randomized experimental designs provide the best information about whether the independent variable caused changes in the dependent variable. That is, if attrition and extraneous variables are controlled, randomized experiments have the highest *internal validity*, which is discussed in chapter 17. The poor quasi-experiments are missing a comparison group, a pretest, or both, so by themselves provide little support for the effectiveness of the intervention. Quasi-experimental designs, if the experimental and comparison groups are very similar, provide some support for the causal effect of the intervention.

Chapter 15

Single-Subject Designs

In this chapter we describe single-subject designs, a subcategory of quasi-experimental time-series designs that can be used with very few participants. These single-subject designs have many of the characteristics that govern traditional group time-series designs, such as the numerous repeated measures on each participant and the initiation and withdrawal of treatment. Using very few participants increases the flexibility of the design but limits the generalizability of the results. The data obtained from these designs usually are not subjected to statistical methods. When statistical methods are applied, the types of analyses used are often unique to these designs.

We define single-subject designs as time-series designs in which an intervention (active independent variable) is given to very few participants—typically four or fewer—not necessarily to only a single subject. In some situations, such as reversal designs, the independent variable is initiated and withheld several times throughout the study. In multiple-baseline single-subject designs, however, the removal of the independent variable is not necessary. Single-subject designs are considered to be quasi-experimental designs because they must include an active independent variable, but there is no random assignment of participants to treatments. The three most frequently encountered single-subject designs are ABAB (or reversal) designs, multiple-baseline designs, and alternating-treatment designs.

REVERSAL DESIGNS

In these designs (Fig. 15.1), A1 stands for the first *baseline* phase, during which the participant is usually observed for a number of time periods. In all single-subject designs, the investigator plots the data for each measure-

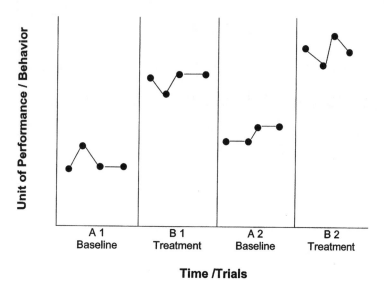

FIG. 15.1.   Hypothetical data for an ABAB single-subject quasi-experimental design.

ment period to determine whether the behavior during baseline (or treatment) is increasing, decreasing, or leveling off. After the baseline has leveled off, the investigator initiates the treatment or active independent variable. B1 refers to the first *intervention* phase. Once the treatment data appear to level off (relatively flat line), the investigator withdraws the treatment and initiates a second baseline phase (A2). The investigator observes this phase for several (three at the minimum) periods (sessions or trials) until the behavior levels off. Then the investigator initiates B2, the second treatment phase. This completes the minimum reversal design, with two A or baseline phases and two B or treatment phases.

What should happen in a typical ABAB single subject study? Figure 15.1 shows schematically what one would expect. During the initial baseline period (A1), there may be some fluctuation of responding, but after the first few periods, the participant's responses (dependent variable) should habituate or level off. During the initial treatment period (B1), behavior should increase (or decrease if the treatment is designed to reduce an undesirable behavior; e.g., aggression). One would expect this behavior to continue to increase up to a point and then level off. Next, during the withdrawal of the treatment (the A2 phase), the expectation is that performance will decrease (although perhaps not as low as the A1 phase) and then begin to stabilize. When the stabilization has occurred, the reintroduction of the treatment (B2 phase) takes place and performance is expected to increase to at least that of the preceding treatment phase. Often this phase is the highest because the second treatment phase is added to any carryover effect from the first treatment phase.

The ABAB single-subject reversal design does not necessarily mean that there only should be two baseline phases and two intervention phases. Many ABAB designs use at least three A and three B phases, whereas some use quite a few more. Increasing the number of A and B phases makes the study more convincing, especially if each A (nontreatment) phase shows a decline or no increase in the desired behavior and each B (treatment) phase shows increases in the desired behavior. When this occurs, there is strong evidence that it is the independent variable that is responsible for changes in the dependent variable (strong internal validity).

In reversal designs, the investigator is not limited to just the phases of A and B. Consider a situation in which after the initial A phase, the investigator initiates a treatment in the B phase. However, the treatment fails to increase performance above that observed during the baseline period. In a single-subject design, the investigator could modify the treatment and introduce it (as C) after the B phase. Thus the design might be something like ABCAC. When making these changes, it is important to reintroduce the baseline phase to test the effectiveness of the new treatment. The point to remember is that a strength of single-subject designs is flexibility. The number of sessions making up any particular phase may be changed, and the researcher is not limited to just an A and B phase.

MULTIPLE-BASELINE DESIGNS

Multiple-baseline single-subject designs were introduced more recently. Multiple-baseline designs were introduced because (a) in clinical situations the removal of treatment is often considered unethical, especially if the treatment appears successful, and (b) many of these studies were being performed in settings in which the patient was responsible for payment for the treatment. Multiple-baseline designs make up a category of single-subject designs and consist of three specific types of designs. These specific designs are *multiple-baseline across participants*, *multiple-baseline across behaviors*, and *multiple-baseline across settings*. In the initial stages of multiple-baseline studies, as many as three baselines may be recorded simultaneously. These baselines may represent the responses of three different participants, the responses of three different behaviors of the same participant, or the responses of the same participant in three different settings. The key to multiple-baseline single-subject studies is that the investigator intervenes at a *randomly selected time* and observes the effect on only one of the baselines while the other two baselines should be unchanged. If there is an observed increase in desired behavior for that particular participant to the treatment, then it appears that the change is due to the introduction of the independent variable. The logic is that if some external event, other than the independent variable, were altering behavior, it would affect all participants, settings, or behaviors, not just one. We will discuss the multiple baseline across subjects design because it is the most common. Its popularity is partially due to the ease of completing this type of study, especially in a clinical setting.

The procedure for carrying out the *multiple-baseline across-subjects design* is as follows. Initially, the investigator selects three (or perhaps four) different participants for the study. All three participants are observed concurrently in a baseline phase, and their responses for each baseline period are plotted on a graph (see Fig. 15.2). Next, the investigator gives the intervention to one (randomly selected) of the participants while continuing to obtain baseline data on the other two participants at the same time. After a given number of periods, the intervention is started with the second participant and continued with the first participant, while the baseline is continued for the third participant. Again, after a number of baseline periods, the intervention is started with the third participant and continued with the first two participants. As demonstrated in Fig. 15.2, the baselines of the participants *not* receiving the intervention should remain stable and not change until the intervention is targeted with that participant.

ALTERNATING-TREATMENT DESIGNS

A third commonly used single-subject design is the alternating treatment design. The term *multielement design* also is used to describe this design. The purpose of this design is to compare the impact of two different treatments within the single subject design framework. The procedure for this design is to establish a baseline on each participant and then introduce the first treat-

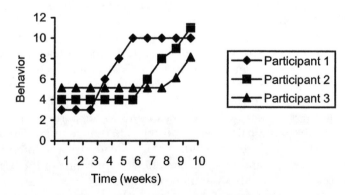

FIG. 15.2.   Hypothetical data for a multiple-baseline across-subjects design.

ment. Once the responses to this treatment become stable, the first treatment is discontinued and a second treatment is introduced. After response stabilization, the second treatment is discontinued and the first treatment is reinstated. The two treatments continue to be alternated until definitive response patterns to each treatment can be discerned. The more phases for each treatment, the fewer data points are required for each phase (Ottenbacher, 1986). Some studies do not implement a baseline prior to the introduction of the treatment. However, Ottenbacher pointed out that a baseline phase helps to demonstrate the impacts of the treatments.

One method to strengthen the alternating treatment design is to counterbalance the order of the treatments among the different participants. Specifically, after baseline, the first participant would get treatment one and then treatment two, while the second participant would get treatment two and then treatment one. The major disadvantage of this design, similar to all within subject/repeated measures designs, is carryover effects. Once a treatment is discontinued there may be transient or permanent changes to the participant which could influence responses to the second treatment. Therefore, the design is more applicable for demonstrating the impacts of treatments that do not have permanent or lasting effects.

MEASUREMENT PERIODS AND INSTRUMENTS

In a reversal design, the number of measurement periods may change between one phase and another. One should wait until the behavior in each phase is stable before starting or withdrawing treatment. This adds to the flexibility of the design. On the other hand, within each measurement period (session), the length of time must be the same.

A second measurement issue to consider when performing single-subject designs is that the type of instrument selected could seriously compromise the study. Each session must yield a score or a number of responses. If there are a limited number of responses per session, then the instrument may not be sensitive enough for the study. When naturally occurring responses are too infrequent, probes may be introduced which allow the investigator to record the desired number of responses. When probes are used, the dependent variable is often expressed as a percentage correct. There are two types of measures (dependent variables) used in single-subject designs: *paper-and-pencil tests* and *behavioral observations* (which are the most common). Certain rules should be followed when using observation.

1. It is best for the observer not to be the teacher, parent, or therapist.
2. It is best to have the observers be as discreet as possible (i.e., be another student or students in the classroom or observers watching through a one-way mirror).

3. The critical responses to be observed should be well defined before the study.
4. More than one observer should be used to record the responses and check reliability.
5. Interrater reliability should be established among observers before the study.

EVALUATION OF THE RESULTS OF SINGLE-SUBJECT DESIGNS

Many early single-subject studies with animals did not use statistical analysis. Instead, the investigators believed that the graphic displays were convincing. However, single-subject studies with humans, especially reversal designs, usually have fewer baseline and intervention periods than animal studies. In addition, single-subject designs often have a problem of *serial dependency* (responses within the same individual are correlated, and thus future responses are partially predictable). Therefore, an increasing emphasis has been given to using some form of statistical analysis in addition to visual analysis.

Visual Analysis of Single-Subject Designs. When evaluating a single subject graph visually, the key is to look for patterns in the data, especially as the phases change from baseline to intervention and back to baseline. Kazdin (1982) discussed the use of certain criteria for visual inspection of single subject designs. One criterion is *level*, which is the amount of change from the last measurement in a phase to the first measurement in the next phase. Sometimes, just examining change in level can be misleading. Because the criterion of level does not always reflect the pattern of a particular phase, one could use *mean level* as a second, more stable criterion. Mean level refers to the average of the points in one phase compared with the average of the points in the next phase. A third criterion for visual analysis (also suggested by Kazdin) was that of *trend*, which indicates a direction of the points within a phase. The trend could be positive, negative, or flat. An additional criterion for visual analysis recommended by Ottenbacher (1986) is *slope*, which refers to the angle of increase or decrease of the measurement points.

Statistical Analysis of Single-Subject Designs. Although visual analysis has been one of the strengths of single-subject designs, sometimes the graphs from these studies are not convincing. Therefore, investigators using these designs have used statistical tests to determine whether interventions have made a difference. There is a disagreement, however, about the best statistical methods. Kazdin (1982) discussed the use of traditional parametric statistical tests, such as an analysis of variance, to compare all phases of an ABAB design. Nonparametric tests are discussed in some detail by Kratochwill and Levin (1992).

CONSIDERATIONS OF INTERNAL AND EXTERNAL VALIDITY OF SINGLE-SUBJECT DESIGNS

Internal validity examines the degree to which one can state that changes in the dependent variable were due to the independent variable. The following problems affect internal validity in single-subject designs. With few participants, there cannot be random assignment of participants to treatments. More important, the order of the treatment phases also cannot be randomly assigned in reversal designs. In multiple-baseline designs, the order in which participants are given the treatment should be randomized, but often it is not. Last, possible carryover effects exist from one phase to another, especially in alternating treatment designs.

One of the important methods of establishing internal validity in single-subject designs is to increase the number of baseline and intervention phases. Reversal designs performed on animals allow for a large number of phases and produce studies that are convincing—that is, that the intervention is causing the change in the dependent variable. Unfortunately, studies with humans often have resulted in only two phases of baseline and treatment in reversal designs. Furthermore, many designs have used less than the desired number of data points to establish stable within-phase responding. Therefore, internal validity, once considered a strength in single-subject designs, is often lacking.

The problems with external validity, or generalizability, for single-subject designs are even more obvious. The random selection of one participant, or even a small number of participants, is unusual because the participants are usually selected because of some particular behavioral or physical problem. What eventually works for one client/participant may not work for another. And, of course, some of the unsuccessful treatments may work for another person. One method to increase external validity for single subject designs is to perform meta-analysis (chap. 35) on frequently used interventions.

Although there has been some criticism on using meta-analysis with single-subject designs, several meta-analyses have been carried out (Scruggs & Mastropieri, 1994; Swanson & Sachse-Lee, 2000). However, there have been criticisms involving the type of effect size to be used and the method of computing the effect size (Gliner et al. 2004).

SUMMARY

Single-subject designs commonly have been used in clinical situations where the opportunity to collect data and observe an intervention on very few participants is provided. The design is considered to be a subcategory of quasi-experimental designs because the independent variable is active but there is no random assignment of participants to groups. In addition to its use with very few participants, the design also provides the investigator with flexibility to alter treatments during the study, especially in reversal designs. The three most commonly implemented single-subject designs are reversal designs, multiple-baseline designs, and alternating-treatment designs.

Internal validity in single subject designs can be strong, especially if the number of phases of baseline and treatment and the number of measurement periods within a phase are increased. Whenever possible, random assignment of order of participants to treatments (multiple baseline across participants) or counterbalance of treatments should be undertaken. External validity is problematic for these types of designs because of the small number of participants and because selection is usually based on a particular behavioral or physical problem. Meta-analysis of single-subject designs has been introduced, but these meta-analyses have not been greeted enthusiastically by all researchers.

Chapter 16

General Design Classifications

In this chapter we look at general design classifications because they are important for determining appropriate statistical methods to be used in data analysis. Within the randomized experimental, quasi-experimental, and also comparative approaches, all designs must fit into one of three categories or labels (between, within, or mixed) that we call general design classifications. These designs classifications do not apply to the associational or descriptive approaches.

GENERAL DESIGN CLASSIFICATIONS

Between-Groups Designs

Between-groups designs are defined as designs in which each participant in the research study is in one and only one condition or group. For example, in a study investigating the effects of medication on the dependent variable, number of symptoms, in hyperactive children, there might be two groups (or conditions or levels) of the independent variable: the current medication and a new medication. In a between-groups design, each participant receives only one of the two conditions or levels: either the current medication or the new one. If the investigator wished to have 30 participants in each group, then 60 participants would be needed to carry out the research. Another example is the DiLorenzo et al. (2004) study, which used a between-groups design to compare two groups of multiple sclerosis (MS) patients, younger and older.

Within-Subjects or Repeated-Measures Designs

Within-subjects designs, the second type of general design classification, are conceptually the opposite of between-groups designs. In these designs, each participant in the research receives or experiences all of the conditions or levels of the independent variable in order to complete the study. If we use the hyperactive children example just given, there still would be two conditions or levels to the independent variable. These conditions again are the usual medication and the new medication. In a within-subjects design, each participant would be given first one medication, then the second medication and would be measured for the number of symptoms on both conditions of the independent variable (i.e., both the new and usual medication). If the researcher wished to have 30 participants for each condition, only 30 participants would be needed to carry out the research, because each participant undergoes both conditions of the independent variable in the research. Because each participant is assessed more than once (i.e., for each condition), these designs are also referred to as repeated-measures designs.

Within-subjects designs have appeal due to the reduction in participants needed and to reduction in error variance because each participant is his or her own control. However, often they may be less appropriate than between-groups designs because of the possibility of *carryover effects*. If the purpose of the study is to investigate conditions that may result in a long-term or permanent change, such as learning, it is not possible for a participant to be in one condition and then "unlearn" that condition to be in the same previous state to start the next condition. Within-subjects designs may be appropriate if the effects of order of presentation are negligible, as when participants are asked to evaluate several topics or when a medication effect would not be long-lasting. *Order effects* can be controlled by presenting the conditions to participants in different orders (e.g., in random orders or counterbalanced so that, for example, half receive condition A first and half receive condition B first). Counterbalancing was used in the *crossover* within-subjects randomized experimental design discussed in chapter 14.

Mixed Designs

A mixed design has at least one between-groups independent variable and at least one within-subjects independent variable; thus they have a minimum of two independent variables. A between-groups independent variable is any independent variable that sets up between-groups conditions. A within-subjects independent variable is any independent variable that sets up within-subjects conditions.

Let's return to our example of investigating the effect of medication type on symptoms in hyperactive children. If medication is a within-subjects independent variable, because all children receive both medications as described earlier, we would additionally need a second independent variable that is a between-groups independent variable in order to complete the criteria for a mixed design. If the researcher hypothesized that boys and girls might respond differently to the new medication, a second independent variable could be the gender of the patient. Gender is a between-groups independent variable with two levels, male and female. Therefore, this example satisfies the criteria for a mixed design: two independent variables, with one a within-subjects variable (medication type) and the other a between-groups variable (gender).

An interesting example of a within-subjects design, which is often analyzed as a mixed design, is the crossover design. If one counterbalances the order of the design and is only interested in the two treatment conditions, then the design is a within-subjects design. However, if one is concerned about the *order* of effects in addition to the treatment effects, then the design has two independent variables. The treatment is the within subjects independent variable and the different orders make up the between-groups independent variable.

MORE DESIGN CONSIDERATIONS

Number of Independent Variables

Between-groups designs and within-subjects designs also may have more than one independent variable (usually no more than three), although the minimum requirement for each of these designs is only one independent variable. If the researcher decides to use more than one independent variable in a between-groups design, these additional independent variables also must be between-groups independent variables or the design would be called mixed design. Likewise, in a within-subjects design, additional variables would have to be within-subjects independent variables or the design would be a mixed design.

Type of Independent Variable

In chapter 6, we described all independent variables as *active* (i.e., the treatment is given to one group but not to a second group) or *attribute* (i.e., the investigator is interested in a quality that is a characteristic of one group of people and that is not characteristic of a second group of people). In a between-groups design, the independent variable may be either an active or an attribute variable. Thus, between-groups designs can use the randomized experimental, quasi-experimental, or comparative approach (see chap. 11). For example, new therapies and interventions are active. Gender and type of disability are attribute independent variables used in between-groups designs.

Change Over Time (or Trials) as an Independent Variable

In within-subjects designs, there can be a third type (neither active nor attribute) of independent variable, called change over time or trials. This third type of independent variable is extremely important in randomized experimental and quasi-experimental designs because pretest and posttest are two levels of this type of independent variable. Longitudinal studies, in which the same participants are assessed at several time periods or ages, are another important case in which change over time is the independent variable.

Consider the following randomized experiment using a *pretest–posttest control-group design*. Participants are randomly assigned (R) to one of two groups, an intervention group (E) that receives a new medication and a control group (C) that receives the usual medication. Participants are measured prior to the intervention (O_1) and after the intervention (O_2), perhaps at the end of the study. The design can be viewed as follows:

$$R \quad E: \quad O_1 \quad X \quad O_2$$
$$R \quad C: \quad O_1 \quad \sim X \quad O_2$$

It is a mixed design because there are two independent variables, with one being a between-groups independent variable and the other being a within-subjects independent variable. The independent variable, type of medication, is the between-groups independent variable because each participant experiences only one of the two conditions (medications). The other independent variable in this study, change over time, is a within-subjects independent variable because participants within each group were measured more than once in the study. This independent variable is referred to as *change over time* (or time of measurement) because the second measurement period took place for each participant at a later time than the first measurement period. Change over time is considered a third type of independent variable rather than an active independent variable because you cannot actively manipulate change over time; the posttest always comes after the pretest.

The Gliner and Sample (1996) study is a common example of a mixed design, a *pretest–posttest control-group design*. In that study, the intervention was given to one group and not given to another group (the active, between groups variable), and participants were assessed before and after the intervention (a change over time, within-subjects variable).

DESCRIBING THE VARIOUS TYPES OF DESIGN

Within the Methods section of a research paper often there is a subsection designated *Design* or *Design/Analysis*. The purpose of this section is to identify the independent variable(s), dependent variable(s), and design in studies that use the randomized experimental, quasi-experimental, and comparative approach. An appropriate procedure is to describe the design in terms of (a) the general type of design (between-groups, within-subjects, or mixed), (b) the number of independent variables, and (c) the number of levels or groups within each independent variable (Winer, 1962). Table 16.1 provides examples of how many researchers describe the between, within, and mixed designs for studies with one, two, and three independent variables.

Single-Factor Designs

If the design has only one independent variable (either a between-groups design or a within-subjects design), then it should be described as a single-factor design. (*Factor* is another name for independent variable; see also appendix C). A between-groups design with one independent variable that

TABLE 16.1
Examples of Design Classification Descriptions in a Research Article

Single factor	One independent variable
Between	Single-factor design with ___ levels
Within	Single-factor repeated-measures design with ___ levels
Mixed	NA
Two factor	Two independent variables
Between	___×___Factorial design
Within	___×___Design with repeated measures on both factors
Mixed	___×___(Mixed) design with repeated measures on the second factor
Three factor	Three independent variables
Between	___×___×___Factorial design
Within	___×___×___Design with repeated measures on all factors
Mixed	___×___×___Design with repeated measures on last (or last two) factors

Note. The dependent variable is not part of the design classification and thus is not mentioned. The number of levels for a specific independent variable is inserted in each blank.

has three levels would be described as a single-factor design with three levels. For example, if there were three dosages of a medication, one-third of the children would get each dose. If the same design was a within-subjects design with three levels, then it would be described as a single-factor, repeated-measures design with three levels. In this case, each child would receive all three dosages, probably in a random order. Note that "between groups" is not stated directly in the first example, but it is implied because there is no mention in that example of repeated measures.

Between-Groups Factorial Designs

When there is more than one independent variable, then the levels of each independent variable become important in the description of the design. For example, suppose a design has three between-groups independent variables, and the first independent variable has two levels (e.g., experimental and control), the second independent variable has three levels (e.g., of socioeconomic status), and the third independent variable has two levels (e.g., male and female). The design is written as a $2 \times 3 \times 2$ factorial design (factorial means two or more independent variables). Again, between groups is not explicitly mentioned but is implied because there is no mention of repeated measures, as there would be in a within-subjects design description. Because the design is a between-groups design, the number of groups needed to carry out the study is 2 multiplied by 3 multiplied by 2; or 12 groups.

Within-Subjects Factorial Designs

On the other hand, if the design is a within-subjects design with two independent variables, each with two levels, then it is described as a 2×2 within-subjects design or, more commonly, a 2×2 factorial design with repeated measures on both factors. For example, if there were two medication levels and all participants received a pretest and a posttest, we would have a 2×2 factorial design with repeated measures on both factors.

Mixed Designs

Such a design might have two between-groups independent variables with two and four levels, respectively, and have one within-subjects independent variable with two levels. It would be described as a $2 \times 4 \times 2$ factorial design with repeated measures on the third factor. This could be one study with two treatments, four ethnic groups, and a pretest and posttest.

In review, when describing a design, each independent variable is given one number, the number of levels for that variable. Thus a design description with three numbers (e.g., 2 × 4 × 3) has three independent variables or factors, which have two, four, and three levels, respectively. A single-factor design is specifically classified or described in words, as done earlier, and not with numerals and multiplication signs. Note that the dependent variable is not part of the design description, so is not considered in this section.

Designs, Classifications, and Statistics

Table 14.1 provided schematic diagrams summarizing each of the quasi-experimental and randomized experimental designs discussed in chapters 13 and 14. Each of these specific designs fits into one of the general design classifications. For example, there is no classification for the one group posttest only design because, as noted in chapter 13, the intervention (X) is not a variable; there is only one level. The one group pretest–posttest design is a *single-factor repeated-measures* (within-subjects) *design with two levels* because the only independent variable is change over time; each participant is tested twice. On the other hand, the poor quasi-experimental posttest only design with nonequivalent groups and the randomized experimental posttest only control-group design are both *single-factor between-groups designs with two levels* because the two groups (E and C) received different levels of the independent variable and there is no repeated measure.

All of the designs with two groups (E and C) and with a pretest and posttest, both quasi- and randomized experimental, are mixed designs. For example, the pretest–posttest control group design is a *2 × 2 factorial design with repeated measures on the second factor* because there are two independent groups (E and C) and there is a repeated-measure (within-subjects) variable, change over time.

The design classification (between-groups, within-subjects, or mixed) determines, in good part, the appropriate type of inferential statistic to use. For example, the single-factor between-groups designs would be analyzed with an independent-samples *t* test or one-way analysis of variance (ANOVA) (chap. 24). The within-subjects designs would be analyzed with the correlated or paired-samples *t* test or repeated-measures ANOVA (if there were more than two levels or measures of the dependent variable) (chap. 25). Mixed designs and others with more than one independent variable would usually be analyzed with a type of factorial ANOVA (chaps. 28 and 29).

Although we demonstrated that most of the specific designs within the randomized or quasi-experimental approaches fit into the three design classifications, the quantitative approaches and design classifications have different purposes. The quantitative approaches describe the rigor of the design and are important in the interpretation of the outcome regarding causality. On the other hand, the design classification determines, for the most part, the statistical analysis to be performed.

SUMMARY

This chapter described the general design classifications of between-groups, within-subjects, and mixed designs. In between-groups designs, each participant is in only one group or condition. In within-subjects or repeated-measures designs, on the other hand, each participant receives all the conditions or levels of the independent variable. In mixed designs, there is at least one between-groups independent variable and at least one within-subjects independent variable. In classifying the design, the dependent variable(s) is not mentioned.

The classifications and descriptions presented in this chapter are for difference questions, using the randomized experimental, quasi-experimental, and comparative approaches to research. Appropriate classification and description of the design are crucial for choosing the appropriate inferential statistic, which is the topic of chapter 23 and several that follow.

Part IV

INTRODUCTION TO THE EVALUATION OF METHODS AND DESIGNS

Internal Validity

Chapters 17–19 describe how to evaluate the merit or validity of a research study. We use the term *research validity* when discussing the merit of a whole study to distinguish it from validity of the measurement of a variable. Based on the work of Cook and Campbell (1979), research validity is divided into four components: (a) *measurement reliability and statistics,* (b) *internal validity,* (c) *overall measurement validity of the constructs,* and (d) *external validity.* In this chapter the focus is on internal validity.

INFERRING CAUSE

A major goal of scientific research is to be able to identify a causal relationship between variables. However, there is considerable disagreement among scholars as to what is necessary to prove that a causal relationship exists. Many of those professing the qualitative or constructivist paradigm do not believe that a causal relationship can be determined. However, most scientists would at least subscribe to some probabilistic statement about the causal relationship between two variables. Researchers also would note that even if they cannot identify all the causes or the most important causal factor of an outcome, they can identify a variable as one (or a partial) cause, under certain circumstances. Porter (1997) provided three criteria that must occur to infer a causal relationship: (a) the independent variable must precede the dependent variable in time; (b) a relationship must be established between the independent variable and the dependent variable (in the behavioral sciences this relationship is usually determined statistically); and (c) there must be no plausible third (extraneous) variable that also could account for a relation between the independent and dependent variables.

Four of the five specific research approaches (experimental, quasi-experimental, comparative, and associational) discussed in chapter 11 attempt to satisfy Porter's three prerequisites. All four can, but do not always, meet the first two criteria, the independent variable preceding the dependent variable and establishing a relationship between variables. The randomized experimental and, to a much lesser extent, the quasi-experimental approaches can be successful in meeting Porter's third condition, elimination of extraneous variables. The comparative and associational approaches are not well suited to establishing causes, but things can be done to control for some extraneous variables. Although the comparative and associational approaches are limited in what can be said about causation, they can lead to strong conclusions about the differences between groups and about associations between variables. Furthermore, they are the *only* available approaches, if the focus of the research is on attribute independent variables. The descriptive approach, as we define it, does not attempt to identify causal relationships or, in fact, any relationships. It focuses on describing variables.

INTERNAL VALIDITY

Cook and Campbell (1979) defined internal validity as "the approximate validity with which we can infer that a relationship is causal" (p. 37). Internal validity depends on the strength or soundness of the design and influences whether one can conclude that the independent variable or intervention caused the dependent variable to change. Although internal validity is often discussed only with respect to randomized and quasi-experiments, we believe the concept also applies to research with attribute independent variables (in nonexperimental studies).

Shadish et al. (2002) proposed a long list of "threats" to research validity. We have found the labels of these threats confusing and more complex than necessary for a basic understanding of internal validity. Another problem with the emphasis on threats to internal validity is that a threat often only instructs you about what might result if the groups are not equivalent. In other words, the threats tell you what is wrong. They do not necessarily provide advice about how to correct the problem. We group the Shadish et al. threats to internal validity into two main types: *equivalence of the groups on participant characteristics* (e.g., equivalence of the intervention and control groups prior to the intervention) and *control of extraneous experience and environmental variables.*

Equivalence of Groups on Participant Characteristics

In research that compares differences among groups, a key question is whether the *groups* that are compared are *equivalent in all respects* prior to the introduction of the independent variable or variables. Using the randomized experimental approach, equivalence is approximately achieved through random assignment of participants to groups, if there are at least 30 in each group. Random assignment of participants to the groups, which is characteristic of randomized experiments but not quasi-experiments, is the best way to ensure equivalent, or at least unbiased, groups. However, in quasi-experimental, comparative, or associational research, random assignment of participants to groups has not or cannot be done.

Equivalence of Groups in Quasi-Experiments. As discussed in chapter 13, other methods, such as random assignment of treatments to similar intact groups, analysis of covariance (ANCOVA), matching, or checking for pretest similarity of groups after the fact, are attempts to make the groups similar. For example, Johnson and Johnson (1991) attempted to match their small group-counseling and control groups on gender, race, age, and IQ. They also found that the pretest scores were not significantly different. Even if one or more of the methods just listed is undertaken to achieve group equivalence in place of random assignment of participants to groups, actual equivalence can *never* be assumed. That is why the specific quasi-experimental designs described in chapter 13 are labeled "nonequivalent groups" designs.

Equivalence of Groups in Comparative Studies. Groups based on attributes (e.g., gender, diagnostic category, self-esteem) are seldom close to equivalent on other participant characteristics, which leads to problems in internal validity. Several techniques can be used to make the groups more similar, at least on some key variables, but they never produce equivalence on all important variables.

For example, DiLorenzo et al. (2002) used analysis of covariance (ANCOVA). In this study, they used duration of illness as the covariate to partially control for group differences on that important variable. Because the older groups had been ill longer than the younger group, ANCOVA helped to adjust for that difference between the groups.

Matching of participants on characteristics other than the independent variable is another method of approaching participant or group equivalence. This technique is especially popular in the comparative approach, where a "diagnostic group" is compared to a "normal" group. For example, Beatty and Gange (1977) compared 26 persons with multiple sclerosis to an equal number of persons without the diagnosis to assess motor and intellectual functioning. Before the study, they matched the participants on age, gender, and education. If participants are not different with the exception of the diagnosis, then the authors could conclude that differences between the two groups *might* be attributed to the disease.

Often in comparative studies, investigators check after the study to see how well matched the groups were with respect to demographic measures collected during the study. If the groups are similar, some degree of internal validity is shown.

Equivalence in Associational Studies. If the research approach is *associational*, there is only one group. (Remember that our associational approach has often been referred to as the *correlational approach*, but we prefer *associational* so that the term is not confused with a correlation coefficient.) In the associational approach, equivalence of participant characteristics comes down to the question of whether those who score high on the independent variable of interest are similar to those who score low, in terms of other attributes that may be correlated with the dependent variable. For example, if the independent variable was education and the dependent variable was income, we should be cautious about interpreting a high correlation as indicating that more education causes a higher income. Are the highly educated participants equal to the poorly educated in terms of other possible causal factors such as IQ, parent's education, and family social status? If it is likely that the high scorers are not equivalent to the low scorers in terms of variables such as age, gender, or ethnicity, statistically controlling for the variables on which the high and low participants are unequal is one method of achieving some degree of this aspect of internal validity within the associational research approach.

Control of Extraneous Experience and Environment Variables

We have grouped several other "threats" to internal validity under a category that deals with the effects of extraneous (variables other than the independent variables) experiences or environmental conditions during the study. Thus, we have called this internal validity dimension *control of extraneous experience and environment variables.* Cook and Campbell (1979) addressed this problem, in part, when discussing threats to internal validity that random assignment does not eliminate (p. 56). Many of these threats occur because participants gain information about the purpose of the study while the study is taking place. One aspect of this dimension has to do with whether extraneous variables or events *affect one group more* than the other. For example, if students learn that they are in a control group, they may give up and not try as hard, exaggerating differences between the intervention and control groups.

Or the opposite may occur and students in the control group overcompensate, eliminating differences between the two groups.

In the associational approach, the issue is whether the experiences of the participants who are high on the independent variable are different from those who are low on the independent variable. Control of extraneous experiences and the environment depends on the specific study, but it is generally better for randomized experiments and for studies done in controlled environments such as laboratories.

Threats to Internal Validity

Table 17.1 provides a current list of threats to interval validity as described by Shadish et al. (2002). Some of the names for the various threats are confusing, but the concepts are important. In Table 17.1 we have added a column for our suggested names and categories.

Shadish, Cook, and Campbell's Threats Related to Equivalence of Groups

Regression. Sometimes the purpose of a quasi-experimental study is to benefit a particular group that, before an intervention, is well above or below average (i.e., the design uses *extreme groups*). For example, children who score in the lowest 10% on some measure might be compared with a nonclinical group. What can happen is that the scores from the low group improve relative to the scores on the pretest even without the intervention. Because these scores were low to start with, children may move or "regress" toward the mean of all scores because of measurement error in the dependent variable; reliability is always less than perfect. Because the pretest is used

TABLE 17.1
Threats to Internal Validity

Shadish, Cook, and Campbell	*Gliner and Morgan*
	Equivalence of groups
Regression	Use of extreme groups
Attrition/mortality	Participant dropouts/attrition during the study
Selection	Bias in assignment to groups
	Control of extraneous variables
Maturation	Changes due to time or growth/development
History	Extraneous environmental events
Testing	Repeated testing, carryover effects
Instrumentation	Instrument/observer inconsistency
Additive and Interactive Threats	Combinations of two or more threats
Ambiguous Temporal Precedence	Did the independent variable occur before the dependent variable?

in the screening, only children who score low on the pretest are selected to be in the "catch-up" group. However, because there is measurement error, some of the students selected to be in this group probably were having a "bad day" and should not actually be in that group. Hence, when tested a second time (posttest), their "true score" is more apt to be reflected, and it would be an increase from the pretest. Therefore, the investigator would not know whether the posttest score was due to the intervention or the statistical problem of regression to the mean. Campbell and Kenny (1999) discussed regression artifacts due to selecting extreme groups and several other related problems.

Attrition (Previously Called Mortality). This threat refers to participants' *attrition from the study.* Problems are created if the percentage who drop out is large, if there is differential loss between or among groups, or both. The result could lead to a biased posttest score, especially if either the intervention or the control condition prompts participants to drop out. For example, if the intervention is found by participants to be onerous or not effective, they may quit the study. Likewise, if participants know they are in the control condition and feel cheated, they may withdraw. Attrition is also a potential problem in comparative and associational longitudinal studies where participants are followed over time. Attention to participants needs and maintaining frequent contacts with them can be helpful in reducing attrition.

Selection Bias. We think this threat should be called *participant assignment bias* because the problem arises from how participants were assigned to a particular group (comparison or intervention) not from how they were selected (sampled) from the population. Problems are created when participants are not randomly assigned to groups, even if a pretest suggests that the groups are similar. The extent of this problem, however, depends on whether there was biased selection/assignment of participants into the groups. There is usually some bias in quasi-experiments; the comparative and associational approaches, by definition, have biased groups.

Shadish, Cook, and Campbell's Threats to Control of Experiences and the Environment

Maturation. The internal validity threat called maturation happens when participants in the study *change as a function of time,* such as from the pretest to the posttest in the case of randomized experimental and quasi-experimental research. Some of these changes could be due to growing older, but other changes are not due to physical maturation. For example, psychiatric patients may get better over time without any treatment. The maturation threat can make it difficult to determine whether it was the intervention or something else related to time that made the difference in the dependent variable.

History. This threat, which we prefer to call *extraneous environmental events*, occurs when something other than the independent variable happens between the pretest and the posttest, especially if it happens to only one group. Consider a situation in which you are interested in the effect of a particular type of therapy and during the period that your intervention is taking place, patients are exposed to information on the merits of your method. Because of the extraneous environmental events threat, it cannot be concluded it was your method and only your method that made the difference in the study.

Testing. This threat most often occurs when the investigator uses *repeated testing* or a pretest and a posttest in the study and the two are identical or similar, resulting in a possible *carryover* from the pretest that might alert the participants about the study and how they should behave. Or, if the study involves learning, the pretest may include information that is on the posttest. It would be difficult to separate what was learned from the pretest from what was learned from the intervention.

Instrumentation. When using the same pretest and posttest in a research design, it is possible that there could be *inconsistency* and the scoring of the test may change, especially if the interval between the pretest and the posttest is relatively long. For example, there could be a *calibration drift* in an instrument that measures heart rate. Even slight changes will prevent the investigator from concluding whether the change was due to the intervention or to the change in calibration. A common problem involving the instrumentation threat is when the pretest and posttest measurements involve raters. It is not uncommon for people to change their criteria over time. Even worse, one or more of the raters may leave the study and have to be replaced with different raters. Repeatedly establishing high interrater reliability is one method of circumventing this problem.

Additive and Interactive Threats. The impact of any one of the preceding threats can be added to one or more of the other threats. Or the impact may depend on the level of (interact with) another threat. Thus, combinations of the threats can be a problem.

Other Threats That Random Assignment Does Not Eliminate. Most of these threats occur because of *contamination*. Participants in different groups communicate or gain information intended for another group while the study is taking place. For example, if participants learn that they are in a control group, they may become *resentful* or *demoralized* and not try as hard, exaggerating differences between the intervention and control groups. Or the opposite may occur, and persons in the control group may *overcompensate* or imitate the experimental group, eliminating differences between the groups.

Likewise, *expectation effects* might make the treatment appear more powerful than if the patients in the intervention condition did not expect good results from a new treatment. One method of preventing expectation effects is to design the study so that the participants don't know (i.e., they are *masked*) whether they are receiving a treatment or not. Use of a *placebo* (no treatment) *control group* can help the researcher estimate and control for *no treatment effects* because even participants in a placebo group may improve some because they know that they are in a study that might be helpful to them. Use of a placebo control group is possible in some studies, but it raises ethical questions. "Treatment as usual" for the control group may be a good alternative as long as the participants do not think they are missing out.

Observer or experimenter bias is another problem; this can be dealt with by "double masking," that is, making both the participant and the tester or evaluator unaware of who is receiving the intervention. Masking of the treatments from the evaluator is often difficult with behavioral interventions, but, at the least, the evaluator should not be someone who has a stake in the success of the treatment.

Ambiguous Temporal Precedence. Remember that Porter (1997) stated that the first criterion for determining cause is that the independent variable (intervention) must precede the dependent variable (outcome or posttests). Occasionally this is unclear in quasi-experiments; it is often a problem in associational studies, and sometimes is a problem in comparative studies. For example, in the study by Redding et al. (1990), introduced in chapter 1, they found a relationship between maternal depression and child mastery behavior, but it is not clear which variable came first. The authors assumed that maternal depression influenced child behavior, but it is plausible that infants who don't seem to be developing well could cause an increase in mothers' depression. The effect is probably bidirectional.

POSTSCRIPT

In this chapter, threats to internal validity were described and related to the specific experimental research designs discussed in chapters 13 and 14. In the next chapter we discuss sampling and external validity. Then in chapter

19 we provide an overview of our framework for evaluating research studies, focusing on the evaluation of internal and external validity. In chapter 37, we provide a more comprehensive framework for evaluating the research validity of articles, and chapter 38, the final chapter, provides narrative evaluations of the four sample studies first presented in chapter 1.

Chapter 18

Sampling and Population External Validity

In this chapter, we discuss sampling as well as population external validity, the extent to which the results generalize to the population of interest. Chapter 19 broadens the discussion of external validity and how it is evaluated. That chapter also provides examples of how we evaluate the internal and external validity of the four studies first discussed in chapter 1.

SAMPLING

Sampling is the process of selecting part of a larger group with the intent of generalizing from the smaller group, called the *sample*, to the *population*, the larger group. If we are to make valid inferences about the population, we must select the sample so that it is *representative* of the population.

With a few notable exceptions, modern survey techniques have proven to be quite accurate in predicting or reporting information about the attitudes of the American public from samples of about 1,000 participants. Historically, however, there have been a number of examples of major miscalculations that can be traced to inadequate sampling techniques. An example is the grossly erroneous prediction, by a *Literary Digest* poll of a very large sample, that Franklin Roosevelt would lose the 1936 presidential election when, in fact, he won by a landslide. One of the problems was that the sample was selected from automobile registrations, telephone directories, and related sources. This led to oversampling of affluent individuals who were not representative of the voting public, especially during the Great Depression. In addition, only about 20% of the selected sample actually returned their questionnaires.

Steps in Selecting a Sample and Generalizing Results

There are many ways to select a sample from a population. The goal is to have an *actual sample* in which each participant represents a known fraction of the *theoretical* or *target population* so that characteristics of the population can be recreated from the sample. Obtaining a *representative sample* is not easy because things can go wrong at three stages of the research process. Figure 18.1 shows the key sampling concepts and the three steps (shown with arrows).

Step 1. Selecting the *accessible population* from the *theoretical population* is the first step. The accessible population should be representative of the theoretical population. However, usually the representativeness of the accessible population is unknown because researchers do not have access to the geographical or socioeconomic range of participants to which they would like to make generalizations. Unfortunately, the theoretical population usually is not specified in published research articles. One has to infer it from the context and the stated inclusion and exclusion criteria. *Inclusion*

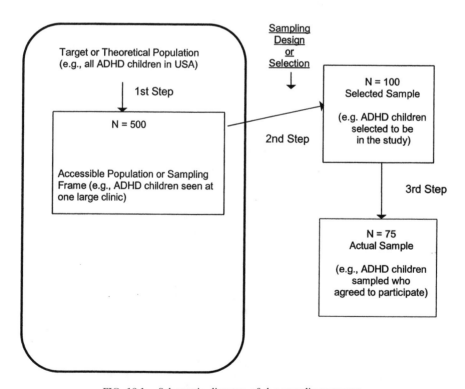

FIG. 18.1.   Schematic diagram of the sampling process.

criteria state what types of persons were included in the sample, (e.g., 5- to 18-year-old males with an ADHD diagnosis). *Exclusion criteria* state what types of persons were not included (e.g., females, children under 5, and those with moderate or severe mental retardation or specified medical conditions).

Step 2.   The process of choosing the *selected sample* from the accessible population is called the *sampling design* or selection of participants. It is described in the method section of an article and is the step over which the researcher has the most control. In some cases, the accessible population is small enough that everyone is asked to participate. From the point of view of external validity, selecting the whole accessible population is similar to selecting a large random sample from a large accessible population. However, if the accessible population is small enough to select everyone, one should consider whether that accessible population is really the one of interest. That is, was step 1 representative of the target or theoretical population of interest?

Step 3.   This includes how the selected sample and the *actual sample* differ. The problem is that participants may not consent to participate (i.e., there may be a low response rate), so the actual sample may be considerably smaller than the selected sample and may be quite unrepresentative of the selected sample. This is often a problem with mailed surveys, especially if the survey is sent to busy people such as clinicians.

Types of Sampling

There are two major types of sampling designs that are used in obtaining the selected sample: probability and nonprobability.

Probability Sampling.   In probability sampling, every participant has a known, nonzero chance of being selected. The participants or elements of the population are usually people, but could be groups, animals, or events. With probability samples, researchers are able to make an estimate of the extent to which results based on the sample are likely to differ from what would have been found by studying the entire population. There are four main types of probability sampling. The most basic is the *simple random sample*, which occurs when all participants have an equal and independent chance of being included in the sample. This technique can be implemented using a random number table to select participants from a list, the sampling frame, of the accessible population.

A similar frequently used technique is *systematic sampling with a random start*. For example, we might randomly select the fourth person on a list as the first participant. If researchers wanted to sample 10% of the accessible population, they would then systematically select every 10th participant, starting with the fourth. With simple random and systematic sampling, the population must be finite and there must be a complete list of potential participants. If the sample is large and the list complete, these two techniques will produce a representative sample.

If some important characteristics of the accessible population such as gender or race are known ahead of time, one can reduce the sampling variation and increase the likelihood that the sample will be representative of the population by using *stratified random sampling*. When participants are geographically spread, it is common to stratify on the basis of geography so that appropriate proportions come from the different regions.

Cluster sampling is a two-stage sampling procedure that is especially useful when the population is spread out geographically and the researcher needs to collect data on site. The usual strategy is to first select a number of clusters/sites (e.g., clinics) randomly and then select all potential participants from these selected clusters.

With a simple random or systematic sample, the descriptive statistics from the sample also describe the population. However, with stratified or cluster sampling, one would need to weight the observations appropriately to describe the population.

Nonprobability Sampling. Nonprobability samples are ones in which the probability of being selected is unknown. Time and cost constraints lead researchers to use nonprobability samples. There are several types of nonprobability samples, including *quota, purposive,* and *convenience.*

The term *convenience sample* has two related meanings. The first is when one selected the *accessible population* by convenience, even if selecting all the persons in the accessible population or a random sample of that accessible population. A sample also is called a convenience one if the researcher selected some participants from the accessible population based on convenience. Researchers later may examine the demographic characteristics of their convenience sample and conclude that the participants are similar to those in the larger population. This does not mean that the sample is, in fact, representative, but it does indicate an attempt by the researcher to check on representativeness. An extended discussion of the types of sampling and the advantages and disadvantages of each can be found in Fowler (2001).

Why Are Nonprobability Samples Used So Frequently?

Because the theoretical population is often infinite and probability sampling is costly, convenience sampling is probably the most common of all sampling methods. In addition to cost and time advantages, researchers, especially those using randomized experimental and quasi-experimental designs, are not primarily interested in making inferences about the population from the descriptive data. These researchers are more interested in whether the treatment has an effect on the dependent variable, and they assume that if the treatment is powerful, the effect will show up in many kinds of participants. Many researchers seem to imply that population external validity is less important than internal validity.

How Many Participants?

The question, "How many participants are needed for this study?" is asked often. One part of the answer depends on whom you ask and what their discipline is (Kraemer & Thiemann, 1987). National opinion surveys almost always have 1,000 or more participants, whereas sociological and epidemiological studies usually have at least several hundred participants. On the other hand, treatment investigations with 10 to 20 participants per group are not uncommon, and in some areas single-subject designs are used. To some extent these dramatic differences in minimum sample sizes depend on differences in types of designs, measures, and statistical analyses, but they also seem to be based in good part on custom.

The size of the sample should be large enough so one does not fail to detect important findings, but a large sample will not necessarily help one distinguish between the merely statistically significant and the societally important findings. *Statistical power analysis* (see chap. 20) can help one compute the sample size needed to find a statistically significant result given certain assumptions (e.g., see Cohen, 1988; Kraemer & Thiemann, 1987).

POPULATION EXTERNAL VALIDITY

In this chapter and the next, we discuss aspects of *research validity*, the validity or quality of the design of a study as a whole. In chapter 17, we discussed *internal validity*, validity related to the approach and design of the study. Now we introduce another aspect of research validity, *population external validity*, which depends on the quality of the sample.

This aspect of external validity is a problem that involves how participants were selected to be in the study. Were participants randomly selected from a particular population, or were they a convenience sample? Because most studies in the behavioral sciences have *not* used probability sampling they cannot be high on population external validity. However, as discussed earlier in this chapter, the issue of population external validity is more complex than an evaluation of the sampling design (i.e., how the sample was selected from the accessible population).

The real question is *whether the actual sample of participants is representative of the theoretical or target population*. To evaluate representativeness, it is helpful to identify (a) the *apparent theoretical population*, (b) the *accessible population*, (c) the *sampling design and selected sample*, and (d) the *actual sample* of participants who completed participation in the study. It is possible that the researcher could use a random or other probability sampling design, but have an actual sample that is not representative of the theoretical population, either due to a low response rate or due to the accessible population not being representative of the theoretical population. The latter problem seems almost universal, in part due to funding and travel limitations. Except in national survey research, we almost always start with an accessible population from the local school district, community, or clinic.

SAMPLING AND THE INTERNAL AND EXTERNAL VALIDITY OF A STUDY

We have discussed the internal and external validity of a study and noted that external validity is influenced by the representativeness of the sample. Much of this chapter has been about how to obtain a representative sample and what problems may arise in the process of sampling. It is important to note, as indicated in Fig. 18.2, that the internal validity of a study is not directly affected by the sampling design or the type of sampling. Thus a study, as is the case with many randomized experiments, may have a small convenience sample and still have high internal validity because random assignment of participants to groups eliminates many threats to internal validity.

Figure 18.2 extends and simplifies Fig. 18.1 to show how the two uses of the word *random* have quite different meanings and different effects on internal and external validity. *Random selection*, or some other probability sampling method, of who is asked to participate in the study is important for high external validity. On the other hand, *random assignment*, or placement of participants into groups, is important for high internal validity. This distinction, which is often confused or misunderstood, is an important one in terms of evaluating the quality of a research study and its internal and external validity.

SUMMARY

Sampling is the process of selecting part of a larger group (the accessible population) with the intent of generalizing from the smaller group (the sample) to the population. We identified two kinds of populations (theoret-

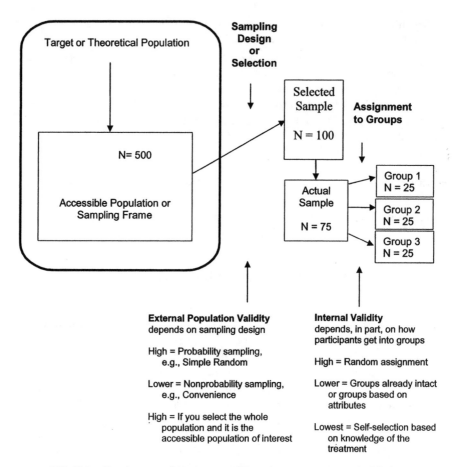

FIG. 18.2.   Random sampling versus random assignment to groups and their
relationships to external and internal validity.

ical/target vs. accessible), and we discussed difficulties in obtaining an accessible population that is representative of the theoretical population of
interest. Sampling (the sampling design) is the method used to select potential participants (the selected sample) from the accessible population.
Convenience sampling is a common but less desirable sampling method
than probability sampling. Finally, we discussed population external validity, noting that it depends on all three steps in the sampling process. Random selection of participants is useful to produce high population external
validity, whereas random assignment of participants to groups is important
for high internal validity.

Chapter 19

Evaluating the Validity of a Research Study: An Introduction

This chapter provides an overview of the evaluation of *research validity*, the validity of a study as a whole. We and others (e.g., Cook & Campbell, 1979) use the term *validity* in two major ways: for the validity of a study (*research validity*) and also for the validity of a single measurement or test (*measurement validity*, chap. 9).

We will further divide *research validity* into two broad types, internal and external, discussed in chapters 17 and 18. *Internal validity* is based on the strength or soundness of the design. This definition of internal validity allows us to evaluate nonexperimental as well as experimental research. Randomized experimental designs are usually high on internal validity, but we believe that one can judge any study's internal validity on a continuum from low to high. *External validity* is based on the extent to which the results can be generalized to the populations, settings, and variables of interest. Again, we think this aspect of research validity can be evaluated for all kinds of studies.

Our research evaluation framework focuses on the main issues under internal and external validity. However, before discussing these dimensions, we would like to put them in the broader context of reliability and validity. Figure 19.1 should help avoid some of the semantic confusion implied above.

RESEARCH VALIDITY VERSUS MEASUREMENT RELIABILITY AND VALIDITY

It is important to distinguish between evidence for the merit or worth of the whole study (*research validity*) as opposed to evidence in support of the quality of a specific instrument or test used in a study (*measurement validity*). Fig-

RELIABILITY	**VALIDITY**
Stability or Consistency	Accuracy and Representativeness

Measurement (or Test) Reliability	**Measurement (or Test) Validity**
The participant gets the same or a very similar score from a specific *test, observation,* or *rating* when it is used for a similar purpose with a similar population. (Chapter 8)	The score accurately reflects/measures what it was designed or intended to measure when used for a similar purpose with a similar population. (Chapter 9)

Research (or Study) Reliability	**Research (or Study) Validity**

If repeated, the *study* would produce similar results. This is called *replication.* Meta analysis examines several similar studies in part to examine the consistency of their results. (Chapter 35)	The results of the study are accurate and generalizable. Two major dimensions of the *validity of a study* are:
	
	▪ **Internal Validity** – strength of design. If high, one can make valid inferences about causes. (Chapter 17)
	  • Equivalence of Groups on Participant Characteristics
	  • Control of Extraneous Experience and Environmental Variables
	
	▪ **External Validity** – If high, the results may generalize to other populations, settings, and variables. (Chapter 18)
	  • Population Validity
	  • Ecological Validity

FIG. 19.1.   Relationships and differences between measurement reliability and validity and research reliability and validity.

ure 19.1 shows that measurement reliability and validity (the upper two boxes) are different from, but related to, research reliability and validity (lower boxes), and the figure shows how all four fit into an overall conception of reliability and validity.

Figure 19.1 demonstrates the relationship between measurement validity and research validity. The horizontal arrow indicates that measurement reliability is a necessary prerequisite for measurement validity (a measure cannot provide evidence for validity if it is not consistent/reliable). The vertical arrow indicates that the validity of a whole study depends to some extent on the reliability and validity of the specific measures or instruments used in the study.

We have not drawn any arrows to or from the research reliability box. Although the concept parallels those in the other boxes, research reliability is not directly an antecedent or outcome of the other concepts. Our major aim in this section is to clarify validity issues. Partly for that reason, we delay discussing *research reliability* and *meta-analysis* until chapter 35.

We discussed measurement reliability and validity in chapters 8 and 9. When evaluating a study, it is important to examine the evidence for the measurement reliability and validity of each instrument and for all the measures as a whole. One can utilize the information from the chapters on measurement reliability and validity, noting that they will influence the overall validity or quality of a study.

At the end of this chapter, we provide an example of a brief evaluation of one of the four sample research studies described in chapter 1 and a few evaluative comments about the other three. The evaluation includes a judgment of measurement reliability and validity, as well as internal and external validity.

EVALUATING RESEARCH VALIDITY

A good study should have moderate to high internal and external validity. However, it is hard, in any given study, to achieve this goal. Using our research validity framework, a reader would evaluate a study from low to high on each of the four scales or dimensions shown in Figs. 19.2 and 19.3. In chapter 37, we provide a comprehensive framework for evaluating the research validity of an article. In that chapter, four of the scales for rating internal and external validity are the same as presented here, but four additional rating scales are included, and there are also several ratings related to how clearly and well the information in the article is presented.

Internal Validity

Figure 19.2 shows two rating scales and several issues under each that we use to evaluate the internal validity of a study.

Equivalence of Groups on Participant Characteristics. A key question for internal validity is whether the groups (e.g., experimental and control) that are compared are equivalent in *all respects* other than the independent variable. Shadish et al. (2002) described a number of specific threats to internal validity, several of which (e.g., selection/assignment and attrition) are participant factors that could lead to a lack of equivalence of the groups.

Randomized experimental designs attempt to achieve group equivalence through random assignment of participants to adequately sized groups. However, in quasi-experimental and nonexperimental research, where participants cannot be randomly assigned, other methods such as random assignment of treatments to similar intact groups, matching, or using analysis of covariance are attempts to achieve *some* degree of group similarity. The top of Fig. 19.2 indicates the key factors we use to rate this di-

INTERNAL VALIDITY

Equivalence of Groups on Participant Characteristics

Based rating on:
   a)   Were the participants randomly assigned to the groups?
   b)   If not, were the attempts to make groups similar (e.g. ANCOVA) or *check* similarity on
        a *pretest* adequate?
   c)   If no randomization, were attempts to make groups similar or check similarity on
        other key variables adequate?
   d)   Was retention during the study high and similar across groups?

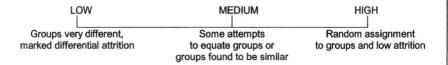

LOW	MEDIUM	HIGH
Groups very different, marked differential attrition	Some attempts to equate groups or groups found to be similar	Random assignment to groups and low attrition

Control of Experiences and Environment Variables (Contamination)

Base rating on:
   a)   Was the study conducted in a controlled environment (e.g., a lab)?
   b)   Were extraneous variables that could affect one group more than the others
        controlled? Did the groups have the same type of environment?
   c)   Was there a no treatment group (placebo) or usual treatment group?
   d)   Were extraneous variables that could affect all groups and obscure the true effect
        controlled? Were attempts to reduce other extraneous influences adequate?

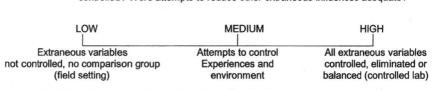

LOW	MEDIUM	HIGH
Extraneous variables not controlled, no comparison group (field setting)	Attempts to control Experiences and environment	All extraneous variables controlled, eliminated or balanced (controlled lab)

FIG. 19.2.   Rating scales to evaluate the internal validity of the findings of a study.

mension from high (random assignment of participants to groups and low attrition) to low (unequal groups, perhaps due to self-*assignment* and high, especially unequal attrition between groups). The comparative and associational approaches are never high and are often low on this dimension.

Control of Extraneous Experience and Environment Variables (Contamination).   We base the rating of this dimension on four issues. First, there is the issue of the degree of control during the study of environmental variables. Obviously, a study in a laboratory setting has better control (less contamination) of variables such as lighting, temperature, and interruptions. Field research would have less control over such variables.

Some of these threats to validity occur because participants gain information about the purpose of the study while it is taking place. One issue is whether extraneous variables or events affect *one group more* than the others. For example, if participants learn that they are in a control group, they may not try as hard, exaggerating differences between the intervention and control groups. Alternately, participants in the control group may overcompensate, eliminating differences between the two groups. One method to prevent some of these external influences is to isolate the intervention group from the control group. For example, when performing research, it might be good to have intervention and control groups from different but similar clinics or schools. A second method to reduce extraneous influences, especially in exploratory studies, is to shorten the time of the intervention in order to lessen the chances for external variables to have an effect on one group or the other. However, this can be a problem for ecological validity, as mentioned later.

A third issue to consider is related to the obvious problem when there is no control group. This type of problem occurs in the one-group poor quasi-experiments and also when one is comparing the effects of two different treatment groups without a no-treatment control group, perhaps for ethical reasons. It could be that neither treatment worked and that both groups got better over time for some other reason. If a control group cannot be included, then the authors need to find a way to document that participants would not have improved over time. This might be done by citing previous research in this area or by delaying the treatment, for at least one of the treatment groups, so that the effects of no treatment can be assessed.

Another issue is whether a third variable could have affected *all groups*, masking the effect of the independent variable. Maturation of participants and placebo or Hawthorne effects are common examples of this situation, especially in the poor quasi-experiments and in nonexperimental designs.

External Validity

External validity was defined by Campbell and Stanley (1963/1966) as follows: "External validity asks the question of generalizability: To what populations, settings, treatment variables, and measurement variables can this effect be generalized?" (p. 5). Some researchers have a tendency to judge external validity as contingent upon internal validity. For example, some might suggest that because the study had poor internal validity, then external validity also must be poor. However, we think that external validity, like internal validity, should be judged separately, before the fact, and not be based on the other. Questions dealing with the external validity of a study are based on the principle that a good study should be rated high on external validity, or, if not, the author should at least be cautious about generalizing the findings to other measures, populations, treatments, and settings.

EXTERNAL VALIDITY

Population

Base rating on:
1)   Representativeness of accessible population vis-à-vis theoretical population
2)   Adequacy of sampling method from accessible population
3)   Adequacy response/return rate

LOW	MEDIUM	HIGH
Actual sample unrepresentative of the theoretical population	Some attempt to obtain good sample	Actual sample representative of theoretical population

Ecological

Base rating on:
1)   Naturalness/representativeness of setting/conditions
2)   Adequacy of rapport with testers/observers.
3)   Naturalness of procedures/tasks
4)   Appropriateness of timing and length of treatment (if any)
5)   Extent to which results are not restricted to a specific time in history

LOW	MEDIUM	HIGH
Unnatural setting, tester, procedures and time	Somewhat artificial (e.g., questionnaire)	Natural setting, tester, procedures and time

FIG. 19.3.   Rating scales to evaluate external validity of the findings of a study.

The key issue for external validity is whether the participants, settings, treatment, and outcome variables are representative of those of interest (i.e., the theoretical or target population, setting, etc.). In this chapter, we divide external validity into two main aspects: *population external validity* and *ecological external validity* (see Fig. 19.3). In chapter 37, we discuss a third aspect of external validity, testing of key subgroups.

Population External Validity.   This aspect of external validity involves how the participants of the study were selected. Before rating the overall population external validity, the theoretical or target population, the accessible population, and the selected and actual samples must be identified as discussed in chapter 18. Three issues were presented in chapter 18 that need to be considered before making an overall rating. First, how representative of the theoretical population is the accessible population? If the group the researcher has access to is the same one as or very similar to the larger population of interest, this aspect would be good. Second, is the selected sample representative of the accessible population? If the whole accessible population is selected or is selected using probability sampling, the second aspect of external population validity is good. Third, is the actual sample representative of the selected sample? If the return or response rate is high (i.e., most of those asked to participate agree to do so), this aspect is good. The overall rating should be based on these three judgments, which condense to whether the actual/final sample of participants represents the theoretical or target population.

It is possible that the researcher used a random or other probability sampling design but the result was a sample that was not representative of the theoretical population. This could be due to a low response rate or to the accessible population not being representative of the theoretical population. The latter problem seems almost universal in the behavioral sciences, in part due to funding and travel limitations. Except in national surveys, researchers commonly start with an accessible population from the local community, clinic or school (i.e., a *convenience sample*).

Ecological External Validity.   The second dimension of external validity evaluates whether the conditions/settings, testers, procedures/tasks, and timing are natural and thus whether the results can be generalized to real-life outcomes. Our evaluation is based on the five issues posed in Fig. 19.3. First, field research is rated higher on ecological external validity than laboratory procedures, which are usually artificial. Sometimes a researcher will use a therapeutic technique that, although representative of the construct, has not been carried out in a similar setting. For high ecological validity, a treatment should be conducted in a realistic setting. Second, the testers or observers should have rapport with the participants. Third, the tasks or procedures should be natural. We think most of the self-report measures, especially questionnaires, are somewhat artificial because they are not direct measures of the participants' actual behavior in a typical environment. Fourth, the intervention, if any, should be presented in a manner and for a period of time that is similar to how it is intended to be used in practice. Cook and Campbell (1979) also include generalization to past and future times under external validity. Thus, we consider here how much a study is likely to be bound to a specific time in history or whether the results will be applicable over a number of years. Attitudes about certain topics (e.g., school vouchers, low-carb diets, or gay marriage) may change over a relatively short period of time so that results may not be generalizable a few years after the study.

An example of a problem with ecological validity is the traditional stranger approach (e.g., see Morgan & Ricciuti, 1969; Spitz, 1965). Although methods varied somewhat, it was typical in the 1960s to test 6- to 12-month-old infants in an unnatural setting (lab playroom) with a male stranger who approached and picked up the baby in a short series of predetermined steps. In the name of experimental control, no attempt was made to have the researcher/stranger's behavior be contingent on the baby's. This procedure, and even the existence of fear of strangers, were criticized by Rheingold and Eckerman (1973), who showed that a slower, more "natural" approach by a female stranger produced almost no crying or attempts to get away. Of course, the determinants of infant fear are complex, but it was clear that early studies were not high on ecological validity. They had traded ecological validity for better control of the environmental and independent variable aspects of internal validity.

Consider another example of a problem in ecological validity. If an educator is interested in the effect of a particular teaching style on student participation, the classroom should be similar to that of a normal classroom. Similarly, if the investigator asked students to come at night for the study, but these students normally attended class during the day, then there is a problem in ecological external validity. The investigator must ask if some representative method was used for selection of the setting and time, or was a convenience method used? For high ecological validity, an intervention should be conducted by a culturally appropriate intervener (teacher, therapist, or tester) for an appropriate length of time.

THE RELATIVE IMPORTANCE OF DIFFERENT VALIDITY CATEGORIES

It is difficult for a single study to achieve high ratings for each of the dimensions of research validity. Typically, researchers sacrifice strength in one dimension to enhance another. Campbell and Stanley (1963/1966) discussed whether a study should be judged more harshly if it is weaker on certain validity dimensions than on others:

> Both types of criteria (internal and external validity) are obviously important, even though they are frequently at odds in that features increasing one may jeopardize the other . . . the selection of designs strong in both types of validity is obviously our ideal. (p. 5)

Cook and Campbell (1979) also addressed the issue in some depth. They suggested that if one is interested in testing a theory, then internal validity and measurement validity of the key constructs have the highest priority. Obviously, the constructs used in the study must represent those in the theory. Also, one would need to show a causal relationship (high internal validity) between or among variables when testing a theory.

Campbell and Stanley (1963/1966) made an oft-quoted statement that "Internal validity is the basic minimum without which any experiment is uninterpretable: Did in fact the experimental treatments make a difference in this specific experimental instance?" (p. 5). However, they followed that quote with the one we already examined about both internal validity and external validity being important and part of their ideal. And they added a final sentence about external validity that has often been overlooked. "This is particularly the case for research on teaching, in which generalization to applied settings of known character is the desideratum" (Campbell & Stanley, 1963/1966, p. 5). If one performs applied research, then emphasis should be placed on external validity, especially if the research involves comparing specific diagnostic groups.

We think that *both* of these dimensions are important for evaluating the quality of *all* types of research: experimental or nonexperimental, theory-driven or applied. Furthermore, we believe that these dimensions can be evaluated separately even though there may well be some conceptual interdependence. Whether to weight internal or external validity more highly probably depends on the purpose of the study. If one is interested in *evidence-based practice* (chap. 34) or whether an intervention works, internal validity should probably be weighted more. However, as Cook and Campbell (1979) pointed out:

> There is also a circular justification for the primacy of internal validity. . . . The unique purpose of experiments is to provide stronger tests of causal hypotheses than is permitted by other forms of research, most of which were developed for other purposes. . . . Given that the unique original purpose of experiments is cause-related, internal validity has to assume a special importance in experimentation since it is concerned with how confident one can be that an observed relationship between variables is causal or that the absence of a relationship implies no cause. (p. 84)

EXAMPLES OF HOW TO USE THE FRAMEWORK

To illustrate how we use this framework and the rating scales in Figs. 19.2 and 19.3 to evaluate research, consider the study by Gliner and Sample (1996) that we used as an example in earlier chapters. The purpose of the study was to increase quality of life for persons with developmental disabilities who were employed in sheltered work or supported employment, using an intervention of community life options. The study attempted to achieve high internal validity by randomly assigning participants to either a community life options intervention or to their present situation. The study also attempted to achieve high ecological external validity by conducting the study in the natural setting. However, obtaining good research validity on all dimensions could not be accomplished. A brief evaluation of the Gliner and Sample (1996) article is provided in the next three paragraphs.

Evidence for *measurement reliability* of the outcome measure, quality of life, was acceptable. This measure had been used in several published studies with similar clients that reported good interrater (.83) and interitem (.83) reliability. Evidence for the *measurement validity* of the intervention and the outcome also seem acceptable. The quality-of-life measure had been used several times with persons with developmental disabilities who had moved out of institutionalized into community settings. However, the measure may have been intended for lower functioning participants.

Internal validity: equivalence of groups on subject characteristics was rated high because participants were randomly assigned to intervention conditions. However, a cautionary note could be raised because random assignment of participants to conditions may not make the groups equivalent with small numbers, as in this study. *Control of experiences and the environment* was constrained, so it was judged to be medium to low. In a community setting, where choice was experienced differently by different participants, it was difficult to insure that the experiences of each group were not influenced by outside variables.

Population external validity was considered to be medium low because the sample was limited to persons in one city, and there was not a random selection of appropriate participants even from that city. Instead, the sample was one of convenience. Thus, both the accessible population and the selected sample might not represent all persons with developmental disabilities. The response rate, however, was high. Because the intervention was a real one and took place in an actual community setting, *ecological external validity* was judged to be relatively high.

The Johnson and Johnson (1991) study on the effect of group counseling, described briefly in chapter 1, was a quasi-experiment because the participants, although matched on some characteristics, could not be randomly signed to the intervention and control groups. For this reason and some problems with control of extraneous variables, the study was rated lower than the Gliner and Sample (1996) study on *internal validity* and thus provides less convincing evidence that the intervention was the cause of changes in the outcomes. The other two studies described in chapter 1 were not experiments and thus were rated even lower on internal validity. The DiLorenzo et al. (2004) study compared older and younger persons with multiple sclerosis, and the Redding et al. (1990) study correlated maternal depression with infant mastery behavior. As nonexperiments with lower internal validity, the investigators of these studies need to be especially careful not to infer that age per se (DiLorenzo et al., 2004) or maternal depression (Redding et al., 1990) have been demonstrated to cause differences in the outcome variables.

External validity, especially ecological external validity, was quite good in the group counseling and multiple sclerosis studies because the settings were natural and rapport with counselors/testers seemed to be good. The mastery study would be rated somewhat lower on ecological validity because the setting (a lab playroom) and tester behavior were somewhat unnatural, in order to control extraneous variables. Population external validity was roughly medium in all these studies because, although the samples were convenience samples, they may have been moderately representative of such participants nationally.

POSTSCRIPT

We deal in more depth in the final two chapters of this book with the dimensions just discussed and with other aspects of the study such as the quality and completeness of the statistical analyses. However, we thought it was desirable to provide an overview of how to evaluate the research validity of a study at this point in the book.

Part V

INTRODUCTION TO INFERENTIAL STATISTICS AND THEIR INTERPRETATION

Introduction to Inferential Statistics and Hypothesis Testing

When performing research, rarely are we able to work with an entire population of individuals. Instead, we usually conduct the study on a sample of individuals from a population. It is hoped that if the relationship is strong and the sample is representative we can infer that the results from our sample apply to the population of interest. Inferential statistics involves making inferences from sample statistics, such as the sample mean and the sample standard deviation, to population parameters such as the population mean and the population standard deviation.

AN EXAMPLE

Suppose we are interested in the relationship between exercise and quality of life in depressed adolescent patients. A reasonable hypothesis is that depressed patients who exercise regularly will have higher quality-of-life scores than those who do not exercise regularly. Inferential statistics provides us with a way to test this hypothesis (i.e., make a decision about the relationship between exercise and quality of life in depressed adolescent patients). To test our hypothesis, we need to reformulate it as two statements or hypotheses, the null hypothesis and the alternative or research hypothesis. However, before we actually specify the null and alternative hypotheses for our study, we need to operationalize our variables. The independent variable, exercise, is defined as either use of a stationary bicycle 45 minutes per day (5 days per week for 6 weeks at a work load of 50% of maximum capacity) or no prescribed exercise. The dependent variable, a quality-of-life inventory (QL), is an indicator of quality of life and is measured as a score between 1 and 100. If our hypothesis is correct, we would expect that subjects who exercise will have a higher quality-of-life index than those who do not exercise regularly, and a higher score on the inventory would indicate improvement in these depressed adolescents. (This assumes an increase from baseline in the intervention group. A difference could also occur if the nonexercising adolescents got worse, but that would not support the hypothesis.)

THE NULL AND ALTERNATIVE HYPOTHESIS

The *null hypothesis* states that the mean QL of the population of those who receive the intervention is equal to the mean QL of the population of those who do not receive the intervention. If the null hypothesis is true, the intervention of exercise has not been successful in changing quality of life. The *alternative hypothesis* states that the mean QL of the population of those who receive the intervention will be greater than the mean QL of the population of those who do not receive the intervention. If the null hypothesis is false, or rejected, the intervention of exercise has been successful in altering quality of life. In most cases, the goal of the research is to reject the null hypothesis in favor of the alternative hypothesis. Note that we have stated the null hypothesis as a "no difference" null hypothesis, that is, that there is no difference between the population means of the treatment and control groups. However, especially in practical applications, the null hypothesis could be stated as some difference between the means of the two populations. Thus to reject the null hypothesis, the treatment group would have to exceed the control group by an amount necessary to make a *functional* difference. This is referred to as a *non nil null hypothesis*. See chapter 21 for more discussion of the non nil null hypothesis.

For our alternative hypothesis we specified that the intervention population mean will be higher (or lower if we were measuring depression and predicting it to decline) than the control group population mean. This is a *directional hypothesis* and is just one method of expressing the alternative hypothesis. Another choice is to specify the alternative hypothesis as nondirectional. A prediction is made that the intervention will be significantly different from the control, but we are not sure of the direction of this difference. A *nondirectional alternative hypothesis* is often used when comparing two different treatment methods. Directional alternative hypotheses are used most often when comparing a treatment to a control condition.

While it may appear that choosing a directional or nondirectional hypothesis is arbitrary, two things are important. First, the type of alternative hypothesis selected should be based on literature or theory. When there is previous research to support the intervention, a directional hypothesis should be used. Sometimes there is not strong support for the intervention. This could be due to conflicting reports from previous studies or to very little research performed with the intervention. In these cases a nondirectional alternative hypothesis should be used. Second, there are statistical consequences (less statistical power) attached to the type of hypothesis. It is more difficult to reject the null hypothesis when using a nondirectional hypothesis. However, if a directional alternative hypothesis is selected, and the result is a statistically significant difference in the opposite direction, the only conclusion is a failure to reject the null hypothesis.

Now that we have stated the null and alternative hypotheses, we need to consider the population of interest for the exercise study. If we are interested in generalizing to all depressed adolescents, that would be our *theoretical or target population*. Perhaps a subset of all depressed adolescents, such as adolescent outpatients, is our theoretical population. However, we often have access only to depressed adolescents who visit one or two clinics in the community. Therefore, these available patients are our accessible population.

If the accessible population is not representative of the theoretical or target population of interest, the inference made from the sample will not tell you about relationships in the population of interest. For example, in our sample study about the effects of an exercise intervention, perhaps the clinics that were used to obtain the accessible population of depressed adolescents had clients who were quite different from *all* depressed adolescents (e.g., in terms of social class and/or ethnicity). If so, the results of the study would apply only to the population from the accessible clinics, not to the broader population of interest. Unfortunately, this is a common problem for population external validity, as discussed in chapter 18.

There is also an external validity problem with the interpretation if the sample is not representative of the accessible population. If, in our exercise study, the accessible clinics had been sampled by convenience rather than with probability (e.g., random) sampling, the 72 participants might have been very different from the others in the accessible population. If so, the results would generalize only to clients similar to those sampled, not the whole accessible population.

THE HYPOTHESIS TESTING PROCESS

Figure 20.1 provides insight into the inferential process using our example. At the far left of the figure is a box representing the population. From the accessible population (depressed adolescent outpatients from the available community clinics) we sample or select, perhaps randomly, 72 adolescents.

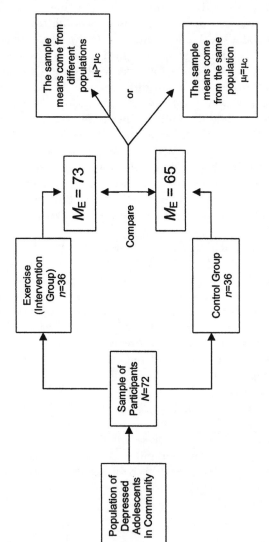

FIG. 20.1. Schematic diagram of the process of making an inference about the difference between two groups.

[This is step (a) in Fig. 20.1.] This step is done best by selecting names from a total list of accessible depressed outpatients in such a way that all available depressed outpatients have an equal chance of being selected for our study. However, frequently, as discussed in chapter 18, the sample is one of convenience, not randomly selected.

In the next step (b), we assign participants to groups. We assign 36 patients to be in the exercise (intervention) group and 36 patients to be in the nonexercise (control) group. Again, it is best to use random assignment, which implies that each patient has an equal chance to be in either group. If the participants cannot be randomly assigned, the study, as discussed in chapter 13, is a quasi-experiment rather than a randomized experiment and a pretest would be needed.

Moving to the right in Fig. 20.1, the next step (c) is to conduct the study. The intervention group (one level of the independent variable) will exercise on a stationary bicycle for 45 minutes per day, 5 days per week, for 6 weeks. The control group (the other level of the independent variable) will continue with their usual daily activities for the next 6 weeks. After 6 weeks we ask the participants to complete the QL inventory; the QL scores are the dependent variable (step d). If we find the mean of the QL scores of the intervention group is 73 and the mean of the QL scores of the control group is 65, the mean of the intervention group is higher, seeming to support our hypothesis that exercise increases quality of life for depressed patients. From these results, can we reject our null hypothesis (that there is no difference between the exercise and no exercise conditions) and support of the alternative hypothesis (that the exercise condition will increase quality of life)? Before we make this decision, a second study is informative.

In order to illustrate a key issue involved in deciding whether to reject the null hypothesis, imagine that we did a similar study. In our new study, we use the same number of participants (also depressed adolescents), the same method of sample selection, and random assignment to groups. However, in this new study, neither group is instructed to exercise for 6 weeks. At the end of the 6-week period we measure the mean quality of life of both groups. Will the means be identical? It is unlikely that the means will be identical because there are individual differences among the members of each sample. Because we are not measuring the whole population, but only two samples from the population, we would expect the means to be different, due to random fluctuation. That is, even without introducing a treatment, and even if the two samples were equivalent in characteristics, we would expect the two means to be somewhat different. Therefore, we need to use inferential statistics to help make the proper decision.

Now back to our original study. After performing the proper statistical test (a *t* test for this example), we can make one of two conclusions. On the one hand, we could conclude that the intervention group mean really is greater than the control group mean. In other words, we can conclude that the intervention group mean represents the mean of a population of participants with a higher quality of life, and the control group mean represents the mean of a population of participants with a lower quality of life. This conclusion defines a statistically significant difference and is demonstrated in the upper portion of the right-hand section (e) of Fig. 20.1. A second conclusion could be that there is no difference between the two means (lower portion of the right-hand section of the figure). In other words, the difference between the means was simply due to random fluctuation. This latter conclusion would imply that the two groups come from the same underlying population and that this amount of exercise does not make a difference in quality of life for depressed patients as defined for our study.

Which conclusion do we make? How much of a difference between the two means is needed before we can conclude that there is a statistically significant difference? Inferential statistics provide us with an outcome (a statistic) that helps us make the decision about how much of a difference is needed. Even after performing inferential statistical procedures on our data, we are still making a decision with some degree of uncertainty.

We stated that there were two possible decisions that we could make based on our sample data. Either we would reject the null hypothesis and conclude that the two groups come from two different populations, or we would not reject the null hypothesis and conclude that the groups come from the same population. The decision to reject or not reject the null hypothesis is determined by subjecting our sample data to a particular statistical test. An outcome that is highly unlikely (i.e., one that results in a low probability value) if the null hypothesis were true leads us to reject the null hypothesis. Most researchers and journals establish this probability value as 5 times in 100, or .05. An outcome that is more likely (probable) will result in a failure to reject the null hypothesis.

TYPE I AND TYPE II ERRORS

Although inferential statistics inform us of the decision to make (e.g., reject or not reject the null hypothesis), there is still a possibility that the decision we make may be incorrect. This is because our decision is based on the probability of a given outcome. Any time we conduct a study based on sample data, four outcomes are possible. Figure 20.2 illustrates the four outcomes. Two of the outcomes are correct decisions and two are errors. The correct outcomes are (a) not reject the null hypothesis when it is true (i.e., there is, in fact, no difference) and (b) reject the null hypothesis when it is false (i.e., a correct decision that there is a difference). The errors are (c) reject the null hypothesis when, in fact, it is true—type I error (i.e., saying

True in the population

Decision based on data from sample		Null is true (No real difference)	Null is false (Really is a difference)
	Reject null	(c) Type I error	(b) Correct decision
	Do not reject null	(a) Correct decision	(d) Type II error

FIG. 20.2.   Type I and Type II errors.

that you found a difference, when there really was no difference)—and (d) not reject the null hypothesis when it is false—type II error (i.e., saying that there was no difference, when there really was a difference).

In the exercise example with depressed patients, the type I error would be made if we concluded, because $p < .05$, that exercise improved quality of life when, in actuality, there was no difference in the population for the quality of life of exercisers and nonexercisers. A type II error would be made if we concluded that there was no improvement when there were real differences in the population. We are never sure whether the decision we have made is correct (reflecting what is actually true in the population) because we are basing our decision on sample data.

STATISTICAL POWER

In the example provided in this chapter (Fig. 20.1), we selected a sample of 72 patients. How do we know how many participants to include in a study? The answer to this question involves the broader topic of statistical power. Statistical power is defined as the probability of rejecting a *false* null hypothesis. In the previous section, we pointed out that there are four outcomes possible in hypothesis testing. Statistical power is based on the outcome (correct decision) presented in Fig. 20.2 as (b), *reject the null hypothesis when it is false.* Because statistical power is the probability of making a correct decision, researchers want to make this probability high. Conventionally, the desired statistical power of a study is set at .80. Because statistical power is inversely related to a type II error, that error would be .20.

Although there are numerous methods to increase statistical power, such as using a directional as opposed to a nondirectional hypothesis or using planned comparisons as opposed to post hoc comparisons, the most common method to increase statistical power is to increase the size of the sample. Determining the necessary sample size always should be a part of planning the study. In order to determine how many participants to include in a study, one must know the significance level (usually established at .05), type of hypothesis (directional or nondirectional), desired power (.8 if possible), and an estimate of the effect size (the size of the relationship between the independent variable and the dependent variable, usually stated in standard deviation units). Where does one obtain effect size information? Effect size information comes from a review of the literature on the topic. Most current research syntheses contain a meta-analysis (chap. 35) that results in at least one effect size estimate.

Once the information has been obtained (significance level, type of hypothesis, amount of power, and effect size), a power table can be used to determine the number of participants. In our current example, for a significance level of .05, directional hypothesis, power of .8, and estimated effect size of .8 (considered a large effect size), the number of participants needed for each of our two groups is 20. On the other hand, had the literature shown that for this type of study, an effect size of .5 was typical, we would need 50 patients in each group to achieve a power of .8. Given an effect size of .5 and only 36 participants in each group, power would be about .66.

Although increasing the number of participants in a study may be the best way to increase statistical power, often this option is not under the control of the investigator. The field of program evaluation provides examples where the number of participants is fixed, often at a number below that desired for adequate power. When this occurs, there are other methods to increase power, such as using homogeneous groups, making sure the instrument/measure has strong evidence for reliability, and sometimes choosing a within subjects design to reduce variability. Lipsey (1990) and Cohen (1988) provided valuable information on this topic.

FINAL POINTS

Four points about inferential statistics and hypothesis testing need to be considered. First, when the null hypothesis is not rejected, it is never actually accepted. The correct conclusion is that the null hypothesis is not rejected. Although one may question the difference between the terms *accept* and *not reject*, the problem with the former is that there could be many reasons why the study did not result in a rejection of the null hypothesis. Perhaps another more powerful or better designed study might result in a rejection of the null hypothesis.

The second point is that a statistically significant difference only shows that there is some relationship between two variables. It does not provide the strength of this relationship. To determine the strength of a difference or an association, effect sizes need to be computed. We address this concept in several later chapters, including the next.

Third, testing the null hypothesis, as already illustrated, is a key part of all types of inferential statistical procedures and four of the research approaches. Our example utilized the randomized experimental design and a t test, but the general process of testing the null hypothesis also applies to the quasi-experimental comparative and associational approaches and to the wide variety of specific statistics (ANOVA, correlation, etc.) that might be used.

Last, in order to provide a fair test of the null hypothesis, there must be adequate statistical power. A power analysis should be planned prior to the study.

Chapter 21

Problems With Null Hypothesis Significance Testing (NHST)

In the last chapter, we discussed the process of null hypothesis significance testing (NHST), which has been an integral part of all inferential statistics (e.g., *t* test, correlation, chi-square) in the biological, behavioral, and social sciences for most of the past century. However, concerns about its use and interpretation have recently increased for two reasons. First, the logic underlying NHST is difficult to understand, appears to be backward, and under certain conditions will always lead to rejection of the null hypothesis. Second, and perhaps more important, null hypothesis significance testing is often improperly used and interpreted in medical and behavioral research. Terms such as *null hypothesis, significance level, statistically significant,* and *power,* which are fundamental to NHST, are often used without an accurate understanding of their technical meanings. As a result, NHST appears to have been overused, and misinterpreted, so much so that many knowledgeable researchers advocated that NHST simply be banned. The purpose of this chapter is to (a) briefly present the logical underpinnings and proper use of NHST, (b) point out common problems accompanying NHST, and (c) make suggestions to increase recognition of misinterpretations of NHST in the published literature. Unfortunately, the topic is too complex to be dealt with completely in a single chapter, so we focus on the major points. However, for a more comprehensive treatment of NHST, we recommend the texts by Harlow, Mulaik, and Steiger (1997) and Kline (2004).

LOGIC OF NHST

The logic underlying NHST is confusing, not only to students but also to instructors and many researchers as well. Cohen (1994) explained this issue well:

What's wrong with NHST? Well, among many other things, it does not tell us what we want to know, and we so much want to know what we want to know that, out of desperation, we nevertheless believe that it does! What we want to know is "Given these data what is the probability that the H_0 (null hypothesis) is true?" But . . . what it tells us is "Given that H_0 is true, what is the probability of these (or more extreme) data?" These are not the same, as has been pointed out many times over the years. (p. 997)

We now apply the logical reasoning about NHST to the example from the last chapter. We put forward a theory that the introduction of an exercise program would result in an improvement in quality of life among depressed adolescent patients. To gain support for our theory, we set up two groups of depressed adolescents, an exercise group and a control group. At the end of a given period, we would compare the mean of the exercise group (M_E) to the mean of the control group (M_C). The logical reasoning, according to NHST, is as follows: If the null hypothesis is true, then the result (the difference between M_E and M_C) will be quite small. However, because the result (the difference between M_E and M_C) turned out to be quite large, the null hypothesis must be false. Cohen (1994) and others point out that the logic of NHST is correct only if stated in absolute terms, reject or do not reject the null hypothesis, not in conditional probabilities. Thus one must be very careful about its use and interpretation.

A second problem involving the logic of NHST, one that has been pointed out by many of its critics (Cohen, 1994; Meehl, 1990; Tukey, 1991), is that the null hypothesis is never actually true, and that there always is some difference between the population means of the two groups. Therefore, rejecting the null hypothesis is merely a matter of having enough participants in each condition, even though the results may be trivial.

BEST PRACTICE

Current best practice in this area is open to debate (e.g., see Harlow et al., 1997). A number of prominent researchers advocate the use of confidence intervals in place of NHST on grounds that, for the most part, confidence intervals provide more information than a significance test, and still include information to determine statistical significance (Cohen, 1994; Kirk, 1996). For those who advocate the use of NHST, the null hypothesis of no difference (the nil null hypothesis) should be replaced by a null hypothesis specifying some nonzero value based on previous research (Cohen, 1994). Thus there would be less chance that a trivial difference between intervention and control groups would result in a rejection of the null hypothesis. If a null hypothesis of no difference is used, the alternative hypothesis should be directional.

Therefore, for NHST to be used properly, the following are necessary. First, the researcher must propose one or a limited number of specific hypotheses. From the example in our previous chapter, we put forward a hypothesis that introduction of an exercise program would result in an increase in quality of life among depressed adolescent patients. Second, a large, accessible population should exist from which the researcher will have the option to draw a random sample large enough to have adequate *power* (i.e., the probability of declaring a result "statistically significant" when the null hypothesis is false). Third, the researcher must have a measure (dependent variable) that has strong psychometric properties, such as sufficient evidence of reliability and validity. Perhaps more important, the measure must have some degree of clinical or practical validity. This means that the researcher should know how much of a difference between and M_E and M_C would produce a clinically significant change in the quality of life of the participants.

Therefore, prior to collecting any data, the researcher should have a specific hypothesis, a representative accessible population, an adequately sized sample, and a clinically valid measure. In addition, the researcher must have a sound methodological approach for carrying out the study. This includes appropriate choices of how many participants will be sampled, how they will be sampled, how they will be assigned to groups, how the data will be analyzed, and an established level of statistical significance, alpha, usually set at .05.

OTHER PROBLEMS WITH NHST

Unfortunately, many research projects conducted in the medical and behavioral sciences are not tied to a specific theory, and they do not have a representative, accessible population, a large enough sample, or a measure that has strong psychometric properties and is clinically valid in the sense described above. This has led to several problems with the way null hypotheses are tested.

Problems Post Hoc Testing

One common problem arises from *post hoc* or after-the-study testing. The problem related to post hoc testing occurs when no hypothesis has been proposed, or a hypothesis is proposed without rationale and justification, and the statistical test is set up only after the data are in hand. Thus, instead of planning to test a hypothesis, one might have collected data on exercise and quality of life, even examined the data, and only then asked how statistical significance is to be established. Both the significance level (α) and power are probabilities that must be calculated a priori (i.e., before the data are collected). To calculate such probabilities after the data are examined is analogous to watching part or all of a horse race and then offering to bet on a horse at the odds established before the race is begun.

Problems With Multiple Significance Tests

Many published papers report a multitude of test statistics and p values, which may lead to type I errors, concluding that results are statistically significant when they are not. The problem related to multiple testing often results from the lack of a good measure for evaluating the theory or no theoretical orientation. The investigator obtains many measures for each participant and tests the statistically significance of each one separately. The probability that one or more of these measures will show statistical significance at the chosen alpha level can become quite high. For a .05 significance test with one measure, the probability of a false positive (type I error) is 5%, which is as it should be. But with 10 different measures, the probability of a false positive is 40%, and with 20 measures it is 64%. Because the hallmark of NHST is that the overall probability of rejecting the null hypothesis when it is true is less than alpha (here 5%), clearly these multiple tests are no longer 5%-level tests. Researchers sometimes try to control possible false positives by using the Bonferroni correction, which returns the true significance level to a 5% NHST, but this method usually decreases the power of the test. One should be extremely cautious about drawing conclusions when several tests of the same hypothesis are conducted, especially when no adjustment has been made for multiple statistical tests.

Misinterpretation of the p Value

Outcomes with lower p values are sometimes interpreted as having stronger treatment effects than those with higher p values; for example, an outcome of $p < .01$ is interpreted as having a stronger treatment effect than an outcome of $p < .05$. The p value indicates the probability that the outcome could happen, assuming a true null hypothesis. It does not indicate the strength of the relationship.[1]

How prevalent is this misinterpretation? Oakes (1986) suggested:

> It is difficult, however, to estimate the extent of this abuse because the identification of statistical significance with substantive significance is usually im-

---

[1]Although p values do not provide information about the size or strength of the effect, smaller p values, *given a constant sample size*, are correlated with larger effect sizes. This fact may contribute to this misconception about p values.

plicit rather than explicit. Furthermore, even when an author makes no claim as to an effect size underlying a significant statistic, the reader can hardly avoid making an implicit judgment as to that effect size. (p. 86)

Oakes found researchers in psychology grossly overestimate the size of the effect based on a significance level change from .05 to .01.

Effect Size

As stated in the American Psychological Association *Publication Manual* (2001), in addition to information on statistical significance, it is important to state the size of the effect. An effect size is defined as the strength of the relationship between the independent variable and the dependent variable. Unfortunately, there are many different effect size measures and little agreement about which to use. In the next chapter and several later ones, especially chapter 36, we discuss various effect sizes and their interpretation in more detail, but there is little consensus about their interpretation.

Assuming that effect size has been computed, how should it be interpreted? Cohen (1988) provided guidelines for interpreting effect sizes as small, medium, or large and provided research examples to support the suggested values. Cohen considered an effect size to be large because it is on the high side of what is usually found in the behavioral science literature. However, Cohen's standards are arbitrary and may be inappropriate in certain situations. It is easy to recommend that effect sizes be reported, but it is more difficult to understand and interpret them.

Should effect size information accompany only statistically significant outcomes? The APA Task Force on Statistical Inference (Wilkinson & the Task Force, 1999) recommended always presenting effect sizes for primary outcomes. The Task Force further stated that "Reporting effect sizes also informs power analyses and meta-analyses needed in future research" (p. 599). On the other hand, Levin and Robinson (2000) were adamant about not presenting effect sizes after nonsignificant outcomes. They note a number of instances of single-study investigations where educational researchers have interpreted effect sizes (as small, medium, or large) in the absence of statistically significant outcomes. Our opinion is that effect sizes should accompany all reported *p* values for possible future meta-analytic use, but their relative size (as small, medium, or large) should not be discussed in a single study in the absence of statistical significance.

Statistical Significance Versus Practical Significance

Another common problem with the interpretation of NHSTs is assuming that statistical significance means practical significance. The problem results in part from the probably unfortunate use of the word *significance*, which to many people implies importance, even practicality. This error involves interpreting a statistically significant difference as a difference that has practical or clinical implications. Although a statistically significant finding *may* have practical or clinical effects, there is nothing in the definition of statistical significance to guarantee that this is the case. Some researchers have advocated always using the word *statistical* before significance when discussing hypothesis testing to distinguish it from practical significance. Others have recommended using effect size to help in the interpretation of practical or clinical significance. We caution, however, that even effect size is not synonymous with practical significance. Consider a commonly cited study that examined aspirin's effect on heart attacks. The study demonstrated that those who took aspirin had a statistically significantly lower probability of having a heart attack than those in the placebo condition. Although, in the case of aspirin, the effect size was considered to be quite low using Cohen's (1988) suggested terminology, the practical importance was quite high, due to the low cost of taking aspirin and the importance of reducing myocardial infarction. Thus, what is a large effect in one context or study may be small in another. We discuss this issue again in the next chapter and in more depth in chapter 36, which describes a relatively new effect size that may help in the interpretation of clinical significance (see also Kraemer et al., 2003).

Perhaps the biggest problem associated with the practical significance issue is the lack of good measures. Cohen (1994) pointed out that researchers probably were not reporting confidence intervals because they were so large. He went on to say, ". . . their sheer size should move us toward improving our measurement by seeking to reduce the unreliable and invalid part of the variance in our measures" (p. 1002).

RECOMMENDATIONS AND CAUTIONS

We have pointed out some major issues regarding NHST. The logic of NHST is difficult to understand, even for researchers, and doesn't tell what we really want to know. Several other common problems were discussed, which should lead readers to be cautious about the interpretation of NHST in research articles. For example, there should be only a few NHSTs in any study, or there should be some attempt to keep the significance level (alpha) at .05. Also, the statistical tests should correspond to the hypotheses that the study was designed to test. A statistically significant p value should not be interpreted as indicating that the result had practical significance. A statistically significant result may or may not be of clinical or practical importance.

Although there are problems with the use and interpretation of NHST, such tests are an important part of the use of inferential statistics. Our suggestion is that descriptive statistics, including especially effect sizes, be used to supplement tests of statistical significance. This suggestion is consistent with recent editorial policy changes of many journals in the behavioral and social sciences and with the American Psychological Association Task Force on Statistical Inference report, which stated that effect sizes should always be reported (Wilkinson & the Task Force, 1999). In addition, we suggest that readers as well as researchers be cautious in interpreting NHSTs. Last, considering all of the problems and controversy surrounding NHST, we quote a solution from Kline (2004): ". . . there is a method that can tell us what we really want to know, but it is not a statistical technique; rather, it is replication, which is not only the best way to deal with sampling error, but replication is also a gold standard in science" (p. 70).

Chapter 22

Using Effect Sizes and Confidence Intervals to Interpret the Results of a Statistical Test

In this chapter, we go beyond NHST and its problems, as discussed in the last chapter, to provide an introduction to effect size and practical or clinical significance to help interpret statistical outcomes. We end this chapter with an example that draws on information from several earlier chapters to illustrate how authors might state their research problem, identify the variables and research questions, select the statistics, and interpret the results using the materials provided in this chapter. The following chapters provide more detailed discussions and examples from published articles of the use and interpretation of many of the common statistical tests.

STATISTICAL SIGNIFICANCE

As a review, Fig. 22.1 shows how to interpret the statistical significance of an inferential test once the probability level (p) is known. In general, if the calculated value of the statistic (t, F, r, etc.) is relatively large, the probability, or p, is small (e.g., .05, .01, .001). If the probability is *less than* the preset alpha level (usually.05), then the results are said to be statistically significant. Thea authors might say that the results are significant at the .05 level, that p < .05, or that they rejected the null hypothesis of no difference or no relationship. Thus, regardless of what specific statistic is used, if the p is small enough, the finding is statistically significant, and the null hypothesis of no difference or no relationship can be rejected.

Value of the statistic[a]	p^b	Null Hypothesis	Interpretation
Small	1.00	Don't Reject	Not Statistically Significant (could be due to chance)
	.50	↓	↓
	.06		
	.05	Reject [c]	Statistically Significant[d] (not likely due to chance)
	.01	↓	↓
Large	<.001		

[a]Large and small values vary for each specific statistic and by the degrees of freedom (df), which are usually based on the number of participants. Statistics textbooks include tables showing what value of a statistic and df are required for $p < .05$.

[b]These are just a sample of p values, which could be any value from 0 to 1.

[c]$p \le .05$ is the typical alpha level that researchers use to assess whether the null hypothesis should be rejected or not. However, sometimes researchers use more liberal levels (e.g., .10 in exploratory studies) or more conservative levels (e.g., .01).

[d]Statistically significant does *not* mean that the results have practical significance or importance.

FIG. 22.1.   Interpreting inferential statistics.

PRACTICAL SIGNIFICANCE VERSUS STATISTICAL SIGNIFICANCE

A common misinterpretation is to assume that statistically significant results are practically or clinically important. But statistical significance is not the same as practical significance or importance. With large samples, statistical significance can be obtained even when the differences or associations are very small/weak. Thus, in addition to statistical significance, it is important to examine the effect size. It is quite possible, with a large sample, to have a statistically significant result that is very weak (i.e., has a small *effect size*). The null hypothesis states that there is no relationship between an independent and dependent variable. A statistically significant result with a small effect size means that we can be confident that there is at least some relationship, but it may not be of any practical importance.

CONFIDENCE INTERVALS

One alternative to null hypothesis significance testing (NHST) is to create confidence intervals. These intervals provide more information than NHST and may provide more practical information. For example, suppose one knew that an increase in scores of more than 5 points, on a particular instrument, would lead to a functional increase in performance. Two different methods of therapy were compared. The result showed that clients who used the new method scored statistically significantly higher than those who used the other method. According to NHST, we would reject the null hypothesis of no difference between methods and conclude that our new method is better. If we apply confidence intervals to this same study, we can determine an interval that we are quite confident contains the *population mean difference*. Using the preceding example, if the lower bound of the confidence interval is greater than 5 points, we can conclude that using this method would lead to a practical or functional increase in performance. If, however, the confidence interval ranged from 1 to 11, the result would be statistically significant, but the mean difference in the population might be as small as 1 point, or as large as 11 points. Given those results, we could not be confident that there would be a *practical* increase using the new method.

EFFECT SIZE

A statistically significant outcome does not give information about the strength or size of the outcome. Therefore, it is important to know, in addition to information on statistical significance, the size of the effect. Effect size is defined as the strength of the relationship between the independent variable and the dependent variable, and/or the magnitude of the difference between levels of the independent variable with respect to the dependent variable. Statisticians have proposed effect size measures that fall mainly into three types or families: the *r* family, the *d* family, and measures of risk potency (see Grissom & Kim, 2005).

The r Family of Effect Size Measures. One method of expressing effect sizes is in terms of strength of association. The most well-known variant of this approach is the *Pearson correlation coefficient, r.* Using the Pearson *r*, effect sizes always have an absolute value less than or equal to 1.0, varying between −1.0 and +1.0 with 0 representing no effect and +1 or −1 representing the maximum effect. This *family* of effect sizes includes many other associational statistics such as rho (ρ or r_s), phi (ϕ), eta (η), and the multiple correlation (R). See chapters 26 and 30 for more discussion of these statistics and effect size measures.

The d Family of Effect Size Measures. The *d* family focuses on the magnitude of the difference that two levels of the independent variable have on the dependent variable, rather than on the strength of association. One way that the effect size (d) is computed is by subtracting the mean of the comparison group from the mean of the intervention group and dividing by the pooled standard deviation of both groups. There are other formulas for d family effect sizes, but they all express effect size in standard deviation units. Thus, a d of .5 means that the groups differ by one half of a standard deviation. Using d, effect sizes usually vary from 0 to +1 or –1, but d can be more than 1. The statistics that utilize d effect sizes are discussed principally in chapters 24 and 25.

Measures of Risk Potency. These measures are based on data with dichotomous independent and dependent variables. There are many such effect size measures, usually expressed as ratios or percentages, including *odds ratios, relative risk reduction,* and *risk difference.* The use of these effect size measures is discussed in chapters 27, 31, and 36.

To summarize, the r effect size is most commonly used when the independent and dependent variables are continuous. The d effect size is used when the independent variable is dichotomous and the dependent variable is continuous. Finally, risk potency effect sizes are used when the independent and dependent variables are dichotomous (binary). However, as implied later in Table 22.1, most effect sizes can be converted from one family to another.

Issues About Effect Size Measures. Unfortunately, there is little agreement about which to use. Although d is the most commonly discussed effect size measure for experimental studies in the behavioral sciences and education, odds ratios and other risk potency effect sizes are most common in medical research. The r family effect sizes, including r and R (multiple correlation), are common in survey research using associational research questions.

There is also disagreement among researchers about whether it is best to express effect size as the unsquared or squared r family statistic (e.g., r or r^2). The squared versions have been used historically because they indicate the percentage of variance in the dependent variable that can be predicted or explained from the independent variable(s). However, Cohen (1988) and others argued that these usually small percentages provide an underestimated impression of the strength or importance of the effect. We, like Cohen, prefer to use the unsquared statistics as our r family indexes, but you will see both in the literature.

Although the 1994 fourth edition of the *Publication Manual of the American Psychological Association* (APA, 1994) recommended that researchers report effect sizes, relatively few researchers did so before 1999 when the APA Task Force on Statistical Inference stated that effect sizes *always* should be reported for primary results (Wilkinson & the Task Force, 1999). The fifth edition (APA, 2001) essentially adopted this recommendation of the Task Force, so in the future most behavioral science journal articles will discuss the size of the effect as well as whether or not the result was statistically significant. Effect sizes should be reported because with large samples, one can have a statistically significant finding with a very weak relationship (small effect size). Knowing the effect size, or at least the information necessary to compute it, is important for meta-analysis, which combines all of the appropriate studies, including those statistically significant and those not significant, to compute an effect size across studies.

INTERPRETING EFFECT SIZES

Assuming that an effect size measure has been computed, how should it be interpreted? Cohen (1988) suggested values for large, medium, and small size effects. Note that these guidelines are based on the effect sizes *usually* found in studies in the behavioral sciences and education. Thus, they do not have absolute meaning; large, medium, and small are only relative to typical findings in these areas. For that reason, we think it would be good practice to use "larger than typical" instead of large, "typical" instead of medium, and "smaller than typical" instead of small. Cohen's guidelines will not apply to all subfields in the behavioral sciences, and they definitely will not apply to fields, designs, or contexts where the usually expected effects are either larger or smaller. It is advisable for authors to examine the research literature to see if there is information about typical effect sizes on the topic and reconsider what are said to be small, large, and typical values. Table 22.1 provides guidelines for interpreting the size of the "effect" for six common effect size measures: d, r, ϕ, R, η, and risk difference.

Cohen (1988) provided research examples of what he labeled small, medium, and large effects to support his suggested d and r family values. Most researchers would not consider a correlation (r) of .5 to be very strong because only 25% of the variance in the dependent variable is predicted. However, Cohen argued that a d of .8 and an r of .5 (which he showed to be mathematically similar) are "grossly perceptible and therefore large differences, as [for example is] the mean difference in height between 13- and 18-year-old girls" (p. 27). Cohen stated that a small effect may be difficult to detect, perhaps because it is in a less well controlled area of research. Cohen's medium size effect is ". . . visible to the naked eye. That is, in the course of normal experiences, one would become aware of an average difference in IQ between clerical and semi-skilled workers . . ." (p. 26).

Effect Size and Practical Significance. The effect size indicates the strength of the relationship and, thus, is relevant for practical significance. Although some researchers (e.g., Thompson, 2002) consider effect size measures to be an index of practical significance, we think that effect size

TABLE 22.1
Interpretation of the Strength of a Relationship (Effect Sizes)

General Interpretation of the Strength of a Relationship	The d Family[a]		The r Family[b]		Risk Potency
	d	r and ϕ	R	η (eta)[d]	RD (%)
Much larger than typical	≥1.00[c]	≥.70	.70+	.45+	≥52
Large or larger than typical	.80	.50	.51	.37	43
Medium or typical	.50	.30	.36	.24	28
Small or smaller than typical	.20	.10	.14	.10	11

[a]d values can vary from 0.0 to +1 or –1.0 infinity, but d greater than one is uncommon.

[b]r family values can vary from 0.0 to +1 or –1.0, but except for reliability (i.e., same concept measured twice), r is rarely above .70. In fact, some of these statistics (e.g., phi) have a restricted range in certain cases; that is, the maximum phi is less then 1.0.

[c]We interpret the numbers in this table as a range of values. For example, d greater than .90 (or less than –.90) would be described as "much larger than typical," d between, say, .70 and .90 would be called "larger than typical," and d between, say, .60 and .70 would be "typical to larger than typical." We interpret the other three columns similarly.

[d]Partial etas from SPSS multivariate tests are equivalent to R. Use R column.

measures are not direct indexes of the importance of a finding. As implied earlier, what constitutes a large or important effect depends on the specific area studied, the context, and the methods. Furthermore, practical significance always involves a judgment by the researcher and/or the consumers (e.g., clinicians, clients, teachers, school boards) of research that takes into account such factors as cost and political considerations. For example, the effect size of taking some medication (e.g., a statin) might be relatively small for heart attacks, but the practical importance could be high because preventing heart attacks is a life-or-death matter, the costs of statins are relatively low, and side effects are relatively uncommon. On the other hand, a therapeutic or curriculum change could have a large effect size but not be practical because of high costs and/or extensive opposition to its implementation.

STEPS IN INTERPRETING INFERENTIAL STATISTICS

The following steps are recommended for interpretation of inferential statistics:

First, the authors should decide whether to reject the null hypothesis, but that is not enough for a full interpretation. If the outcome is statistically significant, the authors should answer at least two more questions. Figure 22.2 summarizes the additional steps about how to more fully interpret the results of an inferential statistic.

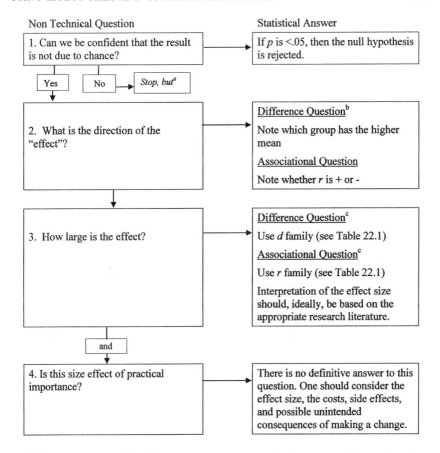

Non Technical Question

Statistical Answer

1. Can we be confident that the result is not due to chance?

If *p* is <.05, then the null hypothesis is rejected.

Yes | No | *Stop, but*[a]

2. What is the direction of the "effect"?

Difference Question[b]

Note which group has the higher mean

Associational Question

Note whether *r* is + or -

3. How large is the effect?

Difference Question[c]

Use *d* family (see Table 22.1)

Associational Question[c]

Use *r* family (see Table 22.1)

Interpretation of the effect size should, ideally, be based on the appropriate research literature.

and

4. Is this size effect of practical importance?

There is no definitive answer to this question. One should consider the effect size, the costs, side effects, and possible unintended consequences of making a change.

[a]With a small sample (*N*), it is possible to have a non significant result (it may be due to chance) and yet a large effect size. If so, replicating the study with a larger sample may be justified.

[b]If there are three or more means or a significant interaction a post hoc test (e.g., Tukey) will be necessary for complete interpretation.

[c]Interpretation of effect size is based on Cohen (1988) and Table 22.1. A "large" effect is one that Cohen states is "grossly perceptible." It is larger than typically found in the area, but does not necessarily explain a large amount of variance.

FIG. 22.2. Steps in the interpretation of an inferential statistic.

Second, the direction of the effect should be stated or shown in a table. Difference inferential statistics compare groups so which group performed better should be stated. For associational inferential statistics (e.g., correlation), the sign is very important, so whether the association or relationship is positive or negative should be clear.

Third, the effect size should be included in the description of the results or, at the least, the information to compute it should be presented. The interpretation of the size is more subjective. If there is little or no research literature about the relationship between the independent variable and the dependent variable used in the study under review, Table 22.1 should be used. If there is relevant research on the variables of interest, what is said to be larger or smaller than typical should be based on that research.

Fourth, the researcher or the consumer of the research (clinician and patient/client) should make a judgment about whether the result has practical or clinical significance or importance. To do so the effect size, the costs of implementing change, and the probability and severity of any side effects or unintended consequences need to taken into account.

AN EXAMPLE OF HOW TO INTERPRET THE RESULTS OF A STATISTICAL TEST

We now provide an example in order to illustrate the points made in this and earlier chapters. *Suppose your research problem was to investigate the presumed effects of an anxiety reduction treatment and trait anxiety on performance on a mathematics achievement posttest.*

Identification of the Variables, Approach, Design, and Measurement. The research problem specifies three variables: the *treatment, trait anxiety inventory score,* and *mathematics achievement.* The latter is the outcome or dependent variable, and the treatment and anxiety scores are the independent or predictor variables because they occurred before the mathematics examination. As such, they are *presumed* to have an effect on posttest mathematics achievement scores. The treatment is an active independent variable, but the participants' trait anxiety is an attribute independent variable because it is a characteristic or attribute of the participants that is assumed not to vary as a result of the treatment, as state anxiety surely would.

If the participants were randomly assigned to the anxiety reduction treatment and to the no-treatment/placebo group, the study would be considered a *randomized experiment, posttest-only control-group design,* and the *equivalence of the groups on participant characteristics* aspect of *internal validity* would be rated high, assuming that there was not high attrition or participant dropout during the study (see chap. 17 for more details).

What is the level of measurement for these three variables? The treatment is dichotomous (*new experimental treatment* or *placebo*). The anxiety inventory score has many ordered levels. These data should be approximately normally distributed. Likewise, the math achievement test has many levels, with more scores probably somewhere in the middle than at the high and low ends, so it is approximately normally distributed.

Research Questions. There are a number of possible research questions that could be asked and statistics that could be used with these three variables. However, we focus on two research questions and two inferential statistics. We discuss the two basic research questions, given the earlier specification of the variables and their measurement. Then we mention a complex research question that could be asked instead of research questions 1 and 2.

1. Is There a Difference Between the New Treatment and No-Treatment Conditions on Their Average Math Achievement Scores?

Type of Research Question. This first question is phrased as a *basic difference question* because there are only two variables, an independent and dependent variable, and the independent variable has only two levels (the new treatment and the control).

Selection of an Appropriate Statistic. The first question should be answered with an *independent samples t test* because (a) the independent variable has only two values, (b) the design is between groups (new treatment and no treatment form two independent groups), and (c) the dependent variable (math achievement) is normally distributed data. The authors also should check other assumptions of the t test (chap. 24) to be sure that they were not markedly violated.

Interpretation of the Results for Question 1. Let's assume that about 50 students participated in the study and that $t = 2.05$. In this case, $p < .05$ and thus t is statistically significant. However, if there were 25 participants this t would not have been significant because the t value necessary for statistical significance is influenced strongly by sample size. Small samples require a larger t to be statistically significant.

If the statistic is significant, it only means the result is highly unlikely if the null hypothesis were true. The direction of the result and the effect size need to be specified (see Fig. 22.2). Let's assume that the new treatment group has the higher mean. If so, we can be confident that participants in the population are at least a little better at mathematics achievement, on average, than persons in the no treatment population. If the difference was not statistically significant, the authors should *not* make any comment about which mean was higher because the difference could be due to chance. Likewise, if the difference was not significant, we think it is best practice not to discuss explicitly or interpret the effect size. But the authors should provide the *Ns*, means, and standard deviations so that effect sizes could be computed if a later researcher wanted to include this study in a meta-analysis.

Because the t was statistically significant, the effect size (probably d) should be given and discussed. For example, if d were .33, there would be a small to medium or typical size effect. This means that the difference was less than typical of the statistically significant findings in the behavioral sciences. A d of .33 may or may not be a large enough difference to use for recommending programmatic changes (i.e., be practically significant).

Confidence intervals might help you decide if the difference in math achievement scores was large enough to have practical significance. For example, say you found (from the lower bound of the confidence interval) that you could only be confident that there was a ½-case-point difference between the treatment and placebo groups; then you could decide whether that was a big enough difference to justify a programmatic change.

2. Is There an Association Between Anxiety Inventory Scores and Math Achievement?

Type of Research Question.   This second question is phrased as a *basic associational question* and *research approach* because there are only two variables and both have many ordered levels.

Selection of an Appropriate Statistic.   The second research question could be answered with a *Pearson correlation* because both the anxiety trait and mathematics achievement scores are probably normally distributed data.

Interpretation of the Results for Research Question 2.   The interpretation of r is based on decisions similar to those already made for t. If $r = -.30$ (with 50 subjects), it would be statistically significant at the $p < .05$ level. If the r is statistically significant, the authors need to discuss the direction of the correlation and effect size. Because the correlation is negative, the author might say that students with *high* anxiety inventory scores tend to perform at the *low* end on math achievement and those with low anxiety scores tend to perform well on math achievement. The effect size of $r = -.30$ is medium or typical. Confidence intervals for the correlation could be helpful in judging practical importance.

Note that if N were 25, the r of $-.30$ would not be significant. On the other hand, if N were 500 and $r = -.30$, p would be $<.0001$. If N were 500, even $r = +.088$ or $-.088$ would be statistically significant, indicating that you could be quite sure the association was not zero, but the effect size would be small, or less than typical.

Complex Research Question and Statistics. In chapters 28–31, we demonstrate the advantages of considering two (or more) independent variables together rather than separately as in questions 1 and 2. There are several statistics, which we discuss in those later chapters, that could be used to consider both the treatment and trait anxiety scores together.

SUMMARY

This chapter provides an introduction to the interpretation of a statistical test beyond knowing whether the result was statistically significant. It emphasizes the importance of having a measure of the effect size or strength of the result. We also point out that judgments about the practical or clinical significance of a result are subtle. Effect sizes help in that judgment but are not enough.

The chapters in the next section of this text deal in more depth with how researchers decide what statistics to use to analyze their data and how they interpret the results from each of the statistics. Examples from published research articles are used to illustrate these points.

Part VI

SELECTION AND INTERPRETATION OF SPECIFIC STATISTICS

Selection of Inferential Statistics:
An Overview

This chapter is an overview of the selection of inferential statistics. It is followed by chapters 24–33, which discuss the use and interpretation of specific statistics in more detail, using examples from clinical research studies. Choosing the proper statistical analysis can be a difficult task, considering the large number of possible choices. However, it is easier if you are familiar with the concepts discussed in previous chapters and summarized here.

RESEARCH APPROACHES AND QUESTIONS

Figure 23.1 shows how the choice of a statistical test follows from the type of research question and purpose of the research. The top line indicates that the general purpose of most studies and thus the common goal of inferential statistics is to explore relationships between variables. We think that it is useful to divide research questions into difference or associational questions or hypotheses, which lead to difference and associational statistics. Although this distinction is somewhat arbitrary, we think it is useful educationally.

Difference Questions. Studies that use the randomized experimental, quasi-experimental, or comparative approach compare groups and test difference questions or hypotheses. Difference questions and statistics are usually used to compare a few groups (e.g., males vs. females, one or more treatments vs. a control group) using each group's average scores on the dependent variable (e.g., number of symptoms).

173

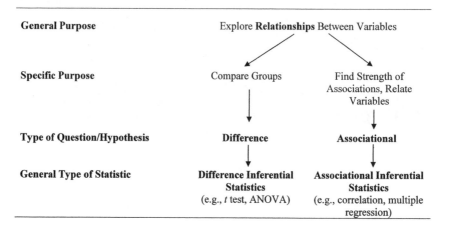

General Purpose	Explore **Relationships** Between Variables	
Specific Purpose	Compare Groups	Find Strength of Associations, Relate Variables
Type of Question/Hypothesis	**Difference**	**Associational**
General Type of Statistic	**Difference Inferential Statistics** (e.g., *t* test, ANOVA)	**Associational Inferential Statistics** (e.g., correlation, multiple regression)

FIG. 23.1. Schematic diagram showing how the purpose and type of research question correspond to the general type of statistic used in a study.

Associational Questions. Associational questions use associational inferential statistics to examine the correlation between two or more variables that usually have many ordered levels. If there is a positive association, persons who have high scores on one variable tend to have high scores on the second variable; those with low scores tend to be low on both variables. On the other hand, if there is a negative association between the two variables, those with low scores on variable 1 tend to have high scores on variable 2 and vice versa. If there is no association, you cannot predict a person's score on the second variable from knowing the first. People who score high on the first variable might be high or low or medium on the second variable.

INDEPENDENT AND DEPENDENT VARIABLES

The number of levels and the scale of measurement determine the type of research question and, therefore, the statistic to use. What is relevant for selecting statistics is the number of variables, especially the number of independent variables and the number of levels or categories within these independent variables.

Number of Levels of the Independent Variable. A difference question is indicated when the independent variable has a few (i.e., two to four) levels. For example, do the experimental and control groups differ on the dependent variable? However, if the independent variable has more than four unordered (nominal) levels, one would usually still ask a difference question and compare the groups. For example, do six ethnic groups differ?

When the independent variable has five or more *ordered* levels, we suggest an associational question and the use of associational inferential statistics. Thus, if the independent variable is continuous (an infinite number of ordered levels within some range) or approximately continuous, associational statistics are used. Note that two-variable associational inferential statistics (e.g., Pearson correlation) are bidirectional, so statisticians would say that there is no independent variable. However, because researchers usually have a causal relationship in mind, we suggest identifying the presumed cause as the independent variable.

Dependent Variables. This variable is also important for the appropriate choice of an inferential statistic. The primary issue with the dependent variable is the level of measurement, which we discuss later.

DESIGN CLASSIFICATIONS

Another key issue for selecting an appropriate statistic is whether the classification is between groups, within subjects, or mixed, as discussed in chapter 16. These classifications apply only to difference questions.

Between-Groups Versus Within-Subjects Single-Factor Designs. If there is only one independent variable or factor, the design must be either between or within because the minimum number of independent variables to have a mixed design is two. To use basic difference statistics, independence of groups or levels must be determined. In *between-groups designs*, each participant is in only one group and participants are independent. In *within-subjects/repeated-measures designs*, either the participants are assessed two or more times (repeated measures) or else two (or more) of them are matched or paired up in some meaningful way, such as members of the same family. For statistical purposes, their scores are not independent (i.e., they are said to be related or correlated samples). Within-subjects designs use statistics that are different from those for the between-groups designs.

Classification in Factorial Designs. When you have two or more independent variables, there are three possible design classifications: all between-groups, all within-subjects, and mixed (between and within). In mixed designs, such as the *pretest–posttest control-group design*, there is at least one between-groups independent variable (experimental vs. control) and at least one within-subjects independent variable (pretest vs. posttest).

SCALE OF MEASUREMENT

For appropriate statistical selection, level or scale of measurement also is important. *Normally distributed* data are the highest level of measurement. *Parametric statistics*, such as the *t* test, analysis of variance (ANOVA), and Pearson correlation, assume that the data are normally distributed. The data from good achievement tests and personality or attitude inventory scales are approximately normally distributed, with most people scoring somewhere in the middle and fewer scoring either high or low. *Ordinal* data have three or more levels ordered from low to high (often ranks), but they are not distributed normally. In contrast, *nominal* data (e.g., ethnic groups) have three or more unordered levels or categories, which are just names or labels. *Dichotomous* variables form a special case. Although dichotomous variables are in many ways like nominal variables, they can be used, especially as independent/predictor variables in multiple regression, as if they were normally distributed variables.

For difference statistics, it is the dependent variable whose level of measurement influences the choice of statistic. The independent variable can be nominal (e.g., ethnic groups) or ordered (e.g., low, medium, and high), but usually has fewer than five ordered levels. For associational statistics, the level of measurement for both or all variables needs to be determined.

ASSUMPTIONS

Every statistical test is based on certain *assumptions*. In general, the parametric statistics (e.g., *t* test, ANOVA, Pearson correlation, multiple regression) have more assumptions that need to be satisfied than nonparametric statistic such as chi-square or the Spearman rho. We include the assumptions underlying statistical tests when we discuss each test in more detail.

SELECTION OF APPROPRIATE INFERENTIAL STATISTICS

Figure 23.2, a decision tree, and the following text are provided to help select an appropriate statistical test. The first step is to determine if the research question or hypothesis is a difference one (i.e., compares groups) or an associational one (associates variables). Our suggestion is that if the independent/predictor variable has five or more ordered levels or categories, the question should be considered an associational one. If the independent variable has two to four categories, it is usually better to treat the

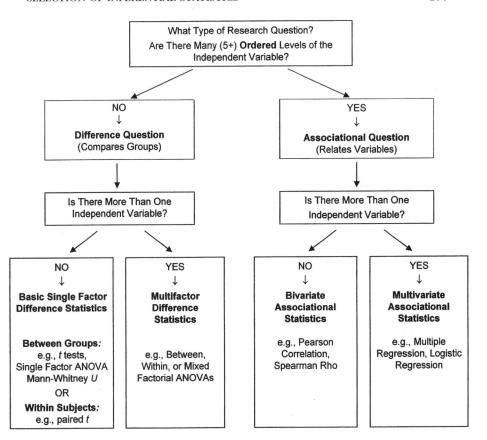

FIG. 23.2.   A decision tree to decide how to select the appropriate inferential statistic.

question as a difference one, especially if the dependent variable has many ordered levels.

The second step is to decide how many independent variables there are in the research question: only one independent variable, or more than one.

Single-Factor Statistics.   If the research question involves a basic, single-factor, difference question, examine the lower left-hand box of Fig. 23.2. Selection of an appropriate statistic is determined by: (a) the level of measurement of the dependent variable and whether assumptions are markedly violated, (b) how many levels/groups/samples there are in the independent variable, and (c) whether the design is between-groups or within-subjects.

For example, if the answers to these questions are (a) the dependent variable is approximately normal (one is never certain the dependent variable is normally distributed in the population, but a frequency distribution from the sample data should approximate a bell-shaped curve), (b) there are two independent groups, and (c) the design is between-groups, you would use an independent-samples *t* test, which is discussed in the next chapter. If assumptions of the parametric test are markedly violated, one should use the equivalent, ordinal nonparametric statistic (e.g., Mann–Whitney *U* test instead of independent-samples *t* test). For this example, it is a serious error to use within-subjects statistics (e.g., paired *t* test) instead of a between-groups statistic (independent *t* test), or vice versa if the design classification were within-subjects. Another serious error that will produce meaningless results is to use a *t* test or Mann–Whitney *U* test when one has a nominal dependent variable.

Bivariate Associational Statistics. If a basic, two variable, associational question is asked, the statistic used depends on both variables. If both are at least approximately normally distributed (and other assumptions met), a Pearson product–moment correlation should be used. If one or both variables are ordinal or parametric assumptions are markedly violated, the Spearman rank order correlation, rho, is appropriate. Correlation is discussed in chapter 26.

Multifactor Difference Statistics. If a complex, multifactor difference question (two or more independent variables) is asked, the appropriate statistic is one of three types of factorial ANOVA. To select the appropriate ANOVA, a decision must be made to determine whether the design classification is between-groups, within-subjects, or mixed. If there is one dependent variable, and it is approximately normally distributed, the factorial ANOVAs corresponding to the design classification should be used. These ANOVAs are similar but have different formulas, so it is important to use the appropriate type. The between-groups factorial ANOVA is discussed in chapter 28 and the mixed ANOVA is discussed in chapter 29.

Multivariate Associational Statistics. If a complex multivariate associational question (two or more independent variables) is asked, two appropriate statistics are multiple regression and logistic regression. We discuss the former in chapter 30 and the later in chapter 31. *Multiple regression* is appropriate when two or more independent variables are used to predict a normally distributed dependent variable. *Logistic regression* is used to predict a dichotomous outcome or dependent variable.

THE GENERAL LINEAR MODEL

It is important to remember that the broad question of whether there is a relationship between independent variable X and dependent variable Y can be answered two ways. If both the independent variable and dependent variable provide approximately normally distributed data with five or more ordered levels, the statistic to use is the Pearson correlation, and that would be our recommendation. However, some researchers choose to divide the independent variable into two or several groups, such as low, medium, and high, and then do a single-factor ANOVA. Conversely, others who start with an independent variable that has a few (two through four) ordered categories may choose to do a correlation instead of a one-way ANOVA. These choices are not wrong, but we do not think they represent best practice.

In the preceding examples, we recommended one of the choices, but the fact that there are two choices raises a bigger and more complex issue. Statisticians point out, and can demonstrate mathematically, that the distinction between difference and associational statistics is an artificial one and that single-factor ANOVA and Pearson correlation are mathematically the same, as are factorial ANOVA and multiple regression. Thus the full range of methods used to analyze one continuous dependent variable and one or more independent variables, either continuous or categorical, are mathematically related (Keppel & Zedeck, 1989). The model on which this is based is called the general linear model; it is "general" in that the kind of independent variable is not specified.

What this means is that if you have a continuous, normally distributed dependent or outcome variable and five or so levels of a normally distributed independent variable, it would be appropriate to analyze it with either a correlation or a one-way ANOVA. Although we recognize that our distinction between difference and associational parametric statistics is a simplification, we think it is useful educationally.

SUMMARY

This chapter serves as an introduction to selection of appropriate statistical methods. In the next eight chapters we discuss conceptually, and in more depth, these statistical methods. We use clinical examples and discuss why the author(s) selected a particular statistical method and how the results of the statistical method were interpreted.

Chapter 24

Single-Factor Between-Groups Designs: Analysis and Interpretation

This chapter includes statistical tests that are used for a design with one independent variable (factor) that has two or more levels, where all participants are in one and only one condition (between groups). The single-factor design includes studies using the quantitative approaches of randomized experimental, quasi-experimental, and comparative. It is important to remember that the appropriate statistical test is the same for each of these quantitative approaches, but interpretation of cause and effect will vary as discussed in chapters 11–17.

We divide this chapter into parametric statistics (*t* test and single-factor analysis of variance [ANOVA]) and nonparametric statistics (Mann–Whitney *U* test and Kruskal–Wallis ANOVA by ranks). Although the chi-square test also could fit here under the category of nonparametric statistics, we save our discussion of chi-square for chapter 27.

There are three major assumptions underlying the use of the *t* test or ANOVA for independent samples.

1. *Independence*. Measures recorded from participants must be independent of each other. In other words, the performance of one participant must not affect the performance of another participant. This assumption must be met for all of the statistics discussed in the present chapter.

2. *Homogeneity of variance*. The variances of the dependent variables of the populations underlying the samples should be equal. ANOVA and *t* are quite sensitive to (affected by) unequal variances. (In this example, the standard deviations, which squared equal the variances, should be approximately equal. Computer programs usually have a test, such as the Levene

test, built in to help the researcher decide whether the variances are signifi-cantly different.)

3. *Normality.* The dependent variable should be normally distributed for each of the populations (groups) from which the samples were selected. ANOVA and *t* are quite robust (still accurate) to deviations from normality. (In the following example, the distribution of IQ scores for each group should be at least approximately symmetrical and shaped like the bell curve, with most scores near the mean and similar numbers of high and low IQ scores.)

Nonparametric statistics are usually applied to data from studies in which the assumptions for using parametric statistics are violated, often be-cause the groups have very unequal variances or the dependent variable is ordinal (and not normally distributed) or nominal.

ANALYZING SINGLE-FACTOR DESIGNS WITH PARAMETRIC STATISTICS

We start with single-factor between-groups designs performed on depend-ent variables that are normally distributed (often said to be interval or ratio scale). For our discussion of parametric statistics, we provide an example by Herpertz et al. (2001). First, we discuss the independent-samples *t* test and then the single-factor or one-way ANOVA.

Herpertz et al. (2001) investigated psychophysiological responses in boys with attention deficit hyperactive disorder (ADHD) compared with boys with this disorder who also had conduct disorder (ADHD + CD). A third group of boys without ADHD served as a comparison or control group. Although the major focus of this study was psychophysiological dif-ferences among the three groups, other dependent variables, including IQ, were also of interest. For purposes of demonstration of the parametric tests, we use the IQ data shown in Table 24.1. Because Herpertz et al. (2001) had three groups in their study (ADHD, ADHD + CD, and control), and each participant in the study was in only one of the three groups, the design was a single-factor between-groups design with three levels. Further-

TABLE 24.1
IQ Data From the Herpertz et al. (2001) Study

	ADHD (n = 21)	*ADHD + CD* (n = 26)	*Non-ADHD* (n = 21)
Mean	95.71	93.50	110.24
Standard deviation	11.08	7.97	11.77

more, because the groups differed on an attribute independent variable, the research approach to the study is considered comparative.

The *t* Test for Independent Samples

For purposes of demonstration, we start by imagining that the Herpertz et al. (2001) study had only two groups. For example, previous work in this area had compared ADHD with non-ADHD groups. If Herpertz et al. (2001) were to replicate this type of study, their design would be a single-factor between-groups design with two levels, ADHD and control. We would perform a *t* test for independent samples to determine whether the two groups differed significantly on the measure of IQ because there was just one independent variable (type of disability), there were only two levels (ADHD and control), and the dependent variable (IQ) was assumed to be normally distributed with equal variances. We express the results of the *t* test as follows. The differences between group means attained statistical significance: $t_{40} = 4.12$, $p < .01$. What does this mean? Conceptually, the *t* test and also the ANOVA (*F* test) are ratios of the variability between groups or conditions to the variability within the groups or conditions. What do we mean by the variability between groups and the variability within groups? In the *t* test, the variability between groups is determined from the difference between the mean of the ADHD group and the mean of the control group. In the present study, the mean of the ADHD group was 95.71 and the mean of the control group was 110.24. Therefore, the difference between the means was 14.53 IQ points in favor of the control group. The variability within groups or conditions is the variability among the individual participants within each group. One would expect there to be some differences in variability among participants within groups because they are different individuals. Other variability might be due to errors made in measurement. The size of the variability within groups can be estimated from the standard deviations within each group, which are shown in Table 24.1. These standard deviations are used as part of the calculation of the within-groups variability. If there is a large amount of variability in IQ among participants within a group, then the standard deviation will be large. On the other hand, if there is little variability, then the standard deviation will be small. Variability within groups is often referred to as error variance.

If the ratio just described is large (i.e., the variability between groups is several times greater than the variability within groups) and given a large enough sample, then it is likely that the result will be *statistically significant*. How does one know the result is statistically significant? To answer this question, we need to understand what is meant by statistical significance. When we use hypothesis testing, we phrase our outcome in terms of the null hypothesis, which, in this case, is the hypothesis that there is no difference between the mean IQ scores in the population of children with ADHD and the mean in the population of children without ADHD. Specifically, we state: If the null hypothesis were true, what is the likelihood that the outcome from the study could happen? If the likelihood were quite small, less than 5 times in 100 for example, p (the probability value) would be <.05, so we would reject the null hypothesis and provide support for the alternative or research hypothesis. (This .05 is the most common significance level, but some researchers use a lower, more conservative level, such as .01, in part because they are less willing to take a chance that they will reject a null hypothesis that is true.) Using the Herpertz et al. (2001) data, the computed probability was less than .01 that the outcome could happen if the null hypothesis were actually true. Therefore, they would reject the null hypothesis that there was no difference in IQ scores between the population means of the two groups. Therefore it is likely that the average IQ in the population of non-ADHD children is at least a little higher than the average IQ of all those with ADHD. We stated the results of our comparison as $t_{40} = 4.12$, $p <$ .01. The subscript number, 40, was the degrees of freedom, which refers to the number of independent pieces of information from the data collected in the study. In the t test, we find the degrees of freedom from the total number of participants minus two. There were 21 participants in each group. Thus there are 40 degrees of freedom for the comparison.

As discussed in chapter 22 and shown in Fig. 22.2, it is not sufficient to state that the result was statistically significant and that the non-ADHD group mean IQ was higher than that of the ADHD group. In addition, an *effect size* should be reported and interpreted, and, if possible, the practical or clinical importance of the finding should be noted. In the Herpertz et al. (2001) study, a d family effect size could be estimated by dividing the difference between the two means (14.53 IQ points) by the pooled standard deviation (11.43). The resulting d value is greater than 1, which is a much larger effect than is typical in the behavioral sciences (see Table 22.1).

Single-Factor ANOVA

In the example from Herpertz et al. (2001) and Table 24.1, there were actually three groups: ADHD, control, and the ADHD + CD group. Again, participants are independent; they are in only one group in the study. Therefore, the design for this study is a single-factor between-groups design with three levels. Again, the dependent variable is IQ, which is normally distributed. Because there are three groups or levels for this study, we could perform three t tests (comparing control with ADHD, ADHD with ADHD + CD, and ADHD + CD with control) to consider all possible paired comparisons. The problem is that the result of doing multiple t tests is that the probability of a type I error is increased substantially. This error occurs when the researcher incorrectly rejects the null hypothesis when it is true. If three separate t tests were performed in this situation, the significance level for each comparison should be reduced to approximately .017 (.05/3 tests) in order to keep the overall significance level at .05. This correction, called *Bonferroni*, divides the alpha level (usually .05) by the number of tests performed. Unfortunately, using the Bonferroni procedure reduces statistical power by changing the significance level (from .05 to .013 in this situation). The more appropriate statistical selection for a single factor design with more than two levels is the single-factor ANOVA which allows the researcher to test the null hypothesis at $p = .05$.

Source Table for Single-Factor ANOVA.   All ANOVA procedures have a source table that displays the results from the ANOVA. Although it is relatively rare for a source table from a single-factor ANOVA to be displayed in a journal article, source tables accompanying factorial designs are more common (see Table 28.2). Table 24.2 shows a *hypothetical* source table for the single-factor ANOVA from the Herpertz et al. (2001) data.

The single-factor ANOVA starts by dividing the sums of squares (SS) into a between-groups component and an error component. The degrees of freedom (df) for the independent variable, called groups, is the number of levels of the independent variable minus one. The df for the error term is computed by subtracting the df for the independent variable from the total df. The total df (not shown in the source table) is the number of participants minus one. Each of the SS is divided by its corresponding df to obtain mean squares (MS). Thus there will be two MS in the single factor ANOVA. The F value, seen in the last column in Table 24.2, is obtained by dividing the MS for groups by the MS for error. As Table 24.2 shows, there is one F value in the source table.

Herpertz et al. (2001) performed a single-factor ANOVA on their IQ data and reported the results in a table. They reported an F of 17.44, which was significant at $p < .0001$. Had they reported this result in the text, it would read as follows: a significant difference was found among the three groups, $F(2, 65) = 17.44$, $p < .0001$. Notice that there are two different de-

TABLE 24.2
Single-Factor ANOVA Source Table (Hypothetical)
From Herpertz et al. (2001)

Source	SS	df	MS	F
Groups	500	2	250	17.44*
Within subjects (error)	931.45	65	14.33	

*$p < .01$.

grees of freedom in the single-factor ANOVA. Sixty-five degrees of freedom are associated with the error variance, similar to the *t* test, and calculated by subtracting the number of groups (3) from the total number of participants (68). Two degrees of freedom are associated with between-groups variance, and they are calculated as the number of groups minus one.

What does an *F* value of 17.44 mean? Herpertz et al. (2001) found, from a statistical table or their computer, that the probability (*p*) was less than .0001. In other words, the probability that the three different mean values could happen, assuming a true null hypothesis, was less than 1 in 10,000, or highly unlikely. Therefore, they rejected the null hypothesis of no difference among the three IQ population means. A significant overall *F* value from an ANOVA tells you only that the population means are not equal. To determine which groups or conditions are significantly different from each other following a significant *F*, a post hoc test must be performed.

There are numerous *post hoc test* alternatives from which to choose. The *Tukey honestly significant difference* (HSD) *test* is considered a middle-of-the-road test between liberal (e.g., the *Fisher least significant difference test* [LSD]) and conservative (e.g., the *Scheffé test* for all comparisons). Most statisticians believe that liberal tests, such as LSD or three *t* tests, allow too high a probability of the type I error.

Herpertz et al. (2001) performed a post hoc test using the Tukey HSD procedure. The results of this test revealed that the non-ADHD (comparison) group IQ was significantly higher than either the ADHD or ADHD + CD group. The ADHD group and the ADHD + CD group did not differ significantly from each other on the dependent variable of IQ.

SPSS and other statistical computer packages provide an index of the *effect size*, eta^2, which corresponds to the overall *F* (see Table 22.1). For our example, eta^2 is .35. Because eta^2 is similar to the squared correlation coefficient, this would imply that approximately 35% of the variance in the study is accounted for by the independent variable. However, we are usually more interested in the size of the effect for pairs of conditions or groups, so one would report *d* effect sizes for the pairs of means that were found to be significant using the Tukey post hoc test. Both the ADHD versus non-ADHD and the ADHD + CD versus non-ADHD comparisons would have *d* values greater than 1.0 so would be very large, and they are probably clinically important differences. It is important to point out that there is some disagreement about how *d* values should be computed in single-factor designs with more than two groups or levels and in factorial designs (Kline, 2004). The issue concerns the measure of variability. Should one use the pooled standard deviation from the two groups in the comparison (Hedges' *g*), or should one uses the square root of the error term, mean square within subjects (Table 24.2), which is more conservative? We favor the former method.

ANALYZING SINGLE-FACTOR DESIGNS
WITH NONPARAMETRIC STATISTICS

Nonparametric analyses often are referred to as distribution-free analyses. Nonparametric tests are "free" of the equal variance and normal distribution assumptions. Actually, each nonparametric analysis has its own sampling distribution. Nonparametric tests should be used when the assumptions of the equivalent parametric statistic are markedly violated, but typically ordinal nonparametric tests are not quite as powerful.

There are many different nonparametric tests (see Siegel & Castellan, 1988). Both of the nonparametric tests discussed next begin by converting the data from all of the groups combined to ranks, by ordering them from the smallest to the largest score, regardless of the particular group or condition. Once the data are ranked, the rankings are used in a formula. Usually this entails summing the rankings from each group. As one might expect, if the sums of the rankings are quite different between or among groups, then they are likely to be significantly different. The computer will indicate the probability, p, or the researcher can look up the result of the formula in a table and draw a conclusion using the same logic as the t test.

Mann–Whitney U Test for Independent Samples

The Mann–Whitney U test is performed when the design is a between-groups design with one independent variable and two levels. It is used when there has been a violation of the assumptions underlying the t test—for example, if in the Herpertz et al. (2001) example the group variances in IQ scores were markedly unequal. The analysis yields a value for the U statistic and a p value associated with it. If the p value is less than the significance level of .05, the null hypothesis is rejected. Because there are only two groups or levels in a comparison, there is no need for a post hoc test following a statistically significant U value.

Kruskal–Wallis One-Way ANOVA by Ranks

This test is the nonparametric analog of the single-factor between-groups ANOVA. It is used when there is one independent variable with more than two levels, participants are in one and only one group, and there has been a violation of the assumptions for parametric statistics. The preliminary steps in the Kruskal–Wallis ANOVA are similar to those of the Mann–Whitney U test. Data are ranked from smallest to largest without respect to group. Then the ranks in each group are summed and applied to the Kruskal–Wallis formula.

The logic underlying the Kruskal–Wallis ANOVA is that if you had three identical distributions of scores and you selected three groups at random, one from each distribution, you would expect their ranks to be distributed equally under the null hypothesis. However, if the ranks were quite different for at least one of the groups, then the null hypothesis would be rejected. Similar to a single-factor ANOVA, a statistically significant Kruskal–Wallis test must be followed by a post hoc test. A common post hoc method for the Kruskal–Wallis ANOVA is to perform Mann–Whitney U tests for each pair of groups, but that is a liberal post hoc comparison, similar to doing three t tests after an ANOVA, so it would be prudent to use the Bonferroni correction.

CONCLUSION

In this chapter we discussed the selection and application of appropriate statistical methods used in single-factor between-groups designs. It should be noted that the suggestions we provided are guidelines, and, especially with respect to nonparametric analyses, there could be other appropriate choices. When selecting a particular statistical analysis, it is desirable to state an appropriate rationale. As a final word of caution, a statistically significant result is not necessarily a clinically significant result. Statistical significance just tells us that it is likely that there is some difference; it does not tell us about the size of the difference (effect) or whether it has clinical or practical importance.

Chapter 25

Single-Factor Repeated-Measures Designs: Analysis and Interpretation

The analyses discussed in this chapter are used in a design with one independent variable, with two or more levels or conditions, and participants are measured under all conditions. These designs are referred to as *within-subjects, dependent-samples,* or *repeated-measures designs,* and we use these terms interchangeably here. This means that participants undergo all conditions of the study or participants are matched on some variable(s) assumed to be related to the dependent variable. The types of research approaches used with single-factor, repeated-measures designs are often randomized experimental or quasi-experimental. The *comparative approach* with a within-subjects design and analysis is used to compare participants who vary on an attribute independent variable if they are matched (e.g., pairs of students with and without attention deficit hyperactivity disorder matched on IQ and gender). The comparative approach is also used when a cohort of participants is followed longitudinally to study developmental change (i.e., they are assessed on the same measures two or more times without any planned intervention between assessments).

To facilitate our discussion of within-subjects designs, we provide an example of a quasi-experiment by Compton et al. (2001). These researchers assessed the therapeutic benefits, response pattern, and safety of the drug sertraline in children with social anxiety disorder. Sertraline, a selective serotonin reuptake inhibitor, is used as a pharmacological treatment of pediatric obsessive-compulsive disorder. In their study, 14 adolescents participated in an open 8-week sertraline drug trial. After an initial fixed dosage level, the dosage during the study was adjusted by the treating psychiatrist with the intent to find an optimal dose for each client. Numerous outcome variables were recorded for this study. All outcome variables were recorded at baseline (pre) and at the end of the 8 weeks (post). Some of the outcome measures also were recorded at the second, fourth, and sixth weeks. For those outcome variables only measured at pre and post, paired-samples *t* tests were performed. For those outcome variables that included all five measurement periods, single-factor repeated-measures analyses of variance (ANOVAs) were performed, accompanied by post hoc comparisons following statistically significant results.

ADVANTAGES OF WITHIN-SUBJECTS DESIGNS

An obvious advantage of using a within-subjects/repeated-measures design is that fewer participants are needed in the study. If the Compton et al. (2001) study had used a between-groups design, they would have needed a separate group of adolescents for each dosage. The repeated-measures design saves time in recruitment of participants, especially, as in our example, if participants have characteristics that are not common. A more important reason for selecting a repeated-measures design is that variability among participants should be reduced. The statistical analysis of single-factor repeated-measures designs is usually a paired *t* test or repeated-measures ANOVA, which conceptually can be thought of as a ratio of the variability between groups to the variability within groups. When we perform a repeated-measures design, each participant undergoes all of the conditions. Therefore, it is expected that any changes from condition to condition (dosages in this example) are due to the nature of a particular condition (treatment), and not variability among participants (error), because the same participant is experiencing each of the conditions. This reduction in error variance would increase the size of the *t* or *F* ratio and result in a greater probability of finding a statistically significant difference if one is actually there.

DISADVANTAGES OF WITHIN-SUBJECTS DESIGNS

Although within-subjects/repeated-measures designs are advantageous in reducing error variance, there are two distinct disadvantages of using repeated-measures designs. First, repeated-measures designs (with the exception of matching) cannot be used in situations in which a lasting effect of a treatment might take place. The problem is often referred to as *carryover effects*. For example, studies of educational or psychological interventions would not use repeated-measures designs because once participants experienced the treatment condition, they could not be expected to "unlearn" the treatment. Because of carryover effects, repeated-measures designs are not seen as frequently as between-group designs in the clinical literature. In studies like that of Compton et al. (2001), the effect of a specific dosage is assumed not to be long-lasting.

One method of circumventing carryover effects while still gaining the advantage of reducing error variance is to use a matching procedure. Participants are grouped into pairs (dyads) or triplets (triads) on the basis of some characteristic that should be related to the dependent variable, for example, intelligence. After participants are matched, one of each pair is assigned (optimally randomly) to group A and the other to group B. Then the study is carried out. Conceptually, the idea of matching is to make each member of the pair or triad as though he or she were the same participant undergoing all conditions. Therefore, designs that use matching are considered to be within-subjects designs and use similar statistical procedures.

A second disadvantage of repeated-measures designs is that the degrees of freedom in the study are reduced. If one did a repeated-measures study with two conditions, it would take half as many participants to gather the same amount of data because each person would be measured twice. For example, consider a between-groups study that compares an intervention condition to a control condition, with 20 participants in each condition. Then, there are 40 participants, or 38 degrees of freedom ($df = [n_1 - 1] + [n_2 - 1]$ for an independent-samples t test). On the other hand, suppose that a repeated-measures design was used. There would be 20 participants in each condition, but because each participant undergoes both conditions, there would be only 20 participants. The degrees of freedom would be $n - 1$ or only 19; thus statistical power is reduced. The decision of which type of design to use involves a trade-off between increased sample size (so increased df) with a between-groups design and reduced error variance with a within-subjects design.

ANALYZING SINGLE-FACTOR WITHIN-SUBJECTS DESIGNS WITH PARAMETRIC STATISTICS

Now we discuss the t test for paired samples and the single-factor repeated-measures ANOVA, which are used with single-factor within-subjects/repeated-measures designs.

The t Test for Paired or Related Samples

This t test is used when there is one independent variable, with two levels, and the participants undergo both conditions, or pairs of participants have been matched on a relevant variable. The dependent variables are normally distributed (often said to be interval or ratio scale), and the variances are approximately equal.

Compton et al. (2001) used the t test for related samples to compare outcome variables measured only at the baseline (pre) and 8 weeks (post) periods. An example of one of the outcome variables used for pretest–posttest data in this study was the behavior avoidance test (BAT). Participants rated their level of subjective distress on a scale from 0 to 100, after two tasks involving social anxiety. The t test was selected because there was one independent variable with two repeated measures (pre and post). Compton et al. (2001) concluded, with respect to the BAT, "A pre-post analysis of subjects' average ratings of subjective distress for these two tasks revealed a significant decrease in subjective distress after the eight-week treatment of sertraline ($t_{13} = 4.27$, $p < .001$)" (p. 568). Notice that the subscript, 13, is the degrees of freedom for this study ($N-1$). The mean and standard deviation are based on the difference scores between pre and post measures. The notation $p < .001$ indicates that the probability of this outcome or one more extreme, assuming a true null hypothesis, is less than 1 in 1,000, a very rare occurrence. The null hypothesis of no difference between conditions was rejected.

An effect size, d, can be computed for this example by dividing the t value by the square root of the degrees of freedom. The effect size is 1.18 and would be considered large in this situation.

Single-Factor ANOVA With Repeated Measures

The single-factor ANOVA with repeated measures is performed in designs with one independent variable, two or more levels, and the participants undergo all conditions or levels of the study. The dependent variable is distributed normally, and variances are similar for each condition. The Compton et al. (2001) study used this statistical test to analyze outcome measures recorded for each participant at all five times: baseline (pre), second week, fourth week, sixth week, and eighth week (post). One of the dependent variables, used to measure overall clinical improvement, was the Clinical Global Impressions Scale–Improvement (CGI–I), with scores ranging from 1 (very much improved) to 7 (very much worse). Compton et al. (2001) stated, "A repeated-measures ANOVA on the psychiatrist's mean CGI-I ratings was conducted to determine in which week a subject's change in clinical status was significantly different from baseline. The main effect for time was significant, indicating that CGI-I ratings declined over time ($F_{4,52} = 19.54$, $p < .001$)" (p. 567). The subscript following the F indicates the two different degrees of freedom used in ANOVA. Four is the number of time periods minus one, whereas 52 is the number of participants measured per time period minus one (13) multiplied by the number of time periods minus one (4). The finding that p was < .001 indicates that the probability of this outcome or one more extreme, assuming a true null hypothesis, is less than 1 in 1,000. Therefore, the null hypothesis that the means for the five time periods were equal was rejected. However, to determine where these differences among times took place, a post hoc test was performed. Compton et al. (2001) stated this outcome as follows: "Using a Bonferroni adjustment, tests of within-subject comparisons across time revealed that a significant change in clinical status relative to baseline occurred by week six of the trial (4.00 versus 2.64, $p < .001$)" (p. 567). There are other post hoc comparisons that could be performed following a statistically significant repeated-measures ANOVA, depending on the question asked. For example, Compton et al. (2001) stated, "Trend analyses were also conducted to identify the form or shape of the relationship between the independent and dependent variable of interest" (p. 567).

The assumptions of *independence, homogeneity of variance,* and *normality* discussed in the previous chapter also need to be considered for the t test for paired samples and the single-factor repeated-measures ANOVA. However, in addition to these assumptions, an additional assumption, sphericity, also must be considered for the single-factor repeated-measures ANOVA. Conceptually, the *sphericity assumption* is satisfied when the correlations among the scores of the different levels are equal. In the Compton et al. (2001) study, because there were five levels of time in the single-factor repeated-measures design, the correlation between baseline and week 2 must be similar to the correlation between baseline and week 4, which must be similar to the correlation between weeks 2 and 4, and so on. Usually, however, the farther apart two time periods are, the lower the correlation coefficient. If the assumption is violated, the type I error is inflated. However, most computer statistical programs have a correction for the violation of the sphericity assumption.

An overall effect size for the repeated measures analysis of variance in the Compton et al. (2001) study was not reported. In this situation, obtaining the overall effect size, eta^2, would be meaningful because the levels of the independent variable differed from each other quantitatively. Thus a large eta^2 would indicate a strong relationship between the drug and time.

ANALYZING SINGLE-FACTOR WITHIN-SUBJECTS DESIGNS WITH NONPARAMETRIC STATISTICS

Nonparametric statistics are used with within-subjects/repeated-measures designs when one of the assumptions underlying use of parametric statistics has been markedly violated. We discuss briefly three nonparametric statistics.

Wilcoxon Signed Ranks Matched Pairs Test

The Wilcoxon matched pairs test is used in a design in which there is one independent variable, with two levels, and the participants undergo both conditions or pairs of participants have been matched on a relevant variable. The dependent variable data are ordinal (and not normally distributed), or there have been violations of assumptions of the t test for paired samples. For example, the Wilcoxon test could have been used instead of the paired-samples t in the Compton et al. (2001) study to compare the pretest and posttest if assumptions had been violated.

Friedman Two-Way ANOVA by Ranks

The Friedman test is used in a repeated-measures design when there is one independent variable, there are three or more levels, and the dependent variable is ordinal (and not normally distributed) or violations of ANOVA assumptions have occurred. Compton et al. (2001) could have used the Friedman test to compare the Global Impressions scale ratings over the five time periods.

Because the Friedman test is carried out on data with more than two levels or conditions, a statistically significant result must be followed by some post hoc comparison to determine specific differences. The Wilcoxon test may be used as a post hoc test in this situation if the Friedman test is statistically significant. Note, however, that using the Wilcoxon test after the Friedman test is analogous to using the least significant difference test after an ANOVA; it is somewhat "liberal" (see chap. 24).

The McNemar Test

The McNemar test is used in designs similar to that for the paired t or Wilcoxon test, but the dependent variable is nominal or dichotomous. The McNemar test is similar to the chi-square test in that frequencies are the unit of measurement and they can be visualized in a cross-tabulation table (see chap. 27). However, because each participant undergoes both conditions of the study, there are important differences from the chi-square test for independence. If the Compton et al. (2001) study had compared participants at pretest and posttest on whether or not they improved, the McNemar test probably would have been used.

SUMMARY

In this chapter we discussed the selection and interpretation of appropriate statistical tests for single-factor within-subjects or repeated-measures designs and provided an example from the literature. The parametric tests that we discussed were the t test for paired or correlated samples and the single-factor repeated-measures ANOVA. We also mentioned three non-parametric tests to be used in single-factor within-subjects/repeated-measures designs, but they are relatively rare in the literature.

The Compton et al. (2001) article did not provide effect size measures. We were able to compute an effect size for the t test for paired samples, but could not compute eta^2 without more information from the repeated measures ANOVA. We again point out that a statistically significant t or ANOVA (even if $p < .001$) does not mean that there was a large effect, especially if the sample was large. In the Compton example, the sample was quite small ($N = 14$) so the findings do reflect a large effect size.

Chapter 26

Basic Associational Designs: Analysis and Interpretation

In this chapter we discuss the selection and application of appropriate statistical methods used with the associational research approach. The basic associational research approach examines the relation between two continuous variables (or at least ones that have many ordered levels) leading to a correlation coefficient. The most common correlation coefficient used to describe the relationships between two continuous variables is the Pearson product–moment correlation, r. When one or both of the variables is not normally distributed or there are violations precluding the use of parametric statistics, the Spearman correlation or the Kendall tau (τ) is usually used. We also discuss common problems associated with the reporting and interpretation of correlation coefficients and the need to present effect sizes and confidence intervals.

When we discuss the relationship between two variables in the associational research approach, technically, neither variable is designated as independent or dependent because a correlation is bidirectional. However, researchers usually have some direction in mind so we continue to use the terms *independent* and *dependent* variable here.

ANALYZING CONTINUOUS VARIABLES WITH PARAMETRIC STATISTICS

Pearson Product–Moment Correlation

The Pearson product–moment correlation provides an index of the strength of the linear relationship between two continuous variables. The Pearson correlation assumes that the distribution of the dependent variable is normal, with equal variance for each value of the independent variable, and assumes that the independent variable is also normally distributed. The Pearson correlation is widely reported in the literature for evaluating measurement reliability where one might test the relationship between two administrations of the same instrument (test–retest reliability) or the relationship between two different observers (interrater reliability) and for measurement validity, testing the relationship between an instrument and some external criterion (see chaps. 8 and 9). However, best practice in the area of reliability suggests the use of intraclass correlation coefficients to estimate reliability, especially interrater reliability, with more than two raters.

The Pearson correlation is expressed as a coefficient, r, which indicates the strength of the association or relationship between two variables. This coefficient has a range of –1 to +1. A positive relationship means that as scores on one variable increase, scores on the other variable also increase. If r is .5 or greater, it is usually considered to be a strong positive relationship, and r values that are below –.5 are considered to be strong negative or inverse relationships between the two variables. An inverse relationship means that a high score on one variable is associated with a low score for the same person on the other variable and vice versa. When the value of r is near zero, it indicates there is no relationship between the two variables; in this case, high scores on the independent variable are associated with high, medium, or low scores on the dependent variable. A zero or a low correlation means that you cannot predict the dependent variable knowing the scores on the independent variable.

Correlation coefficients were used in a study by Dierker et al. (2001), who were interested in the accuracy of three different dimensional rating scales for detecting anxiety and depressive disorders in a school-based survey of ninth-grade youths. Part 1 of their study investigated the relationships among the three rating scales. A sample of 632 youths completed the three rating scales, which were the Center for Epidemiologic Studies–Depression Scale (CES–D), the Revised Children's Manifest Anxiety Scale (RCMAS), and the Multidimensional Anxiety Scale for Children (MASC). Pearson correlation coefficients were obtained for all relationships among the three rating scales using the composite scores for each instrument. Because Dierker et al. predicted differences due to gender, separate correlations were completed for females and males.

Dierker et al. placed the results from their correlations in a table. However, if they had reported their results in the text, they probably would have reported one correlation as follows: "A statistically significant relationship between CES-D and MASC for males was found, $r = .50$, $df = 348$, $p < .01$." The degrees of freedom for a Pearson correlation coefficient are the number of participants in the analysis minus two. Degrees of freedom refer to the number of independent pieces of information from the data collected in the study and are closely associated with the number of participants with data on both variables. There were 350 male participants and the degrees of freedom for this correlation were 348.

Statistical Significance. As with any inferential statistic, one must be cautious about the interpretation of statistically significant correlation coefficients. There is an inverse relationship between the number of participants in the study (degrees of freedom) and the size of the coefficient needed to obtain statistical significance. In other words, studies with a large number of participants might find statistically significant correlation coefficients, but they may be trivial. If we examine a table of critical values for the Pearson correlation, we find that with 350 participants in a study, a correlation of about .11 is all that is needed to obtain statistical significance at $p <$ .05, given a nondirectional hypothesis or two-tailed test. Therefore, it is useful with correlation coefficients, as well as other inferential statistics, to obtain an index of effect size and/or confidence intervals.

Effect Sizes. A statistically significant outcome gives an indication of the probability that a result as extreme as this could happen, assuming the null hypothesis is true. It does not describe the strength of the relationship between the independent and dependent variables, which is what an effect size does. In other words, how much of the outcome can be predicted from knowing the value of the independent variable? One can calculate an effect size for every statistic. It is especially easy to perform this operation for a Pearson correlation because one effect size that is often used is r^2. This describes the amount of shared variance or the variance in the dependent variable that could be predicted from the independent variable. For example, in the present study, the r^2 for the correlation (.50) between CES–D and MASC for males is .25. This would indicate that only one quarter of the variance between the two measures was common to both. Three quarters of the variance is unexplained. Note that r^2 for a correlation of .11, which would be statistically significant with $n = 350$, is .0121; thus only about 1% of the variance is shared.

There is a disagreement among researchers about whether to use r^2 or r as the measure of effect size. Cohen (1988) provided rough guidelines for interpreting the effect size of correlation coefficients. He considered Pearson r values around +.1 or −.1 to be weak relationships, values around +.3 or −.3 to be medium strength, and values of +.5 or −.5 or more to be strong. Even though a correlation (r) of .50 means that you can predict only 25% of the variance in the dependent variable if you know the independent variable, Cohen argued that we could consider this a large effect because it is about as high as correlations between measures of *different concepts* get in the applied behavioral sciences.

Vaske, Gliner, and Morgan (2002) suggested that a more descriptive terminology would be that .1 is a *minimal relationship*, .3 is a *typical relationship* (one that is common for the behavioral sciences but could differ across disciplines), and .5 or more is a *substantial* (stronger than usual) *relationship* between two *different* concepts. In chapter 22, we proposed that correlations of these sizes be labeled *less than typical, typical,* and *greater than typical,* respectively, to emphasize that they are relative to literature in the field.

Note that in the Dierker et al. (2001) study, the authors measured the same concept, anxiety, using two different measures, so it is not surprising that these correlations are .7 or higher. Because the strength of a correlation is attenuated by the extent of its reliability, it is common to find a correlation between two measures of the same concept correlated about .7.

Confidence Intervals.   Perhaps a better alternative to dealing with statistical significance and effect size, and one that is currently recommended by many methodologists, is to report the results from a correlation coefficient as a confidence interval. The reason for presenting a confidence interval is that showing a "statistically significant" *r* is only showing that it is nonzero. Thus a highly significant *r* may be completely trivial. A confidence interval delineates the magnitude and the error of estimation of *r* and is computed using the same information needed to determine statistical significance. Specifically, this information includes the value of *r*, the sample size used to determine *r*, and a table called the Fisher *z* transformation table. Thus, Dierker et al. (2001) might have stated the following as an example of a confidence interval: "The 95% confidence interval for the relationship between CES–D and MASC for males was between .42 and .58." In other words, they could be 95% confident that the actual (population) value of the relationship between the two variables would be found within this interval.

Correlation Matrix.   It is relatively rare to see only a single correlation coefficient or even two or three correlation coefficients in a study. When more than a few correlations are reported, correlation matrices commonly are used. A correlation matrix is a table of correlation coefficients that shows how all variables are related to each other. In the Dierker et al. (2001) study, the correlations obtained in phase 1 of the study for the three different dimensional rating scales were presented in a correlation matrix. Table 26.1 shows the correlations among each of the instruments for females and males separately.

A table displaying a correlation matrix has the variables ordered horizontally across the top row of the table and vertically down the first column of the table. In many correlation matrices, the values are displayed in either the upper right corner or in the lower left corner of the table, but not both, which would be redundant because the same values would be present. How-

TABLE 26.1
Correlations Among the Three Rating Scales for Females and Males

	CES–D	*RCMAS*	*MASC*
CES–D	—	.76**	.54**
RCMAS	.66**	—	.72**
MASC	.50**	.70**	—

Note. Correlations for females ($n = 350$) are listed above the diagonal and males ($n = 282$) below the diagonal. Significance: **$p < .01$.

ever, in their 2001 study, Dierker et al. used the lower left corner of the table to present the correlation matrix for males and the upper right for females. Also, in each row there is one cell with a dash. This denotes a variable correlated with itself. All of the dashes taken together are referred to as the diagonal. To interpret a correlation matrix, one reads down the first column to find the variable of interest. Next, you proceed across to find the other variable of interest. Where these two variables intersect is the correlation coefficient for the two variables. For example, the correlation for females between the CES–D and the RCMAS is $r = .76$; the correlation between the same two variables for males is $r = .66$.

Although correlation matrices are common in journal articles, one should use caution in interpreting them because often statistically significant relationships occur that were not originally hypothesized. To interpret these relationships outside of a theory or working hypothesis is often referred to as *"fishing" for statistical significance* and is not considered best practice.

USING NONPARAMETRIC ASSOCIATIONAL STATISTICS

Spearman Rank Order Correlation Coefficient and Kendall Tau Coefficient

When there are many ordered levels of both variables, one should use a nonparametric statistic if either the independent or dependent variable is ranked (or measured on an ordinal scale and not normally distributed) or if other assumptions underlying parametric associational statistics (linearity or equal variance) are violated. Two nonparametric statistics that are used to assess the relationship between ordered independent and dependent variables are the Spearman rank order correlation (rho or r_s) and the Kendall tau (τ). The Spearman correlation, the more common of the two, provides an index of the strength of a monotonic relationship (i.e., an increase in scores on one variable is accompanied by an increase or decrease in scores on the other variable, but this change in scores is not necessarily linear). Both the Spearman correlation and the Kendall tau are performed on ranked data rather than original scores. When the sample is relatively small and some of the rankings are the same for different participants (ties), the Kendall tau is the appropriate nonparametric choice.

MISLEADING CORRELATION COEFFICIENTS

Earlier, we discussed problems related to interpreting statistical significance and correlation coefficients. There are other situations that one must pay attention to that could lead to overestimation or underestimation of the correlation coefficient. A few common examples are as follows. For a more in-depth explanation, see Shavelson (1996). The first is referred to as restriction of the range. This occurs when the range of one of the variables used to compute the correlation coefficient is limited. This often happens with selected or homogeneous groups, but also could happen if the scale of one of the variables has limited range. The result is usually a reduction in the size of the correlation coefficient. A second common example is when outliers, or extreme scores, occur in a relatively small sample. This can change the relationship between variables from linear to curvilinear and vice versa. A third example is the combining of groups. This occurs when samples from two different populations are combined. For example, Dierker et al. (2001) presented correlation coefficients separately from females and males. Had they combined these two samples, they might have obtained completely different values. A fourth example is the use of extreme groups. This happens when we perform correlations on participants that were selected because they represent just the high and low ends of a particular scale, and no participants in the middle range. This tends to inflate the correlation coefficient.

It is not uncommon to make incorrect inferences from correlation coefficients. We only can make inferences about causes if the design is a well-constructed, randomized experiment. Correlation coefficients are most common in associational, noncausal research approaches; hence one should not infer causation from correlation. However, the correlation— even in the absence of causation—might be strong, moderate, or weak. In chapter 30, we examine linear regression, used when the researcher wants to predict values of the dependent or outcome variable from the independent variable based on the strength of a correlation.

The Chi-Square Test and Accompanying Effect Size Indices

In chapter 26, we described statistical methods used to test the significance of a relationship between two variables that were either continuous or had many ordered categories or levels. The purpose of the present chapter is to describe a statistical test, the *Pearson chi-square* (χ^2) *test for independence*, that examines the relationship between two variables that are dichotomous or nominal level, with a few nonordered categories. Nominal scale data provide less information than interval or ordinal scale data. The finer the gradations on the measurement scale, the more information is transmitted, as long as there is evidence for reliability and validity. We recommend that data not be divided into a few categories if the data are continuous or have a number of ordered levels, unless the measure to be divided has been validated against an external criterion that justifies using "cut points."

When there are more than two categories of at least one of the variables and these categories are ordered (i.e., ordinal scale), such as education level, which might vary from a little to a lot, power is lost if a χ^2 test to analyze the data is used. We recommend that such data be analyzed by using nonparametric statistics for ordinal data. Examples of these statistics are Kendall's tau correlation (chap. 26) if both variables have more than two ordered levels, or a Mann–Whitney U test (chap. 24) if one of the two variables has only two levels and the other is ordered. There is also a chi-square test, which is not discussed in this book, for the *goodness of fit* of one sample of nominal data to some theoretical distribution or known distribution.

In this chapter, the data to be considered are frequencies. Specifically, our interest is in how many people (the frequency count) fall into a particular category, relative to a different category. There are two major requirements of the χ^2 test. The first is that frequencies represent counts. The second is that each participant can be assigned to only one category or cell.

The χ^2 test for independence tests the association between two variables. Under the null hypothesis, the two variables are assumed to be independent of each other. For this chapter, we first discuss a χ^2 with only two categories of each variable, often referred to as a two by two contingency table, and then expand our discussion to χ^2 tests where there are more than two nonordered categories for at least one of the variables. Examples are provided for both situations. As with our discussion of other tests of statistical significance, we also discuss effect size measures that describe the strength of relationship between two nominal scale variables.

THE CHI-SQUARE (χ^2) TEST WITH ONE DEGREE OF FREEDOM

Chi-square tests with two categories of each variable were used in a study by Wolfe, Scott, Wekerle, and Pittman (2001), who were interested in the relationship between past maltreatment, current adjustment, and dating violence in a community sample of adolescents. For the first part of this study, the authors performed a number of χ^2 tests examining the relationship between different demographic variables and maltreatment classification based on the Childhood Trauma Questionnaire. These results were presented in a table providing the frequency of each of the four cells and the associated χ^2 value. For the Wolfe et al. example, we examined the first demographic variable, living in intact family or not, and maltreatment classification (yes or no). Table 27.1 shows the frequency data and percentages.

A χ^2 statistic for these data was reported as $\chi^2 = 19.81**$. The value of 19.81 is the computed χ^2 for this example. To arrive at this value, expected frequencies are generated for each cell in the contingency table by multiplying the corresponding row and column totals together and then dividing by the total sample. The expected frequencies are the frequencies we would expect if the two variables were not related. To obtain each cell value, the expected frequency is subtracted from the observed frequency

TABLE 27.1
Relationship Between Family Intactness and Maltreatment
Classification (Adapted From Wolfe et al., 2001)

	Maltreatment Classification		
Status of Family	Maltreated	Not Maltreated	Total
Not intact family	125 (44%)	159 (56%)	284 (100%)
Living in intact family	337 (30%)	782 (70%)	1,169 (100%)

Note. $\chi^2(df = 1, N = 1,453) = 19.81**$.

(the actual cell frequencies), squared, and divided by the expected frequency. The four cell values are added to determine the χ^2 value.

There is one degree of freedom for this χ^2. In our previous chapters, degrees of freedom were associated with the sample size for either the whole study or specific groups. In the χ^2 test, degrees of freedom are associated with the number of categories within each variable. For any χ^2, the degrees of freedom are determined by multiplying the number of rows minus one times the number of columns minus one. In the present example, the degrees of freedom are two rows minus one times two columns minus one, equals one.

The two asterisks following the χ^2 value indicated that it was statistically significant at $p < .01$. Statistical significance is determined by comparing the computed χ^2 value, 19.81, to a value in the χ^2 table associated with $p < .01$ and one degree of freedom. This table value is referred to as the critical value. A critical value of 6.63 in the χ^2 table corresponds to the .01 level for one degree of freedom. Any χ^2 value that is as large as or larger than this critical value has a probability of occurrence of less than 1 in 100, assuming a true null hypothesis. Because our value of 19.81 exceeds 6.63, it is considered to be statistically significant, $p < .01$. A statement summarizing this result is that there was a statistically significant relationship between the variables intactness of family and maltreatment classification.

INTERPRETATION OF THE CHI-SQUARE TEST
WITH ONE DEGREE OF FREEDOM

Percentages. Perhaps the simplest method of interpreting the χ^2 test with one degree of freedom is to convert each cell frequency to a percentage and examine the relationships among these cell percentages. One could calculate percentages so that either the row or column percentages add to 100%. A general rule is to calculate row percentages so that they add to 100% if in the table, as here, the independent variable is a row variable, or vice versa if the independent variable is the column variable. Sometimes the independent variable is obvious, such as when there is a treatment. At other times, however, as in the present study, there has been no manipulation. In this case, one should determine the likely order of occurrence of the variables. For example, we assume that the independent variable is intact family because it is presumed to precede the variable of maltreatment classification. The independent variable of intact family is a row variable, so row percentages will help guide the interpretation. As shown in Table 27.1, the frequencies were converted to row percentages by dividing each cell frequency by the row total; thus the row percentages will add to 100%. For those not living in an intact family, the ratio of not maltreated to maltreated was close to 1 to 1. For those living in an intact family, the ratio of not maltreated to maltreated was more than 2 to 1 (70% to 30%). Thus adolescents from intact families are less likely (30%) to be maltreated than those from not-intact families (44%).

Phi as an Effect Size. For a χ^2 test with one degree of freedom, a common effect size indicator of the strength of the relationship between the two variables is phi (φ). Phi is a nonparametric measure of association or correlation between two variables when both are dichotomous (i.e., have two levels). Like the Pearson product–moment correlation, discussed in the last chapter, a strong association would be indicated by a φ coefficient of +.5 or –.5 or further from zero (Cohen, 1988). No association would be indicated by a coefficient near zero. However, a disadvantage of φ is that the size of φ is restricted by the row and column percentages. The closer the two row percentages are to the two column percentages, the higher is the upward limit of φ (Nunnally & Bernstein, 1994). In the Wolfe et al. (2001) example, the maximum possible value that φ could have is 0.72. The actual φ in this study was 0.12, which using Cohen's guidelines would be considered a small effect.

Strength of Association Measures Involving Risk. In addition to the effect size measure, φ, there are three measures of association often used in epidemiology with a two by two (2×2) contingency table to express the risk of clinical-level outcomes. These measures are relative risk, risk difference, and odds ratio. The three measures can be understood from the Wolfe et al. (2001) example in Table 27.1.

The *relative risk* is determined by first computing the percentages of those who are maltreated within not-intact and intact families. In our example, these two percentages are 44% for not-intact family and 30% for intact family. A ratio is then obtained by dividing the not-intact percentage by the intact percentage. In the present example, the relative risk is 1.47 or 44%/30%. Thus the relative risk of receiving a classification of maltreated from a not-intact compared with an intact family is 1.47 or approximately one and a half times as high.

Risk difference is obtained with the same percentages as relative risk, except that instead of computing a ratio, a percentage difference is computed by subtracting the percent maltreated in intact families from the percent in not-intact families, or 44% minus 30%. Thus there is a 14% greater risk of receiving a classification of maltreated if one comes from a not-intact family. The risk difference is very close to the phi coefficient for all 2×2 contingency tables. In the example, the risk difference (0.14) is close in magnitude to φ, which was 0.12.

Odds ratio, which is the most commonly reported of these measures, is determined by first computing the ratio of those who are maltreated to those who are not maltreated within not-intact and intact families. In our example, these two ratios are 0.79 for not-intact family (125/159) and 0.43 for intact family (337/782). The odds ratio is then obtained by dividing the not-intact family ratio by the intact family ratio. In our present example, the odds ratio is 1.83 (0.79/0.43), indicating that the odds of receiving a classification of maltreated from a not-intact family are 1.83 times as high as those from an intact family. It should be noted that odds ratios are often provided as a result of a logistic regression, as reported by Wolfe et al. (2001). The major limitation of the odds ratio as an effect size index is that the upper limit may approach infinity if one of the cells is quite small relative to the other cells. Thus, it is difficult to decide what represents a large odds ratio, compared with effect sizes that accompany parametric tests such as r and d. Although odds ratios intuitively seem to be meaningful to nonstatisticians, they can be quite misleading.

Which of the three measures of effect size involving risk presented here is the most appropriate? Rosenthal (2001) examined the three effect size measures and recommended risk difference. As stated earlier, the risk difference is very close to the φ coefficient, and partly, "For that reason, the risk difference index may be the one least likely to be quite misleading under special circumstances . . ." (p. 135).

THE CHI-SQUARE TEST WITH GREATER THAN ONE DEGREE OF FREEDOM

Although a 2×2 contingency table analyzed by a χ^2 is commonly observed and relatively easy to interpret, there are many cases in which the number of rows, columns, or both exceeds two. For example, a study published by Zeanah et al. (2001) compared an intervention group (IG) with a comparison group (CG) to examine outcomes for infants and toddlers in foster care. The four outcome categories for foster children were reunification with birth parents, termination of parental rights, surrender, and placement with a relative. Table 27.2 shows the relationship between the treatment group and outcome type.

TABLE 27.2
Frequency of Outcome Type by Group Membership

Outcome Type	Group Membership	
	Intervention Group	*Comparison Group*
Reunification	33 (34.7%)	71 (49.0%)
Termination	42 (44.2%)	30 (20.7%)
Surrender	8 (8.4%)	17 (11.7%)
Relative placement	12 (12.6%)	27 (18.6%)

A statistically significant χ^2 was reported for these data ($\chi^2[df = 3$, $N = 240] = 16.13$, $p < .01$). The value 16.13 is the χ^2 for this example. There are three degrees of freedom for this χ^2 (four rows minus one times two columns minus one). Again, the relationship was statistically significant, $p < .01$.

INTERPRETATION OF THE CHI-SQUARE TEST WITH MORE THAN ONE DEGREE OF FREEDOM

Percentages. Similar to the χ^2 with one degree of freedom, cell frequencies should be converted to percentages to detect patterns. The percentages following the frequencies for each cell are this time column percentages because the independent variable is group membership, a column variable (see Table 27.2). When performing a χ^2 with more than one degree of freedom, a bar graph of the percentages is often a meaningful method to facilitate interpretation. Figure 27.1 displays the percentage data from Table 27.2.

The largest percentage discrepancies for the two groups were for reunification and termination; the authors reported, "An examination of the frequency table indicated that this difference was due to the fact that the IG had more than twice as many terminations as the CG and the IG had significantly fewer reunifications" (p. 217). That is, "More children were freed for adoption . . . than before the intervention" (p. 214).

Two by Two Contingency Tables. A second method to facilitate interpretation of the chi-square test with more than one degree of freedom is to examine meaningful comparisons by setting up two by two contingency ta-

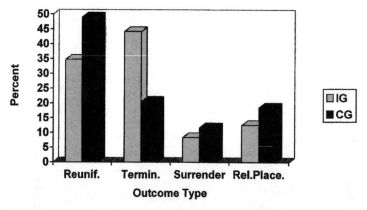

FIG. 27.1. Frequency of outcome type by group membership, presented as a bar graph.

bles. In our present example, a two by two table could be established comparing the intervention group and the comparison group on reunification and termination. A phi value could be computed or a measure of associated risk could be established. There are other methods to construct two by two contingency tables from larger tables, such as the chi-square corner test or combined category chi-square test (Rosenthal & Rosnow, 1991). We point out that the comparisons must be meaningful, usually established prior to the study, and related to the original hypotheses.

SUMMARY

The chi-square (χ^2) test for independence is the appropriate statistical test for determining the association between two nominal scale variables, where each participant can be included in only one cell of the contingency table. The 2 × 2 contingency table is the most common contingency table analyzed by χ^2. Interpretation of outcomes from this table is facilitated by converting frequencies to row or column percentages and calculating effect size measures such as the risk difference index or φ. Chi-square tests on contingency tables with more than two levels in the columns, rows, or both are often more difficult to interpret, but bar graphs are useful in conveying accurately and succinctly the relationship between two variables. Also, reduction to two by two contingency tables is recommended.

Chapter 28

Between-Groups Factorial Designs: Analysis and Interpretation

The last four chapters discussed the analysis of single-factor designs, which include only one independent and one dependent variable. However, many studies include designs with more than one independent variable. In this chapter, we introduce an example of a study with a second between-groups independent variable, discuss the advantages of analyzing more than one independent variable at a time, and demonstrate how between-groups factorial designs are analyzed and interpreted. Between-groups designs are distinguished by each participant being included in only one group in the study. In the next chapter, we continue our discussion of factorial designs by introducing a repeated-measures independent variable as the second independent variable, creating a mixed design.

REASONS FOR ADDING A SECOND (OR MORE) INDEPENDENT VARIABLE

There are two major reasons for adding a second independent variable in a study. The first reason is that it provides the researcher more information. When we have two independent variables in a single study, we can determine how each independent variable works by itself and determine how the two independent variables work together or interact. How an independent variable, by itself, affects the dependent variable is referred to as a *main effect*. How two independent variables interact on the dependent variable is referred to as an *interaction effect*. In a study with two independent variables, there will be two main effects (one for each independent variable) and an interaction effect. We would like to emphasize that the term *effect* can be misleading because it seems to imply a causal relationship. As noted in earlier chapters, this inference is not justified if the independent variable is an attribute (such as age or gender) and may not be justified with an active independent variable unless the study is a well-designed randomized experiment. Thus one should be cautious about interpreting a significant main effect as meaning that the independent variable caused the difference in the dependent variable.

Consider a study by Conners et al. (2001), who were interested in the effects of two independent variables on an attention deficit hyperactivity disorder (ADHD) outcome assessment measured by a composite score. In one of their analyses, the two independent variables were treatment type and treatment site. In this analysis, there was one main effect for treatment and a second main effect for site. There is also an interaction effect between treatment and site.

The second reason for using a two-factor design instead of two single-factor designs is that *error variance* is more precisely estimated. Error variance is variability attributed to individual differences among participants. Often these differences are due to assessments not measuring a construct reliably. At other times these differences are due to age, gender, or site differences among participants. It is the latter type of error we are trying to reduce. If we introduce a second independent variable, such as site, then part of the error variance due to this variable could be removed and distributed as a second independent variable. Conners et al. (2001) were primarily interested in the active independent variable, type of treatment. The other independent variable, site, was not important by itself, but if it was statistically significant, it would reduce error variability in the study.

The study by Conners et al. (2001) had a 4×6 factorial design. Seven- to 9-year-old children who met *Diagnostic and Statistical Manual of Mental Disorders*, 4th edition text revision (*DSM–IV–TR*; American Psychiatric Association, 2000) criteria for ADHD combined type were randomly assigned to one of four treatments at the screening site. The four levels of the first independent variable were four types of treatment: medication management, behavior therapy, a combination of these treatments, and community comparison, which was composed of children who were assessed and then referred to local community care resources. The six levels of the second independent variable were six participating university sites. The key dependent variable, the composite score, was converted to a standard score for each participant. This standard score was then compared with baseline scores, yielding a change score for each time period. Negative scores indicated a reduction in symptoms. The average change score for each treatment after 14 months can be seen in Table 28.1.

TABLE 28.1
Composite Outcome by Treatment 14 Months
Post Baseline, From Conners et al. (2001)

Treatment	n	M	SD
Combined	145	−2.23	1.35
Medication management	144	−1.82	1.61
Behavior therapy	144	−1.42	1.47
Community comparison	146	−1.29	1.36

ANALYSIS OF TWO-FACTOR DESIGNS

Two-factor designs are analyzed with a two-factor analysis of variance (ANOVA) if both independent variables are between-groups independent variables and the ANOVA assumptions of independence, homogeneity of variance, and normality are not markedly violated (see chap. 24 for more discussion of these assumptions). For those studies with two independent variables and a dependent variable that is measured on ordinal scale, there are not many options. These studies are sometimes analyzed with nonparametric techniques applied to one independent variable at a time, but the interaction effect is lost. There are more sophisticated techniques, such as log-linear analysis for categorical data, that are beyond the scope of this book.

Source Table for a Two-Factor ANOVA. ANOVA procedures have an accompanying source table, which for the Conners et al. (2001) study is Table 28.2.

The two-factor ANOVA starts by dividing the sums of squares (*SS*) into a between-groups component and an error component. Next, as shown in Table 28.2, the between-groups component is divided into a *SS* for independent variable A (treatment), a *SS* for independent variable B (site), and the remainder is the interaction *SS*, A × B. The degrees of freedom (*df*) for independent variable A are the number of levels or types of treatment

TABLE 28.2
Two-Factor ANOVA Source Table From Conners et al. (2001)

Source	SS	df	MS	F
Treatment (A)	77.88	3	25.96	13.49*
Site (B)	83.02	5	16.60	8.63*
Treatment × site (A × B)	52.56	15	3.50	1.82
Within subjects (error)	1,067.76	555	1.92	

*$p < .01$.

(four) minus one. The df for independent variable B are the number of sites (six) minus one. The interaction df are computed by multiplying the df for independent variable A (three) times the df of independent variable B (five). The df for the error term are computed by subtracting the sum of the df for independent variable A, independent variable B, and the interaction from the total df. The total df (not shown) is the number of participants minus one. Each of the four SS is divided by its corresponding df to obtain mean squares (MS). Thus there will be four MS.

Each of the three F values, seen in the last column in Table 28.2, is obtained by dividing the MS for that source of variation by the MS for error. As Table 28.2 shows, there are four MS and three F values in the source table. Thus, in a two-factor ANOVA, there are three F values and three questions that can be answered: one about each main effect and the interaction. To get a clearer picture of the role of the source table in a two-factor ANOVA, let's examine the data from the study by Conners et al. (2001).

Questions Answered in the Two-Factor ANOVA.   In the single-factor design, one hypothesis is tested: the effect of that independent variable on the dependent variable. In the two-factor design, three null hypotheses were tested: that (a) the means of the four conditions of independent variable A (treatment type) are equal, (b) the means of the six sites of independent variable B are equal, and (c) the interaction of independent variables A and B is zero.

Describing the Results in the Text.   Although we have presented the data from the Conners et al. (2001) two-factor ANOVA in a source table, it is not uncommon to have authors report their results in the text to save space. The data from Table 28.2 might be reported as follows: There were significant differences among four treatment conditions ($F_{3,555} = 13.49$, $p < .001$). There was also a significant effect of site ($F_{5,555} = 8.63$, $p < .001$). The interaction was significant at the .05 probability level but not the .01 probability level ($F_{15,555} = 1.82$, $p = .029$). When presenting the results in text form, the degrees of freedom for that effect and the error are given as subscript numbers.

INTERPRETATION OF THE RESULTS
FROM A TWO-FACTOR ANOVA

A first step toward interpretation of the two-factor ANOVA could be to compute an overall eta^2 (η^2), which would determine how much of the variance in the dependent variable, composite score, was estimated by the treatment, the site, and the interaction between the two independent variables. However, in the Conners et al. (2001) publication, there was no discussion of the site differences or interaction, probably because they were not the focus of their article, which was one of many from this large, multisite project. Like Conners et al., we start our interpretation of the results by focusing on the main effect of treatment type. Then we make up simplified, hypothetical results to illustrate a significant interaction.

Interpretation of Significant Main Effects. As noted, there was a significant main effect for treatment, which indicates that all of the means were not equal. Table 28.3 shows which pairs of means were significantly different based on a post hoc test comparing each pair of treatments. Notice that the combined (medication management and behavior therapy) treatment was statistically significantly better than each of the other three at $p < .05$. Likewise, medication management was better than behavior therapy ($p = .015$) and community comparison ($p = .001$). However, behavior therapy was not significantly better than the community comparison ($p = .451$).

Remember that statistical significance does not tell us about the size or strength of the relationship (effect size, ES) between treatment group variable and the composite score. Conners et al. (2001) could have computed η^2 for the main effect of treatment. This would provide an estimate of the relationship of all of the treatments to the dependent variable, the composite score. This value (computed from the data presented in Table 28.2) was .06, indicating that the treatment accounted for about 6% of the variance of the dependent measure in the study. We feel that best practice in this situation would be to compute effect sizes comparing individual treatments, as Conners et al. (2001) did. They computed the Cohen delta (or d), which is presented in Table 28.3 in the ES column. Note that the ES for the statistically significant contrasts between the combined treatment and the other three vary from roughly small (0.28) to medium (0.58) to large (0.70), according to Cohen's general guidelines (see Table 22.1 for effect size interpretations). Conners et al. also discussed several ways, suggested by Krae-

TABLE 28.3
Effect Sizes and Significance for Post Hoc Contrasts
Between Treatments, From Conners et al. (2001)

Contrast	p	ES
Combined > Med Management	.012	0.28
Combined > Behavioral	.000	0.58
Combined > Community	.000	0.70
Med Management > Behavioral	.015	0.26
Med Management > Community	.001	0.35
Behavioral ≈ Community	.451	0.09

Note. One-tailed hypothesis ES = Cohen delta; Med Management = medication management; Behavioral = behavior therapy; Community = community comparison.

mer (1992), of assessing the clinical importance of the findings. One index used to indicate a clinically meaningful effect, when comparing two types of psychotherapeutic treatments, is d ES of 0.2 or more.

Interpretation of an Interaction Effect.   Table 28.2 showed that there were significant main effects for treatment, site, and a statistically significant (at p < .05) interaction between treatment and site. Best practice is to interpret the interaction effect first because it provides more accurate, less potentially misleading information. To simplify the discussion of interaction effects, let us assume that the design had only two treatments (behavior therapy and community comparison) and three sites. The hypothetical findings for this 2 × 3 design are shown in Fig. 28.1.

A first step in the examination of a statistically significant interaction is to plot the cell means. When setting up an interaction plot, the dependent variable is placed on the y (vertical) axis. When there are two independent variables, a guideline is to place the attribute independent variable (site) on the x axis and graph the active independent variable (type of treatment) with separate lines, as we have in Fig. 28.1. In a *disordinal interaction,* the lines on the graph cross. An interaction is said to be *ordinal* if the lines are clearly not parallel but do not cross within the graph. When there is no interaction, the lines are approximately parallel to each other. Although a plot of the data is informative to guide interpretation, statistical significance can be determined only by follow-up statistical procedures.

One way to do these statistical procedures is referred to as *simple main effects* analyses and *post hoc comparisons.* Simple main effects analysis is a statistical procedure that takes advantage of the information already compiled from computing the two-factor ANOVA. Performing simple main effects is similar to performing single-factor ANOVAs on each of the two independ-

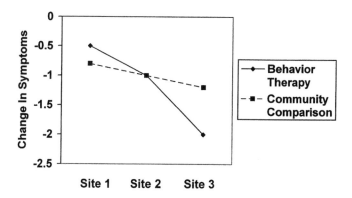

FIG. 28.1.   Hypothetical findings for a simplified 2 × 3 design showing a statistically significant interaction.

ent variables in Fig. 28.1, one level at a time. If simple main effects were performed for the independent variable of site, there would be three simple main effects, one for each site. Each simple main effect would be tested to determine whether there was a significant difference between behavior therapy and community comparison. In our hypothetical study, there was no significant simple main effect for site 1 or site 2, but there was a significant simple main effect for site 3. We might conclude that the significant interaction resulted from site 3 children doing better (more reduction in symptoms) from behavior therapy than from community resources, whereas site 1 and site 2 students did equally well in both treatments.

Simple main effects analysis could have been performed for the two treatment conditions instead of the three site conditions. However, if there were statistically significant differences for either of the treatment conditions, follow-up post hoc analyses would have to be performed, similar to a single-factor ANOVA, because there are three levels in each of the treatment conditions.

SUMMARY

We described the results of a recent study that used a two-factor ANOVA as the main statistical analysis, and we discussed why the researchers chose it. In addition to stating whether the results were statistically significant, the investigators discussed the size and clinical importance of the differences among the treatments. Last, we pointed out how to interpret a significant interaction effect.

Chapter 29

Pretest–Posttest Comparison Group Designs: Analysis and Interpretation

The pretest–posttest comparison group design, a randomized experimental design, is one of the most extensively used methods to evaluate clinical research, but it is often overanalyzed with more than one analysis when one is sufficient. We discuss parametric approaches that are often used to analyze this design and the strengths and limitations of each approach. We then comment on common nonparametric approaches. Last, we discuss methods to analyze this design when the treatment groups are not randomized (intact).

DESIGN DESCRIPTION

The simplest case of the pretest–posttest comparison group design has one treatment group and one comparison group. Prior to the pretest, participants are randomly assigned to groups or conditions. Random assignment is an important feature of the pretest–posttest comparison group design and separates it from nonequivalent (nonrandomized) group designs, which are quasi-experiments. Each group is measured prior to the intervention and after the intervention. Typically, one group receives a new treatment and the other group receives the usual treatment or a placebo. The purpose of this design is to allow the investigator to evaluate the new treatment relative to the previously used treatment. Figure 29.1, modified from Wood, Trainor, Rothwell, Moore, and Harrington (2001), provides a schematic diagram of the sequence of the pretest–posttest comparison group design.

The design is classified as a mixed design because there are two independent variables, a between-groups independent variable, the treatment,

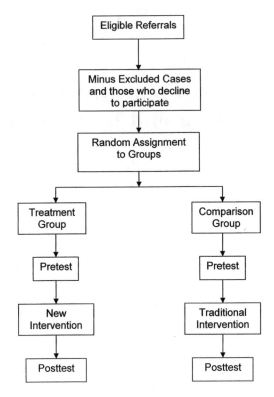

FIG. 29.1. Schematic diagram of the sequence of the pretest–posttest comparison group design (adapted from Wood et al., 2001).

and a within-subjects or repeated-measures independent variable, change over time from pretest to posttest. Time is a within-subjects independent variable because two or more measures are recorded for each person. Although the simplest description of the design has two levels of treatment and two levels of time, as seen in Fig. 29.1, it is not uncommon to have three levels of treatment, such as two treatments and a control group, or more than two repeated measures. The number of levels of an independent variable makes a difference in the type of analysis selected, as does the scale of measurement of the dependent variable.

ANALYSIS WITH TWO LEVELS OF TREATMENT AND TWO LEVELS OF TIME

Let's start with the example of the study by Wood et al. (2001). The objective of this study was to compare a group therapy treatment with a routine care treatment ". . . in adolescents who had deliberately harmed themselves on at least two occasions within a year" (p. 1246). The Wood et al. (2001) study had two levels of the between-groups independent variable, group therapy and routine care. Also, there were two levels of the within-subjects independent variable, a pretest and a posttest 7 months later. Adolescents were randomly assigned to groups. The study fits the criteria for a pretest–posttest comparison group design. The authors used a number of dependent variables; however, for our example, we selected suicidal thinking measured by the Suicidal Ideation Questionnaire. This 30-item questionnaire has scores ranging from 0 to 180, with high scores indicating higher suicidal ideation. In Fig. 29.2 we demonstrate how the study could be analyzed using several different statistical procedures, some appropriate and some not appropriate.

Analysis of Pretest to Posttest Scores Within Each Group. One approach is to compare, within each group separately, from pretest to posttest, and if the treatment condition shows a significant change but the comparison condition does not, then the treatment is assumed to be successful. Unfortunately, it is not uncommon for both treatment and comparison groups to show gains (with the treatment being statistically significant and the comparison not), even though the difference in gain between the two groups is quite small. Although these results seem to indicate that the treatment worked, the improvement could be due partially to something else (e.g., maturation), and the results do not show that the new treatment worked

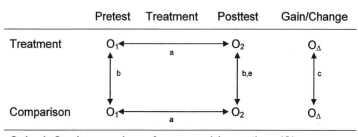

O ⟷ O A comparison of measures/observations (O).

a. Analysis of pretest to posttest within each group. Not recommended.
b. Analysis of pretest and posttest scores separately. Only the posttest comparison is useful but not as powerful as approaches c, d, e.
c. Gain score analysis. Usually a good approach.
d. Mixed analysis of variance (not shown). The interaction F provides the same information as the gain score analysis.
e. ANCOVA (with adjusted posttests) the most powerful approach if assumptions are met. We suggest that this be done using multiple regression.

FIG. 29.2. Comparison of five approaches to analyzing the pretest–posttest comparison group design.

better than the comparison treatment. This procedure should not be used to analyze the pretest–posttest comparison group design.

Analysis of Pretest Scores and Posttest Scores Separately. It is not uncommon to see this design analyzed by making one comparison between pretest scores of the two groups and then making a second comparison between posttest scores of the two groups. If there was no statistically significant difference at the pretest comparison and a statistically significant difference at the posttest comparison, then a conclusion is reached that the treatment was successful. The problem with this approach is that because participants were randomly assigned to groups, a statistical test comparing the pretest scores of the two groups only tests the randomization between the two groups and would be expected to be statistically significant 5% of the time. In addition, adding a pretest analysis to the posttest analysis inflates the type I error above 5%. The posttest analysis between the two groups is all that is necessary, assuming that the number of participants is relatively large. A statistically significant difference between the two groups at the posttest in favor of the treatment group would lead to the conclusion that the treatment is successful relative to the control group with this measure. The major problem with this approach is that it does not take advantage of pretest scores as does the gain score analysis and ANCOVA, and thus the analysis is less powerful than those analyses.

Gain Score Approach. The gain or change score approach is the most straightforward approach for the analysis of this design. The gain score approach involves subtracting the pretest scores from the posttest scores within each group. This creates just one independent variable with only two groups or levels, the treatment group and the comparison group. The gain scores become the dependent variable. As reported in chapter 24, the proper analysis for this design is an independent-samples t test. This tests whether the means of the gain scores for the two groups are equal. However, one should be cautious when using the gain score approach because the reliability of gain scores is often suspect, especially if there is not evidence for strong reliability of the measurement instrument. The gain score approach used by Wood et al. (2001) is described in the statistical analysis section: ". . . changes from baseline were calculated for the outcomes, and t tests for independent samples were used to compare the two arms of the trial" (p. 1248). They found no statistically significant difference between the two groups for suicidal thinking, and they reported their results in the form of confidence intervals for the group difference in mean gain scores (Table 29.1).

TABLE 29.1
Change From Baseline to 7 Months on Suicidal
Ideation Questionnaire (Wood et al., 2001)

	Baseline			Change From Baseline to 7 Months		
	n	Mean	SD	n	Mean	SD
Group therapy	32	89.1	44.4	27	47.3	50.5
Routine care	28	83.9	51.1	28	39.7	46.7
Mean difference		5.2			7.6	
95% CI of difference		(−19.5 to 29.9)			(−18.8 to 33.9)	

Mixed Analysis of Variance Approach.   This is a less common approach to the analysis of the pretest–posttest comparison group design. Because the design is a mixed design, this analysis appears to be the proper analysis. Because there are two independent variables in this design, the analysis yields three different F ratios, one for between groups, one for change over time, and an interaction between treatment and time. The only F of interest for this design is the treatment by time interaction. It has been demonstrated that the interaction F provides identical information to the gain score t (or F if there are more than two groups), which, as demonstrated earlier, is a simpler approach. Therefore, we do not recommend this analysis of the pretest–posttest comparison design.

Analysis of Covariance.   This approach, favored by many researchers, is a statistical method used to reduce error variance. When used in the analysis of the pretest–posttest comparison group design, the analysis of covariance (ANCOVA) changes the design from a mixed design to a single-factor design. The ANCOVA makes use of differences in the pretest scores among conditions to reduce error variance by adjusting posttest scores. Once these adjustments have been made to the posttest scores, the analysis is applied only to the posttest scores. Use of ANCOVA in the pretest–posttest comparison group design allows the researcher to use the pretest as the covariate and to adjust posttest scores based on a significant linear relationship between the pretest scores (covariate) and posttest scores (variate). It should be noted that gain scores, instead of posttest scores, could be adjusted using ANCOVA. The rationale behind this approach is that there are usually pretest differences between the treatment and control groups prior to the intervention. Examination of the pretest scores from the Wood et al. (2001) study (Table 29.1) demonstrates that the pretest scores are higher (i.e., worse) for the group therapy condition by about 5 points prior to the intervention. Thus the ANCOVA approach would adjust that group's posttest scores downward based on the linear regression between pretest and posttest scores.

Although the ANCOVA approach is common with the pretest–posttest comparison group design, two assumptions must be satisfied. The first is that the relationship between the pretest scores and the posttest scores must be linear. The second assumption is that the regression slopes for each pretest–posttest relationship must be homogeneous (regression lines must be parallel). This latter assumption is often not satisfied in the analysis of the pretest–posttest comparison group design, leading to two problems. First, research is often reported using ANCOVA without satisfying this assumption, making the conclusions invalid. Second, the researcher, after discovering the violation, must reanalyze the data using one of the other approaches mentioned above. A better solution to the problem is to use the ANCOVA approach through multiple linear regression.

Multiple Linear Regression Approach. Because ANCOVA is a special case of multiple regression, it can be performed using multiple regression. This statistical approach, although less common than other approaches used with this design, is a powerful approach (H. C. Kraemer, personal communication, October 13, 2002). We discuss multiple regression in the next chapter; however, it is important to present the topic here, at least briefly, because of its relevance for this design. With this regression approach, the posttest scores become the dependent or criterion variable. The independent or predictor variables are the pretest scores (the covariate), the groups (treatment and comparison), and the interaction between the pretest scores and the groups. The multiple regression analysis yields tests of significance for each of the predictor variables. This allows the researcher to test both of the preceding assumptions of the ANCOVA using multiple linear regression. However, if the ANCOVA assumptions are not met, the analysis still appropriately assesses the impact of the treatment on the posttest scores.

Recommendations. Kraemer (personal communication, October 13, 2002) recommended, in order of power from least to most, posttest-only analysis, gain score analysis, and ANCOVA performed by multiple regression. The ANCOVA, if assumptions are satisfied, is considered to be more powerful than the gain score approach because the variability due to error is reduced (Stevens, 1999).

ANALYSIS WITH MORE THAN TWO LEVELS OF THE TREATMENT VARIABLE

The example by Wood et al. (2001) had just two conditions or groups with a pretest and a posttest. However, if there were three or more groups, the three methods recommended earlier would still apply. For the posttest-only analysis, a single-factor ANOVA (instead of a t test) would be applied to the posttest scores of the three groups. Assuming a significant F is found, it would be followed by appropriate post hoc tests to identify specific differences. Likewise, for the gain score approach with three conditions, a single-factor ANOVA would be used instead of the independent-samples t test, after gain scores were obtained. Again, because there are more than two conditions, a post hoc test must follow the single-factor ANOVA, if there was a statistically significant overall F. For the ANCOVA approach, performed through multiple regression, the variable coding is a little more complex for three or more groups, but the analysis is appropriate.

ANALYSIS WITH NONPARAMETRIC MEASURES

When the data to be analyzed in the pretest–posttest comparison group design are ordinal (and not normally distributed) or nominal/dichotomous, nonparametric analyses should be undertaken. With ordinal data, a gain score approach could be used. Then a Mann–Whitney U would be applied if there are just two conditions, or a Kruskal–Wallis test would be used for more than two conditions. ANCOVA cannot be used in this situation.

Often when clinical importance is being considered, posttest data are dichotomized based on a clinically relevant cut point and then a statistical analysis is performed. It is recommended that if continuous data are to be dichotomized for clinical relevance, then effect size indices such as number needed to treat or absolute risk ratio be reported without significance testing.

NONEQUIVALENT (INTACT) GROUP DESIGNS WITH A PRETEST AND POSTTEST

An essential feature of the pretest–posttest comparison group design is random assignment of participants to groups. When this feature cannot be accomplished (e.g., using different hospitals or classrooms as intact groups), the design is quasi-experimental and referred to as a nonequivalent groups design with a pretest and posttest. With this design, the ANCOVA should not be applied because the population means on the covariate cannot be assumed to be equal (Huck, 2004). Thus the posttest-adjusted means could be biased. We recommend the gain score approach be used to analyze the nonequivalent groups pretest–posttest design. Stevens (1999) pointed out, "The fact is that inferring cause-effect from intact groups is treacherous, regardless of the type of statistical analysis. Therefore, the task is to do the best we can and exercise considerable caution . . ." (p. 324).

EFFECT SIZE AND THE PRETEST–POSTTEST
COMPARISON GROUP DESIGN

Perhaps the most common effect size computation results from the pretest–posttest comparison group design due to its use in meta-analysis (chap. 35). The most frequently used effect size index for this design is Hedges' g from the d family of effect sizes. There is some debate about the best method to compute d for this design.

One method to compute d commonly used with randomized experiments is to use only posttest measures of the treatment and comparison groups. Thus d would be computed by subtracting the posttest score of the comparison group from the posttest score of the treatment group and dividing by the pooled standard deviation of the posttest scores of both groups. The major advantage of this method of computation is its simplicity, and there are no complications due to pretest scores or gain scores. Another advantage is that effect sizes that are determined from dichotomous data, such as odds ratios or phi, also are based on posttest score performance.

A disadvantage for meta-analyses of computing d values from posttest scores is that it eliminates combining randomized experimental designs and quasi-experimental designs, which need to utilize the pretest scores. One solution to this problem is to compute the effect size form the gain scores. In this method, the gain scores of the comparison group would be subtracted from the gain the treatment group and divided by the pooled standard deviation of the posttest scores (Lipsey & Wilson, 2001).

CONCLUSION

In conclusion, many different statistical approaches have been used to analyze the randomized-experimental, pretest–posttest comparison group design. Analysis of pretest to posttest change with each group is not recommended. Comparisons of posttest scores or gain scores are appropriate, as is the mixed ANOVA. However, the ANCOVA using multiple linear regression appears to be the best statistical approach because if the assumptions are satisfied it is the most powerful analysis. If the ANCOVA assumptions are not satisfied, the analysis can still be used and the researcher does not have to reanalyze the data. We urge caution in interpreting results from analysis of the quasi-experimental version of this design; i.e., when participants have not been randomly assigned to groups (there are intact groups). We also advise against the statistical analysis of data that have been dichotomized artificially, but suggest that descriptive indices such as effect sizes be reported.

Use and Interpretation
of Multiple Regression

Multiple regression is a frequently used statistical method for analyzing data when there are several independent variables and one dependent variable. Although it can be used in place of analysis of variance, it is most commonly used in the associational approach. For example, Logan and King (2002) were interested in parents' ability to identify signs of depression in their adolescent children. They hypothesized that prior use of mental health services, impact of the adolescent's emotional/behavioral problems on the family, presence of substance abuse, adolescent–parent communication, and parental depression would be related to a parent's ability to identify depression in the adolescent. In this example, the independent variables, which are referred to in multiple regression as predictor variables, are service use, impact on family, presence of substance abuse, adolescent–parent communication, and parental depression. The dependent variable, which in multiple regression is called the criterion or outcome variable, is parental ability to identify depression. Multiple regression was appropriate for this analysis because the variables are approximately normally distributed (some predictor variables could be dichotomous), and the research question asked how the many independent variables combined to predict the dependent variable.

CORRELATION AND BIVARIATE REGRESSION

In chapter 26, we discussed how the strength of the relation between two continuous variables could be indicated with a Pearson product–moment correlation coefficient. One of the research questions in the study by Logan and King (2002) was whether the level of communication between the parent and the adolescent was related to the parent's ability to identify depression in the adolescent. The Pearson product–moment correlation was $r = .40$, $p < .01$. According to Cohen (1988), this indicates a medium to large effect, somewhat larger than typical in the behavioral sciences. An additional step would be to form a *bivariate* (two variables) *regression equation* so that one could predict a parent's ability to identify depression in his or her adolescent in the future from the level of parent–adolescent communication. This is referred to as simple linear (or bivariate) regression. Therefore, if you knew the level of communication between the parent and the adolescent, you could predict the parent's future ability to identify depression in the adolescent. How well? The r^2 gives one indication, which in this example would be .16. How do we interpret r^2 in this situation?

The r^2 is the amount of shared variance between the two variables. We could say that there is some underlying relationship, which is common to both the level of adolescent–parent communication and a parent's ability to identify depression that explains about 16% of the variance. Another way of looking at the problem is to focus on the parent's ability to identify depression, which in this case is the y variable. We call the dependent variable y or, in regression, the criterion variable. Adolescent–parent communication is referred to as the independent variable or predictor variable. From these data, we can conclude that adolescent–parent communication accounts for only 16% of the variance of parents' ability to identify depression. Looking at it from another direction, we could say that 84% of the variance in predicting a parent's ability to identify depression is unexplained or could be explained by other variables. This leads to multiple regression, which includes adding independent variables to improve the prediction of the dependent or criterion variable.

Similar to the Pearson product–moment correlation, in multiple regression a multiple R is computed; it is a correlation of the combination of the independent variables with the dependent variable. The multiple R tells how strong a relationship exists between the predictor variables and the criterion variable. The goal is to find a combination of independent variables that explains the most variance in the dependent variable. Multiple regression is used to predict or explain the relationship between the combination of the independent variables and the dependent variable. As with correlation, it does not indicate that the independent variables *caused* the change in the dependent variable.

COMPUTING MULTIPLE REGRESSION

The computation of multiple regression starts from a *correlation matrix* among all of the variables of interest, including the dependent variable. Then a linear combination of the variables is created so that the overall correlation, R, of the independent variables and the criterion variable is maximized, and the error in the prediction is minimized. For each of the independent variables a partial correlation is computed. This is a measure of the relationship between the independent variable and the criterion variable, keeping the other independent variables constant. From the partial correlations, *unstandardized coefficients* are calculated. These coefficients can then be used to create a formula that is a linear combination of independent variables to predict the criterion variable. Note that there are many possible linear combinations based on *different* sets of independent variables. Multiple linear regression finds the best linear combination of variables to predict the criterion variable only for those independent variables actually entered into the equation.

If the regression coefficients are converted to standardized or *z scores*, then comparisons can be made among the coefficients to determine the relative strength among each of the variables used in a particular analysis. A *t* test value is computed to examine the statistical significance of the relationship of each of the independent variables with the criterion variable. The *t* value tells whether the independent variable significantly contributes to the regression, assuming all the other independent variables are in the equation. Note that just because a predictor variable is not statistically significant in an analysis does not necessarily mean that variable should be dropped from the equation. The variable could still be making a contribution to the overall R^2. Furthermore, it is possible, but not common, to have a significant R^2, even if none of the individual predictor variables alone are statistically significant.

There are several assumptions related to multiple regression. As with other inferential statistics, if the assumptions are not met, there can be problems interpreting the results. One important assumption of multiple linear regression is that the independent variables are related to the dependent variable in a *linear* (straight-line) fashion. If the data do not meet this assumption (e.g., the independent variables are related in a *curvilinear* fashion to the dependent variable), then multiple regression is not appropriate. Another important assumption is that the independent variables should be correlated with the dependent variable, but not highly correlated with each other. If the independent variables are highly correlated with each other, there will be the problem of *multicollinearity*. When there is multicollinearity in the data, methods such as transforming or combining variables might change the data to meet this assumption. Most of the other assumptions related to multiple regression concern error; errors should be independent, constant, and normally distributed. Residual plots can help in identifying problems with error not meeting the assumptions.

In multiple regression analysis, the criterion variable should be approximately *normally distributed*, usually having many ordered values. Two other statistical methods used to predict a criterion variable from several predictor variables, *discriminant analysis* and *logistic regression,* are discussed in the next chapter. In these latter two methods, the criterion variable has nominal categories; it is usually dichotomous.

There are several different forms or methods of analysis with multiple linear regression. These include hierarchical multiple regression, simultaneous multiple regression, stepwise multiple regression, and all possible models.

HIERARCHICAL MULTIPLE REGRESSION

Logan and King (2002) were interested in many independent variables and how they combined to predict parents' ability to identify depression. From other information they collected, they knew that service initiated prior to the past year was a variable they wanted to control. Thus, they utilized hierarchical multiple regression.

When using hierarchical multiple regression, variables are entered in steps, and the *change in R^2* is examined at each step. The decision of the order to enter each variable into the equation is decided ahead of time by the investigator. Usually these decisions are based on a careful conceptualization of the problem and result in the testing of particular hypotheses. In their 2002 study, Logan and King determined that the variable, whether mental health service was initiated prior to the past year, needed to be controlled, so they entered it first. This is considered the first step. The R for this step was .27, with an adjusted R^2 of .05. The adjusted R^2 indicates that 5% of the variance in parents' ability to identify depression was predicted from the variable of prior service use. The R, as an effect size measure, would be interpreted by Cohen (1988) as a small to medium effect (see Table 22.1).

In the second step, the independent variables of impact on family, presence of substance abuse, adolescent–parent communication, and parental depression were added. The multiple R for this step was .56, with an adjusted R^2 of .31. Thus adding the other independent variables increased the precision of predicting parents' ability to identify depression from .05 to .31 or an increase of 26% in predictable variance.

Table 30.1 shows, for both steps in the multiple regression, the degrees of freedom, the F value, and an adjusted R^2. The level of significance for each of the steps (indicated with asterisks) is also shown. To understand how much each predictor is contributing to the R^2, *standardized coefficients* (β weights) are computed for each predictor. Note that on the second step, two of the five new factors were considered to be statistically significant, assuming an alpha level of .05. In addition, the F value indicates whether the

TABLE 30.1
Prediction of Parents' Ability to Identify Adolescent
Depression Using Multiple Regression (From Logan & King, 2002)

	β	df	F	Adj. R^2
Step 1		1,40	3.06*	.05
Past use of services	.27			
Step 2		5,36	4.67***	.31
Past use of services	.12			
Impact on family	.37**			
Presence of substance disorder	−.30**			
Adolescent–parent communication	.22			
Parental depression symptoms	.15			

*$p < .10$. **$p < .05$. ***$p < .01$.

combination of the predictors at that step is significantly predicting the criterion variable. In this example, the $F = 4.67$, $p < .01$, indicates that the combination of predictors on the second step significantly predicts the criterion variable, parents' ability to identify depression.

Usually with multiple regression it is helpful to form a *regression equation.* This is done with the unstandardized coefficients (not shown in Table 30.1). The equation then could be used in the future to predict parents' ability to identify depression in adolescents from these independent variables, assuming a similar sample of participants.

SIMULTANEOUS MULTIPLE REGRESSION

In this method, all of the predictor variables are entered simultaneously instead of in steps. As with the other methods, the best linear combination of variables is determined using a *least squares fit,* which is a method for maximizing the prediction accuracy. In least squares fit, the computer tries to fit the regression line so that the squared deviations (the distance between the scores and the prediction line) are minimized. Thus, the prediction line is as close as possible to all of the scores. The simultaneous regression method could have been used by Logan and King (2002) if the researchers did not have any prior knowledge that past use of services or some other variable needed to be controlled.

STEPWISE MULTIPLE REGRESSION

The stepwise multiple regression approach is similar to hierarchical multiple regression, but the computer instead of the researcher decides the order and how many of the potential predictors are used. The stepwise regression procedure describes how much more each independent or predictor variable has contributed to the prediction from the predictor variable(s) already used.

Although stepwise linear regression makes a lot of sense conceptually, several problems have been associated with this approach (see Thompson, 1995, for a critical review of this procedure). Researchers should probably use this approach only as an exploratory procedure. One of the basic problems with this approach is that because of the potentially large number of predictor variables that could be entered into the equation, the probability of a type I error is considerably larger than the usual alpha of .05. A second, and perhaps more important, objection with the stepwise approach is that the computer rather than the researcher is making the decision on which variables should be included in the equation. This is especially the case when one enters a large number of predictor variables into the stepwise analysis with little thought given to particular hypotheses or theories. Many statisticians associate this approach with the term "data mining" or "snooping." Third, the approach takes advantage of possible small differences in correlations when entering variables and thus is not likely to be replicated in another sample.

SUMMARY

Multiple regression is a commonly used statistical approach to predict a criterion variable from a linear combination of predictor or independent variables. We described three different multiple regression approaches: hierarchical, simultaneous, and stepwise. Stepwise multiple regression is not recommended because of the problems already pointed out. Hierarchical multiple regression, on the other hand, is recommended because it encourages the investigator to test a particular hypothesis and enter variables in a carefully controlled manner.

Chapter 31

Logistic Regression and Discriminant Analysis: Use and Interpretation

Predicting the probability that an event will or will not occur, as well as identifying the variables useful in making the prediction, is important in the health sciences; it is central to risk research. Two statistical techniques can be used appropriately to predict a dichotomous dependent variable: discriminant analysis and logistic regression. In the last chapter, we discussed linear regression, used when the dependent variable is continuous. Discriminant analysis can be used with a dichotomous dependent variable, but the method requires several assumptions for the predictions to be optimal. The Grimm and Yarnold (1995) book provides more extensive, but still nontechnical, chapters on discriminant analysis and on logistic regression than we present here.

LOGISTIC REGRESSION

This chapter focuses primarily on logistic regression, which requires fewer assumptions than discriminant analysis. Even when the assumptions required for discriminant analysis are satisfied, logistic regression still performs well so it is the more commonly used statistic in clinical research. In logistic regression, the probability of an event occurring is estimated. Logistic regression models can include one or more independent (predictor) variables that may be either dichotomous or continuous. Logistic regression with one independent variable is called *bivariate logistic regression*; with two or more independent variables, logistic regression is called *multiple logistic regression*. These should not be confused with *multinomial logistic regres-*

sion, where the dependent variable has more than two categories. In this chapter, the focus is on dichotomous outcomes of the dependent variable with several independent variables. Thus, we focus on multiple logistic regression often just called logistic regression.

In linear regression, the regression coefficient represents the amount of change in the dependent variable for one-unit change in the independent variable. Logistic regression coefficients are typically expressed as the *odds of an event* (outcome) occurring. The odds of an outcome is the ratio of the probability that the outcome occurs to the probability that it does not. Thus, if the probability of an event occurring is .8, the odds of the event is .8 divided by the probability of it not occurring (.2) or .8/.2 = 4.0. In everyday language, this means that the odds are 4 to 1. An *odds ratio* (OR) is simply the ratio of two odds. For example, if the odds of an event is 4 for boys (i.e., the risk is 4 of 5 = .80) and the odds of the same event is 3 for girls (i.e., the risk is 3 of 4 = .75), the OR relating gender to the event is 4/3 = 1.33.

Odds ratios are central to logistic regression, just as the correlation coefficient is central to linear regression. The null value of an OR is 1.0 (or a correlation coefficient of 0) and indicates random association. When a positive association increases, the correlation coefficient increases from 0 to 1 and the OR increases from 1 to infinity. As a negative association increases, the correlation coefficient decreases from 0 to −1 and the OR decreases from 1 to 0.

An Example

A study by Mick, Biederman, Faraone, Sayer, and Kleinman (2002) used logistic regression analysis to assess the association between the presence or absence of attention deficit hyperactivity disorder (ADHD, the dependent variable) and three primary independent variables (prenatal exposure to maternal cigarette smoking, drug abuse, and alcohol use). The study was based on 280 ADHD cases and 242 non-ADHD controls.

The ADHD group and the control group, which was obtained from pediatric outpatient clinics, differed on the three primary independent variables (tobacco, alcohol, and drug abuse or dependence during pregnancy) and nine "background" independent variables. These variables included conduct disorder (CD) in the offspring/child, maternal age at the time of the child's birth, maternal depression, ADHD in either parent, CD and/or antisocial personality disorder in either parent, child's age, and the number of Rutter's indicators of adversity (0, 1, 2, or 3). These 12 independent or predictor variables were entered simultaneously to examine their association with ADHD (yes or no), when all the others were included in the model. The estimated OR for a given independent variable is often said to be "controlled for" or "adjusted for" the other independent variables in the model.

Interpreting Logistic Regression

From the Mick et al. (2002) data, we computed a *bivariate odds ratio* (*OR*) for exposure to smoking and ADHD. Of the 280 ADHD children, 44 were exposed to smoking. Thus, the odds of exposure among the 280 ADHD children was 44 (exposed) divided by 236 (not exposed) = .186. The odds for the 242 non-ADHD children was 16 (exposed) divided by 228 (not exposed) = .071. The OR then is .186 divided by .071, or 2.62.

The null hypothesis is that the population OR is equal to 1. If the null hypothesis were true (OR = 1), membership in the two categories of the dependent variable would be unrelated to the independent variable. The ADHD children had odds 2.62 times higher than the non-ADHD children, which in this case is a nonrandom association.

An OR should not be interpreted as a *risk ratio* (*RR*). It is a common error to confuse OR and RR and say, for example, that the risk among ADHD children was 2.62 times higher than among the non-ADHD children. In this study, the risk was .157 (44/280) among ADHD children and .066 (16/242) among non-ADHD children, for an RR of .157/.066 = 2.38. Note that the RR is smaller than the OR of 2.62. The OR always seems to indicate a stronger association than the RR does. When the probabilities are very low, as in the ADHD example, the exaggeration is not large. When the probabilities are higher, the difference between the OR and RR is much larger. For example, if the risk is .70 in one group and .50 in a second group, the OR would be 2.33 but the RR would be 1.40. The distinction between the OR and the RR should be kept in mind, and the OR should not be interpreted as if it were an RR.

One also should be cautious about interpreting the OR as an effect size. Epstein (2003) and others have raised questions about the value of the OR as an index of practical significance. Other effect size measures (e.g., number needed to treat or risk difference, to be discussed in chap. 36) suggest that the association of two dichotomous variables is much weaker than either the OR or RR imply. Nevertheless, the significance of the OR is a good indicator of nonrandomness. Thus, despite reservations about the interpretation of the OR, logistic regression continues to be widely used.

In logistic regression, significance tests are provided for each independent variable. These tests of significance are often based on the *Wald statistic*, which has a chi-square distribution with 1 degree of freedom (*df*). The Wald statistic is just the square of the ratio of the logistic regression coefficient to its standard error. Unfortunately, when the absolute value of the regression coefficient is large, the estimated standard error is too large, leading the researcher to fail to reject the null hypothesis, when it should be rejected (i.e., a type II error). As an alternative, the significance of an OR can be examined using a confidence interval. If the confidence interval overlaps 1.00 (no association), the null hypothesis is retained; otherwise, it is rejected.

As is the case with linear regression, the contribution of individual variables in logistic regression is difficult to determine. The contribution of each variable depends on the other variables in the model. This is a problem particularly when independent variables are highly correlated.

A test for whether the combination of independent variables has a greater than chance ability to predict the status of people on the dependent variable in logistic regression is called a *goodness-of-fit test*. The goal is to identify a "good" set of independent variables (a model) that helps predict or explain group membership on the dependent variable.

Another way to assess whether the model fits the data in logistic regression is the *classification table*, which compares the predictions to the observed outcomes. For example, the Mick et al. (2002) study had 280 ADHD cases and 242 non-ADHD controls. If the independent variables in their model had correctly predicted that all 280 ADHD children would have ADHD and that all 242 non-ADHD children would not have the disorder, the classification table would indicate that the model correctly classified 100% of the subjects. However, if the Mick et al. model had correctly classified only 50% of the subjects, the findings would suggest that the independent variables were not at all useful in predicting ADHD. The researchers could have done equally well by chance.

In logistic regression, a "risk score" for each individual in the population can be computed using the regression coefficients multiplied by the individual's characteristics on the independent variables. The Framingham Risk Score, for example, identifies individuals at risk of heart problems, using age, gender, obesity, cigarette smoking, cholesterol levels, and so on.

Interpreting the Mick et al. Model

Table 31.1 summarizes the Mick et al. (2002) results. The OR for each independent variable is the "common" OR relative to all the other variables included in the model. The 95% confidence interval indicates that if the study were repeated 100 times, 95 of such confidence intervals would contain that population parameter or OR. The statistical significance column is based on Wald's chi-square. If p was less than .05, the null hypothesis of randomness was rejected. The OR is statistically significant if the confidence interval for an OR does not include 1.0. In Table 31.1, the OR for cigarette exposure was 2.1; the 95% confidence interval ranged from 1.1 to 4.1 and

TABLE 31.1
Increased Risk for ADHD Associated With Exposure
to Cigarettes, Alcohol, and Drugs During Pregnancy
(Adapted From Mick et al., 2002)

	Odds Ratio	(95% CI)	Statistical Significance
Cigarette exposure	2.1	(1.1–4.1)	$p = .02$
Alcohol exposure	2.5	(1.1–5.5)	$p = .03$
Drug exposure	0.8	(0.3–2.0)	$p = .6$
CD in offspring/child	8.5	(3.1–23.5)	$p < .001$
Maternal age at child's birth	1.0	(0.9–1.1)	$p = .9$
Maternal depression	1.8	(0.9–3.4)	$p = .1$
ADHD in either parent	6.6	(3.2–13.9)	$p < .001$
CD/ASPD in either parent	0.9	(0.5–1.6)	$p = .6$
Rutter's indicators of adversity (vs. none)			
One	1.7	(0.9–2.7)	$p = .08$
Two	1.6	(0.9–2.8)	$p = .1$
Three or more	4.1	(1.9–8.7)	$p < .001$
Subject's age in years	0.9	(0.8–.95)	$p < .001$

Note. ADHD = attention deficit hyperactivity disorder; CD/ASPD = conduct disorder and/or antisocial personality disorder.

the statistical significance level was $p = .02$, which was judged to be significant because it was <.05.

The OR for subject's age is 0.9 ($p < .001$), and the confidence interval is quite narrow (0.8–0.95) and does not include 1.00. An OR significantly less than 1 indicates a negative association. In other words, older children (high age) are less likely to be in the ADHD group. Note that the OR of 0.9 for subject's age was statistically significant ($p < .001$), whereas the same OR of 0.9 was not statistically significant for CD/antisocial personality disorder in either parent ($p = .60$), and the larger OR of 1.8 for maternal depression also was not statistically significant ($p = .10$). These findings illustrate the problems of interpreting the magnitude of the OR in terms of clinical and practical significance. An OR of 0.9 or 1.1 may have major implications in one situation and be trivial in another. The ORs and p values just described serve as a warning not to interpret the magnitude of the OR without further information.

DISCRIMINANT ANALYSIS

Although this chapter has focused on logistic regression, it is helpful to briefly describe discriminant analysis, which sometimes can be used instead of logistic regression. Like logistic regression, discriminant analysis can be used to predict a dichotomous outcome variable (e.g., ADHD vs. non-

ADHD) from a combination of several independent variables (such as those listed in Table 31.1). A discriminant function prediction equation is a *linear* combination of the independent variables meant to discriminate between the two outcome groups, similar to the risk score used in logistic regression. However, in logistic regression, the combination of independent variables is not necessarily linear. In discriminant analysis, the weights for each independent variable are selected based on how well they classify participants into the two groups, as is also true in logistic regression.

Stone, Lemanek, Fishel, Fernandez, and Altemeier (1990) had a dichotomous outcome (type of handicapping condition: autistic or other) and five independent variables. They performed a discriminant analysis and found that three of the independent variables (appropriate toy play, functional play, and imitation) combined to significantly discriminate between the two groups (autistic and nonautistic). Furthermore, they reported that 82% of the autistic children and 100% of the nonautistic children were classified correctly.

ADDITIONAL CONSIDERATIONS

As is true of all regression models, logistic regression can be conducted in a simultaneous, hierarchical, or stepwise matter. In the Mick et al. (2002) study, all the independent variables were *entered simultaneously* to determine how much each contributed to the model. In hierarchical *logistic regression*, a set of independent variables is entered first. These are often the variables considered to be background (or control) variables and of less interest to the researchers. The remaining independent variables (those of primary interest to the researchers) are then added to determine if they increase the predictive power of the model. In *stepwise logistic regression*, each independent variable is entered (or removed) one at a time into the model, based on the level of statistical association between the independent and dependent variables. However, best practice indicates that variables should be included or excluded from models based on past research or theoretical arguments, not just on their level of statistical significance. Thus, our recommendation is not to use stepwise methods.

Finally, it is important to remember the distinction between statistical significance and practical significance. If the sample is large, a finding can be statistically significant and yet be of trivial practical significance. The size of the OR is an index of the "strength of the relationship," although its exact interpretation is problematic. Notice that we did not say the "strength of the effect," which could imply that there is a causal link between the independent variables and the dependent variable. One can never infer causality simply from correlation analyses. In a situation in which subjects are randomly assigned to treatment groups, logistic regression analyses can be used to assess the causal effects of treatments and conditions. However, in the absence of experimental control of the independent variables, causal hypotheses might be formulated to be tested in future randomized experiments, but causal inferences should be avoided.

Chapter 32

Selection and Use of Inferential Statistics: A Summary

The interpretation of many of the inferential statistics found in applied journals was discussed in chapters 24–31. In the present chapter, we summarize and also include discussion about some additional statistics. Several figures are presented to help in the selection and interpretation of appropriate statistical tests. When reading a research article, the statistic mentioned in that article can be looked up in the figures in this chapter to get a better idea of why the authors chose that statistic.

In previous chapters we divided research questions into difference questions and associational questions. *Difference questions* compare groups and utilize the statistics, which we call *difference inferential statistics* (see the left side of Fig. 32.1). These statistics (e.g., *t* test and analysis of variance) are identified in Figs. 32.2 and 32.4. *Associational questions* examine the association or relationship between two or more variables (see the right side of Fig. 32.1). They utilize *associational inferential statistics* (correlation and regression) and are shown in Figs. 32.3 and 32.5.

It is worth noting that there may be more than one appropriate statistical analysis for a given design or configuration of variables; thus, Figs. 32.2–32.5 just provide guidelines. As we show in the later section on the general linear model (GLM), many difference statistics have an analog associational statistic.

USING FIGURES 32.2 TO 32.5

We also have made a distinction in previous chapters between two kinds of inferential statistics: basic and complex. For *basic* (or bivariate) *statistics,*

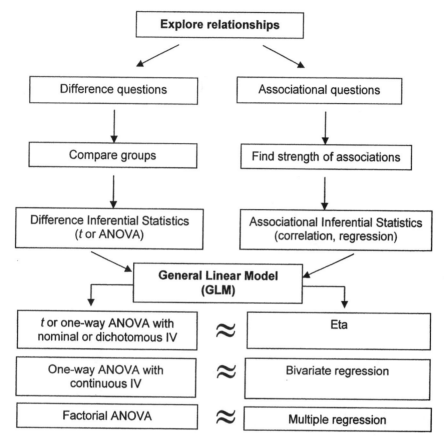

FIG. 32.1.   A schematic showing how the general linear model is related to the purposes for and types of inferential statistics.

shown in Figs. 32.2 and 32.3, there is *one* independent and *one* dependent variable. For *complex* difference and associational *statistics*, shown in Figs. 32.4 and 32.5, there are three or more variables. We call them complex rather than multivariate, because there is not unanimity about the definition of multivariate, and several such complex statistics (e.g., factorial ANOVA) are not usually classified as multivariate.

To help understand these figures, the following guidelines are provided:

1. Decide how many variables there are in the research question or hypothesis. If there are only two variables, refer to Figs. 32.2 or 32.3. If there is *more* than one independent and/or one dependent variable (i.e., three or more variables) to be analyzed, refer to Figs. 32.4 or 32.5.

BASIC (TWO-VARIABLE) QUESTIONS AND STATISTICS

2. If the independent variable is nominal (has unordered levels) or has a few (two to four) ordered levels, refer to Fig. 32.2. The research question is a *basic,* two-variable, *difference question* to compare groups. Then determine: (a) whether there are two *or* more than two levels (also called categories, groups, or samples) of the *independent* variable, (b) whether the design is between groups or within subjects/repeated measures, and (c) whether the measurement of the *dependent* variable is (i) normally distributed and parametric assumptions are not markedly violated or (ii) ordinal or (iii) nominal or dichotomous. The answers to these questions lead to a specific box and recommended statistic in Fig. 32.2.

For a brief review of the concepts of variables, levels, design classifications (between and within), measurement scales (nominal, ordinal, etc.), and assumptions, refer to chapter 23 and appropriate earlier chapters (e.g., 6, 7, and 16).

Note that the chapters in which we discussed the statistics shown in the figures are given in parentheses in the appropriate box in the figure. For example, Fig. 32.3 indicates that the *independent samples t test* and *one-way ANOVA* were discussed in chapter 24. The article that we selected to illustrate ANOVA was by Herpertz et al. (2001), who compared three groups of boys (ADHD, ADHD + CD, and comparison) on psychophysiological and other measures (e.g., IQ). Notice that, as discussed in chapter 24, Herpertz et al. had (a) three levels of the independent variable, (b) a between or independent groups design, and (c) a normally distributed dependent variable, IQ, so the appropriate box in Fig. 32.2 is in the top row, second from the right side. In chapter 24, we also described how the *Kruskal–Wallis* nonparametric test (see Fig. 32.2) could have been used to compare the three groups of boys if the ANOVA assumptions had been markedly violated.

To illustrate the *paired samples t test* and *repeated-measures ANOVA*, we chose an article by Compton et al. (2001), who assessed the benefits of sertraline in adolescents with social anxiety disorder in an open 8-week trial. They applied the paired *t* test to assess whether there was a change from the baseline to the end of the trial on the behavior avoidance test. Repeated-measures ANOVA was selected to determine whether there was clinical improvement compared to the baseline at 2, 4, 6, and 8 weeks. Notice that these statistics were used because there was one group of adolescents assessed repeatedly (within subjects design).

3. If both variables are nominal or dichotomous, a difference question (refer to the bottom row of Fig. 32.2) or an associational question (refer to the bottom row of Fig. 32.3) could be asked. Note, in the second to bottom

Scale of Measurement of Dependent Variable → COMPARE →	One Factor or Independent Variable with 2 Levels or Categories/Groups/Samples		One Independent Variable 3 or more Levels or Groups	
	Independent Samples or Groups (Between)	Repeated Measures or Related Samples (Within)	Independent Samples or Groups (Between)	Repeated Measures or Related Samples (Within)
Dependent Variable is Approximately **Normally Distributed** and Assumptions Not Markedly Violated (MEANS)	INDEPENDENT SAMPLES t TEST or ONE-WAY ANOVA (Ch. 24)	PAIRED SAMPLES t TEST (Ch. 25)	ONE-WAY (SINGLE FACTOR) ANOVA (Ch. 24)	GLM REPEATED MEASURES ANOVA (Ch. 25)
Dependent Variables Clearly **Ordinal** or Parametric Assumptions Markedly Violated (MEAN RANKS)	MANN-WHITNEY (Ch. 24)	WILCOXON (Ch. 25)	KRUSKAL-WALLIS (Ch. 24)	FRIEDMAN (Ch. 25)
Dependent Variable **Nominal** or **Dichotomous** (COUNTS)	CHI-SQUARE (Ch. 27)	MCNEMAR (Ch. 25)	CHI-SQUARE (Ch. 27)	COCHRAN Q TEST (Ch. 25)

FIG. 32.2. Selection of an appropriate basic difference inferential statistic.

Level (scale) of Measurement of **Both Variables** ↓	RELATE ↓	Two Variables or Scores for the Same or Related Subjects
Both Variables are **Normally Distributed** and Assumptions not Markedly Violated	SCORES	PEARSON (r) or BIVARIATE REGRESSION (Ch. 26)
Both Variables at Least **Ordinal** Data or Assumptions Markedly Violated	RANKS	KENDALL TAU or SPEARMAN (Rho) (Ch. 26)
One Variable is **Normally Distributed** and One is **Nominal**		ETA
Both Variables are **Nominal** or **Dichotomous**	COUNTS	PHI or CRAMER'S V (Ch. 27)

FIG. 32.3.   Selection of an appropriate basic associational inferential statistic.

row of Fig. 32.3, that we have included *eta*, an associational statistic for one nominal and one normally distributed variable. Eta often is used as an effect size measure for ANOVAs.

A study by Wolfe et al. (2001) was selected to illustrate the applicability of *chi-square* (Fig. 32.2) and also *phi* (Fig. 32.3). They examined the relationship between family intactness (yes or no) and maltreatment classification (maltreated in the past or not). Note that both variables were dichotomous. Phi could have been used as an index of the effect size or strength of the association.

4. If both variables have many (we suggest five or more) *ordered* levels, refer to Fig. 32.3 (top two rows). The research question would be a *basic* two-variable (bivariate) *associational question*. Which row to use depends on *both* variables. If both are normally distributed, then selection of the *Pearson product–moment correlation* or *bivariate regression* is recommended. (Regression should be selected if one has a clearly directional hypothesis, with an independent and dependent variable. Correlation is chosen if one is simply interested in how the two variables are related.) If one or both variables are ordinal (ranks or grossly skewed) or other assumptions of the Pearson correlation are markedly violated, the second row (*Kendall's tau* or *Spearman rho*) is a better choice.

Dierker et al. (2001) chose *Pearson correlations* to study the association or relationship between depression (CES–D scale) and anxiety (RCMAS). Note that both variables had many levels ranging from low to high, and these variables were at least approximately normally distributed.

COMPLEX (THREE OR MORE VARIABLE) QUESTIONS AND STATISTICS

It is possible to break down a complex research problem or question into a series of basic (bivariate) questions and analyses as above. However, there are advantages to combining several bivariate questions into one complex analysis; additional information is provided and a more accurate overall picture is obtained.

5. If there is one normally distributed dependent variable and two (or perhaps three or four) independent variables, each of which is nominal or has a few (two to four) ordered levels, refer to the top row of Fig. 32.4 and one of three types of factorial ANOVA. These analyses of variance (ANOVA) statistics answer *complex difference questions.*

Conners et al. (2001) selected *factorial ANOVA* to study the effects of four types of treatment and six treatment sites (a 4 × 6 factorial design) on a composite change or improvement scores in children with ADHD. Note that there are two between-groups independent variables (treatment type and site) and one dependent variable (improvement in ADHD symptoms).

6. Note, in Fig. 32.4, that there are no appropriate common complex difference statistics if the dependent variable is ordinal. *Log-linear analysis* is a nonparametric analysis in which there are two or more categorical independent variables and a dependent variable, which is also categorical. Log-linear analysis was applied in a study by Compton et al. (2000), who examined whether differences in gender, age group, and race (independent variables) were related to social phobia (high or low). All of these variables were categorical, and most were dichotomous. Log-linear analysis can handle complex patterns of interactions and variables.

7. The statistics in Fig. 32.5 are used to answer *complex associational questions.* If there are two or more independent or predictor variables and one normally distributed dependent variable, the top row of Fig. 32.5 and multiple regression are appropriate.

Multiple regression was chosen by Logan and King (2002) to study the extent of parents' ability to identify signs of depression in their adolescents

Dependent Variable(s) ↓	Two or More Independent Variables		
	All Between Groups	**All Within Subjects**	**Mixed (Between & Within)**
One **Normally Distributed** Dependent Variable	Factorial ANOVA or ANCOVA (Ch. 28)	Factorial ANOVA or GLM with Repeated Measures on all Factors	Factorial ANOVA or GLM with Repeated Measures on some Factors (4/03)
Ordinal Dependent Variable	None Common	None Common	None Common
Dichotomous Dependent Variable	LOG-LINEAR ANALYSIS	None Common	None Common

FIG. 32.4.   Selection of an appropriate complex (two or more independent variables) difference statistic.

(the dependent variable). They examined whether a combination of several independent variables would predict the degree to which parents could identify depression. Those independent variables could be continuous and/or dichotomous.

8. If the dependent variable is dichotomous or nominal, consult the bottom row of Fig. 32.5. Discriminant analysis is appropriate when the independent variables are continuous. Logistic regression is a better choice when some or all of the independent variables are dichotomous or assumptions of discriminant analysis are violated.

One Dependent or Outcome Variable ↓	Several Independent or Predictor Variables		
	All Continuous	**Some Continuous Some Dichotomous**	**All Dichotomous**
Normally Distributed (Continuous)	MULTIPLE REGRESSION (Ch. 30)	MULTIPLE REGRESSION (Ch. 30)	MULTIPLE REGRESSION (Ch. 30)
Dichotomous or Nominal	LOGISTIC REGRESSION OR DISCRIMINANT ANALYSIS (Ch. 31)	LOGISTIC REGRESSION (Ch. 31)	LOGISTIC REGRESSION (Ch. 31)

FIG. 32.5.   Selection of an appropriate complex associational statistic.

Mick et al. (2002) selected *logistic regression* to study whether children who had been diagnosed with ADHD (the dependent variables) seemed to be influenced by prenatal exposure to smoking, alcohol and/or drug use. These and several of the "control" variables were dichotomous (e.g., parent smoked or did not smoke).

EXCEPTIONS

Occasionally there are research articles in which a dichotomous *dependent variable* was used with a *t* test or ANOVA. Also there are articles in which either or both variables were dichotomous, and Pearson correlation or regression was used. Because of the special nature of dichotomous variables, this is not incorrect, as would be the use of a nominal (three or more unordered levels) dependent variable with these associational parametric statistics. However, we think that it is generally a better practice to apply the same statistics with dichotomous variables that are used with nominal variables. The exception is that it is appropriate to include dichotomous (sometimes called *dummy*) independent variables in multiple regression (see Fig. 32.5 again).

SOME OTHER MULTIVARIATE (COMPLEX) STATISTICS

When there is a design similar to that appropriate for a *t* test or ANOVA but there are *two or more* normally distributed dependent variables that are moderately interrelated, it is desirable to consider treating the variables simultaneously with a *multivariate analysis of variance* (MANOVA). Marmorstein and Iacono (2003) chose MANOVA to study differences between depression (yes or no) and conduct disorder (yes or no) on a linear combination of several dependent variables (e.g., grade point average, number of school suspensions, number of substance abuse symptoms) considered together.

Canonical correlation is a correlation of a linear combination of several (set 1) independent variables with a linear combination of several (set 2) dependent variables. Toppelberg, Medrano, Morgens, and Nieto-Castanon (2002) used canonical correlation in a study of bilingual children, referred for psychiatric services, to control for variable combinations acting as potential confounds. Set 1 variables included bilingual language skills and the Child Behavior Check List; set 2 included potential "confounds" of IQ, immigration depth, and maternal education.

Path analysis is a multivariate analysis in which strength of relationships among several variables is represented by figures showing the "paths" among variables. *Structural equation models* (SEM) are models that describe relationships among latent (unobserved) variables. Path analysis and SEM are related statistics; both provide tests of the accuracy of the proposed model and both are said by proponents to provide evidence of "causal linkages" from nonexperimental designs. However, the American Psychological Association Task Force on Statistical Inference stated that "The use of complicated 'causal modeling' software rarely yields results that have any interpretation as causal effects" (Wilkinson & the Task Force, 1999, p. 600).

Donenberg, Emerson, Bryant, Wilson, and Weber-Shifrin (2001) applied SEM to conduct a path analysis to explore the relationships of adolescent psychopathology to risky sex, drug/alcohol use, and needle use; peer influence mediated these linkages. Several distinct paths were identified; for example, aggression was related to risky sexual behaviors, and delinquency was linked to drug/alcohol use.

THE GENERAL LINEAR MODEL

Testing the *relationship between variables can be answered in two ways.* This is not obvious from Figs. 32.2–32.5. Using these figures we recommended one of the choices, but statisticians point out, and can demonstrate mathematically, that the distinction between difference and associational statistics is artificial. Figure 32.1 shows that although we have made a distinction between difference and associational inferential statistics, they both serve the purpose of exploring and describing relationships (top box) and both are subsumed by the *general linear model* (middle box); that is, all common parametric statistics are relational. Thus, the full range of methods used to analyze one continuous dependent variable and one or more independent variables, either continuous or categorical, are mathematically equivalent. The relationship between the independent and dependent variables can be expressed by an equation with terms for the weighted values of each of the independent/predictor variables plus an error term.

The bottom part of Fig. 32.1 indicates that a t test or one-way ANOVA with a nominal or dichotomous independent variable is analogous to eta, which is a correlation coefficient for a nominal independent variable and a continuous dependent variable. Likewise, a one-way ANOVA with a continuous independent variable is analogous to bivariate regression. Thus, if there is a continuous, normally distributed dependent/outcome variable and there are five or so levels of a normally distributed independent variable, it would be appropriate to analyze it with either regression or a one-way ANOVA. Finally, as shown in the lowest boxes in Fig. 32.1, factorial ANOVA and multiple regression are analogous mathematically.

Although our distinction between difference and associational parametric statistics is a simplification, we think it is useful educationally. Hopefully this summary of a large number of statistics and the general linear model is helpful in terms of understanding the selection and interpretation of many of the statistics that are published in research articles.

Interpretation of Alpha, Factor Analysis, and Principal Components Analysis

This chapter discusses three complex descriptive statistics that did not fit well into the last chapter. They are commonly found in journal articles as measures of reliability or validity and for reducing a large number of related variables to meaningful composite variables. Chapters 8 and 9 in this book provide broader overviews of what we label measurement reliability and measurement validity.

These statistics often are discussed in articles when researchers describe the reliability or validity of their measures or the development of aggregated, summated, or composite scores used in a study. First, we discuss the use and interpretation of one measure of reliability: Cronbach's alpha. Then we discuss exploratory factor analysis (EFA) and principal components analysis (PCA). Because EFA and PCA are used to prepare a large data set for more efficient inferential analyses of the research questions in a study, they are commonly found in the methods section of an article. The primary examples cited in this chapter are based on a modified Dimensions of Mastery Questionnaire (DMQ) data set, which is described, analyzed, and interpreted in a textbook by Leech, Barrett, and Morgan (2005), some of which is reprinted here.

CRONBACH'S ALPHA

Several types of statistics, especially correlations, are used to assess reliability, but in this chapter we only discuss Cronbach's coefficient alpha, which is probably the most commonly reported measure of reliability. Alpha is a measure of the *internal consistency* of a composite or summated scale. It is typically used when the researcher has several Likert-type items (ratings from *strongly disagree* to *strongly agree*) that are summed or averaged to make a composite score or summated scale. Alpha is based on the average correlation of each item in the scale with every other item. In the behavioral science literature, alpha is widely used because it provides a measure of reliability that can be obtained from one testing session or one administration of a questionnaire.

Leech et al. (2005) computed three alphas to provide evidence for the internal consistency reliability of the three mathematics attitude scales: motivation, competence, and pleasure. The motivation scale score was composed of six items that were rated on 4-point Likert scales, from very atypical (1) to very typical (4). Did these items go together (interrelate) well enough to add them together for use as a composite variable labeled *motivation*? That is, what is the internal consistency reliability of the math attitude scale that was labeled *motivation*?

Table 33.1 lists the items included in this scale, their labels, and a matrix showing the interitem correlations of every item in the scale with every other item. Note that the second and fourth items in the list were reversed (4 = 1, 3 = 2, etc.) before alpha was computed. This is necessary for alpha to be computed correctly.

Table 33.2, which is labeled Item–Total Statistics, provides three pieces of information for each item in the scale. The two we find most useful are the *corrected item–total correlation* and Cronbach's alpha if that item was deleted. The former is the correlation of each specific item with the sum/total of the *other* items in the scale. If this correlation is moderately high, .40 or above, the item is probably at least moderately correlated with most of the other items in the proposed scale and will make a good component of this

TABLE 33.1
Interitem Correlation Matrix for the Motivation Scale Items

	item01 motivation	item04 reversed	item07 motivation	item08 reversed	item12 motivation
Practice math until do well	1.00	—	—	—	—
(Don't) give up easily instead of persisting	.25	1.00	—	—	—
Prefer to figure out problems without help	.46	.55	1.00	—	—
(Do) keep at it long if problem challenging	.30	.58	.59	1.00	—
Try to complete math even if it takes long	.18	.38	.34	.40	1.00
Explore all possible solutions	.17	.32	.36	.31	.60

TABLE 33.2
Item–Total Statistics for the Motivation Scale Items

	Corrected Item–Total Correlation	Squared Multiple Correlation	Cronbach's Alpha if Item Deleted
Practice math until do well	.38	.23	.80
(Don't) give up easily instead of persisting	.60	.54	.75
Prefer to figure out problems without help	.68	.52	.72
(Do) keep at it long if problem challenging	.63	.59	.74
Try to complete math even if it takes long	.52	.87	.77
Explore all possible solutions	.48	.85	.77

summated rating scale. Items with lower item–total correlations do not fit into this scale as well, psychometrically. If the item–total correlation is negative or too low (less than .30), the authors should examine the item for wording problems and conceptual fit and may want to modify or delete such items. The last column describes what the alpha would be if an item were deleted. This can be compared to the alpha for the scale with all six items included, which was .79. Deleting a poor item usually will make the alpha increase, but it probably will make only a small difference in the alpha, unless the scale has only a few items (e.g., fewer than five) because alpha is based on the number of items as well as their average intercorrelations.

As with other reliability coefficients, alpha should be above .70; however, it is common to see journal articles where one or more scales have somewhat lower alphas (e.g., in the .60–.69 range), especially if there are only a small number of items in a scale. A very high alpha (e.g., greater than .90) probably means that the items are somewhat repetitious or that there may be more items in the scale than are really necessary for a reliable measure of the concept for research purposes. A common error is to compute a single overall alpha when there are several scales such as motivation, competence, and pleasure. The overall alpha is only meaningful if there is an overall summated scale such as overall math attitude, but frequently, and in this example, there was no such overall score. Thus, three separate alphas (for motivation, competence, and pleasure) were computed and reported.

Leech et al. (2005) wrote, for the method section, the following sentences about the reliability of the motivation scale and the other two scales.

> To assess whether the six items that were summed to create the motivation score formed a reliable scale, Cronbach's alpha was computed. The alpha for the six items was .79, which indicates that the items form a scale that has reasonable internal consistency reliability. Similarly, the alpha for the competence scale (.80) indicated good internal consistency, but the .69 alpha for the pleasure scale indicated minimally adequate reliability. (p. 67)

EXPLORATORY FACTOR ANALYSIS AND PRINCIPAL COMPONENTS ANALYSIS

Exploratory factor analysis (EFA) and principal components analysis (PCA) are methods that are used to help investigators represent a large number of relationships among normally distributed variables in a simpler (more parsimonious) way. Both of these approaches allow the computer to determine which, of a fairly large set of items, "hang together" as a group or are answered most similarly by the participants. A related approach is *confirmatory factor analysis*, in which one tests very specific models of how variables are related to underlying constructs (conceptual variables). It is not discussed here but is, along with EFA, in Thompson (2004).

The primary difference, conceptually, between exploratory factor analysis and principal components analysis is that in EFA, one postulates that there is a smaller set of unobserved (latent) variables or constructs that underlie the variables that actually were observed or measured. In PCA, one is simply trying to mathematically derive a relatively small number of variables to convey as much of the information in the observed/measured variables as possible. In other words, EFA is directed at *understanding* the relations among variables by understanding the constructs that underlie them, whereas PCA is simply directed toward enabling one to use fewer variables to provide the same information that one would obtain from a larger set of variables. There are actually a number of different ways of computing factors for factor analysis; one of these methods, *principal axis factor analysis*, is used when describing EFA for this chapter.

Conditions for Exploratory Factor Analysis and Principal Components Analysis

There are two main conditions necessary for factor analysis and principal components analysis. The first is that there need to be relationships between the variables. Further, the larger the sample size, especially in relation to the number of variables, the more reliable the resulting factors usually are. Sample size is less crucial for factor analysis to the extent that the communalities of items with the other items are high, or at least relatively high, and variable. Principal axis factor analysis should never be done if the number of items/variables is greater than the number of participants.

Assumptions for Exploratory Factor Analysis and Principal Components Analysis

The methods of extracting factors and components that are discussed in this book do not make strong distributional assumptions; normality is important only to the extent that skewness or outliers affect the observed correlations or if significance tests are performed (which is rare for EFA and PCA). Because both principal axis factor analysis and principal components analysis are based on correlations, independent sampling of participants is required and if the variables are related to each other (in pairs) it should be in a linear fashion. Finally, at least many of the pairs of variables should be correlated at a moderate level. Factor analysis and principal components analysis are seeking to explain or reproduce the correlation matrix, which would not be a sensible thing to do if the correlations all hover around zero. If correlations are too high, this may cause problems with obtaining a mathematical solution to the factor analysis problem.

Exploratory Factor Analysis

In Leech et al. (2005), a principal axis factor analysis on the mathematics attitude variables was performed. Factor analysis was more appropriate than PCA because they believed that there were latent variables underlying the variables or items measured. In this example, the authors had beliefs about the constructs underlying the mathematics attitude questions; they believed that there were three constructs: *motivation, competence,* and *pleasure.* They wanted to see if the items that were written to index each of these constructs actually did "hang together." That is, they wished to determine empirically whether participants' responses to the motivation questions were more similar to each other than to their responses to the competence items, and so on. This is considered exploratory factor analysis, even though the authors had some ideas about the structure of the data, because the hypotheses regarding the model were not very specific. For example, they did not have specific predictions about the size of the relationship of each observed variable to each latent variable.

Factor analysis programs generate a number of tables depending on which options are chosen. A *correlation matrix* would show how each of the 14 items was associated with each of the other 13. Some of the correlations were high (e.g., +.60 or −.60 or further from zero) and some are low (i.e., near zero). The high correlations indicate that two items are associated and will probably be grouped together by the factor analysis.

Total variance explained indicates how the variance is divided among the 14 possible factors. In this example four factors had *eigenvalues* (a measure of explained variance) greater than 1.0, which is a common criterion for a factor to be useful. When the eigenvalue is less than 1.0, this means that the factor explains less information than a single item would have explained. Most researchers would not consider the information gained from such a factor to be sufficient to justify keeping that factor. Thus, if the researchers had not specified otherwise, the computer would have looked for the best four-factor solution by "rotating" four factors. Because the authors believed there were three constructs and specified that they wanted only three factors rotated, only three were rotated.

The authors used an *orthogonal rotation* (*varimax*). This means that the final factors would be as uncorrelated as possible with each other. As a result, we can assume that the information explained by one factor is independent of the information in the other factors. Rotated factors are easier to interpret. Rotation makes it so that, as much as possible, different items are explained or predicted by *different* underlying factors, and each factor explains more than one item. This is a condition called *simple structure.* Although this is the *goal* of rotation, in reality, this often is not achieved. One thing that often is examined in the rotated matrix of factor loadings is the extent to which simple structure is achieved.

Within each factor (to the extent possible), the items are sorted from the one with the highest absolute *factor weight* or *loading* for that factor to the one with the lowest loading on that first factor. Loadings resulting from an orthogonal rotation are correlation coefficients of each item with the factor, so they range from −1.0 through 0 to +1.0. A negative loading just means that the question needs to be interpreted in the opposite direction from the way it is written for that factor (e.g., "I am a little slow catching on to new topics in math" has a negative loading from the competence factor, which indicates that the people scoring higher on this item see themselves as lower in competence). Usually, factor loadings lower than .30 or .40 are considered low, which is why the authors suppressed such loadings. On the other hand, loadings of .40 or greater are typically considered high. This is just a guideline, however, and one could set the criterion for "high" loadings as low as .30 or as high as .50. Setting the criterion lower than .30 or higher than .50 would be very unusual.

Every item has a weight or loading from every factor, but in a "clean" factor analysis almost all of the loadings beyond +.40 or −.40 in the rotated factor matrix would be in only one column or factor. Notice in Table 33.3 that two items (*prefer to figure out problems without help,* and *feel happy after solving a hard problem*) have loadings above .40 for two factors. This is common but undesirable, in that one wants only one factor to predict each item.

Leech et al. (2005) wrote about the results as follows:

> Principal axis factor analysis with varimax rotation was conducted to assess the underlying structure for the fourteen items of the Math Motivation Questionnaire. Three factors were requested, based on the fact that the items were designed to index three constructs: motivation, competence, and pleasure. After rotation, the first factor accounted for 21.5% of the variance, the second factor accounted for 16.6%, and the third factor accounted for 12.7%. The table [33.3] displays the items and factor loadings for the rotated factors, with loadings less than .40 omitted to improve clarity.
>
> The first factor, which seems to index competence, loads most strongly on the first four items, with loadings [shown] in the first column. Two of the

TABLE 33.3
Factor Loadings for the Rotated Factors

Item	Factor Loading			Communality
	1	2	3	
Slow catching on to new topics	−.90			.77
Solve math problems quickly	.78			.60
Practice math until do well	.78			.66
Have difficulties doing math	−.57			.59
Try to complete math even if takes long		.72		.50
Explore all possible solutions		.67		.45
Do not keep at it long if problem challenging		−.62		.53
Give up easily instead of persisting		−.60		.56
Prefer to figure out problems without help	.41	.59		.61
Really enjoy working math problems			−.80	.48
Smile only a little when solving math problem			.58	.37
Feel happy after solving hard problem	.49		−.54	.54
Do not get much pleasure out of math			.52	.38
Eigenvalues	3.02	2.32	1.78	
Percent of variance	21.55	16.62	12.74	

Note. Loadings <.40 are omitted.

items indexed low competence and had negative loadings. The second factor, which seemed to index motivation, was composed of the five items with loadings in column 2 of the table. "I prefer to figure out the problem without help" had its highest loading on the second factor, but had a cross-loading over .4 on the competence factor. The third factor, which seemed to index (low) pleasure from math, comprised the four items with loadings in the third column. "I feel happy after solving a hard problem" had its highest loading from the pleasure factor, but also had a strong loading from the competence factor. (pp. 83–84)

Principal Components Analysis

Principal components analysis is most useful if one simply wants to reduce a relatively large number of variables to a smaller set of variables that still captures the same information. These new composite variables are called *components* or *factors*. Principal components analysis was selected by Rohde et al. (2001) to evaluate the multidimensional concept of attention-deficit/hyperactivity disorder in Brazilian adolescents. They extracted two factors: (a) hyperactivity-impulsivity composed of eight *DSM–IV* symptoms and (b) inattention, which also included eight symptoms.

Researchers usually give names to a component in a fashion similar to that used in EFA; however, there is no assumption that this indicates a latent variable that underlies the measured items. Often, a researcher will aggregate (add or average) the items that define (have high loadings for) each component, and use this composite variable in further research. Actually, the same thing is often done with EFA factor loadings; however, the implication of the latter is that this composite variable is an index of the underlying construct such as motivation to study math.

DEVELOPING AGGREGATED OR SUMMATED SCALES

As implied earlier, it is common to read that a researcher used a measure based on the sum or average of several items such as a set of Likert-type ratings like those intended to measure mathematics motivation, competence, and pleasure. Figure 33.1 shows a flow chart of two different methods that

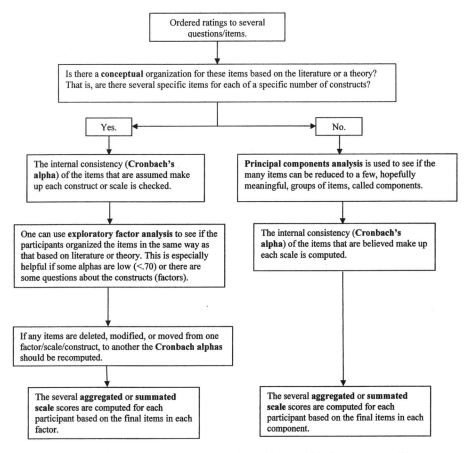

FIG. 33.1.   Two common strategies for making multiple-item summated/ composite scales.

researchers might use to decide which items to combine or aggregate and how they would check the reliability of the resulting multiple item scale. Note that both methods to develop these summated or aggregated scales utilize Cronbach's alpha to check reliability. The first (left-hand) method is used when the researcher has a conceptual plan for the organization of the items, as Leech et al. (2005) did for the three mathematics attitude scales. The second (right-hand) method is used when there is not a clear conceptualization ahead of time and the computer is used to help reduce a larger number of items to a smaller number of groups or sets of items. The second method begins with a principal components analysis, and the first method may utilize exploratory factor analysis, especially if the alphas for the conceptual plan are not acceptable. Both of these methods are common in the literature.

Part VII

APPLICATION CHAPTERS

Chapter 34

Levels of Evidence for Evidence-Based Practice

In previous chapters we have discussed evaluation of the research process including statement of hypotheses, selection of an appropriate sample, formulation of an appropriate design, choice of the appropriate data analysis, and interpretation of this analysis. Evaluation of research also compliments the process of evidence-based practice. Regardless of whether studies were carried out in clinical or applied settings, or whether they included an intervention, they provide evidence that may guide practitioners in the future. A large part of the concept known as evidence-based practice is using research to compile evidence. Evidence-based practice, according to Law (2002), "is now part of every health care discipline and professional education program. While everyone agrees that it is important to use evidence in practice, the challenges of finding, evaluating, and using evidence are substantial" (p. xv). An example of these challenges is as follows.

Holm (2000) presented an invited address entitled "Our Mandate for the New Millennium: Evidence-Based Practice" to the national conference of occupational therapists. For many, it was an introduction to a topic that had largely been ignored by disciplines with an emphasis on therapeutic procedures. Holm started her lecture by asking the audience, who were mostly clinicians, how they would respond if their patients asked them a simple, yet important question: "How do you know that what you do and how you do it really works?" She supplemented this question by asking the therapists if they could provide a summary of research that, for example, would describe the number of patients who benefited from a particular option and those who did not. She described additional information that would be needed to answer the question, such as the frequency and duration of each intervention that would be included. She stated that it is doubt-ful that this evidence could be provided today.

What is *evidence-based practice* (EBP)? According to Sackett, Rosenberg, Gray, Haynes, and Richardson (1996), it is "explicit and judicious use of current best evidence in making decisions about the care of individual patients" (p. 71). The underlying idea behind EBP is that decisions about interventions in clinical areas should be based on the strength of the evi-dence.

Current best evidence is, however, not necessarily only research evi-dence. "This focus on research evidence can lead practitioners to misin-terpret evidence-based practice to be a form of practice that is based solely on research study evidence and that is devoid of evidence based on clini-cal experience and the client's own needs and desires" (Tickle-Degnen, 1999, p. 538). On the other hand, information collected from clinical ex-perience, expert testimony, and discussions with other professionals is subject to bias. Therefore, an important aspect of evidence-based practice is that it should be used to integrate research findings with these other, more subjective, pieces of evidence, rather than use of research as the sole source of evidence.

LEVELS OF EVIDENCE

Evidence-based practice makes the assumption that not all evidence should be treated as having equal value or weight. There are several rating schemes or classifications provided to evaluate the levels of evidence from strong to weak (Holm, 2000; Sackett, 1989). Law (2002), in her book entitled *Evi-dence-Based Rehabilitation,* described three different rating schemes or levels classifications. Table 34.1 provides a summary of these rating schemes.

TABLE 34.1
Hierarchy of Levels of Evidence for Evidence-Based Practice

Level	Description
I	Evidence from one or more systematic reviews of well-designed randomized con-trolled trials
II	Evidence from one randomized control trial with large sample size ($N > 500$)
III	Evidence from one or more systematic reviews incorporating randomized control trials and observational studies
IV	Evidence from randomized control trials with small sample size
V	Evidence from quantitative studies using quasi-experimental designs or comparative designs
VI	Evidence from qualitative studies and case reports
VII	Evidence from expert opinion

What do these rating scales have in common? First, quantitative research is viewed more positively than qualitative research. Second, internal validity is given more weight than external validity. Third, multiple studies on a topic are viewed more favorably than a single study. Last, studies with large sample size are rated higher than studies with small sample size. Each of these statements is viewed in more detail in the following sections.

Quantitative Versus Qualitative Evidence

As discussed in chapter 3, quantitative and qualitative research approaches represent two different paradigms or philosophies of how research should be conducted and interpreted. Although there are wide differences within each of these paradigms, there are also considerable consistencies among qualitative and quantitative researchers. Chapters 2 and 10 point out that the types of data, data collection methods, and data analyses are substantially different for the two paradigms.

Typically in these classification of evidence schemes, qualitative research is seen near the bottom. One reason for this view is that most of these classification schemes come from the field of medicine, where objective data and randomized control trials are viewed as the pinnacle. When participants are randomly assigned to groups, criticisms of bias in the study, although not totally removed, usually are reduced considerably. In qualitative research, random assignment into groups is rarely done. Data collection bias also is considered a problem because the researcher as observer is often the only instrument in the study. Not only does the researcher collect the data and code it into different categories, but the researcher also interprets the data. Because these are necessary parts of good qualitative research, they cannot help but give the appearance of strong subjective influence.

Internal Validity Versus External Validity

Studies with strong internal validity are usually considered to provide more valuable evidence than studies with strong external validity in these classification schemes. What do we mean by strong *internal validity*? As discussed in chapter 17, a requirement for strong internal validity is that participants have been randomly assigned to groups. This does not mean that the randomization process makes the groups equal or equivalent, although the larger the number of participants, the greater is the possibility of equivalence. Random assignment of participants to groups means that there is no bias between the groups in the participant characteristics prior to introduction of the independent variable. Therefore, studies viewed as randomized experimental are given more weight than those that are quasi-experimental, where participants could not be randomly assigned to groups. Studies where the independent variable is an attribute, such as ones using the comparative and/or associational approaches, are viewed as having less internal validity, and are given significantly less weight in the evidence based practice evaluation schemes.

Strong population *external validity* means that the method of selection of participants should allow the researchers to generalize the results of the study to the population of interest. However, if one study is low in internal validity and a second is high in internal validity, the latter is viewed more favorably even if the low internal validity study has strong external validity (where participants were randomly selected to be in the study from the population of interest). Studies that are tightly controlled are viewed as higher, even though they may have less generalizability to the population. Qualitative studies are usually viewed as low in internal validity, which is another reason that evidence from them is given lower weight than studies with high internal validity.

A major reason that internal validity has been given more weight in these classification schemes than external validity is meta-analysis (see the next section and chap. 35). Previously, studies with strong internal validity but relatively low external validity, due to convenience sampling, have been criticized. However, when large numbers of studies have been included in a meta-analysis, even though the majority of these studies might have used convenience sampling, the large number of participants with different demographic characteristics increases external validity substantially.

Multiple Studies Versus a Single Study

Evidence from a single, rigorously designed study, although persuasive, is still not nearly as convincing as a synthesis of multiple, well-designed studies on the same topic. Often, the problem with single studies is that they have not been replicated, or when replication is attempted the results do not hold up. Worse, many of the replication attempts that fail are not published in journals. In order to solve this problem, a whole new methodology, meta-analysis, was developed. Meta-analysis is a method to synthesize research on a particular topic by combining the results of many studies dealing with the topic. These studies are combined averaging an effect size index from each study. Briefly, the effect size expresses the difference between the treatment or intervention group and the control or comparison group divided by a common measure of variability. Prior to the use of meta-analysis, one might read a review on a particular topic and see that some studies might favor the treatment, whereas other studies might suggest that the treatment is not effective. It was difficult to obtain an overall judgment about the effectiveness of the treatment. Meta-analysis solves this problem by obtaining an overall effect size average indicating the degree of success or lack thereof of the intervention. For example, Connor, Glatt, Jackson, and Melloni (2002) did a meta-analysis on the pharmacologic interventions for aggression-related behaviors in attention deficit hyperactivity disorder (see chap. 35 for discussion of this study). Meta-analyses have become more common in all fields, and collaborations have been formed such as the Cochrane Collaboration (for medical research) or the Campbell Collaboration (for social science research) that provide research syntheses in a wide range of topics. We discuss meta-analysis in more detail in the next chapter.

Large Sample Size Versus Small Sample Size

Although single studies on a topic have not been held in favor, those single studies that have a large sample size have been given more weight in the evidence-based practice evaluation schemes than studies with a small sample size. The reason for this is that, given appropriate sampling, there is less chance for error as we add more participants to a study. Not only is there less variability with larger numbers, but more important, there is more statistical power, the power to reject a false null hypothesis. Researchers hope to reject a hypothesis of no difference (the null hypothesis) and conclude that the intervention was successful. When the study has a small sample size, there could be greater variability. This means that the intervention could have worked, but because the sample size was relatively small, one might not have the statistical power to reject a false null hypothesis. Therefore, one might give up on the intervention, when it was not given a fair test. What constitutes a large as compared to a small sample size is somewhat arbitrary, but statistical power can be determined for various sample sizes providing an estimate of the effect size (see chap. 20).

In these evidence-based practice classification systems, studies that combine a large sample size with strong internal validity are valued. It should be noted that, other things being equal, a large sample size is preferred to a small sample size. However, *many* studies with small sample sizes are preferred to one study with a large sample size. Better yet are many studies with large sample sizes.

PROBLEMS WITH THE USE OF LEVELS OF EVIDENCE HIERARCHIES

A few years ago a colleague taught a research class to undergraduate students. As part of the course, the students were required to gather evidence for any particular intervention related to a therapy that was of interest. The students presented their findings in a poster session. It was interesting that the students evaluated the evidence similar to the classification schemes presented earlier. If one particular intervention had a number of randomized experimental studies, then this was considered to be strong evidence. On the other hand, if most of the studies were associational, comparative, descriptive, or qualitative, this was considered poor evidence. Unfortunately, the students gave little consideration to the specific results of the individual studies.

Levels of evidence hierarchies evaluate the rigor and design of a study, but describe little about the specific results of the study. What exactly did the authors find about the intervention condition as compared to the previously used intervention? This is usually what a practicing therapist or clinician would like to know from a single or multiple studies. What were the findings? When the investigator compared the two groups (or more than two in some situations) were there differences? Were these differences judged to be statistically significant? Even if the differences were statistically significant, what was the effect size and were the results of practical importance? (Remember that in studies with large sample sizes, performing tests of statistical significance on the data is usually a trivial exercise because the statistical power is so great that any difference between the two groups will result in a statistically significant difference.) Without knowledge of how to evaluate research, it is difficult to make a judgment about these issues. Chapter 36 discusses the use of various effect sizes measures to assist in making decisions about clinical significance or importance.

THE PROCESS OF EVIDENCE-BASED PRACTICE

Often when we think of evidence-based practice, we think of the clinician becoming a researcher, using practice to run clinical trials. Of particular interest is the view that good, systematic research practice makes one a better practitioner. Although training the practitioner/researcher might be the goal of every academic program, realistic expectations are less. What might be expected of the current practicing clinician toward the use of evidence-based practice? The view taken here is that the current practicing clinician must be a consumer of research. That is, clinicians must be able to understand the current research in the field to be able to evaluate interventions. It also means that there is a process to evidence-based practice. One purpose of this text is to help the practitioner evaluate the research process through examples from articles selected from representative disciplines.

Sackett, Richardson, Rosenberg, and Haynes (2000) suggested five steps in the practice of evidence-based medicine. These steps are:

Step 1. Converting the need for information into an answerable question.

Step 2. Tracking down the best evidence with which to answer the question.

Step 3. Critically appraising that evidence for its validity, impact, and applicability.

Step 4. Integrating the critical appraisal with clinical expertise and with the patient's unique biology, values, and circumstances.

Step 5. Evaluating our effectiveness and efficiency in executing steps 1–4 and seeking ways to improve them both for next time. (p. 4)

This process usually begins with asking a meaningful and answerable question, a question that is directly related to an issue of concern about practice. If the question is not one of concern, there will be little interest in pursuing evidence of support. This is not uncommon in research—for example, when students are attempting to select a thesis topic. Once this question has been defined, a search of the literature begins. This could include review of relevant journals, recent texts, and electronic databases. Once the literature is searched and relevant articles retrieved, the next step is to systematically evaluate these articles. (It should be noted that although this seems like a horrendous task for the practicing clinician, there are certain short cuts. For example, the Cochrane collaborative publishes meta-analyses on a wide range of topics. In addition, there are many meta-analyses being published in most professional journals.) Not all published studies are of equal value; some are better designed than others, some have used improper statistical techniques, some have limited statistical power, and some have poor external validity that makes application to a specific population untenable. The task of the therapist, as evidence-based practitioner, is to ask a question, collect the literature, and be able to evaluate both individual articles and systematic reviews toward answering the specific question. Even after all of these have been accomplished, the therapist still must make a decision as to the usability of the information within the specific context of practice.

SUMMARY

Because the "practice" in evidence-based practice is usually an intervention or treatment, the most relevant research to evaluate the effectiveness of that intervention is experimental research using the same or a very similar intervention. As discussed in chapters 17 and 19, randomized experimental designs provide the best evidence for a causal relationship between the intervention and the outcome. Qualitative and nonexperimental research can provide some useful evidence, especially when experimental studies are not available or practical. For example, studies of the effectiveness of a treatment or practice that took place in the past, extended over a long period of time, or where an intervention would be unethical have to be nonexperimental. In these, the comparative (ex post facto) or associational approaches may provide the only relevant evidence. Clinical judgments and qualitative evidence also may supplement or enrich the data from quantitative studies, even data from randomized experiments.

In chapter 37, we provide a framework for a comprehensive evaluation of research articles, including both experimental and nonexperimental studies. There we take a more balanced approach to the relative merits of internal and external validity because we recognize that there are several purposes or goals that a research study might have in addition to or instead of the "what works" goal of evidence-based practice. For some studies, the goal is description of a phenomenon or participants' views. In others the goal is prediction or the identification of relationships among variables. For those purposes internal validity is still important, but we don't think it is dominant. Chapter 19 presented a discussion of this balanced view of the relative importance of the internal and external validity dimensions.

Chapter 35

Meta-Analysis: Formulation and Interpretation

Meta-analysis is a research synthesis of a set of studies that uses a quantitative measure, effect size, to indicate the strength of relationship between the treatment or other independent variable and the dependent variables. For the health care professions, the internationally known Cochrane Collaboration publishes systematic reviews of the effects of health care interventions (see Antes & Oxman, 2001). Not all research syntheses are meta-analyses. Often, the purpose of a research synthesis is to provide a description of a subject area, illustrating the studies that have been undertaken. In other cases, the studies are too varied in nature to provide a meaningful effect size index. The focus of this chapter, however, is on research syntheses that result in a meta-analysis.

One advantage of performing a meta-analysis includes the computation of a summary statistic for a large number of studies. This summary statistic provides an overall estimate of the strength of relationship between independent and dependent variables. Previously, research syntheses were divided into those studies that supported a particular hypothesis and those that did not support this hypothesis, making it difficult to form a conclusion. A second advantage of meta-analysis is that it provides evidence of the reliability of a research finding. Researchers have more confidence in the findings of multiple studies than in the results of a single study. A third advantage is that it takes into account studies that failed to find statistical significance and may not have been published perhaps because of a lack of statistical power (reduced sample size). A fourth advantage of meta-analysis is increased external validity. Many studies, strong in internal validity (design characteristics), do not use a representative sample of subjects. This limits the generalization of results. However, including many studies increases the variation of the sample and strengthens external validity.

Although there are many advantages to meta-analysis, there also has been considerable criticism. The most frequent criticism of meta-analysis is that it may combine "apples and oranges." Synthesizing studies that might differ on both independent and dependent variables brings into question the usefulness of the end product. Furthermore, many studies have similar independent and dependent variables, but differ in the strength of design. Should these studies be combined? Another criticism concerns small sample size. Introducing a large proportion of studies with inadequate statistical power into a meta-analysis could introduce bias into the overall effect size. Kraemer, Gardner, Brooks, and Yesavage (1998) demonstrated that the effect sizes generated from underpowered studies were likely to be poor estimates of the population effect sizes. Last, even though the statistics used in meta-analysis are quite sophisticated, the end product will never be better than the individual studies that make up the meta-analysis.

In this introduction we use, as an example, a meta-analysis published by Connor et al. (2002) that demonstrated pharmacological interventions were effective for aggression related behaviors in attention deficit hyperactivity disorder (ADHD). We discuss the criteria for inclusion and exclusion of certain studies, the selection and computation of an effect size for an individual study, and the computation of an overall effect size and other statistical indices. We recognize that this chapter is brief and recommend the text by Lipsey and Wilson (2001) as an introduction to meta-analysis, and we recommend the edited text by Cooper and Hedges (1994) for the more sophisticated reader.

The Connor et al. (2002) meta-analysis included 28 studies investigating the effects of stimulants on overt and covert aggression-related behaviors in children with ADHD. They divided their effect size indices from these studies into those of overt aggression (28) and those of covert aggression (7). They found that the intervention was effective, yielding an overall weighted mean effect size (expressed as d) for overt aggression of .84, and covert aggression of .69. They concluded that stimulant effects for aggression-related behaviors in children with ADHD produced effect sizes similar to those of core ADHD symptoms.

Criteria for Review

Although much of the focus of meta-analysis is on statistical procedures, perhaps the most important part of a meta-analysis is the planning of inclusion and exclusion criteria for selecting a study into the meta-analysis. These inclusion and exclusion criteria are often related to internal validity and external validity. Most researchers feel that meta-analyses composed of randomized control trials (RCT) represent the "gold standard" for clinical research. A randomized control trial is distinguished by random assignment of participants to treatment and comparison groups, creating an unbiased selection factor. However, there are some researchers who acknowledge the strengths of an RCT and its emphasis on internal validity, but remind us of the importance of strong external validity. This is summarized in the following statement by Egger, Smith, and Schneider (2001):

> The patients that are enrolled in randomized trials often differ from the average patient seen in clinical practice. Women, the elderly and minority ethnic groups are often excluded from randomized trials. Similarly, the university hospitals typically participating in clinical trials differ from settings where most patients are treated. In the absence of randomized trial evidence from these settings and patient groups, the results from observational database analyses may appear more relevant and more readily applicable to clinical practice. (p. 213)

In the study by Connor et al. (2002), the inclusion/exclusion criteria focused on the disability (ADHD), the aggression-related behaviors independent of core ADHD behaviors, peer-reviewed articles, type of research design, age, and type of measure (rating scale). The authors did not separate articles by design type into RCT and non-RCT, but established a quality rating for each study based on psychometric properties of the rating scale, drug-free washout period prior to the study, random assignment to groups, within-subjects (crossover) versus between-groups design, and single- or double-"blind" studies.

Statistical Computations for Individual Studies

Type of Effect Size. There are numerous types of effect size indices. We discuss some of these in chapters 22, 36, and several other chapters. The most common effect size indices used in meta-analyses are d, r, and odds ratio (OR), although risk ratio (RR) and number needed to treat (NNT) also have been used.

Briefly, the effect size d indicates the strength of a relationship between an independent and dependent variable in standard deviation units. In general, d is used when most of the studies to be included in the meta-analysis have an independent variable that is dichotomous, intervention versus control group, and a dependent variable that is continuous. The d effect size is computed by dividing the difference between the intervention and control group means by either the standard deviation of the control group, or the pooled standard deviation of the treatment and control groups. Connor et al. (2002) selected d as the effect size index for their studies. It should be noted that there are actually three different d effect size indices dependent on whether the difference between means is divided by the standard deviation of the control group only (Glass's Δ) or by the pooled standard deviation of both the treatment and control groups (Cohen's d and Hedges' g). In Cohen's d the pooled standard deviation is computed using the population standard deviation estimate. In Hedges' g the pooled standard deviation is computed using estimates of the sample standard deviation estimate. Connor et al. (2002) used Cohen's d.

The effect size r is usually used when most of the studies have continuous independent and dependent variables. Odds ratios are used as effect sizes when most of the studies have dichotomous independent and dependent variables, often resulting from chi-square analysis or logistic regression analysis.

There are two important points to remember about the computation of effect sizes for individual studies. First, effect size indices can be computed from significance tests when the means and standard deviations of the measures have not been provided in the study. For example, if a study compared a treatment group with a control group and reported the results of a t test, but did not report means and standard deviations, a d value could be computed from t as follows: $d = 2t/\sqrt{df}$. Second, effect sizes indices can be converted from one effect size to another. For example, if the researchers chose to use the effect size d as their effect size index for the meta-analysis, but a few studies to be included express effect size as r, then r can be converted to d as follows: $d = 2r/\sqrt{1 - r^2}$.

Number of Effect Sizes.   Each study in the meta-analysis should yield at least one effect size. It is not uncommon, however, to observe studies that compare a treatment group with a control group on many measures. An effect size could be computed for each measure of the study. However, when studies have more than one measure, the measures are usually related or correlated, and computing more than one effect size yields redundant information and gives too much weight to that particular study. Therefore, the researcher should select one representative measure from the study or use a statistical method to determine a representative measure. A common statistical method is to compute a weighted mean of the related measures of the study. However, there are more sophisticated methods for computing a representative effect size when there are correlated measures that make use of the strength of the correlations.

If the researcher is convinced that some of the measures in the study are representative of different constructs (i.e., independent of each other) more than one effect size may be computed from that study. For example, in the Connor et al. (2002) meta-analysis, there were 28 studies, but 35 effect size indices. Aggression-related behaviors were divided into overt and covert aggression based on extensive clinical support. These two types of measures were considered independent of each other. According to the authors, when individual studies had more than one measure of each type of aggression, ". . . effect sizes for each discrete measure were averaged to arrive at a maximum of one overt aggression effect size and one covert aggression effect size per study" (p. 254).

Weights. For the most part, each study included in the meta-analysis is based on a different sample size. Studies with larger sample sizes are likely to be better estimates than studies with small sample sizes. Therefore, in order to take sample size into consideration when the effect sizes are averaged, a weight is computed for each effect size. Effect sizes also can be weighted by other important indices, such as quality of the study.

Computation of Combined Effect Size for Studies and Related Statistics

When all studies that meet the criteria for inclusion in the meta-analysis have been coded and effect size data entered, a *combined effect size* can be computed. Frequently there is an effect size computed for each construct. In the Connor et al. (2002) meta-analysis, two different mean effect sizes were computed, one for the construct of overt aggression ($d = .84$) and one for the construct of covert aggression ($d = .69$). Each of these mean effect sizes was based on a weighted average. Connor et al. (2002) computed their weighted average by ". . . weighting each value of d by its corresponding sample size and quality rating" (pp. 254–255). In addition to a mean effect size index computed for each construct, a confidence interval, usually 95%, also is obtained. Analyses also are performed to test for statistical significance and to test for homogeneity as discussed next.

A common method of testing for *statistical significance of the mean effect size* is called the Stouffer method and is based on adding z values. Connor et al. (2002) obtained their z values by multiplying each effect size, d, by the square root of the sample size. This procedure, computation of a z value, is done for each effect size in the meta-analysis. An overall z value is obtained, yielding a corresponding p value. If the p value is less than .05, a statistically significant outcome is assumed. For example, Connor et al. (2002) combined 18 independent effect sizes of clinicians' ratings. They found, "The combined z test of these effects was significant, indicating that stimulant treatment reduces clinicians' ratings of aggression ($z = 6.53$, $p < .0001$ . . .)" (p. 256).

The second statistical analysis common to meta-analysis is the *test for homogeneity of the effect size* distribution. Is the mean effect size of a particular construct representative of the population effect size? How much variability should be expected around the mean effect size? The assumption is made that if the distribution is homogeneous, then the variability around the effect size is no greater than would be expected from sampling error (Lipsey & Wilson, 2001). However, if the variability around the mean effect size is large (effect size distribution is heterogeneous), then it appears that each effect size is not estimating a common population mean. In order to test for a homogeneous distribution, a common test used is the Q test. If Q is statistically significant, the null hypothesis of homogeneity is rejected and the researcher assumes a heterogeneous distribution. Another statistical test that can be used to test for a homogeneous effect size distribution is the χ^2 test of goodness of fit. Connor et al. (2002) reported a significant mean effect size indicating that stimulant treatment reduces clinicians' ratings of aggression. They followed up this finding by testing the mean effect size distribution for homogeneity using the χ^2 test of goodness of fit. Their result was statistically significant, rejecting the null hypothesis of a homogeneous distribution.

Follow-Up Procedures

When a test for homogeneity of effect size distribution is statistically significant, the researcher can take a number of steps to explain the heterogeneity (Lipsey & Wilson, 2001).

Assume a Random Effects Model. *Before* undertaking the task of computing a meta-analysis, it is important to consider what generalizations will be made from the resulting effect size estimate. There are two models from which to choose, one with fixed effects and one with random effects. In a *fixed effects model*, the researcher is attempting to generalize only to studies that are the same as those included in the meta-analysis. The effect size generated from each study would be an estimate of the population effect size except for random error due to sampling variability. In other words, if each study had an infinite sample size, all of the studies would yield identical effect sizes. In the *random effects model*, there is random error due to subject level sampling, similar to the fixed effects model, and also random error due to study level sampling (problems in sampling of studies into the meta-analysis.) Study level sampling variability could be due to differences in how therapeutic procedures were carried out or due to different settings of the study. The random effects model does not propose a single underlying effect size identical in all studies; instead, the effect sizes are presumed to be randomly distributed, with the average as representative of these studies. When the test for homogeneity of effect size distribution is significant, *one possibility* is that the data fit a random effects model.

Identify Systematic Variability. The most common follow-up procedure when a test for homogeneity of effect size distribution is statistically significant is to attempt to identify the variability that is contributing to the heterogeneity. Most often, the researcher has in mind, prior to the meta-analysis, certain hypotheses about which variables might contribute to variability in the mean effect size. These variables (such as strength of research design, sample subgroups, gender, etc.) are usually referred to as *moderator* variables. In the Connor et al. (2002) study they found 13 studies of *parent-rated* overt aggression. In these studies, the stimulant significantly reduced parents' ratings of aggression. The heterogeneity statistic was significant. Therefore, Connor et al. introduced moderator variables to help explain the heterogeneity. Diagnosis was one moderator variable that was introduced. "Parent-reporter effect sizes obtained from 10 samples of children with a primary diagnosis of ADHD (mean $d = .910$) were significantly larger than those obtained from two studies of children with ADHD and mental retardation (MR) (mean $d = 0.173$ [contrast $z = 4.70$, $p < .0001$])" (p. 256).

In some cases, heterogeneity may be assumed, but introduction of moderator variables fails to be related to the mean effect size. Connor et al. (2002) found a significant relationship between stimulant treatment effect and the reduction of *clinicians' ratings* of overt aggression in 18 studies. Even though the group of effect sizes was significantly heterogeneous, Connor et al. failed to find any moderator variables that were significantly related to the mean effect size for clinicians' ratings. They concluded, "These findings suggest that factors other than those coded in the present meta-analysis are responsible for the variability in this group of effect sizes" (p. 256).

Meta-analysis is a valuable tool for both the researcher and the clinician. Summarizing the results of many studies as an effect size index provides important strength of relationship information. Caution always should be used concerning the types of studies that went into the meta-analysis; especially, one should be aware of design issues.

Chapter 36

Effect Sizes and Clinical Significance

Behavioral scientists are interested in answering three basic questions when examining the relationships between variables (Kirk, 2001). First, is an observed result real or should it be attributed to chance (i.e., statistical significance)? Second, if the result is real, how large is it (i.e., effect size)? Third, is the result large enough to be meaningful and useful (i.e., clinical or practical significance)? In this chapter, we treat clinical significance as equivalent to practical significance.

CLINICAL SIGNIFICANCE

The clinical significance of a treatment is based on external standards provided by clinicians, patients, and/or researchers. Unfortunately, to date there is little consensus about the criteria for these efficacy standards. Several such criteria are: lowering the percentage of treated clients with negative outcomes or at risk, eliminating the problem, or attaining normative levels of function (meeting or exceeding the cut score) at the end of treatment. Jacobson, Roberts, Berns, and McGlinchey (1999) defined clinical significance as a change that results in normal functioning due to therapy, and they suggested approaches for identifying patients who made statistically reliable changes that were clinically significant according to their definition.

Judgments by the researcher and the consumers (e.g., clinicians and patients) regarding clinical significance should consider factors such as clinical benefit, cost, and side effects. Although there is no formal statistical test of clinical significance, we suggest using an effect size measure to assist in interpreting clinical significance. In this chapter, we review briefly the d and r effect size measures and expand the discussion of measures of risk potency (e.g., odds ratio) introduced in chapter 27. Finally we present a relatively new effect size, AUC, which stands for area under the curve. However, for ease of understanding, this measure could be called the probability of a superior (better) outcome of one treatment over another. AUC integrates many of the other effect size indices and is directly related to clinical significance. Grissom (1994) and Kraemer et al. (2002) provide more information on this relatively new effect size. Each of these measures, however, has limitations that require the clinician to be cautious about interpretation. Guidelines are offered to facilitate the interpretation and understanding of clinical significance.

PROBLEMS WITH STATISTICAL SIGNIFICANCE

A statistically significant outcome indicates only that there is likely to be at least some relationship between the variables. In other words, the p value indicates the probability that an outcome this extreme could happen, if the null hypothesis were true. Statistical significance, however, does not provide information about the strength of the relationship (effect size) or whether the relationship is meaningful (clinical significance).

Sometimes researchers misinterpret statistically significant results as showing clinical significance. However, it is quite possible, with a large sample, to have a statistically significant result from a weak relationship between variables (i.e., a small effect size). In addition, sometimes researchers misinterpret nonstatistically significant results as "proving" the null hypothesis—for example, as showing that two treatments have equivalent effects. However, a nonsignificant result may not be due to a small effect size, but to unreliable measures, inadequate designs, insensitive analyses, or other determinants of low power. Because the presence or absence of statistical significance does not give information about the size or importance of the outcome, it is critical to know the effect size (i.e., the strength of the relationship between the independent variable and the dependent variable).

EFFECT SIZE MEASURES

Statisticians have proposed many effect size measures. They fall mainly into three types or families: the r family, the d family, and measures of risk potency.

The r Family. One method of expressing effect sizes is in terms of strength of association, with statistics such as the Pearson product–moment correlation coefficient, r, used when both the independent and the dependent measures are ordered. Such effect sizes vary between -1.0 and $+1.0$, with 0 representing no effect. This family of effect sizes also includes associational statistics such as the Spearman or Kendall rank correlation coefficients, and the multiple correlation coefficient (R).

The d Family. These effect sizes are used when the independent variable is binary (dichotomous) and the dependent variable is ordered. The d family effect sizes use different formulas, but they all express the mean difference in standard deviation units. Effect sizes for d range from minus to plus infinity, with zero indicating no effect; however, it is unusual to find d values in the applied behavioral sciences much greater than 1.

Measures of Risk Potency. These effect sizes are used when both the independent and the dependent variable are binary. There are many such effect sizes, but in this chapter we discuss five common ones: odds ratio, risk ratio, relative risk reduction, risk difference, and number needed to treat (NNT). Odds ratios and risk ratios vary from 0 to infinity, with 1 indicating no effect. Relative risk reduction and risk difference range from -1 to 1, with zero indicating no effect. Finally, NNT ranges from 1 to plus infinity, with very *large values* indicating no treatment effect.

AUC. Finally we discuss one index that can be used when the independent variable is binary, but the dependent variable can be either binary or ordered (Grissom & Kim, 2005). This measure ranges from 0% to 100%, with 50% indicating no effect, and it has a unique status in that it was originally proposed to address clinical significance.

Unfortunately, there is little agreement about which effect size to use for each situation. The most commonly discussed effect size in the behavioral sciences, especially for experiments, is d, but the correlation coefficient, r, and other measures of the strength of association are common in survey research. In medical journals, an odds ratio is most common.

In the remainder of this chapter, we discuss the use and interpretation of each of the above measures and discuss the advantages and disadvantages of each of the above measures as indicators of clinical significance. In this discussion, we focus on positive association only—that is, effect sizes ranging from the value that indicates no effect to the value indicating maximal effect. (If association were negative, one need only change the sign of one variable, or switch two categories to make a negative association positive.)

INTERPRETING d AND r EFFECT SIZES

Table 36.1 expands Table 22.1, providing general guidelines for interpreting the size of the effect for five measures discussed in this chapter. As discussed in chapter 22, Cohen (1988) provided research examples of what he labeled small, medium, and large effects suggested by d and r values. Most researchers would not consider a correlation (r) of .5 to be very strong because only 25% of the variance in the dependent variable is predicted. However, Cohen argued that when the two variables measure different constructs, an r of .3 is typical and .5 is about as large as correlations in applied behavioral sciences get. When, as in test–retest reliability measures, the two variables measure the same construct, typical correlations are much higher; for example, .7 or more.

Cohen (1988) also pointed out that effects with a d of .8 are "grossly perceptible and therefore large differences . . ." (p. 27). Cohen's medium size effect is "visible to the naked eye. That is, in the course of normal experiences, one would become aware of an average difference . . ." (p. 26). Kazdin and Bass (1989), based on a review of psychotherapy research, found that d was approximately .8 when comparing a new active treatment against an inactive (treatment withheld) placebo. Comparing a new effective treatment with a usual or comparison treatment would produce a d of about .5.

The d and r guidelines in Table 36.1 are based on the effect sizes commonly found in studies in the applied behavioral sciences. They do not have absolute meaning; Cohen's "large," "medium," and "small" were meant to be relative to typical findings in behavioral research in general. For that reason, we suggest using "larger than typical" instead of "large,"

TABLE 36.1
Interpretation of the Strength (Effect Size) of a Positive Relationship

General Interpretation of the Strength of a Relationship	d	r	2 × 2 Associations		
			AUC	RD	NNT
Much larger than typical	≥1.00	≥.70	≥76%	≥52%	≤1.9
Large or larger than typical	.80	.50	71%	43%	2.3
Medium or typical	.50	.30	64%	28%	3.6
Small or smaller than typical	.20	.10	56%	11%	8.9

Note. We interpret the numbers in this table as a range of values. For example, a d greater than .90 (or less than –.90) would be described as much "larger than typical," in the applied behavioral sciences, a d between say .70 and .90 would be called "larger than typical," and d between say .60 and .70 would be "typical to larger than typical." We interpret the other columns similarly.

"typical" instead of "medium," and "smaller than typical" instead of "small." However, as suggested by the Kazdin and Bass (1989) results, it is advisable to examine the research literature to see if there is information about typical effect sizes *in that context*. The standards then expressed in Table 36.1 would need to be adjusted accordingly.

There are disadvantages of the d and r effect sizes as measures of clinical significance. First, they are relatively abstract, and consequently may not be meaningful to patients and clinicians, or even to researchers. They were not originally intended to be indexes of clinical significance and are not readily interpretable in terms of how much *individuals* are affected by treatment.

INTERPRETING MEASURES OF RISK POTENCY

Clinicians must make categorical decisions about whether or not to use a treatment (medication, therapy, hospitalization), and the outcomes also are often binary. For example, a child is classified as having ADHD or not, or being at risk for some negative outcome or not. In comparing two treatments, a positive outcome might indicate that the patient is sufficiently improved (or not) to meet the criteria for a clinically significant change. These binary decisions and outcomes provide data in a 2×2 contingency table.

The *phi coefficient*, which applies the formula for the Pearson or Spearman correlation coefficient to 2×2 data, is sometimes used here. For example, phi was computed from the outcome of giving the Salk vaccine to half of several hundred thousand children to see if it prevented polio. The effect of receiving the vaccine seemed by the r standards in Table 36.1 to be small (phi = .01). However, the more different the distributions of the two binary variables, the more restricted the range of phi. For example, in the Salk vaccine case, less than 1% in either group developed polio, but approximately 50% of the study sample received the vaccine. Thus, the maximal possible value of phi was .02, considerably less than theoretical maximum of 1.0. In the Salk example, the observed phi was about halfway between random (0) and its maximal value (.02), rather than 1% of the way if it was judged on the usual r scale. For this reason it is difficult, if not possible, to extract clinical meaning from phi.

All the measures described below are used when researchers and clinicians have a 2×2 contingency table to express the risk of clinical level outcomes (i.e., the success or failure of a treatment). In some cases, a 2×2 table results when initially continuous outcome data are dichotomized (e.g., when responses on an ordered outcome measure in a clinical trial are reclassified as "success" and "failure"). Such dichotomization not only results in a loss of information, but, as Kraemer (1992) pointed out, dichotomizing

TABLE 36.2
Several Measures of Effect Size When the Failure Rate Included
Both "Not Improved" and "Somewhat Improved" Patients

	Failure (Not Improved and Somewhat)	Successes (Very Improved)	Odds
Comparison group	84%	16%	5.25
Treatment group	62%	38%	1.63

Note. OR = 3.22; RR = 1.35; RRR = 26%; RD = 22%; NNT = 4.55; AUC = 61%.

TABLE 36.3
Several Measures of Effect Size When the Failure
Rate Included Only "Not Improved" Patients

	Failure (Not Improved)	Success (Somewhat and Very Improved)	Odds
Comparison group	68%	32%	2.13
Treatment group	10%	90%	.11

Note. OR = 19.12; RR = 6.80; RRR = 85%; RD = 58%; NNT = 1.72; AUC = 79%.

can result in inconsistent and arbitrary effect size indexes due to different choices of the cut point or threshold for failure, whatever effect size is used.

In order to illustrate the risk potency effect sizes and the associated interpretation problems, we present the examples in Tables 36.2 and 36.3. Although these are hypothetical examples, they are similar to recently published data from a randomized controlled trial (RCT), where 50% of the subjects were randomly assigned to each group. The tables show the percent of subjects in the treatment and comparison groups for each of two outcomes, failure and success. Table 36.2 shows results when "failure" includes both "not improved" and "somewhat improved" responses, whereas Table 36.3 includes only "not improved" as "failures." Any response not classified as "failure" is considered a "success."

Odds Ratio. OR, the most commonly reported of these measures, is determined by first computing the odds, the ratio of the percentage judged to fail (failure rate) to the percentage judged as successes (success rate) within both the comparison and intervention groups. In Table 36.2, these two ratios are 5.25 (84/16) for the comparison group and 1.63 (62/38) for the intervention group. The odds ratio is then obtained by dividing the comparison group odds of failure by that of the intervention group. The odds ratio is 3.22 (5.25/1.63), indicating that the odds of failing to improve for a comparison group member are 3.22 times as high as those from the treatment group. If one compared the odds of *success* in the treatment group to that in the comparison group, one would get the same OR. Easier yet, one could compute the cross-product ratio: $(84 \times 38)/(16 \times 62) = 3.22$.

A major limitation of the odds ratio as an effect size index is that the magnitude of the odds ratio may approach infinity if the outcome is rare or very common, even when the association is near random or no effect. The magnitude of the OR varies strongly with the choice of cut point. For example, the only difference between Table 36.2 and Table 36.3 is the choice of cut point, but the OR in Table 36.3 is 19.12, whereas that in Table 36.2 is 3.22. Thus, there are no agreed-on standards for what represents a large odds ratio because some very large odds ratios are obtained for situations very close to random association. Consequently, odds ratios can be quite misleading as an effect size indicating clinical significance.

Risk Ratio. RR is determined by dividing the *failure rate* of the comparison group by the failure rate of the treatment group, or by dividing the *success rate* of the treatment group by that of the comparison group. In Table 36.2, if one compares failure rates, the relative risk is 1.35 or 84/62. Risk ratios are always less than odds ratios. In Table 36.3, the risk ratio of failure is 6.80. The choice of cut point and which risk ratio (failure or success) is chosen change the magnitude of the risk ratio, making it hard to interpret. Once again, because the RR may approach infinity when the risk in the denominator approaches zero, there can be no agreed-on standards for assessing the magnitude or clinical significance of RR.

Relative Risk Reduction. RRR is computed by subtracting the treatment group failure rate from the comparison group failure rate, and dividing by the latter, or by subtracting the comparison group success rate from the treatment group success rate and dividing by the former. RRR can vary between 0 and 1.0. In Table 36.2 the failure RRR is 26% ($84 - 62/84$) but in Table 36.3 it is a much larger 85%. Because the "failure" RRR may be very small when the "success" RRR is large, RRR is difficult to interpret in terms of clinical significance, and there are no agreed-upon standards for judging its magnitude.

Risk Difference. RD, also called absolute risk reduction (ARR), is computed by subtracting the percent of failures in the treatment group from the percent in the comparison group (i.e., 84% minus 62%), or, equivalently, by subtracting the percent of successes in the comparison group from that in the treatment group. In either case, in Table 36.2, RD is 22%. Risk difference can vary from 0% to 100%. When the RD is near zero, it indicates near random association. If the success or failure rates are extreme, the RD is likely to be near 0%. For example, in the Salk data, the RD was only .041% because polio was rare in the comparison group so the absolute risk of polio could not be reduced much by the vaccine. It is troublesome to note that the RD is often very near zero when the odds ratio and one of the risk ratios are very large.

Number Needed to Treat. NNT is a relatively new measure (Laupasis, Sackett, & Roberts, 1988) that has been recommended for improving the reporting of effect sizes. However, it has not yet been widely used (Nuovo, Melnikov, & Chang, 2002). NNT is the number of patients who must be treated to generate one more success or one less failure than would have resulted had all persons been given the comparison treatment. Alternatively, in risk studies, it is the number who would need to be exposed to the risk factor to generate one more problem case than if none had been so exposed.

Mathematically, NNT is the reciprocal of the risk difference. A result of 1.0 means the treatment is perfect, that every treatment subject succeeds and every comparison subject fails. The larger the NNT, the less effective is the treatment relative to the comparison. In Table 36.2, NTT is $1/.22$ or 4.55. This means that out of every 4.55 patients treated, 3.55 would get the same results as they would have had if they had been in the comparison group, and there would be one "excess" success due to treatment. In other words, 3.55 subjects would be exposed to the costs or risks of the treatment with no benefit, and only one subject out of 4.55 would gain whatever benefit the treatment confers. Although this measure of effect size has been received positively by clinicians, we find it somewhat difficult to understand and, as with the interpretation of other effect sizes indexes, the context of the study needs to be considered.

In the Salk data, the NNT was 2,439. Because the benefit was the prevention of serious disability or death and the cost and risks of the vaccine were very low, subjecting 2,438 subjects to the vaccination who did not benefit from it was considered acceptable to save one person from polio. If the outcome had been the common cold, and the treatment involved a drug with both high cost and side effects, an NNT of 2,439 would have been clinically unacceptable.

AUC or the Probability of a Better Outcome. This relatively new effect size might substitute for either *d* family measures or measures of risk potency. It represents the probability that a randomly selected participant in the treatment group has a better result than a randomly selected one in the comparison group. As shown in Table 36.1, one can define guidelines for interpreting AUC that correspond to those for *d.* For example, a medium or typical effect size of $d = .5$ corresponds to AUC = 64%. Thus, when comparing a treatment subject against a comparison subject, 64% of the time the treatment subject would have a better response.

In situations where measures of risk potency are used, $RD = 1/NNT = 2 \times AUC - 1$. Thus, as in Table 36.1, one can present standards for RD and NNT that correspond to those for d. For example, a medium or typical effect size of $d = .5$ corresponds to AUC = 64%, which corresponds also to RD = 28% and to NNT = 3.6 subjects. An AUC of 50% corresponds to a d or RD of 0 and an NNT of infinity; all indicate no effect. The computation of AUC from d is provided in Kraemer et al. (2003).

AUC is of special interest because it can be computed based on clinical judgments alone. One could randomly select pairs of subjects, one of each pair in the treatment and one in the comparison group, and submit their clinical records to experts with group membership masked. The experts would then be asked which of the two had a better outcome. The proportion of the pairs for which the experts selected the treatment group subject as better off is an estimate of AUC. For this reason, AUC has special appeal as a measure of clinical significance.

Finally, AUC helps us understand the problem of cut points. When one imposes dichotomization on an ordered outcome, there is a tacit declaration that all variation above the cut point and all below the cut point have no clinical relevance. All that matters in comparing the outcome for one subject to another is whether the outcome lies above or below the cut point. Thus in a cancer trial, where survival past 5 years is a "success," someone who survives 5 years + 1 day is considered as having an equivalent outcome to someone who survives 50 years, and someone who survives 5 years – 1 day as having an equivalent outcome to someone who survives 1 day. If this reflects good clinical judgment, then a treatment patient who survived 50 years is considered tied with a comparison group patient who survived 5 years + 1 day, and the tie is randomly broken in computing the AUC. The more such ties there are, the more the AUC is reduced from its original value computed from the ordered scores. The relevant question in comparing Tables 36.2 and 36.3 is whether clinicians think that "somewhat improved" is clinically equivalent to "not improved" or instead to "very improved."

SUMMARY

Which of the measures of effect size presented here is the most appropriate for reporting clinical significance? Clearly, r family effect sizes address a problem that none of the other effect sizes address—association between two ordered variables. When one of the variables is binary (dichotomous) and the other ordered, the d family effect sizes are familiar to researchers but, like r, d is not designed for and probably not very helpful to patients and clinicians. However, d can easily be converted to AUC, which is very helpful to patients and clinicians.

When both of the variables are binary, despite their popularity with medical researchers, odds ratios, risk ratios, and relative risk reduction are best avoided. One could easily convert risk difference or number needed to treat to AUC, and thus have a clinically useful effect size comparable to that derived from d.

Nuovo et al. (2002) pointed out that the Consolidated Standards on Reporting Trials (CONSORT) statement (Altman et al., 2001) recommends reporting the number needed to treat (NNT) or the risk difference (RD). However, often RD can seem unimpressively small, and NNT may seem very large, suggesting very little effect of treatment. In many such cases with small RD or large NNT, one of the risk ratios and one of the relative risk reduction measures and, most of all, the odds ratio can give an inflated impression of the size of the effect, thus exaggerating apparent clinical significance. For this reason, our preferred effect size for understanding clinical significance would tend to be AUC, but remember that d, NNT, and RD are all mathematically equivalent and can be converted to AUC.

We have provided some general guidelines for interpreting measures of clinical significance. It is not possible, however, to provide any fixed standards that a clinician could use to conclude that an effect size was clinically significant. It makes a difference whether the treatment is for a deadly disease like polio, or for the common cold, and whether the treatment is risky and costly or perfectly safe and free. The context in which an effect size is used matters in interpreting the size of the effect; the effect size only facilitates consideration of clinical significance in the context of its use.

EVALUATION OF RESEARCH VALIDITY

Framework for a Comprehensive Evaluation of the Research Validity of a Study

OVERVIEW

This chapter summarizes and integrates many of the concepts from the preceding chapters, and it expands our framework (presented briefly in chap. 19) to evaluate the quality of the design and analysis of a quantitative study (i.e., the *research validity* of a study). This framework uses several research validity rating scales adapted from those developed by Gliner and Morgan (2000) and Morgan, Gliner, and Harmon (1999). Here we discuss key concepts and present several figures and tables that provide the information needed to make a comprehensive evaluation of the research validity of an empirical quantitative study. The four studies described and evaluated briefly in chapters 1 and 19 are evaluated using this expanded framework in chapter 38.

The Cook and Campbell Framework

Our framework is based on four research validity constructs originally proposed by Campbell and Stanley (1963/1966) and updated by Cook and Campbell (1979) and by Shadish et al. (2002). Our evaluation plan also was influenced by the recent What Works Clearinghouse (n.d.) framework called the Design and Implementation Device (DIAD) (http://w-w-c.org/reports/study_standards_final.pdf) endorsed by the Campbell Collaboration (n.d.; www.campbellcollaboration.org). The What Works system is designed specifically to evaluate intervention research. A major difference between our framework and the What Works framework (and most discussions of Cook and Campbell) is that our framework is designed to be used with both experimental (i.e., intervention) and nonexperimental research approaches.

Several issues came up using Cook and Campbell's (1979) criteria for validity. Specifically their terminology and their many "threats" to validity posed four types of problems. First, there was confusion about the uses of certain common research terms. For example, the term *validity* for Cook and Campbell refers to the design of the whole study, but a more common use refers to the validity of a measurement or test. To make matters more confusing, Cook and Campbell divided the validity of a study into four aspects now labeled *statistical validity, internal validity, construct validity*, and *external validity*.

Second, validity has sometimes been assumed to be all or nothing, a study or test was or was not valid. We think research validity should be assessed on eight continua, from high to low, as discussed in this chapter. Third, Cook and Campbell's specific threats to validity were hard to remember because many have peculiar names (e.g., history, interactions with selection, and mortality). Fourth, it was easy to lose track of the main issues because there are many different threats to validity that deal with very specific, sometimes uncommon, situations. It was easy not to see the forest, only the trees.

Other Evaluation Frameworks

Many of the books that discuss the evaluation of research studies (e.g., McMillan & Wergin, 2002; Pyrczak, 2003) have a broader or less focused framework than ours, emphasizing how completely, appropriately, and clearly the various parts (title, abstract, introduction, results, and discussion) of the article were written. Although we pose a few evaluation questions about how the study was written, the emphasis here is on the method section of an article. A study that is poorly written or inadequately justified, but well designed, may have less impact than if it was well written. However, good writing should not substitute for a poor design.

Of course, the importance or significance of the research problem is a key issue, but its evaluation is beyond the scope of this book and is best done by content experts in the area of study. (Indirect evaluation of the importance of the content is provided if the article is published in a peer reviewed journal; see question 17, later in this chapter.) A well-designed study on a trivial topic will not add much to the knowledge in a field. On the other hand, a poorly designed study, especially if convincingly written, may be accepted uncritically and even set the field back because the results are misleading.

Our Evaluation Framework

The evaluation framework described in this chapter is based on 19 questions. Some request descriptive information about the design and some ask for an evaluative rating. These questions are numbered and presented in bold throughout the chapter. Chapter 38 is a narrative evaluation of the four sample studies using these 19 questions and the 8 rating scales provided in this chapter.

The 19 questions are divided into three main groups. Questions 1–8 are about describing/naming key aspects of the design and methods, including the variables, research questions/hypotheses, approach, design, and support for the reliability and validity of each key measure.

The heart of the evaluation is questions 9–16, which utilize, in part, the answers to questions 1–8 to make eight evaluative ratings. These ratings fall under four main headings or aspects of research validity. We label these four key dimensions or aspects of research validity: (a) measurement reliability and statistics (question 9), (b) internal validity (questions 10 and 11), (c) measurement validity of the constructs (questions 12 and 13), and (d) external validity (questions 14–16).

Questions 17–19 are general evaluation questions about peer review (17), the link between literature and/or theory and the research questions (18), and the clarity and accuracy of the authors' title, abstract, and discussion, given the evaluation of the aspects of research validity (19). These last three questions are intended to provide a general estimate of three aspects of the article not well covered by our evaluation of the design.

As mentioned earlier, our research evaluation framework maintains the four dimensions of research validity identified by Cook and Campbell, but somewhat modifies the labels to help prevent the confusions mentioned above and to focus on the main issues. Before discussing these dimensions, we want to review reliability and validity in a broader context. Doing this also should help avoid some of the potential semantic confusion.

It is important to distinguish between the merit or worth of the study as a whole (*research validity*) as opposed to the quality of the measurement of each separate variable or test used in the study (*measurement validity*). As shown in Fig. 37.1, measurement reliability and validity (top two boxes) are different from, but related to, aspects of research validity (middle boxes), all four of which determine the overall research validity of a study (bottom box). Within each box, we list the number of the question we use to evaluate that aspect of validity. The horizontal arrow (1) from measurement reliability (Q7) to measurement validity (Q8) indicates that reliability or consistency is a necessary (but not sufficient) precursor for the validity of a measure. The vertical arrow (2) from measurement reliability (Q7) to overall measurement reliability and statistics (Q9) indicates that an important

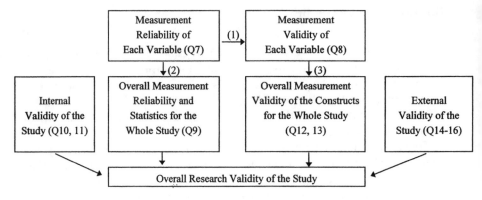

FIG. 37.1.   Schematic diagram showing how the overall research validity of a study depends on the four major aspects or dimensions of research validity and, in turn, on the measurement reliability and validity of the several variables.

determinant of the quality of the statistical analysis is the strength of the support for the reliability of the specific instruments used. Likewise the vertical arrow (3) from measurement validity (Q8) to overall measurement validity of the constructs (Q12, Q13) indicates that this dimension is dependent on the evidence for the measurement validity of all of the variables.

Ideally a study should be rated high on each of the four main evaluation criteria or dimensions of research validity (shown in the middle row of boxes of Fig. 37.1). However, there are always trade-offs and few, if any, studies are high on all criteria. Furthermore, the weight that researchers give to each of the criteria varies. For example, experimental researchers, especially medical researchers who do randomized clinical trials and meta-analyses for evidence-based practice, give more weight to internal validity. Survey researchers tend to value population external validity, and qualitative researchers value ecological external validity. Our experience and the sample studies we evaluate at the end of this chapter indicate that usually studies compromise one or more aspects of external validity to achieve high internal validity or vice versa.

ANALYSIS OF THE DESIGN AND METHODS

Variables and Their Measurement Levels

1. What were the key *independent*/antecedent/predictor *variable(s)*? For *each*:
   (a) Is it an active, attribute, or change over time independent variable?

(b) **What is the *number* of *levels*/categories?**

(c) **What is the level of *measurement* (nominal, dichotomous, ordinal, or approximately normal), especially if the independent variable is an attribute?**

In chapter 6, we make an important distinction between *active* (sometimes called manipulated) *independent variables* and *attribute independent variables* that are characteristics of the participants. This distinction is important because it divides quantitative research studies into two main types: experimental (with one or more active independent variable) and nonexperimental (with only attribute variables). See Table 11.1 and Fig. 11.1 for more detail about this distinction and its implications.

Table 37.1 provides definitions for the traditional *measurement* terms and how they differ from ours based on Kraemer (personal communication, 1999). Chapter 7 provides more details about why we use these somewhat nontraditional measurement terms and also more information about variables and their measurement. In experiments, the level of measurement for the active independent variable is usually not stated but is often dichotomous or nominal, producing two or more groups to compare.

2. **What were the key *dependent*/outcome *variable(s)*? For *each*, what is the level of *measurement*?**

TABLE 37.1
Traditional Measurement Terms and Our Recommended Terms

Traditional Term	Traditional Definition	Our Term	Our Definition
Nominal	Two or more *unordered* categories	Nominal	Three or more *unordered* categories.
—	—	Dichotomous	Two categories, either ordered or unordered.
Ordinal	*Ordered* levels, in which the difference in magnitude between levels is not equal	Ordinal	Three or more *ordered* levels, but the frequency distribution of the scores is *not* normally distributed.
Interval and ratio	Interval: *ordered* levels, in which the difference between levels is equal, but there is no true zero. Ratio: *ordered* levels; the difference between levels is equal, and there is a true zero.	Approximately normal	Many (at least five) *ordered* levels or scores, with the frequency distribution of the scores being approximately normally distributed.

As stated earlier, Table 37.1 can be used to identify the level or scale of measurement. The level of measurement helps determine the appropriateness of the statistics used in the study. Again, refer to chapters 6 and 7 for more details.

Research Hypotheses/Questions, Approaches, and Design

3. What were the main *research questions* or hypotheses?

Most studies have several questions or hypotheses, often spelled out in the introduction and/or method section of the article. Chapter 12 provided examples of descriptive, difference, and associational research questions and the types of statistics that are commonly used with each of them. Chapters 22–32 provide concrete examples of the research questions posed by a number of studies and discussions of how those questions were answered with the results of statistical tests.

4. What was the *research approach* (i.e., descriptive, associational, comparative, quasi-experimental, and/or randomized experimental) *for each question?*

Note that studies with a number of research questions may have more than one approach. Table 37.2 and the answers to question 1 help one decide which approach was used for each research question. Some studies have one or several descriptive research questions, especially about the dependent variables. However, almost all quantitative studies published in peer-reviewed journals go beyond the purely descriptive approach to compare groups and/or associate/relate variables. Thus, most studies also will use one (or more) of the other four approaches (see also chap. 11). If a study has an active independent variable we would call it an experimental study even if the researcher also asks questions using attribute independent variables such as gender. Studies with no active independent variables are called nonexperimental or observational; they often have comparative, associational, and descriptive research questions.

Identifying the research approach is important because the approach influences the internal validity of a study and inferences about whether the independent variable *caused* any change in the dependent variable. In general, the randomized experimental approach produces the best evidence for causation. Neither the comparative nor the associational approaches are well suited to providing evidence about causes. Quasi-experimentation is usually in between.

TABLE 37.2
A Comparison of the Five Basic Quantitative Research Approaches

Criteria	Randomized Experimental	Quasi-Experimental	Comparative	Associational	Descriptive
Random assignment of participants to groups by the investigator	Yes	No	No	No (only one group)	No groups
Independent variable is active	Yes	Yes	No (attribute)	No (attribute)	No independent variable
Independent variable is controlled *by the investigator*[a]	Always	Sometimes	No	No	No
Independent variable has only a few levels/categories[b]	Usually	Usually	Usually	Typically 5+ or-dered levels	No
Associations between variables or comparison of groups	Yes (comparison)	Yes (comparison)	Yes (comparison)	Yes (association)	No

[a]Although this is a desired quality of randomized experimental and quasi-experimental designs, it is not sufficient for distinguishing between the randomized experimental and quasi-experimental approaches.

[b]This distinction is made for educational purposes and is only "usually" true. In the associational approach, the independent variable usually is *assumed to be continuous*; i.e., it *has many ordered levels/*categories. We consider the approach to be associational if the independent variable has five or more *ordered* categories. Except for this difference and a difference in the statistics typically used with them, the comparative and associational approaches are the same. Note that there are associational statistics that can be used when there are a few, nominal levels of the independent variable.

5. What was the *general design classification, if* the approach is randomized experimental, quasi-experimental, or comparative?

If the study has randomized experimental, quasi-experimental, or comparative research question(s), the design classification can be identified using chapter 16 and Table 16.1. This requires knowing (a) the number of *factors* (i.e., independent variables), (b) the number of *levels/values* of each factor, and (c) whether the *design* is *between groups, within subjects* (repeated measures) or *mixed.* For example, a design might be described as a 3 × 2 (mixed) factorial design with repeated measures on the second factor. This means that there are two independent variables, the first with three levels/ groups and the second with two levels or, in this case, measured at two times because there are repeated measures. This classification of designs applies to not only the randomized experimental and quasi-experimental approaches (which is typical) but also to comparative approach questions, where there is no active/manipulated independent variable. Note that the mentioned 3 × 2 mixed design could be the typical experimental or quasi-experimental pretest–posttest design with three groups (e.g., two treatments and a control) or it could be a longitudinal (two ages) design comparing three types of participants (e.g., securely attached vs. avoidant vs. disorganized) over time.

6. What was the *specific experimental design* name *if* the approach is randomized experimental or quasi-experimental?

The names of specific randomized experimental or quasi-experimental designs are provided in Table 14.1, an overview schematic diagram of most of the common designs and their names (see also chaps. 13 and 14). Randomized clinical trials (RCT) usually use pretest–posttest comparison (control) group designs.

Note that if the specific research question/hypothesis and *approach* are *associational,* the analysis will usually be done with some type of correlation or multiple regression, and questions 5 and 6 are not applicable.

Measurement Reliability and Validity for Each Key Variable

Questions 7 and 8 require an evaluation based on the principle that in a good study each key variable should be measured *reliably* and *validly*. Therefore, you should evaluate these aspects of *each* measured variable. Chapters 8 and 9 discuss measurement reliability and validity and point out that instruments are not valid or invalid per se. The data they produce are reliable and valid to some extent, for some purpose, and with some population, based on the evidence available.

7. Was the *measurement reliability* for *each* key variable acceptable?
(a) What type(s) of evidence for reliability were presented?
(b) Was the evidence or support for *each* key variable acceptable?
(*No, Maybe, Yes*)

Were test–retest, parallel forms, internal consistency, and/or interrater reliability evidence cited or obtained, and how strong is the *evidence* for the *reliability of the measurement* for each key variable? Table 37.3 and chapter 8 help identify what type(s) of reliability evidence were provided. (Note that active independent variables and demographic variables seldom have information about measurement reliability or validity, but in some cases they ought to). However, for most attribute independent variables and for dependent variables, the method section should report some evidence to support measurement reliability.

A reliability coefficient of .70 or higher is usually considered necessary for a variable to be measured with acceptable reliability, but in a complex study a few reliability coefficients above .60 are common and marginally ac-

TABLE 37.3
Measurement Reliability and Validity (for Q7a and Q8a)

Measurement Reliability: Stability or Consistency	Measurement Validity: Accuracy or Correctness

The participant gets the same or very similar score from a test, observation, or rating. There is evidence for reliability of:
a. *Participants' responses*
  1. *Test–retest reliability*—stability over time
  2. *Parallel forms reliability*—consistency across presumably equivalent versions of the instrument
  3. *Internal consistency*—items that are to be combined are related to each other
b. *Observers' responses*
  4. *Interrater reliability*—different observers or raters give similar scores
	The score accurately reflects/measures what it was designed or intended to. Several sources of evidence can be used to support the validity of a measure:
	a. *Content evidence*—all aspects of the construct are represented in appropriate proportions
	b. *Evidence based on response processes*
	c. *Evidence based on internal structure*
	  1. Factorial—factor analysis yields a theoretically meaningful solution
	d. *Evidence based on relations to other variables*
	  1. Convergent—based on theory, variables predicted to be related are related
	  2. Discriminant—variables predicted not to be related are not
	  3. Criterion-related evidence
	    a. Predictive—the test predicts some criterion in the future
	    b. Concurrent—test and criterion are measured at the same time
	  4. Validity generalization
	e. *Evidence based on consequences of testing*

TABLE 37.4
Evaluating Measurement Reliability Coefficients (for 7b)

Correlation Coefficient	Support for Reliability
+.90	Acceptable[a]
+.80	Acceptable[b]
+.70	Acceptable[b]
+.60	Marginally acceptable[b]
+.50	Not acceptable
+.30	Not acceptable
+.10	Not acceptable
−.10	Not acceptable[c]
−.30	Not acceptable[c]
−.50	Not acceptable[c]
>−.50	Not acceptable[c]

Note. Statistical significance is not enough for measurement reliability. Examine the size and direction of the correlation.

[a]Useful for decisions about individual selection, placement, etc.

[b]Useful for research, but probably not for decision about individuals.

[c]Check data for probable errors in coding or conceptualization.

ceptable. Were reliability coefficients reported? It is desirable, but unusual, to obtain more than one type of reliability evidence (e.g., test–retest and internal consistency) for each measure. If the instruments had been used before, the author may only refer to another study and not provide actual coefficients; in this case it is probably reasonable to assume that the reliability was adequate. However, researchers who plan to use an instrument in their research should obtain the cited document(s) and personally check the evidence. Table 37.4 is one good way to evaluate evidence for the measurement reliability of each measure.

8. Was the evidence for *measurement validity* for *each* key variable acceptable?

   (a) What type(s) of evidence to support measurement validity are reported?

   (b) Was the evidence or support for *each* key variable acceptable? (*No, Maybe, Yes*)

In terms of the *validity of each measure,* authors often only cite previous studies that used the instrument without providing details about the evidence for validity; it seems reasonable to assume that such published studies provide acceptable evidence, but one should always be prudent when

TABLE 37.5
Evaluating Measurement Validity Coefficients (for 8b)

Correlation Coefficient	Support for Validity
+/−.60 or higher	Acceptable, but[a]
+/−.50	Acceptable[b,c]
+/−.30	Acceptable[b,c]
+/−.10	Maybe[b,c]

[a]If a validity coefficient is quite high (e.g., >.60), the same or very similar concepts probably are being measured, rather than two separate ones, so such high correlations may be more like measurement reliability than measurement validity.

[b]We base the strength or level of support for measurement validity on Cohen's (1988) effect size guidelines. For correlations: $r = .1$ is a small effect size so weak support for validity, $r = .3$ is a medium or typical effect size, and $r = .5$ is a large effect size and strong support. However, the correlation *must be statistically significant*. Thus, a correlation of +/−.20 would provide some support for validity only if r was significant but *no support* if r was not significant.

[c]Criterion and convergent evidence for validity would be expected to produce positive (+) correlations, unless the concepts are hypothesized to be negatively related (e.g., anxiety and GPA).

evaluating the validity of self-report measures. Table 37.5 provides one way to evaluate measurement validity when the evidence provided is a correlation coefficient (see also chap. 9).

In summary, for *each* key measure or variable, one should evaluate the evidence for measurement reliability and validity. Note that, as shown in Fig. 37.1, measurement reliability is a necessary precursor of measurement validity, and both reliability and validity (top boxes) influence aspects of research validity.

EVALUATION OF THE FOUR KEY DIMENSIONS OF RESEARCH VALIDITY

The four key criteria and eight evaluative dimensions for the validity of a study are based on the writings, as discussed earlier, of Cook and Campbell. A high-quality study should have moderate to high ratings on each of the four dimensions of research validity, as indicated by ratings on *each* of the eight scales shown in Figs. 37.2 to 37.5, using the criteria listed in these figures and discussed later. The ratings in Figs. 37.2 to 37.5 can be made using at least two strategies. First, as was done in chapter 19, a global evaluation can be made for each rating scale using the several issues listed on the scale and in the text to guide the evaluation. Second, we have provided an article evaluation form and rubrics in appendix A to provide another way to arrive at the evaluation rating for each of the eight research validity dimensions. This method involves tallying up answers to a series of *no, maybe, yes* answers

---

OVERALL MEASUREMENT RELIABILITY AND STATISTICS (for Q9)

Base rating on:
  a) Overall reliability of instruments/ measures
  b) Appropriateness of power
  c) Appropriateness of statistical techniques
  d) Adequate presentation of the statistical results including effect size
  e) Appropriateness of interpretation of the analysis

LOW   MEDIUM   HIGH
|_____|_____|
No on all   Yes on all

FIG. 37.2.   Evaluating the statistics and measurement reliability of the findings of a study.

to questions about what we think are the key issues for each of the eight dimensions. This second method is more mechanical and may miss some subtleties that experienced reviewers would want to make. However, we think this method will be helpful to less experienced readers and those who need a detailed, quantitative evaluation.

Overall Measurement Reliability and Statistics

9. **What is the overall rating of** *measurement reliability and statistics*? **Base the rating and comments on the following:**

   (a) **Was the overall measurement reliability of the variables acceptable?** (*No, Maybe, Yes*)

   (b) **Was the power appropriate?** (*No, Maybe, Yes*)

   (c) **Was the choice/use of statistics appropriate?** (*No, Maybe, Yes*)

   (d) **Was there adequate presentation of the statistical results, including effect size?** (*No, Maybe, Yes*)

   (e) **Was the interpretation of statistical results appropriate?** (*No, Maybe, Yes*)

This first dimension of research validity emphasizes the importance of the overall measurement reliability as well as the inferential statistics. Question 9 requests an overall rating of the study from low through medium to high based on five issues (see Fig. 37.2 and also chaps. 8 and 20–32).

9a. First, there is the issue of whether the *variables as a group are measured reliably*. Question 9 considers an overall rating of the measurement reliability of all the instruments. A principle often emphasized in measurement classes is that if a test does not consistently measure the construct, it can not be accurately measuring it. Likewise, a study's validity is reduced if one or more of the key measures are relatively unreliable.

9b. Second, can a statistically significant relationship be detected, assuming that such a relationship exists? The ability to detect a statistically significant difference is most commonly referred to as *power*, or the ability to reject a false null hypothesis. Although adequate power is based, in part, on having enough participants in the study, there are other methods of increasing power (Lipsey, 1990). Some of these methods include decreasing variability and increasing reliability of the dependent variable, or increasing the strength and consistency of administering the independent variable. Cook and Campbell (1979) brought up a second side to the issue of power, which involves having too much power, especially with respect to the number of participants in a study. For the most part, the problem arises when an exceptionally large sample size yields a statistically significant, but perhaps trivial, relationship. The trend toward estimating effect sizes in current research is one way of resolving this problem (see especially chaps. 22 and 35 for more about power and/or ES).

9c. A third issue to consider involves the *selection of the proper statistical method* to assess whether a relationship between the independent and dependent variable actually exists. Selection and interpretation of statistics have been discussed in more detail in chapters 23–32. Sometimes researchers select the wrong statistic, such as a *t* test or correlation with a nominal dependent variable. However, Cook and Campbell (1979) pointed out, more often problems involve violation of assumptions underlying statistical tests or problems in making several or many comparisons without adjusting the alpha level. Such problems often result in a Type I error. Our own experience suggests that not adjusting the alpha level is more common than selection of an inappropriate statistic.

9d. Fourth, were the statistical results presented adequately? Effect sizes should be given or, at least, the necessary information (e.g., M, SD, N) is presented so effect sizes can be computed. Discussion of several effect size measures is presented in chapter 36 and in many of the earlier chapters on statistics.

9e. The fifth issue to consider involves making the *proper interpretation* of the statistical analysis. Sometimes the correct statistic is selected, but the investigator misinterprets the findings, concluding more from the data than is actually provided. For example, if one has a significant interaction from the analysis of a factorial ANOVA, one should examine the simple effects rather than the main effects, which may be misleading. These issues are discussed in more detail in chapters 24–31.

Internal Validity

Internal validity is based on the strength or soundness of the design. This definition of internal validity allows us to evaluate nonexperimental as well as experimental research. Randomized experimental designs are usually high on internal validity. We believe that one can and should judge the internal validity of any study on a continuum from low to high.

Internal validity is important because it indicates how confident we can be that the relationship between an independent and dependent variable is a cause and effect relationship. Although it is important to use the appropriate statistical analysis, the statistical method does not determine causation. Causation is inferred primarily from the research approach. Thus, although "correlation does not indicate causation," the same is true for t tests and analysis of variance (ANOVA), if the approach was comparative. In general, randomized experimental designs provide the best evidence for causation (high internal validity). The comparative and associational approaches, at best, provide suggestions about possible causes. The strength of a quasi-experiment affects how much confidence we can place in whether the independent variable is a cause of the dependent variable (see chap. 17). Our evaluation framework divides internal validity into two dimensions: *equivalence of the groups* on *participant characteristics* (question 10) and *control of extraneous experience and environment variables* (question 11).

10. **What is the evaluation of the *equivalence of the groups on participant characteristics*? Base the rating and comments on:**
    (a) **Was there random assignment of participants to the groups?** (*No or Yes*)
    (b) **If no random assignment, were the participants in each group matched, made, or found to be similar on a pretest?** (*No, Maybe, Yes*) **If random assignment was done, (b) and (c) should be scored as *yes*.**
    (c) **If no random assignment, were the participants in each group matched, made, or found to be similar on other key participant characteristics (e.g., age, gender, IQ, etc.)?** (*No, Maybe, Yes*)
    (d) **Was the retention (low attrition) of subjects during the study high and similar across groups?** (*No, Maybe, Yes*)

In the *randomized experimental, quasi-experimental,* and *comparative* approaches, a key question is whether the *groups* that are compared are *equivalent in all respects except the independent variable* or variables, *before* the procedures of the study take place. There are a number of specific "threats" to internal validity, several of which are "participant" factors, that could lead to a lack of equivalence of the participants in the two (or more) groups and thus influence the relationship with the dependent variable. This dimension is often called *selection bias*, because it should be rated low if the participants choose which group they will be in (self-selection or assignment to groups). The phrase *assignment bias* is less likely to be confusing because random sampling or selection of subjects is *not relevant* to the rating of internal validity. Sampling or *selection to be in the study is relevant* to population external validity, which is question 14. The top section of Fig. 37.3 should be used to evaluate this aspect of internal validity.

10a. The way to assure that the groups are unbiased and close to equivalent is by *randomly assigning the participants to adequately sized groups*. If random assignment to groups is not possible, randomly assigning treatments to intact groups (strong quasi-experiments), matching, analysis of covariance (ANCOVA), or checking for demographic similarity of groups (10b and 10c) are all methods of achieving a medium level of this aspect of internal validity. If the groups were known to be dissimilar and no attempts were made to confirm the similarity of the groups or make the groups similar with matching, ANCOVA, and so on, the rating would be low. Associational approaches also would be rated low unless attempts were made to control for other key variables.

If the approach is *associational*, there is only one group. In that case, this aspect of internal validity comes down to the question of whether participants who score high on the independent variable of interest are equivalent to those who score low, in terms of other attributes that may be correlated with the dependent variable. It is likely that the high scorers on an attribute independent variable such as anxiety are *not* equivalent to the low scorers in terms of variables such as age, social status, education, and especially other psychological characteristics. Thus, studies using an associational approach (as well as the comparative approach) usually should be rated low on this dimension. Statistical controls may increase this aspect of internal validity to medium for the associational approach, as well as the quasi-experimental and comparative approaches, by making the groups more similar, but such techniques cannot produce high internal validity.

10d. Thus, randomized experiments are rated high on this aspect of internal validity, *unless* there is markedly different attrition (dropouts) between groups or high overall attrition during the study. It is not good if too many people drop out during the study, especially if they are mostly in one group or the other.

11. **What is the evaluation of the *control of extraneous experience and environment variables*?**

   (a) **Was the study conducted in a controlled environment?** (*No, Maybe, Yes*)

INTERNAL VALIDITY

Equivalence of Groups on Participant Characteristics **(for Q10)**

Base rating on:
  a) Were the participants randomly assigned to the groups?
  b) If not, were attempts to make groups similar (e.g., ANCOVA) or *check* group similarity
     on a pretest adequate?
  c) If no randomization, were attempts to make groups similar or check similarity on
     other key variables adequate?
  d) Was retention during the study high and similar across groups?

LOW	MEDIUM	HIGH
Groups very different, Marked differential attrition	Some attempts to equate groups or groups found to be similar	Random assignment to groups and low attrition

Control of Extraneous Experiences and Environment Variables **(For Q11)**

Base rating on:
  a)   Was the study conducted in a controlled environment?
  b)   Did the groups have equivalent environments, except for the independent variable?
  c)   Was there a no or usual treatment control group?
  d)   Were attempts to reduce other extraneous influences adequate?

LOW	MEDIUM	HIGH
Extraneous variables not controlled, no comparison group (Field setting)	Attempts to control experiences and environment	All extraneous variables controlled, eliminated or balanced (controlled lab)

FIG. 37.3.   Rating scales to evaluate the internal validity of the findings of a study.

(b) Did the groups have equivalent environments? (*No, Maybe, Yes*)

(c) Was there a no treatment (placebo) or usual treatment comparison group? (*No, Maybe, Yes*)

(d) Were there adequate attempts to reduce other extraneous influences? (*No, Maybe, Yes*)

We use the issues just listed and in the lower half of Fig. 37.3 to make the evaluation of this dimension of research validity. Several "threats" to internal validity have been grouped under a category that deals with the effects of extraneous (those variables not of interest in this study) experiences or environmental conditions during the study, also called *contamination*. (See chap. 17 for a discussion of these threats.)

   In general, well-controlled laboratory-type settings offer less contamination and field or natural settings offer less control (more contamination) of extraneous variables. This dimension of validity is rated lower if extraneous variables or events, such as different environments or teachers, affect one group more than the other(s). In the *associational approach*, the issue is whether the experiences of the participants who are high on the independent variable are different from those who are low on the independent variable. In *experimental studies*, if participants know what group they are in, that may affect their motivation and contaminate the results. In experiments without a no treatment (placebo) control group, any changes could be due to maturation or some other variable that the groups had in common.

In laboratory experimental designs, these experiential and environmental variables are usually quite well controlled, but in field experimental designs, and especially in the comparative and associational approaches, such experiences may be inadequately controlled. In general, there is a trade-off between high control of extraneous variables and high ecological validity. It is difficult to have both.

If a study is rated low or medium on either or both of the two described dimensions of internal validity, the authors should not use terms such as *effect, impact*, and *determine* that imply cause and effect. Phrases such as *may affect, presumed cause*, or *possible determinant* are more cautious, but it is probably best to avoid causal terms and to just describe the results as indicating that there is a relationship or difference.

Overall Measurement Validity of the Constructs

This dimension is often labeled *construct validity*, but that may be confusing because the same phrase has been used for one type of evidence for measurement validity. Parts of this question were dealt with in question 8. Now, we can make an *overall judgment* of the validity of the operational definitions of the several key variables in the study using Fig. 37.4. This judgment has two main aspects: the *construct validity of the intervention* or active independent variable (question 12), and measurement or *construct validity of the outcomes* (or dependent variables) *and* any attribute independent variables (question 13).

12. **What is the evaluation of the construct *validity* of the *intervention* (if any)?**
    (a) **Was the intervention (active independent variable) operationally defined and implemented a valid way, based on an existing body of empirical and/or theoretical research? (*No, Maybe, Yes*)**
    (b) **Was the intervention described in enough detail for it to be replicated? (*No, Maybe, Yes*)**
    (c) **Was there a manipulation check or verification to be sure that the intervention was presented as planned? (*No, Maybe, Yes*)**

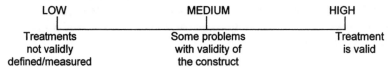

**OVERALL MEASUREMENT VALIDITY
OF THE CONSTRUCTS**

Construct Validity of the Intervention or Treatment (for Q12)

Base rating on:
  a) Appropriateness (validity) of the operational definition of the active independent
  variable (treatment/intervention), if any, to the construct of interest
  b) Is there enough detail presented to replicate the intervention?
  c) Was there a manipulation check?

LOW	MEDIUM	HIGH
Treatments not validly defined/measured	Some problems with validity of the construct	Treatment is valid

Measurement or Construct Validity of the Measured Variables (for Q13)

Base rating on:
  a) Have the measures been used with similar participants?
  b) Was adequate evidence for the validity of outcomes presented?
  c) Was adequate evidence for the validity or attribute independent variables presented?

LOW	MEDIUM	HIGH
Measures not validly defined/measured	Some problems with validity of the constructs	Measures are valid

FIG. 37.4.   Evaluating the measurement validity of a study.

Was the active independent variable (treatment or intervention) implemented appropriately? Was it based on commonly shared empirical or theoretical concepts, and was it described in enough detail so it could be replicated? Was there a "manipulation check" to see if the intervention was
presented as planned and described in the study protocol? If there is no active independent variable (intervention), this rating is not applicable.

13. **What was the overall evaluation of the measurement or construct va-
    lidity of the outcomes (dependent variables) and attribute inde-
    pendent variables?**
    (a) **Have the measures been used with similar participants?**
    (b) **Was adequate evidence for the validity of the outcomes based on
        existing empirical and/or theoretical research presented?**
    (c) **Was adequate evidence for the validity of the attribute inde-
        pendent variables presented?**

This question has to do with whether the attribute independent variables and dependent variables are measured validly and are appropriately defined so that they represent the concepts under investigation. The validity of the outcomes and measured (attribute) independent variables depends, in part, on whether the measures are appropriate for the types of participants in the study.

The issue is whether these operational definitions are representative of the intended concepts and constructs. Sometimes the intervention and outcomes are not based on commonly shared and/or theoretically derived ideas. If so, the overall ratings (Q12 and Q13) should be low.

External Validity

"External validity asks the question of generalizability: to what populations, settings, treatment variables, and measurement variables can this effect be generalized?" (Campbell & Stanley, 1963/1966, p. 5). In our evaluation framework, external validity has three aspects: *population external validity* (question 14), *ecological external validity* (question 15), and *testing of subgroups* (question 16). These dimensions examine how representative the population and setting are of the target or theoretical population and setting.

14. **What is the evaluation of the overall *population external validity*? Base the rating on answers to the following:**
    (a) **Was the accessible population representative of the theoretical population?** (*No, Maybe, Yes*)
    (b) **Was the selected sample representative of the accessible population?** (*No, Maybe, Yes*)
    (c) **Was the actual sample representative vis-à-vis the selected sample? That is, was the response rate acceptable?** (*No, Maybe, Yes*)

This aspect of external validity is a participant selection or sampling issue that involves how participants were *selected to be in the study*. Were they randomly selected from a particular population, or were volunteers used? Most quantitative studies in the social sciences have not used random selection of participants, but the issue of population external validity is more complex than whether there was a random sample; as shown in chapter 18 and Fig. 18.1, it depends on three steps in the sampling process.

In order to evaluate these three steps, first *identify* (a) the *theoretical population*, (b) the *accessible population*, (c) the *sampling design* and *selected sample*, and (d) the *actual sample* of participants involved in the study. It is possible that the researcher could use a random or other probability *sampling* technique (step 2), but have an actual sample that is not representative of the theoretical population, either due to a low response rate (step 3) or due to the accessible population not being representative of the theoretical population (step 1). The latter problem seems almost universal, in part due to funding and travel limitations. Except in national survey research, researchers almost always start with an accessible population from the local school district, community, or clinic that is probably not fully representative of the target population of interest.

Ratings now can be made for each subquestion (14a, 14b, and 14c) in the top section of Fig. 37.5. Finally, an overall rating can be made of whether the *actual sample of participants is representative of the theoretical or target population.*

There is an important distinction between *random sampling* (or selection of subjects from the population), which influences population external validity, and *random assignment* (of participants to *groups*), which influences the participant equivalence aspect of internal validity.

15. **What is the evaluation of the overall *ecological external validity?* The rating and comments are based on:**

    (a) **Was the setting (or conditions) natural and representative of the target setting?** (*No, Maybe, Yes*)

    (b) **Was the rapport with testers or observers good?** (*No, Maybe, Yes*)

    (c) **Were the procedures or tasks natural and representative of the behavioral concepts of interest?** (*No, Maybe, Yes*)

    (d) **Was the timing and length of the treatment or intervention appropriate? (NA if not an experiment because no intervention is done)** (*No, Maybe, Yes, NA*)

    (e) **Will the results apply to more than the specific time in history that the study was done?** (*No, Maybe, Yes*)

Ecological validity is an aspect of external validity that has to do with the conditions/settings, testers, procedures or tasks, and times. We evaluate each of these five aspects of ecological validity in terms of how representative they are of the target or intended settings and so on, and thus whether the results can be generalized. Because the target settings, testers, procedures, and tasks are usually "natural" we use that term here. We rate each of the five aspects of ecological validity and then provide an overall judgment using the middle scale in Fig. 37.5.

15a. A study in a field setting (e.g., home or school) is higher on this aspect of ecological external validity than one in a laboratory setting, especially if the lab conditions are highly artificial.

15b. The rapport or quality of the relationship between tester/observer and the participants is important. Differences between the participants and researcher/tester in personal style, ethnicity, gender, and/or age may re-

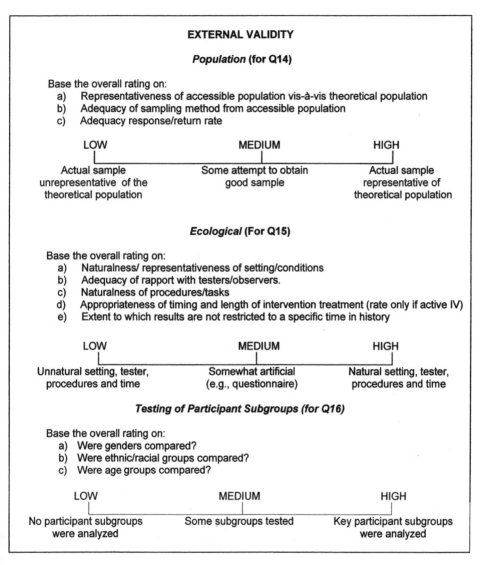

EXTERNAL VALIDITY

Population **(for Q14)**

Base the overall rating on:
   a)   Representativeness of accessible population vis-à-vis theoretical population
   b)   Adequacy of sampling method from accessible population
   c)   Adequacy response/return rate

LOW	MEDIUM	HIGH
Actual sample unrepresentative of the theoretical population	Some attempt to obtain good sample	Actual sample representative of theoretical population

Ecological **(For Q15)**

Base the overall rating on:
   a)   Naturalness/ representativeness of setting/conditions
   b)   Adequacy of rapport with testers/observers.
   c)   Naturalness of procedures/tasks
   d)   Appropriateness of timing and length of intervention treatment (rate only if active IV)
   e)   Extent to which results are not restricted to a specific time in history

LOW	MEDIUM	HIGH
Unnatural setting, tester, procedures and time	Somewhat artificial (e.g., questionnaire)	Natural setting, tester, procedures and time

Testing of Participant Subgroups **(for Q16)**

Base the overall rating on:
   a)   Were genders compared?
   b)   Were ethnic/racial groups compared?
   c)   Were age groups compared?

LOW	MEDIUM	HIGH
No participant subgroups were analyzed	Some subgroups tested	Key participant subgroups were analyzed

FIG. 37.5.   Rating scales to evaluate the external validity of the findings of a study.

duce rapport. Interviewers may be able to increase rapport by "getting to know" the interviewee.

15c. Most of the procedures that utilize self-report measures, especially questionnaires, are at least somewhat artificial because they are not direct measures of the participant's actual behavior.

15d. In experiments, sometimes the intervention or treatment is too short to be representative of how the intervention would actually take place if widely implemented. (This rating is not applicable if the study is not an experiment.)

15e. The topic of the study or phrasing of the questions may restrict its usefulness to approximately the time in history that it was conducted. Results related to topics about current events or trendy issues may soon become outdated. For example, attitudes about topics such as school vouchers, low-carb diets, or gay marriage may change over time. Other topics are more timeless and their results may stay relevant for decades.

16. **What is the evaluation of the extent to which important participant**
    subgroups **were** *tested/compared* **on the effect of the intervention or independent variable?**
    (a) **Were gender differences analyzed/compared?** (*No, Maybe, Yes*)
    (b) **Were two or more ethnic or racial groups analyzed/compared?** (*No, Maybe, Yes*)
    (c) **Were two or more age groups analyzed/compared?** (*No, Maybe, Yes*)

Rate how broadly the *intervention* was tested statistically across important subgroups of participants. Do the results of the intervention for one gender, ethnicity, or age group hold for the other gender, ethnicities, or ages? Due to financial and time constraints, many, probably most, research projects delimit the participants to a few of the demographic groups, in part to have enough power to detect differences. Gender comparisons are quite common, but often a single age or ethnicity is used. Or there is a range of ages or ethnicities but there are not enough participants in the smaller groups to analyze age or ethnic differences.

If the focus of the study is on an attribute independent variable such as type of disability, the question becomes, "Are differences on the dependent variable specific to a certain gender, age, or ethnicity (i.e., is there an interaction with gender, age, or ethnicity)?" Or do the noted disability differences apply to both genders, all ages, and all ethnicities? Similar logic would apply to testing of these important subgroups for ordered or continuous attribute independent variables that were the focus of a nonexperimental study. If the focus of the study is on gender, age, or ethnicity as the main independent variable, that subquestion (16a, 16b, or 16c) would be considered "not applicable" for this rating.

OTHER ISSUES

17. Was there adequate *peer review?* (*Yes, Maybe, No*)

Question 17 is about the extent of peer review of the article or document. Most consumers of research will read newspaper or newsletter articles summarizing research studies. These may not give much detail about the methods used, but they usually provide some information about the source from which the article was written. Newspaper articles often are based on published peer-reviewed articles or presentations at professional meetings, which had some sort of peer review. However, the journalist may have left out important details.

If the source is a scholarly journal, the chances are that the peer review was at least moderately extensive and strict. *Peer review* means that the article was evaluated by other experts (peers) in the field, usually without knowing who the author of the article was (i.e., masked or "blind" review). One way to indirectly evaluate the quality of the peer review is to compare rankings of the journal that published the article to others in the same general discipline. For example, if many authors refer to articles in a specific journal, it would be considered to have high status; see ranks in *Journal Citation Reports. Social Sciences Ed.* (1994–present). Another common method of evaluating the quality of the journal is to obtain the percentage of articles that are accepted by the journal. The lower the percentage accepted, the higher the status of the journal.

If the association that publishes the journal is made up primarily of practitioners who are only secondarily interested in research, the peer review of the design and analysis is likely to be less strict because practitioner reviews focus more on the importance of the problem, application, and implications. Presentations at professional meetings, even research oriented meetings, are usually less strictly reviewed, especially if the judgment to accept was based on a summary or abstract of the paper.

Furthermore, presentations to nonscholarly audiences or at events like press conferences are even less likely to be reviewed by independent scholars or researchers and thus do not have peer review. Finally, studies whose main or sole source is dissemination in a popular article or an article in a popular magazine or newspaper would not have had peer review.

If a study provides clinically significant results on an important topic, one would assume that it would be published in a peer-reviewed journal, at least within a few years of completion. It is not a good sign if a somewhat older study has only been presented at a conference, published in the trade or popular press, or posted on an Internet web site. If the study was not published in a peer-reviewed journal, that may well indicate that there are serious flaws in the study or that the study lacked sufficient new, important findings to be published in a peer-reviewed source.

18. **Did the authors adequately present the case for the theoretical importance and/or practical relevance of their research questions and design?** (*No, Maybe, Yes*)

This question asks how well the research questions follow from the literature and/or theory used to support their importance. The theoretical background and rationale for the study are usually provided in the introduction of the study. Thus, does the introduction make a good case for the importance of the study and the relevance of the research questions to the problem of interest?

19. **Did the authors interpret their findings adequately? That is, were the title, abstract, and discussion clear and accurate (or overstated and misleading) given the evaluation of the several aspects of research validity?** (*No, Maybe, Yes*)

Finally, question 19 is a summary question that evaluates the title abstract and especially the discussion and conclusions for indications of inaccuracy or misleading statements, given your previous analysis of the study. Often in popular articles the editor or writer will overstate the findings to make them seem more impressive or be more easily understood by the public. Thus, in a popular magazine or newspaper discussion of a study with relatively low internal validity (because of lack of proper control groups or lack of equivalence of groups), the journalist may report or imply that the independent variable caused the dependent variable, had an impact on, or determined the outcome. These overstatements may not have been made in the actual article by the researcher, who may have presented the conclusions more cautiously and appropriately, given the relatively low internal validity of the study. Likewise, a study based on an unrepresentative sample of people or on one gender may be overgeneralized, perhaps without any mention of the types of participants used, or at least implying that there is no problem in making more general statements. The astute consumer should become aware of these possible overinterpretations and evaluate the article appropriately.

There are other questions that could be asked about a research article, such as questions about its readability, clarity, and so forth, but we believe that we have discussed the major dimensions and thus we have not tried to be exhaustive in our coverage.

SUMMARY

This chapter provides an integrated review of most of the important concepts presented throughout the book. Answers to the 19 questions provide a comprehensive evaluation of a research study, especially its methods. To do this evaluation, one must identify the key variables and their characteristics (type and level of measurement). We also identify the research questions, approaches, and design. Based on Cook and Campbell (1979), we discussed the four aspects of research validity. Then we provided eight rating scales, and rubrics for using them, to evaluate the main dimensions of research validity. These eight key dimensions of research validity are:

1. Measurement reliability and statistics.
2. Internal validity: equivalence of the groups on participant characteristics.
3. Internal validity: control of extraneous experience and environmental variables.
4. Construct validity of the intervention or treatment.
5. Measurement or construct validity of the measured variables.
6. Population external validity.
7. Ecological external validity.
8. External validity: testing of subgroups.

Finally, we discussed briefly three additional issues that are related to the quality of the written presentation of the research. These issues are whether there was peer review, how well the research questions are justified and linked to the literature, and how clearly and accurately the authors discuss the results.

In the next chapter, we use the framework and questions from this chapter to provide narrative evaluations of the four sample research studies introduced in chapters 1 and 19. Each of these four studies also is rated from low to high on the eight research validity dimensions. In appendix A we provide a form that might be used to guide evaluations. Appendix B is a completed evaluation form for one of the four studies showing how we might use the form to produce numerical ratings of research validity. Finally, appendix C is a side-by-side comparison of the four studies using the numerical scores.

Evaluations of Four Sample Articles

To illustrate how to use this framework to evaluate research validity, we consider four studies that vary in the approach used but have a number of features in common: They all were published in peer-reviewed journals, made a reasonable case for the research questions and methods based on literature and theory, and interpreted the results with appropriate caution given the strengths and weaknesses of the methods used. Thus, questions 17–19 would not produce major differences in the evaluations. However, there were differences in the strength of various aspects of the design and methods as discussed next. We evaluate each of the four studies in turn using global judgments and narratives to rate each of the eight research validity scales described in chapter 37. In the appendixes, we provide a proposal for how one might do numerical ratings of the research validity of the four studies. Appendix A is a *Research Validity Evaluation Form* that could be used to make and record numerical ratings of the eight dimensions. Appendix B is a completed evaluation form, and appendix C presents side-by-side numerical ratings and comments about the strengths and weaknesses of each study.

The evaluation form (appendix A) provides one possible method for making a comprehensive and detailed numerical evaluation of the research validity of a study. There are advantages and disadvantages to such a detailed evaluation. On the positive side, attention is given to all, or almost all, of the key factors of the research design and presentation that influence the research validity of a study. Doing a comprehensive evaluation forces one to read the paper carefully, especially the methods section, and encourages critical reading of not only what is said but what is implied and what is left out.

On the other hand, using the evaluation form and assigning points to the scales makes the evaluation somewhat mechanical and tedious. In appendix A, the evaluation of each of the eight research validity dimensions is based on assigning points (*no* = 0, *maybe* = 1, *yes* = 2) to the answers of each of three to five subquestions. Scores for each dimension and overall could be computed as described in appendix A.

A more subjective and global approach to the eight key ratings may, at times, be more appropriate. However, we have found that such global ratings are hard to make for less experienced evaluators. The subquestions are intended to facilitate consideration of the key issues for each dimension of research validity.

There is, of course, some degree of subjective judgment involved with both the global ratings in this chapter and when using the numerical evaluation form and subquestions in appendix A. Thus, different knowledgeable evaluators would probably produce somewhat different ratings for the eight key dimensions (questions 9–16). However, we believe that reliability would be quite high and the mean difference in ratings would be small.

Another important consideration is how the eight research validity ratings should be weighted if one were required to provide an overall or composite score. In appendix A we suggest that it could be based on equal weights for the eight dimensions, an average percentage score for questions 9–16. How one might do this is described in appendix A and illustrated in appendixes B and C for the sample studies. Of course, as discussed in chapters 19 and 34, some researchers would place more weight on internal validity and others on external validity, so it would be hard to obtain agreed-on differential weights for the eight research validity dimensions.

Furthermore, these eight research validity dimensions focus on the design and analysis of studies and deemphasize the importance and originality of the topic or research problem. These latter points obviously are key aspects of an overall rating of whether a research grant should be awarded or an article published and in a broader rating of the quality of an article they and questions 17–19 would have to be given substantial weight.

A comprehensive evaluation, using either narratives and global ratings (this chapter) or the numerical evaluation form (appendix A), can be used with any research study. However, such detailed evaluations are most appropriate for studies that are critical to some decision such as whether to publish a paper, use a design as a model for replication, or adopt a procedure or instrument for use in a study. In many cases, the briefer overview evaluation presented in chapter 19 may be adequate.

Next, we provide a narrative evaluation and global rating for each of the four sample studies. Table 38.1 reprints questions 9–16 (from chap. 37), which are the focus of the following evaluations.

TABLE 38.1
Evaluation Questions for the Eight Dimensions of Research Validity

9. What is the overall rating of *measurement reliability and statistics*? Base the rating and comments on the following:
   (a) Was the overall measurement reliability of the variables acceptable? (*No, Maybe, Yes*)
   (b) Was the power appropriate? (*No, Maybe, Yes*)
   (c) Was the choice/use of statistics appropriate? (*No, Maybe, Yes*)
   (d) Was there adequate presentation of the statistical results, including effect size? (*No, Maybe, Yes*)
   (e) Was the interpretation of statistical results appropriate? (*No, Maybe, Yes*)

10. What is the evaluation of the *equivalence of the groups on participant characteristics*? Base the rating and comments on:
    (a) Was there random assignment of participants to the groups? (*No or Yes*)
    (b) If no random assignment, were the participants in each group matched, made, or found to be similar on a pretest? (*No, Maybe, Yes*) If random assignment was done, (b) and (c) should be scored as yes.
    (c) If no random assignment, were the participants in each group matched, made, or found to be similar on other key participant characteristics (e.g., age, gender, IQ, etc.)? (*No, Maybe, Yes*)
    (d) Was the retention (low attrition) of subjects during the study high and similar across groups? (*No, Maybe, Yes*)

11. What is the evaluation of the *control of extraneous experience and environment variables*?
    (a) Was the study conducted in a controlled environment? (*No, Maybe, Yes*)
    (b) Did the groups have equivalent environments? (*No, Maybe, Yes*)
    (c) Was there a no treatment (placebo) or usual treatment comparison group? (*No, Maybe, Yes*)
    (d) Were there adequate attempts to reduce other extraneous influences? (*No, Maybe, Yes*)

12. What is the evaluation of the construct *validity* of the *intervention* (if any)?
    (a) Was the intervention (active independent variable) operationally defined and implemented a valid way, based on an existing body of empirical and/or theoretical research? (*No, Maybe, Yes*)
    (b) Was the intervention described in enough detail for it to be replicated? (*No, Maybe, Yes*)
    (c) Was there a manipulation check or verification to be sure that the intervention was presented as planned? (*No, Maybe, Yes*)

13. What was the overall evaluation of the measurement or construct *validity* of the outcomes (dependent variables) and attribute independent variables?
    (a) Have the measures been used with similar participants?
    (b) Was adequate evidence for the validity of the outcomes based on existing empirical and/or theoretical research presented?
    (c) Was adequate evidence for the validity of the attribute independent variables presented?

14. What is the evaluation of the overall *population external validity*? Base the rating on answers to the following:
    (a) Was the accessible population representative of the theoretical population? (*No, Maybe, Yes*)
    (b) Was the selected sample representative of the accessible population? (*No, Maybe, Yes*)
    (c) Was the actual sample representative vis-à-vis the selected sample? That is, was the response rate acceptable? (*No, Maybe, Yes*)

(Continued)

TABLE 38.1
(Continued)

15. What is the evaluation of the overall *ecological external validity*? Base the rating and comments on:
    (a) Was the setting (or conditions) natural and representative of the target setting? (*No, Maybe, Yes*)
    (b) Was the rapport with testers or observers good? (*No, Maybe, Yes*)
    (c) Were the procedures or tasks natural and representative of the behavioral concepts of interest? (*No, Maybe, Yes*)
    (d) Was the timing and length of the treatment or intervention appropriate? (*No, Maybe, Yes, NA*) (*NA* if not an experiment because no intervention is done)
    (e) Will the results apply to more than the specific time in history that the study was done? (*No, Maybe, Yes*)
16. What is the evaluation of the extent to which important participant *subgroups* were *tested/compared* on the effect of the intervention or independent variables?
    (a) Were gender differences analyzed/compared? (*No, Maybe, Yes*)
    (b) Were two or more ethnic or racial groups analyzed/compared? (*No, Maybe, Yes*)
    (c) Were two or more age groups analyzed/compared? (*No, Maybe, Yes*)

STUDY 1: A RANDOMIZED EXPERIMENT

The purpose of the first study (Gliner & Sample, 1996) was to increase quality of life for persons with developmental disabilities who were employed in sheltered work or supported employment, using an intervention of community life options. The key independent variables were the intervention (vs. no intervention), the type of employment (sheltered vs. supported), and change over time (pretest and four follow-ups at 6-month intervals). The Quality of Life Index (QLI) had three subscales so there were three outcome/dependent measures. The approach was randomized experimental because participants were randomly assigned to either the community life option or their present situation. The specific experimental design was a pretest–posttest control group design (with follow-up assessments). The general design classification was 2 (treatments) × 2 (settings) × 5 (pretest plus 4 posttests) with repeated measures on the last variables.

The QLI had been used in several published studies that reported good interrater (.83) and interitem (.83) reliability coefficients. The published studies also provided evidence in support of the measurement validity of the QLI with similar clients.

The study attempted to achieve high internal validity by randomly assigning participants to the groups. The study also attempted to achieve high external ecological validity by carrying out the conditions in the actual community setting. However, obtaining good research validity on all eight dimensions could not be accomplished. A summary example of a narrative evaluation is provided in the following paragraphs.

Measurement reliability and statistics were judged overall to be medium high. Evidence for the reliability of the measures was acceptable. However, statistical power was constrained because there were a limited number of persons who fit the criteria to be in the study (persons with developmental disabilities who were employed in supported or sheltered work). Thus, the ability to detect a relationship was inadequate unless the effect was large. The choice of statistics, presentation of the results and their interpretation were all judged to be acceptable.

Internal validity: equivalence of groups on participant characteristics was rated high. Participants were randomly assigned to intervention conditions. However, a cautionary note should be raised because random assignment of participants to conditions may not make the groups equivalent with small numbers. There was not much attrition (5 out of 40) over the 2 years of the study, and it was quite evenly spread across the groups. This dimension was rated high but not the maximum due to the caution about sample size, which resulted in the groups being different on one pretest measure before the intervention.

Control of extraneous experience/environment variables was constrained by an emphasis on ecological validity so it was judged to be medium to low. In a community setting, where choice was experienced differently by different participants, it was difficult to insure that the experiences of each group were not influenced by outside variables.

In terms *of construct validity of the* independent *variable*, the intervention seems appropriately named and generalizable. This dimension was rated medium high.

The *measurement or construct validity* of the *dependent variable* was medium. Quality of life for persons with developmental disabilities had been used several times with this population to measure quality of life among individuals who had moved out of institutionalized settings into community settings. However, the instrument may not have been appropriate for measuring changes following intervention in only one life area. In addition, the instrument may have been intended for lower functioning participants.

Population external validity was not high because the sample was limited to persons in one city, and there was not a random selection of appropriate participants even from that city. Instead the sample was one of convenience. Thus, the accessible population might not represent all persons with developmental disabilities. We rated this dimension medium.

Ecological external validity was judged to be high. Because the intervention was a real one, of appropriate length, and took place in an actual community setting, rapport with the testers was adequate, but the quality of life measure was an interview measure so it was not fully representative or natural. The type of intervention and outcome were not particularly tied to the early 1990s when the study was done. Our rating was high.

The eighth dimension of research validity is *testing of subgroups*. Because of the small sample, age, gender, and ethnic subgroups were not compared for differential effects of the intervention. Thus, the study was low medium on this dimension.

The paper had two additional data sources (subjective ratings of improvement by two recreational therapists who were familiar with the participants and three case studies), making it a multimethod approach to the topic. We do not evaluate the case studies, but the design of the part of the study that used the subjective ratings raises some design and evaluation issues. These subjective ratings were made only for the intervention group and only at the end of the first and second years of the intervention. Thus, there was no pretest and there was no comparison group. The design for this aspect of the study would be a poor quasi-experiment, a one group posttest only design. If this aspect of the design had been all there was, internal validity would be rated low.

STUDY 2: A QUASI-EXPERIMENT

This study (Johnson & Johnson, 1991), titled "Using Short-Term Group Counseling with Visually Impaired Adolescents," used the quasi-experimental approach because there was an active independent variable (group counseling), but the participants could not be randomly assigned to the two groups (counseling or no counseling). There was potentially another independent variable (change over time) because there were pretests and posttests on the three dependent variables: self-concept, attitudes toward blindness, and locus of control. Three hypotheses stated that group counseling would produce more improvement in each of the three dependent variables. The specific experimental design is a pretest–posttest nonequivalent comparison group design, even though the researchers attempted to match the groups on age, IQ, race, and sex. The general design classification is a 2 × 2 factorial design with repeated measures on the second factor; however, the authors chose to use the gain score approach to the analysis, making the design, as analyzed, a single-factor between-groups design with two levels.

The evidence in support of the measurement reliability and validity of the three dependent or outcome measures was indirect, based on brief references to published studies and dissertations. A positive point is that the instruments had been used successfully with visually impaired adolescents.

With regard to *measurement reliability and statistics,* as just described the reliability of the instrument seems to be adequate, although no coefficients are provided. Power would be considered inadequate with only 14 subjects (7 per group), but the effect size turned out to be very large so the three *t* tests were all statistically significant. The selection of the gain score t test was appropriate, but only t and p values were presented; descriptive statistics for the pre- and posttests would have been desirable and helpful for the interpretation of results. We rated this dimension medium.

The *internal validity: equivalence of the groups* was pretty good given that random assignment was not possible. The groups turned out not to be significantly different on any of the three pretest scores, which is good; however, with only seven in each group, lack of significance is not surprising due to the lack of power to detect real differences. The researchers attempted to match the groups on age, IQ, sex, and race. Again, the existence of nonsignificant group differences in age and IQ is good but not surprising given the low power available. The fact that only seven sets of parents agreed to allow their child to be in the therapy group may indicate that the other parents were more dubious or suspicious of the treatment, even though that was not apparent from pretest group differences. The retention rate over the 4-week study period was apparently 100% for both groups. We rated this dimension medium high.

Internal validity: control of extraneous experience and environment variables was reasonably good. Although the group counseling was done at a rehabilitation center, the participants were only there during the sessions. For the remainder of the study, both the therapy and the control group participants were in their home/uncontrolled environments, which might have differed in important ways. Furthermore, other experiences of the groups were not the same during the study, in part because the control group data were collected during the end of the school year and the treatment group was conducted in the summer. It also was possible that some participants in the two groups knew each other and that there was contamination or influence of one group on the other. On the positive side, there was a no treatment control group. Overall, we rated this dimension medium to low.

Construct validity of the intervention seemed pretty good. The treatment was outlined in some detail and seemed to be well grounded in the group counseling and visual impairment literature, but exact replication of the 12 sessions would not be possible. During the final session the group critiqued the group process. We rated this aspect of research validity medium high.

Overall construct validity of the measured variables seemed okay. As stated earlier, the evidence to support the measurement validity of the three outcome measures was indirect from apparent successful use with other usually visually impaired persons. We rated this as medium. One should always be cautious when interpreting the validity of data from self-report inventories.

External population validity was okay but not particularly good. These visually impaired adolescents were from one school district in North Carolina. This accessible population was clearly one of convenience. The authors state that because these students were all congenitally visually impaired and all but one had some usable vision, they had a limited range of visual ability characteristics, which limits generalizability. It appears that invitations to participate were sent to all congenitally visually impaired teenagers in the school district. Eighteen agreed to participate, but the number asked was not stated so the response rate is unknown. We rate this dimension as medium.

External ecological validity depends on how natural or representative the intended setting, testers, procedures, and times are. Except for the therapy sessions at the rehab center, the setting (home or school) was natural. The rapport with the testers/researchers was probably very good, at least for the therapy group. The tasks were not fully natural because they were paper-and-pencil inventories rather than behavioral observations of locus of control, and so on. Twelve sessions of group therapy over 4 weeks seems to be appropriate for this type of intervention. Finally, the effects of group therapy would not be restricted to a specific time in history; it should have broad applicability over many decades. Our rating for ecological external validity was medium high.

External validity: testing of subgroups was greatly constrained by the very small sample, which meant that meaningful comparisons were unlikely. Thus, no age, gender, or ethnic comparisons in regard to the effect of the intervention were made. We rated this dimension as low.

STUDY 3: A NONEXPERIMENTAL, COMPARATIVE APPROACH

The purpose of this study (DiLorenzo et al., 2004) was to compare older (60–85 years old) and younger (29–59 years old) persons with multiple sclerosis (MS) on physical functioning, mental health, and quality of life. The independent variable, age, is an attribute that for this study had two levels, older and younger. The duration of illness was another independent variable (covariate). There were many dependent variables that fell into the three broad categories of physical functioning, mental health, and quality of life. The approach was basically comparative (older vs. younger), but duration of illness was used as a covariate. The design could be considered a single-factor design with two levels. There is no specific experimental design name because the study was nonexperimental.

Overall measurement reliability and statistics was quite good. The many dependent variables were assessed with published instruments, most or all of which had been used with persons with MS. However, no specific reliability coefficients for the instruments were reported, probably due to space limitations of the journal. Power was not high with 30 in each group, so the lack a of significant difference on most variables could be due to lack of power.

The choice of a statistic (ANCOVA) may be appropriate, but the article is not clear with regard to whether they tested covariance assumptions, which are especially important because they used an attribute independent variable. Effect sizes were not presented or discussed, but means and standard errors were given so effect sizes could be computed. The results were interpreted appropriately, except more caution in interpreting the nonsignificant results as indicating "no difference" would have been better. We rated measurement reliability and statistics to be moderately high.

Equivalence of the groups on participant characteristics could not be high because this was a nonexperimental study using the comparative approach. However, the younger and older groups were matched in terms of gender and were quite similar in terms of race, marital status, and education (nearly 100% Caucasian in both groups, about two-thirds married in both groups, and about one-third in each group were college graduates). The groups were different, not surprisingly, in duration of illness and in percentage currently employed. As noted earlier, duration was used to adjust the means of the dependent variables so that statistically the groups would be more similar on that dimension. Because the study involved only a one-time interview there was no attrition during the study. Overall, the equivalence of the groups was judged to be medium, which is pretty good for a nonexperiment.

Control of extraneous experience and environmental variables is unlikely to be high for a nonexperimental field study because the environment and experiences of the participants in the two groups (older and younger) were uncontrolled and could have been very different. For example, most of the older group experienced, as children, the Depression and World War II, whereas the younger group were postwar and baby boomers. Current friends and experiences also could be different. On the other hand, both groups had the same illness and went to the same MS center in the same city so they shared somewhat the same environment and experiences. We rated control of extraneous variables low to medium.

Construct validity of the intervention (if any) is not applicable because there is no intervention in a nonexperimental study, which has only attribute independent variables.

Construct validity of the measured variables was judged to be medium. Age was no doubt assessed accurately as was duration of illness from the medical records. The validity of the dependent variables was probably acceptable because the researchers used published instruments that had been found to be appropriate for MS patients. However, no details about evidence for validity of these self-report measures were presented.

External population validity was judged to be medium high. The accessible population was from one large comprehensive care center for MS in the Northeast so might not be fully representative of the national population of adults with MS, but subjects were randomly selected from the medical charts of all patients diagnosed with MS for at least 5 years. The response rates were slightly less than 50%, so not high.

External ecological validity was rated medium high. The setting was the patients' homes using a telephone interview for efficiency and so that non-ambulatory patients could easily participate. Rapport with the interviewer was probably okay, but the telephone and structured nature of the interview probably reduced rapport somewhat. The self-report interview ratings are a somewhat unnatural way to assess quality of life, physical health, and mental health. There is no intervention in a nonexperimental study so there was no rating of its appropriateness. Because this is a cross-sectional rather than longitudinal design, it is possible that the older patients might self-report less depression and better current quality of life than the younger cohort will when they get older. However, the finding that older MS patients have more physical limitations but similar perceived quality of life will probably be applicable to future generations, so the study is not highly bound to this time in history.

External validity: testing of subgroups was rated as low. The study did not discuss gender or ethnic differences; there were very few racial minorities. Because age was the main independent variable, testing age differences is not applicable to this dimension.

STUDY 4: NONEXPERIMENTAL, ASSOCIATIONAL

This study (Redding et al., 1990) examined the relationship between maternal depression and infants' mastery behavior in a nonclinical sample of 1- and 2-year-olds and their mothers. The attribute independent variable was the degree of self-reported maternal depression. The three dependent variables were infant competence at the mastery tasks (puzzles), their persistence at the more challenging tasks, and task pleasure, all observed in a laboratory playroom. Puzzles of varying difficulty were presented one at a time to the infants. The approach was associational because maternal depression had many ordered levels. The study was nonexperimental so there was no specific design name, and there was no general design classification.

The *overall measurement reliability and statistics* was rated high to medium. Interrater reliability for the observations of three dependent variables ranged from .83 to .96. The independent variable, maternal depression, used a common published instrument, the Beck Depression Inventory, known to have good reliability. Power ($N = 40$) was probably adequate when examining the bivariate correlations of the three dependent variables with maternal depression, but was not adequate to examine the age groups separately or for multivariate statistics. Because the results were reported as

Pearson correlations, effect sizes (mostly large) were available but were not explicitly discussed. The results were interpreted appropriately and cautiously.

Equivalence of the groups on participant characteristics was low, as might be expected with a nonexperimental study using the basic associational approach. With this approach there is only one group, so this dimension is based on whether mothers who were relatively high on the independent variable, maternal depression, were similar to mothers who were low on depression in their personal and demographic characteristics. There was, of course, no random assignment to the groups and no pretest. It seems likely that mothers who report that they are relatively more depressed would differ from other mothers in many ways. A positive aspect is that there was no attrition during the study.

Control of extraneous experience and environmental variables was rated low to medium. The study was conducted in a laboratory playroom, so the environment was pretty well controlled and essentially the same for all children. Mothers were in the room but were instructed to refrain from assisting or encouraging the child, so attempts were made to reduce extraneous variables. As in other associational approach studies, there was no control group.

Construct validity of the intervention was not applicable because there was no intervention.

Construct validity of the measured variables was judged to be medium. The Beck Depression Inventory has been widely used with nonclinical as well as clinical samples. Published evidence to support validity is available, but not specified in this brief article. The validity of self-reports of depression is always open to question. Similar mastery tasks and measures had been used in other published studies, but no specific evidence for their validity was presented here. Toddlers' mood variability and other potentially confounding variables could raise questions about the validity of the mastery behavior measures.

External population validity was rated medium low. The target or theoretical population was probably normally developing 1- and 2-year-olds in the United States, but the accessible population and selected sample were ones of convenience. The sample was predominately middle-class, Caucasian, and from one Western city. The response rate is unknown, but no doubt some mothers declined the invitation to participate.

External ecological validity was rated as medium low. Although the laboratory playroom somewhat resembled a child's room in a home, it and the structured task procedures were clearly somewhat artificial. The tester attempted to obtain good rapport with the mother and the child, but the controlled nature of the tasks and prescribed tester behaviors no doubt reduced rapport. There was no intervention so (d) is not applicable. The study does not seem to be constrained to any particular time in history. Depression is an ongoing problem, and mastery behavior in children is of timeless interest.

External validity: testing of subgroups was rated as medium low. Child gender relationships with maternal depression were not reported and minorities were too few to analyze. However, relationships were reported for each age separately as well as for both ages combined.

Research Validity Evaluation Form

Reviewer_____ **Date**_____
Reference Citation:

1. **Key independent variables** (Name of variable, type, # levels, measurement)
   1.
   2.
   3.

2. **Key dependent variables** (Name of variable, measurement)
   1.
   2.
   3.

3. **Main research questions or hypotheses**

4. **Research approach for each question**

5. General design classification (if approach is experimental or comparative)

6. Specific experimental design name (if the approach is randomized or quasi-experimental)

Instructions for Using the No, Maybe, Yes Ratings

For questions 7–19, we ask you to make a rating of: No or Maybe or Yes for each of the subquestions. For questions 7 and 8, "No" means that the evidence for reliability (or validity) of the data from the variable was unacceptable. "Yes" means that reliability (or validity) data were acceptable. "Maybe" means that the evidence was not clear or, perhaps, marginal.

7. Measurement reliability (types of evidence and support for each variable)

Key Variable	Type of Evidence	Acceptable Support?		
1.		No	Maybe	Yes
2.		No	Maybe	Yes
3.		No	Maybe	Yes
4.		No	Maybe	Yes
5.		No	Maybe	Yes
Overall Rating		No	Maybe	Yes

8. Measurement validity (type of evidence and support for each key variable)

Key Variable	Type of Evidence	Acceptable Support?		
1.		No	Maybe	Yes
2.		No	Maybe	Yes
3.		No	Maybe	Yes
4.		No	Maybe	Yes
5.		No	Maybe	Yes
Overall Rating		No	Maybe	Yes

Instructions for Scoring Questions 9–16

For the following scales, answer each of the subquestions (e.g., 9a, 9b, etc.) as no, maybe, or yes. Consider No = 0, Maybe = 1, and Yes = 2 for each subquestion. For example, in question 9, if a = yes, b = no, c = maybe, d = no and e = yes, then the points would be 2, 0, 1, 0, 2. Next, add the points (i.e., 5) and convert to a percentage (i.e., 5 out of 10 or 50%), which should be recorded on the Summary Rating Form at the end of this appendix. For question 15 when subquestion 15d is not applicable, base the percentage on subquestions that were actually rated. (See appendixes B and C for examples of how to compute the proposed scores for each question and the overall research validity.)

9. **Overall measurement reliability and statistics**
   a. Overall measurement reliability acceptable?   No   Maybe   Yes
   b. Appropriate power?   No   Maybe   Yes
   c. Appropriate choice of statistics and testing assumptions?   No   Maybe   Yes
   d. Adequate presentation of results, including effect size?   No   Maybe   Yes
   e. Appropriate interpretation of statistics?   No   Maybe   Yes

   Summary Rating   Low 0   Medium 5   High 10

Comments

10. **Equivalence of the groups on participant characteristics**
   a. Random assignment to groups? (assume no if not stated)   No   Yes
   b. Groups similar or were made similar on pretest? (If yes for a. above, score as yes here)   No   Maybe   Yes
   c. Groups similar on other key variables? (If yes for a., score as yes here)   No   Maybe   Yes
   d. Adequate retention (low attrition/mortality)?   No   Maybe   Yes

   Summary Rating   Low 0   Medium 4   High 8

Comments

11. Control of extraneous experience and environment variables

a. Was the study conducted in a controlled
environment (e.g., a lab)?   No   Maybe   Yes

b. Did the groups have equivalent
environments except for the independent
variable?   No   Maybe   Yes

c. Was there a no-treatment (placebo) or
usual-treatment control group?   No   Maybe   Yes

d. Were there adequate attempts to reduce
other extraneous influences?   No   Maybe   Yes

Summary Rating	<u>Low</u>	<u>Medium</u>	<u>High</u>
	0	4	8

Comments

12. Construct validity of the intervention (if any)

a. Was it adequately defined/operationalized
based on the theory and literature?   No   Maybe   Yes

b. Is there enough detail to replicate the
intervention?   No   Maybe   Yes

c. Was there a "manipulation check" to be
sure that the intervention was presented
as planned?   No   Maybe   Yes

Summary Rating	<u>Low</u>	<u>Medium</u>	<u>High</u>
	0	3	6

Comments—If there is no intervention, omit this rating; it is NA.

13. Overall measurement or construct validity of the measured variables

a. Have the measures been used with
similar participants?   No   Maybe   Yes

b. Was adequate evidence for the validity
of outcomes presented?   No   Maybe   Yes

c. Was adequate evidence for the validity
   of measured or attribute independent
   variables presented?   No   Maybe   Yes

Summary Rating   <u>Low</u>   <u>Medium</u>   <u>High</u>
                          0   3   6

Comments

14. Population external validity
Target/theoretical population? _____
Accessible population? _____
Selected sample? _____ How sampled? _____
Actual sample? _____ Return rate? _____

a. Representativeness of accessible population
   re target?   No   Maybe   Yes

b. Representativeness of selected sample
   re accessible?   No   Maybe   Yes

c. Representativeness of actual sample
   re selected?   No   Maybe   Yes

Summary Rating   <u>Low</u>   <u>Medium</u>   <u>High</u>
                          0   3   6

Comments

15. Ecological external validity
Target setting _____
Target outcome _____

a. Naturalness/representativeness of
   setting/conditions?   No   Maybe   Yes

b. Adequacy of rapport with testers/observers?   No   Maybe   Yes

c. Naturalness/representativeness of
   procedures/tasks?   No   Maybe   Yes

d. Appropriateness of timing and length of
   intervention treatment?
   (rate only if active IV)   No   Maybe   Yes

e. Results apply to more than a specific
   time in history?   No   Maybe   Yes

Summary Rating	<u>Low</u>	<u>Medium</u>	<u>High</u>
	0	4 or 5	8 or 10

Comments—If d. is NA, base the percentage on the number of points out of 8.

16. **Testing of participant subgroups**
    a. Were gender differences analyzed/
       compared?   No   Maybe   Yes
    b. Were two or more ethnic or racial groups
       analyzed/compared?   No   Maybe   Yes
    c. Were two or more age groups analyzed/
       compared?   No   Maybe   Yes

Summary Rating	<u>Low</u>	Medium	<u>High</u>
	0	3	6

Comments—If gender, ethnicity, or age is the main focus of the study, base the number of points on the other two ratings, so out of 4.

17. **Peer review?** Was it adequate?   No   Maybe   Yes
    Comments/Explanation

18. **Literature/theory to results** Was the case made? No   Maybe   Yes
    Comments

19. **Interpretation of results** Were they appropriate? No   Maybe   Yes
    Comments

Summary Research Validity Rating Form

Transfer each score (e.g., 5/10) and the percentage (e.g., 50%) to this table. If an overall score is needed, average the percentages.

Question	Score	Percent
9. Overall measurement reliability and statistics	_____	_____
Internal Validity		
10. Equivalence of the groups on participant characteristics	_____	_____
11. Control of extraneous experience and environment variables	_____	_____
Validity of Constructs		
12. Construct validity of the intervention (if any)	_____	_____
13. Measurement or construct validity of outcomes and other measures	_____	_____
External Validity		
14. Population external validity	_____	_____
15. Ecological external validity	_____	_____
16. Testing of subgroups	_____	_____
Total		_____
Average Percent		_____

Comments

Completed Research Validity Evaluation Form

Reviewer:

Reference Citation: *Redding, R. E., Harmon, R. J., & Morgan, G. A. (1990). Relationships between maternal depression and infants' mastery behaviors.* Infant Behavior and Development, *13, 391–395.*

1. **Key independent variables** (Name of variable, type, # levels, measurement)

   1. *The degree of self-reported maternal depression, attribute, many levels, probably normal*
   2. *NA*
   3. *NA*

2. **Key dependent variables** (Name of variable, measurement)

   The three dependent variables were all observed in a laboratory playroom. Puzzles of varying difficulty were presented one at a time to the infants.

   1. *infant competence at the mastery tasks (puzzles), probably normal*
   2. *persistence at the more challenging tasks, probably normal*
   3. *task pleasure, probably normal*

3. **Main research questions or hypotheses**

   This study examined the relationship between maternal depression and infants' mastery behavior in a nonclinical sample of 1- and 2-year-olds and their mothers.

4. **Research approach for each question**

   The approach was associational because maternal depression had many ordered levels.

329

5. **General design classification** (if approach experimental or comparative)

   The study was non-experimental so there was no specific design name, and there was no general design classification.

6. **Specific experimental design name** (if the approach randomized or quasi-experimental) *NA*

7. **Measurement reliability** (types of evidence and support for each variable)

Key Variable	Type of Evidence	Acceptable Support?		
1. *Maternal depression*	*Literature*	No	Maybe	⟨Yes⟩
2. *Infant competence*	*Interrater*	No	Maybe	⟨Yes⟩
3. *Persistence*	*Interrater*	No	Maybe	⟨Yes⟩
4. *Task pleasure*	*Interrater*	No	Maybe	⟨Yes⟩
5. *NA*		No	Maybe	Yes
Overall		No	Maybe	⟨Yes⟩

   Generally good evidence of reliability for the four key measures.

8. **Measurement validity** (type of evidence and support for each key variable)

Key Variable	Type of Evidence	Acceptable Support?		
1. *Maternal depression*	*Literature*	No	⟨Maybe⟩	Yes
2. *Infant competence*	*Literature*	No	⟨Maybe⟩	Yes
3. *Persistence*	*Literature*	No	⟨Maybe⟩	Yes
4. *Task pleasure*	*Literature*	No	⟨Maybe⟩	Yes
5. *NA*		No	Maybe	Yes
Overall		No	⟨Maybe⟩	Yes

   No reported validity measures, but all had been used successfully in other studies. Maternal depression is self-reported.

Instructions for Rating Questions 9–16

For the following scales, answer each of the subquestions as no, maybe, or yes. Consider No = 0, Maybe = 1, and Yes = 2 for each subquestion (a, b, c, etc.). For example, in question 9, if a = yes, b = no, c = maybe, d = no, and e = yes, then the points would be 2, 0, 1, 0, 2. Next, add the points (i.e., 5) and convert to a percentage (i.e., 5 out of 10 or 50%), which should be recorded

on the Summary Rating Form at the end of this appendix. In question 15
when subquestion 15d is not applicable, base the percentage on subquestions that were actually rated. (Also see appendixes B and C for examples.)

9. **Overall measurement reliability and statistics**
   a. Overall measurement reliability
      acceptable?   No   Maybe   (Yes)

   b. Appropriate power?   No   (Maybe)   Yes
   c. Appropriate choice of statistics and
      testing assumptions?   No   Maybe   (Yes)
   d. Adequate presentation of results,
      including effect size?   No   Maybe   (Yes)
   e. Appropriate interpretation of statistics? No   Maybe   (Yes)

   Summary Rating   Low   Medium   High
                          0   5   (9)   10

Comments

*Interrater reliability for the observations of three dependent variables ranged from .83-.96.
The independent variable, maternal depression, used a common published instrument, the
Beck Depression Inventory, known to have good reliability. Power (N = 40, p<.05, two tailed)
was examined for the bivariate correlations of the three dependent variables with maternal
depression. The power to detect a relatively large effect size (>.40) was high, but power to detect a medium effect size (.3) was only 50%. Furthermore, power was not adequate to examine the age groups separately or for multivariate statistics. Because the results were reported
as Pearson correlations, effect sizes (mostly large) were available but were not explicitly discussed. The results were interpreted appropriately and cautiously.*

10. **Equivalence of the groups on participant characteristics**
    a. Random assignment to groups?
       (assume no if not stated)   (No)   Yes

    b. Groups similar or were made similar
       on pretest? (If yes for a. above, score
       as yes here)   (No)   Maybe   Yes

    c. Groups similar on other key
       variables? (If yes for a.,
       score as yes here)   (No)   Maybe   Yes

    d. Adequate retention (low attrition/
       mortality)?   No   Maybe   (Yes)

    Summary Rating   Low   Medium   High
                           0   (2)   4   8

Comments

This dimension was rated low, as might be expected with a non experimental study using the basic associational approach. With this approach there is only one group so this dimension is based on whether mothers who were relatively high on the independent variable, maternal depression, were similar to mothers who were low on depression in their personal and demographic characteristics. It seems likely that mothers who report that they are relatively more depressed would differ from other mothers in many ways. There was, of course, no random assignment to the groups and no pretest. A positive aspect is that there was no attrition during the study.

11. Control of extraneous experience and environment variables

a. Was the study conducted in a
   controlled environment (e.g., a lab)?   No   (Maybe)   Yes

b. Did the groups have equivalent
   environments except for the
   independent variable?   No   (Maybe)   Yes

c. Was there a no-treatment (placebo)
   or usual-treatment control group?   (No)   Maybe   Yes

d. Were there adequate attempts to
   reduce other extraneous influences?   No   (Maybe)   Yes

Summary Rating   <u>Low</u>   (3)   <u>Medium</u>   <u>High</u>
                          0   4   8

Comments

This dimension was rated low to medium. The study was conducted in a laboratory playroom so the environment was pretty well controlled and essentially the same for all children. Mothers were in the room but were instructed to refrain from assisting or encouraging the child so attempts were made to reduce extraneous variables. There was no control group.

12. Construct validity of the intervention (if any)

a. Was it adequately defined/opera-
   tionalized based on the theory
   and literature?   No   Maybe   Yes

b. Is there enough detail to replicate
   the intervention?   No   Maybe   Yes

c. Was there a "manipulation check" to
   be sure that the intervention was
   presented as planned?   No   Maybe   Yes

Summary Rating   <u>Low</u>   <u>Medium</u>   <u>High</u>   (NA)
                      0   3   6

Comments—If there is no intervention, omit this rating; it is NA.

This was not applicable because there was no intervention.

13. Overall measurement or construct validity of the measured variables

a. Have the measures been used with
   similar participants?　　　　　　　　No　　(Maybe)　Yes

b. Was adequate evidence for the
   validity of outcomes presented?　　No　　(Maybe)　Yes

c. Was adequate evidence for the validity
   of measured or attribute independent
   variables presented?　　　　　　　　No　　(Maybe)　Yes

Summary Rating　　　　Low　　　　Medium　　　High
　　　　　　　　　　　　0　　　　　　(3)　　　　　6

Comments

This was judged to be medium. The Beck Depression Inventory has been widely used with non-clinical as well as clinical samples. Published evidence to support validity is available, but not specified in this brief article. The validity of self-reports of depression is always open to question. Similar mastery tasks and measures had been used in other published studies, but no specific evidence for their validity was presented here. Toddlers' mood variability and other potentially confounding variables could raise questions about the validity of the mastery behavior measures.

14. Population external validity

Target/theoretical population? *All mothers and infants in the US*
Accessible population? *Mothers in the Denver area*
Selected sample? *Volunteers to advertisements* How sampled? *Convenience*
Actual sample? *Contacted moms who agreed to participate* Return rate? *Probably Medium*

a. Representativeness of accessible
   population re target?　　　　　　　No　　(Maybe)　Yes

b. Representativeness of selected
   sample re accessible?　　　　　　(No)　　Maybe　　Yes

c. Representativeness of actual
   sample re selected?　　　　　　　No　　(Maybe)　Yes

Summary Rating　　　　Low　　　　Medium　　　High
　　　　　　　　　　　　0　　(2)　　3　　　　　6

Comments

This was rated medium low. The target or theoretical population was probably normally developing 1- and 2-year-olds in the US, but the accessible population and selected sample were ones of convenience. The sample was predominately middle class, Caucasian, and from one western city. The response rate is unknown, but no doubt some mothers declined the invitation to participate.

15. **Ecological external validity**
    Target setting *homes of mothers and infants*
    Target outcome *natural mastery behaviors of infants*

    a. Naturalness/representativeness of
       setting/conditions?   (No)   Maybe   Yes

    b. Adequacy of rapport with testers/
       observers?   No   (Maybe)   Yes

    c. Naturalness/representativeness of
       procedures/tasks?   No   (Maybe)   Yes

    d. Appropriateness of timing and length
       of intervention treatment? (rate only
       if active IV)   No   Maybe   Yes

    e. Results apply to more than a specific
       time in history?   No   Maybe   (Yes)
       Summary Rating   <u>Low</u>   <u>Medium</u>   <u>High</u>
                                  0   (4) or 5   8 or 10

**Comments—If d. is NA, base the percentage on the number of points
(out of 8).**

This was rated as medium low. Although the laboratory playroom somewhat resembled a child's room in a home, it and the structured task procedures were clearly somewhat artificial. The tester attempted to obtain good rapport with the mother and the child, but the controlled nature of the tasks and prescribed tester behaviors no doubt reduced rapport. There was no intervention so (d) is not applicable. The study does not seem to be constrained to any particular time in history. Depression is an ongoing problem, and mastery behavior in children is of timeless interest.

16. **Testing of subgroups**

    a. Were the gender differences   (No)   Maybe   Yes
       analyzed/compared?

    b. Were two or more ethnic or racial   (No)   Maybe   Yes
       groups analyzed/compared?

c. Were two or more age groups
analyzed/compared?   No   Maybe   ⟨Yes⟩

   Summary Rating   <u>Low</u>   <u>Medium</u>   <u>High</u>
                          0   ②   3   6

**Comments—If gender, ethnicity, or age are the main focus of the study,
base the number of points on the other two ratings, so rated ⟨2 out of 6⟩.**

*This was rated as medium. Child gender relationships with maternal depression were not re-
ported and minorities were too few to analyze. However, relationships were reported for each
age separately as well as for both ages combined.*

17. Peer review? Was it adequate?   No   Maybe   ⟨Yes⟩

   Comments/Explanation

18. Literature/theory to results Was the
case made?   No   Maybe   ⟨Yes⟩

   Comments

19. Interpretation of results Were they
appropriate?   No   Maybe   ⟨Yes⟩

   Comments

Summary Rating Form

Transfer each score (e.g., 5/10) and the percentage (e.g., 50%) to this table. If an overall score is needed, average the percentages.

Question	Score	Percent
9. Overall measurement reliability and statistics	9	90
Internal Validity		
10. Equivalence of the groups on participant characteristics	2	25
11. Control of extraneous experience and environment variables	3	38
Validity of Constructs		
12. Measurement validity of the intervention (if any)	NA	NA
13. Measurement validity of outcomes and other measures	3	50
External Validity		
14. Population external validity	2	33
15. Ecological external validity	4	50
16. Testing of subgroups	2	33
Total		319
Average Percent		46

Comparative Numerical Evaluations of the Four Sample Studies

	Evaluation Percentages			
Question	Study 1	Study 2	Study 3	Study 4
9. Overall measurement reliability and statistics	80%	60%	70%	90%
Internal Validity				
10. Equivalence of the groups on participant characteristics	88%	63%	50%	25%
11. Control of extraneous experience and environment variables	33%	38%	25%	38%
Validity of Constructs				
12. Construct validity of the intervention (if any)	67%	67%	—	—
13. Measurement or construct validity of outcomes and other measured variables	50%	50%	50%	50%
External Validity				
14. Population external validity	50%	50%	67%	33%
15. Ecological external validity	80%	80%	75%	50%
16. Testing of subgroups	0%	0%	0%	33%
Average %	56%	51%	48%	46%

A side-by-side comparison indicates that in terms of overall research validity, based on the average percentages, all four studies were in the middle range (46% to 56%). These somewhat similar percentages are not too surprising because all four were published in peer-reviewed journals. However, they all had areas of weakness, in part because they were small-scale, clinically relevant studies.

All of the studies had middling population external validity, with study 3 having a somewhat better sample. The samples, as is often the case, may not be representative of the population of interest. On the other hand, measurement reliability and statistics, except for low power and lack of detail about reliability, was quite good for all four. The ecological external validity of, especially, the first three studies was quite good.

Testing of participant subgroups was low, in part because the relatively small samples prevented adequate comparisons of gender, age, and ethnicity/racial subgroups. This markedly lowered the average ratings.

The studies did vary considerably, as expected, on internal validity, which is considered to be the most important dimension by experimental researchers, including those who do randomized clinical trials, meta-analyses of what interventions work best, and evidence-based practice. The randomized experiment (study 1) rated the highest and the comparative and associational studies rated the lowest. The quasi-experiment (study 2) was rated in between on internal validity overall.

Confusing Terms

PARTIALLY SIMILAR TERMS FOR DIFFERENT CONCEPTS[1]

- Cronbach's *alpha* ≠ *alpha* (significance) level
- *Chi-square* for independence (two samples) ≠ *chi-square* for goodness of fit (one sample)
- *Dependent* variable ≠ *dependent* samples design or statistic
- *Discriminant* analysis ≠ *discriminant* evidence for measurement validity
- *Factor* (i.e., independent variable) ≠ *factor* analysis
- *Factorial* design ≠ *factorial* evidence for measurement validity
- *Independent* variable ≠ *independent* samples
- *Levels* (of a variable) ≠ *level* of measurement
- *Odds* ratio ≠ *odds*
- *Ordinal* scale of measurement ≠ *ordinal* interaction
- *Outcome* (dependent) variable ≠ *outcome* (results) of the study
- Research *question* ≠ questionnaire *question* or item
- *Random* assignment of participants to groups ≠ *random* assignment of treatments to groups
- *Random* assignment (of participants to groups) ≠ *random* selection (or sampling of participants to be included in the study) ≠ *random* order ≠ *random* selection of times to intervene

---

[1]Italicized terms are listed alphabetically; ≠ means "not equal to."

- Odds *ratio* ≠ risk *ratio*
- *Related* samples design ≠ variables that are *related*
- Random *samples* ≠ paired/related *samples* ≠ independent *samples*
- Measurement *scale* ≠ a rating *scale* ≠ summated/composite *scale* ≠ semantic differential *scale*
- *Theoretical* research ≠ *theoretical* population
- Measurement *validity* ≠ research *validity*

DIFFERENT TERMS FOR SIMILAR CONCEPTS[2]

Variables (see chap. 6)

- Active independent variable ≈ manipulated ≈ intervention ≈ treatment
- Attribute independent variable ≈ measured variable ≈ individual difference variable
- Change over time ≈ change between trials ≈ change between measures
- Dependent variable ≈ DV ≈ outcome ≈ criterion ≈ endogenous
- Independent variable ≈ IV ≈ antecedent ≈ predictor ≈ presumed cause ≈ factor ≈ *N*-way (e.g., 2-way) ≈ exogenous
- Levels (of a variable) ≈ categories ≈ values ≈ groups

Measurement (chap. 7)

- Categorical variable ≈ usually nominal, but many ordered variables have discrete categories
- Continuous variable ≈ normally distributed ≈ interval scale
- Dichotomous ≈ binary ≈ dummy variable ≈ nominal with two categories
- Interval scale ≈ numeric ≈ continuous variable ≈ quantitative ≈ scale data
- Normal ≈ (approximately) normally distributed variable ≈ interval and ratio data ≈ quantitative
- Nominal scale ≈ unordered categorical variable ≈ qualitative ≈ discrete
- Ordered variable ≈ ordinal or interval scale

---

[2]Terms are listed alphabetically within the categories (e.g., Variables). The term we use most often is listed on the left. Similar terms (indicated by ≈) used by other researchers and/or us are listed to the right. In a few cases an → is shown to indicated "leads to."

- Ordinal scale ≈ unequal-interval scale ≈ discrete ordered categorical variable
- Psychometric properties ≈ evidence for measurement reliability and validity

Measurement Reliability (chap. 8)

- Alternate forms reliability ≈ equivalent forms ≈ parallel forms ≈ coefficient of equivalence
- Internal consistency reliability ≈ interitem reliability ≈ Cronbach's alpha
- Interrater reliability ≈ interobserver reliability
- Measurement reliability ≈ reliability ≈ test, instrument, or score reliability
- Test–retest reliability ≈ coefficient of stability

Validity (chaps. 9, 17, and 37)

- Measurement reliability and statistics ≈ statistical (conclusion) validity
- Measurement validity ≈ test, instrument, or score validity ≈ validity
- Measurement validity of the constructs ≈ construct validity
- Random assignment → internal validity
- Random sampling → external validity
- Research validity ≈ validity of the study

Data Collection Techniques (chap. 10)

- Observer report ≈ researcher observation
- Participants ≈ subjects
- Questionnaire ≈ survey
- Self-report ≈ participant report or rating ≠ participant observation
- Summated scale ≈ aggregated scale ≈ composite

Research Approaches and Questions (chaps. 11 and 12)

- Associational approach ≈ correlational ≈ survey ≈ descriptive
- Associational questions ≈ correlational questions
- Comparative approach ≈ causal comparative ≈ ex post facto
- Descriptive approach ≈ exploratory research
- Difference questions ≈ group comparisons

Designs (chaps. 13–16)

- Between groups ≈ independent samples ≈ uncorrelated samples
- Comparison group ≈ control group
- Factorial design ≈ two or more independent variables ≈ complex design
- Nonexperimental research (comparative, associational, and descriptive approaches) ≈ some writers call all three descriptive
- Poor quasi-experimental designs ≈ preexperiment
- Quasi-experiment ≈ better quasi-experimental designs
- Random assignment to groups ≈ how subjects get into groups ≈ randomized design → high *internal* validity
- Randomized experiment ≈ true experiment ≈ randomized clinical trial ≈ randomized control trials ≈ RCT
- Single factor design ≈ one independent variable ≈ basic design
- Within subjects ≈ repeated measures ≈ related samples ≈ paired samples ≈ matched groups ≈ correlated samples ≈ within groups ≈ dependent samples

Threats to Internal Validity (chap. 17)

- Additive and interactive threats ≈ combinations of two or more threats
- Attrition/mortality threat ≈ high dropout rate (from the study)
- Contamination ≈ low control of extraneous variables
- History threat ≈ extraneous environmental events
- Instrumentation threat ≈ observer or instrument inconsistency
- Maturation threat ≈ growth/developmental changes
- Nonequivalent groups ≈ biased groups ≈ intact groups ≈ nonrandomized assignment
- Placebo effect ≈ Hawthorne effect ≈ expectancy effect
- Regression (to the mean) threat ≈ use of extreme groups
- Selection threat ≈ self-assignment to groups ≈ biased groups ≈ nonrandomized assignment
- Testing threat ≈ carryover effects

Sampling (chap. 18)

- Accessible population ≈ sampling frame
- Actual sample ≈ sample ≈ final sample

- Convenience sampling ≈ nonprobablility sampling ≈ biased sampling
- Random selection ≈ random sampling ≈ probability sampling → high *external* population validity
- Response rate ≈ return rate ≈ percent of selected sample consenting/ participating
- Selected sample ≈ participants sampled
- Theoretical population ≈ target population ≈ population of interest

Statistics (chaps. 20–36)

- Alternative hypothesis ≈ research hypothesis ≈ H_1
- ANOVA ≈ F ≈ analysis of variance ≈ overall or omnibus F
- Associate variables ≈ relate ≈ predict → correlation or regression
- Basic inferential statistics ≈ univariate statistic (one IV and one DV) ≈ also called bivariate statistics
- Chi-square for independence ≈ two-sample chi-square
- Chi-square for goodness of fit ≈ one-sample chi-square
- Compare groups ≈ test differences → t or ANOVA
- Complex inferential statistics ≈ multifactor statistics (more than one IV) ≈ multivariate statistics (usually more than one DV)
- Data mining ≈ fishing ≈ snooping ≈ multiple significance tests (without clear hypotheses or theory)
- Mann–Whitney U test ≈ Wilcoxon Mann–Whitney test ≠ Wilcoxon matched pairs test
- Mixed ANOVA ≈ split-plot ANOVA ≈ (sometimes called repeated-measures ANOVA)
- Multiple regression ≈ multiple linear regression
- Null hypothesis ≈ H_0
- Odds ratio ≈ OR
- Orthogonal ≈ independent ≈ perpendicular to
- Post hoc test ≈ follow-up ≈ multiple comparisons
- Relationship between variables ≈ relation between variables
- Repeated-measures ANOVA ≈ within-subjects ANOVA
- Significance level ≈ alpha level ≈ α
- Significance test ≈ null hypothesis significance test ≈ NHST
- Single-factor ANOVA ≈ one-way ANOVA

References

Altman, D. G., Schultz, K. F., Moher, D., Egger, M., Davidoff, F., Elbourne, D., Gotzsche, P. C., & Lang, T. (2001). The revised CONSORT statement for reporting randomized trials. *Annals of Internal Medicine, 134,* 663–694.

American Educational Research Association, American Psychological Association, & National Council on Measurement in Education. (1999). *Standards for educational and psychological testing.* Washington, DC: American Educational Research Association.

American Psychiatric Association. (2000). *Diagnostic and statistical manual of mental disorders* (4th ed. text revision). Washington, DC: Author.

American Psychological Association. (1994). *Publication manual of the American Psychological Association* (4th ed.). Washington, DC: Author.

American Psychological Association. (2001). *Publication manual of the American Psychological Association* (5th ed.). Washington, DC: Author.

Antes, G., & Oxman, A. D. (2001). The Cochrane Collaboration in the 20th century. In M. Egger, G. D. Smith, & D. G. Altman (Eds.), *Systematic reviews in health care* (2nd ed., pp. 211–227), London: BMJ.

Bartko, J. J., & Carpenter, W. T. (1976). On the methods and theory of reliability. *Journal of Nervous and Mental Diseases, 163,* 307–317.

Beatty, W. W., & Gange, J. J. (1977). Neuropsychological aspects of multiple sclerosis. *Journal of Nervous and Mental Disease, 164,* 42–50.

Campbell, D. T., & Kenny, D. A. (1999). *A primer on regression artifacts.* New York: Guilford Press.

Campbell, D. T., & Stanley, J. C. (1966). *Experimental and quasi-experimental designs for research.* Chicago: Rand McNally. (Originally published 1963)

Campbell Collaboration. (n.d.). *What helps? What harms? Based on what evidence?* Retrieved August 18, 2004, from www.campbellcollaboration.org

Cohen, J. (1988). *Statistical power analysis for the behavioral sciences* (2nd ed.). Hillsdale, NJ: Lawrence Erlbaum Associates.

Cohen, J. (1994). The world is round ($p < .05$). *American Psychologist, 49,* 997–1003.

Compton, S. N., Grant, P. J., Chrisman, A. K., Gammon, P. J., Brown, V. L., & March, J. S. (2001). Sertraline in children and adolescents with social anxiety disorder: An open trial. *Journal of the American Academy of Child and Adolescent Psychiatry, 40,* 564–571.

Compton, S. N., Nelson, A. H., & March, J. S. (2000). Social phobia and separation anxiety symptoms in community and clinical samples of children and adolescents. *Journal of the American Academy of Child and Adolescent Psychiatry, 39,* 1040–1046.

Connor, D. F., Glatt, S. J., Lopez, I. D., Jackson, D., & Melloni, R. H. (2002). Psychopharmacology and aggression I: A meta-analysis of stimulant effects on overt/covert aggression-related behaviors in ADHD. *Journal of the American Academy of Child and Adolescent Psychiatry, 41,* 253–261.

Conners, C. K., Epstein, J. N., March, J. S. Angold, A., Wells, K. C., Klaric, J., Swanson, J. M., Arnold, L., Abikoff, H. B., Elliot, G. R., Greenhill, L. L., Hechtman, L., Hinshaw, S. P., Hoza, B., Jensen, P. S., Kraemer, H. C., Newcome, J. H., Palham, W. E., Severe, J. B., Vitiello, B., & Wigal, T. (2001). Multimodal treatment of ADHD in the MTA: An alternative outcome analysis. *Journal of the American Academy of Child and Adolescent Psychiatry, 40,* 159–167.

Cook, T. D., & Campbell, D. T. (1979). *Quasi-experimentation: Design and analysis issues for field settings.* Boston: Houghton Mifflin.

Cooper, H., & Hedges, L. V. (Eds.). (1994). *The handbook of research synthesis.* New York: Russell Sage Foundation.

Cronbach, L. J. (1990). *Essentials of psychological testing* (5th ed.). New York: HarperCollins.

Dierker, L. C., Albano, A. M., Clarke, G. N., Heimberg, R. G., Kendall, P. C., Merikangas, K. R., Lewinson, P. M., Offord, D. R., Kessler, R., & Kupfer, D. J. (2001). Screening for anxiety and depression in early adolescence. *Journal of the American Academy of Child and Adolescent Psychiatry, 40,* 929–936.

DiLorenzo, T., Hapler, J., & Picone, M. A. (2004). Comparison of older and younger individuals with multiple sclerosis: A preliminary investigation. *Rehabilitation Psychology, 49,* 123–125.

Donenberg, G. R., Emerson, E., Bryant, F. B., Wilson, H., & Weber-Shifrin, E. (2001). Understanding AIDS-risk behavior among adolescents in psychiatric care: Links to psychopathology and peer relationships. *Journal of the American Academy of Child and Adolescent Psychiatry, 40,* 642–653.

Egger, M., Smith, G. D., & Schneider, M. (2001). Systematic reviews of observational studies. In M. Egger, G. D. Smith, & D. G. Altman (Eds.), *Systematic reviews in health care* (2nd ed., pp. 211–277). London: BMJ.

Epstein, D. H. (2003). Problems with odds ratios. *American Journal of Geriatric Psychiatry, 160,* 190–191.

Fowler, F. J., Jr. (2001). *Survey research methods* (3rd ed.). Thousand Oaks, CA: Sage.

Gaito, J. (1980). Measurement scales and statistics: Resurgence of an old misconception. *Psychological Bulletin, 87,* 564–567.

Gaito, J. (1986). Some issues in the measurement-statistics controversy. *Canadian Psychology, 27,* 63–68.

Gliner, J., Gliner, G., Cobb, B., Alwell, M., Winokur, M., Wolgemuth, J., & Newman-Gonchar, B. (2004). *Meta-analysis of single subject designs.* Technical Report, What Works in Transition. Ft. Collins: Colorado State University, School of Education.

Gliner, J. A., & Morgan, G. A. (2000). *Research design and analysis in applied settings: An integrated approach.* Mahwah, NJ: Lawrence Erlbaum Associates.

Gliner, J. A., & Sample, P. (1996). A multimethod approach to evaluate transition into community life. *Evaluation & Program Planning, 19,* 225–233.

Goodwin, L. D., & Leech, N. L. (2003). The meaning of validity in the new standards: Implications for measurement courses. *Measurement and Evaluation in Counseling and Development, 36*(3), 181–192.

Grimm, L. B., & Yarnold, P. R. (Eds.). (1995). *Reading and understanding multivariate statistics.* Washington, DC: American Psychological Association.

Grissom, R. J. (1994). Probability of the superior outcome of one treatment over another. *Journal of Applied Psychology, 79,* 314–316.

Grissom, R. J., & Kim, J. (2005). *Effect sizes for research.* Mahwah, NJ: Lawrence Erlbaum Associates.

Harlow, L. L., Mulaik, S. A., & Steiger, J. H. (Eds.). (1997). *What if there were no significance tests?* Mahwah, NJ: Lawrence Erlbaum Associates.

Harmon, R. J., Morgan, G. A., & Glicken, A. D. (1984). Continuities and discontinuities in affective and cognitive-motivational development. *Child Abuse and Neglect, 8,* 157–167.

Hendricks, B., Marvel, M. K., & Barrington, B. L. (1990). The dimensions of psychological research. *Teaching Psychology, 17,* 76–82.

Herpertz, S. C., Wenning, B., Mueller, B., Qunaibi, M., Sass, H., & Herpertz-Dahlmann, B. (2001). Psychophysiological responses in ADHD boys with and without conduct disorder: Implications for adult antisocial behavior. *Journal of the American Academy of Child and Adolescent Psychiatry, 40,* 1222–1230.

Holm, M. B. (2000). Our mandate for the new millennium: Evidence-based practice, 2000 Eleanor Clarke Slagel lecture. *American Journal of Occupational Therapy, 54,* 575–585.

Huck, S. W. (2004). *Reading statistics and research* (4th ed.). Boston: Allyn & Bacon, Longman.

International Committee of Medical Journal Editors. (1997). Uniform requirements for manuscripts submitted to biomedical journals. *Journal of the American Medical Association, 277,* 927–934.

Jacobson, N. S., Roberts, L. J., Berns, S. B., & McGlinchey, J. B. (1999). Clinical significance of treatment effects models for defining and determining the description, application and alternatives. *Journal of Consulting and Clinical Psychology, 67,* 300–307.

Johnson, C. L., Jr., & Johnson, J. A. (1991). Using short-term groups counseling with visually impaired adolescents. *Journal of Visual Impairment & Blindness, 85,* 166–170.

Journal citation reports. Social science ed. (1994). (CD-ROM. Annual electronic resource). Philadelphia: Thompson/ISI.

Kazdin, A. (1982). *Single-case research designs.* New York: Oxford University Press.

Kazdin, A. E. (Ed.). (2003). *Methodological issues and strategies in clinical research.* Washington, DC: American Psychological Association.

Kazdin, A. E., & Bass, D. (1989). Power to detect differences between alternative treatments in comparative psychotherapy outcome research. *Journal of Consulting and Clinical Psychology, 57,* 138–147.

Keppel, G., & Zedeck, S. (1989). *Data analysis for research designs.* New York: W. H. Freeman.

Kerlinger, F. N. (1986). *Foundations of behavioral research* (3rd ed.). New York: Holt, Rinehart & Winston.

Kirk, R. E. (1996). Practical significance: A concept whose time has come. *Educational and Psychological Measurement, 56,* 746–759.

Kirk, R. E. (2001). Promoting good statistical practices: Some suggestions. *Educational and Psychological Measurement, 61,* 213–218.

Kline, R. B. (2004). *Beyond significance testing.* Washington, DC: American Psychological Association.

Kraemer, H. C. (1992). Reporting the size of effects in research studies to facilitate assessment of practical or clinical importance. *Psychoneuroendocrinology, 17,* 527–536.

Kraemer, H. C., Gardner, G., Brooks, J. O., III, & Yesavage, J. A. (1998). Advantages of excluding underpowered studies in meta-analysis: Inclusionist versus exclusionist viewpoints. *Psychological Methods, 3,* 23–31.

Kraemer, H. C., Jacob, R. G., Jeffery, R. W., & Agras, W. S. (1979). Empirical selection of matching factors in matched-pairs and matched-blocks small-sample research designs. *Behavior Therapy, 10,* 615–628.

Kraemer, H. C., Morgan, G. A., Leech, N. L., Gliner, J. A., Vaske, J. J., & Harmon, R. J. (2003). Measures of clinical significance. *Journal of the American Academy of Child and Adolescent Psychiatry, 42,* 1542–1529.

Kraemer, H. C., & Thiemann, S. (1987). *How many subjects? Statistical power analysis in research.* Newbury Park, CA: Sage.

Kratochwill, T., & Levin, J. (Eds.). (1992). *Single-case research design and analysis.* Hillsdale, NJ: Lawrence Erlbaum Associates.

Kuhn, T. S. (1970). *The structure of scientific revolutions* (2nd ed.). Chicago: University of Chicago Press.

Laupacis, A., Sackett, D. L., & Roberts, R. S. (1988). An assessment of clinically useful measures of the consequences of treatment. *New England Journal of Medicine, 318,* 1728–1733.

Law, M. (Ed.). (2002). *Evidence-based rehabilitation.* Thorofare, NJ: Slack, Inc.

Leech, N. L., Barrett, K. C., & Morgan, G. A. (2005). *SPSS for intermediate statistics: Use and interpretation.* Mahwah, NJ: Lawrence Erlbaum Associates.

Levin, J. R., & Robinson, D. H. (2000). Rejoinder: Statistical hypothesis testing, effect-size estimation, and the conclusion of coherence of primary research studies. *Educational Researcher, 29,* 34–36.

Lincoln, Y. S., & Guba, E. G. (1985). *Naturalistic inquiry.* Newbury Park, CA: Sage.

Lipsey, M. W. (1990). *Design sensitivity: Statistical power for experimental research.* Newbury Park, CA: Sage.

Lipsey, M. W., & Wilson, D. B. (2000). *Practical meta-analysis.* Thousand Oaks, CA: Sage.

Logan, D. E., & King, C. A. (2002). Parental identification of depression and mental health service use among depressed adolescents. *Journal of the American Academy of Child and Adolescent Psychiatry, 41,* 296–304.

MacTurk, R. H., & Morgan, G. A. (Eds.). (1995). *Mastery motivation: Origins, conceptualizations and applications.* Norwood, NJ: Ablex.

Marmorstein, N. R., & Iacono, W. G. (2003). Major depression and conduct disorder in a twin sample: Gender, functioning, and risk for future psychopathology. *Journal of the American Academy of Child and Adolescent Psychiatry, 42,* 225–233.

McMillan, J. H., & Wergin, J. F. (2002). *Understanding and evaluating educational research* (2nd ed.). Upper Saddle River, NJ: Merrill Prentice Hall.

Meehl, P. (1990). Why summaries of research on psychological theories are often uninterpretable. *Psychological Reports, 66*(Monogr. Suppl. I-V66), 195–244.

Mental measurements yearbooks. (1938–present). Lincoln, NE: Buros Institute of Mental Measurements, University of Nebraska.

Mick, E., Biederman, J., Faraone, S. V., Sayer, J., & Kleinman, S. (2002). Case-control study of attention-deficit hyperactivity disorder and maternal smoking, alcohol use, and drug use during pregnancy. *Journal of the American Academy of Child and Adolescent Psychiatry, 41,* 378–385.

Morgan, G. A., Busch-Rossnagel, N. A., Barrett, K. C., & Harmon, R. J. (2005). *Dimensions of mastery questionnaire: A manual about its development, psychometrics, and use.* Unpublished document is available from G. A. Morgan at the School of Education, Colorado State University, Fort Collins, CO 80523-1588.

Morgan, G. A., Gliner, J. A., & Harmon, R. J. (1999). Evaluating the validity of a research study. *Journal of the American Academy of Child and Adolescent Psychiatry, 38,* 480–485.

Morgan, G. A., Harmon, R. J., & Maslin-Cole, C. A. (1990). Mastery motivation: Definition and measurement. *Early Education and Development, 1,* 318–339.

Morgan, G. A., Maslin-Cole, C. A., Harmon, R. J., Busch-Rossnagel, N. A., Jennings, K. D., Hauser-Cram, P., & Brockman, L. (1993). Parent and teacher perceptions of young children's mastery motivation: Assessment and review of research. In D. Messer (Ed.), *Mastery motivation in early childhood: Development, measurement and social processes* (pp. 109–131). London: Routledge.

Morgan, G. A., & Ricciuti, H. N. (1969). Infants' response to strangers during the first year. In B. M. Foss (Ed.), *Determinants of infant behavior* (pp. 272–353). London: Methuen.

National Commission for the Protection of Human Subjects of Biomedical and Behavioral Research. (1978). *The Belmont report: Ethical principles and guidelines for the protection of human subjects of research* (DHEW Publication [OS] 78-0012). Washington, DC: U.S. Government Printing Office.

Nunnally, J. C., & Bernstein, I. H. (1994). *Psychometric theory* (3rd ed.). New York: McGraw-Hill.

Nuovo, J., Melnikov, J., & Chang, D. (2002). Reporting number needed to treat and risk difference in randomized controlled trials. *Journal of the American Medical Association, 287,* 2813–2814.

Oaks, M. (1986). *Statistical inference: A commentary for the social and behavioral sciences.* New York: Wiley.

Ottenbacher, K. (1986). *Evaluating clinical change.* Baltimore, MD: Williams & Wilkins.

Phillips, D. C. (1992). *The social scientist's bestiary.* Oxford, England: Pergamon.

Phillips, D. C., & Burbules, N. C. (2000). *Postpositivism and educational research.* Lanham, MD: Rowman & Littlefield.

Porter, A. C. (1997). Comparative experiments in education research. In R. M. Jaeger (Ed.), *Complementary methods for research in education* (2nd ed., pp. 523–544). Washington, DC: American Educational Research Association.

Pross, C. (1992). Nazi doctors, German medicine, and historical truth. In G. J. Annas & M. A. Grodin (Eds.), *The Nazi doctors and the Nuremberg Code* (pp. 32–52). New York: Oxford University Press.

Pyrczak, F. (2003). *Evaluating research in academic journals.* Glendale, CA: Pyrczak.

Redding, R. E., Harmon, R. J., & Morgan, G. A. (1990). Relationships between maternal depression and infants' mastery behaviors. *Infant Behavior and Development, 13,* 391–395.

Rennie, D., Yank, V., & Emanuel, L. (1997). When authorship fails: A proposal to make contributors accountable. *Journal of the American Medical Association, 278,* 579–585.

Rheingold, H. L., & Eckerman, C. O. (1973). Fear of the stranger. In H. W. Reese (Ed.), *Advances in child development and behavior* (pp. 185–222). New York: Academic Press.

Rohde, L. A., Barbosa, G., Polanczyk, G., Eizlrik, M., Rasmussen, E. R., Neuman, R. J., & Todd, R. D. (2001). Factor and latent class analysis of *DSM-IV* ADHD symptoms in a school sample of Brazilian adolescents. *Journal of the American Academy of Child and Adolescent Psychiatry, 40,* 711–718.

Rosenthal, R. (2001). Effect sizes in behavioral and biomedical research. In L. Bickman (Ed.), *Validity and social experimentation* (pp. 121–139). Thousand Oaks, CA: Sage.

Rosenthal, R., & Rosnow, R. L. (1991). *Essentials of behavioral research: Methods and data analysis* (2nd ed.). Boston: McGraw-Hill.

Sackett, D. L. (1989). Rules of evidence and clinical recommendations on the use of antithrombotic agents. *Chest, 25,* 2S–3S.

Sackett, D. L., Richardson, W. S., Rosenberg, W., & Haynes, R. B. (Eds.). (2000). *Evidence-based medicine: How to practice and teach EBM.* New York: Churchill Livingstone.

Sackett, D. L., Rosenberg, W. M., Gray, J. A., Haynes, R. B., & Richardson, W. S. (1996). Evidence-based medicine: What is it and what isn't it. *British Medical Journal, 312,* 71–72.

Salant, P., & Dillman, D. A. (1994). *How to conduct your own survey.* New York: Wiley.

Scruggs, T. E., & Mastropieri, M. A. (1994). The effectiveness of generalization training: A quantitative synthesis of single subject research. In T. E. Scruggs & M. A. Mastropieri (Eds.), *Advances in learning and behavioral disabilities* (Vol. 8, pp. 259–280). Greenwich, CT: JAI.

Shadish, W. R., Cook, T. D., & Campbell, D. T. (2002). *Experimental and quasi-experimental designs for generalized causal influence.* Boston: Houghton Mifflin.

Shavelson, R. J. (1996). *Statistical reasoning for the behavioral sciences* (3rd ed.). Needham Heights, MA: Allyn & Bacon.

Shuster, E. (1997). Fifty years later: The significance of the Nuremberg code. *New England Journal of Medicine, 337,* 1436–1440.

Sieber, J. E. (1992). *Planning ethically responsible research: A guide for students and internal review boards.* Newbury Park, CA: Sage.

Siegel, S., & Castellan, N. J. (1988). *Nonparametric statistics for the behavioral sciences* (2nd ed.). New York: McGraw-Hill.

Smith, M. L. (1981). Naturalistic research. *Personnel and Guidance Journal, 59,* 585–589.

Spitz, R. A. (1965). *The first year of life.* New York: International Universities Press.

Stevens, J. P. (1999). *Intermediate statistics: A modern approach* (2nd ed.). Mahwah, NJ: Lawrence Erlbaum Associates.

Stevens, S. S. (1951). Mathematics, measurement and psychophysics. In S. S. Stevens (Ed.), *Handbook of experimental psychology* (pp. 1–49). New York: Wiley.

Stone, W. L., Lemanek, K. L., Fishel, P. T., Fernandez, M. C., & Altemeier, W. A. (1990). Play and imitation skills in the diagnosis of autism in young children. *Pediatrics, 86,* 267–272.

Strube, M. J. (2000). Reliability and generalizability theory. In L. G. Grimm & P. R. Yarnold (Eds.), *Reading and understanding more multivariate statistics* (pp. 23–66). Washington, DC: American Psychological Association.

Swanson, H. L., & Sachse-Lee, C. (2000). A meta-analysis of single-subject intervention research for students with LD. *Journal of Learning Disabilities, 33,* 114–136.

Thompson, B. (1995). Stepwise regression and stepwise discriminant analysis need not apply here: A guideline editorial. *Educational and Psychological Measurement, 55,* 525–534.

Thompson, B. (2002). "Statistical," "practical," and "clinical": How many kinds of significance do counselors need to consider? *Journal of Counseling & Development, 80,* 64–71.

Thompson, B. (2004). *Exploratory and confirmatory factor analyses: Understanding concepts and applications.* Washington, DC: American Psychological Association.

Tickle-Degnen, L. (1999). Evidence-based practice forum: Organizing, evaluating, and using evidence in occupational therapy practice. *American Journal of Occupational Therapy, 53,* 537–539.

Toppelberg, C. O., Medrano, L., Morgens, L. P., & Nieto-Castanon, A. (2002). Bilingual children referred for psychiatric services: Associations of language disorders, language skills, and psychopathology. *Journal of the American Academy of Child and Adolescent Psychiatry, 41,* 712–722.

Tukey, J. W. (1977). *Exploratory data analysis.* Reading, MA: Addison-Wesley.

Tukey, J. W. (1991). The philosophy of multiple comparisons. *Statistical Science, 6,* 100–116.

Vaske, J. J., Gliner, J. A., & Morgan, G. A. (2002). Communicating judgments about practical significance: Effect size, confidence intervals and odds ratios. *Human Dimensions of Wildlife, 7,* 287–300.

Velleman, P. F., & Wilkinson, L. (1993). Nominal, ordinal, interval, and ratio typologies are misleading. *American Statistician, 47,* 65–72.

Wazana, A. (2000). Physicians and the pharmaceutical industry: Is a gift ever just a gift? *Journal of the American Medical Association, 283,* 373–380.

What Works Clearinghouse. (n.d.). *WWC study review standards.* Retrieved August 18, 2004, from http://w-w-c.org/reports/study_standards_final.pdf

White, R. W. (1963). Ego reality in psychoanalytic theory: A proposal regarding independent ego energies. *Psychological Issues* (Monogr. II, Vol. 3, No. 3). New York: International Universities Press.

Wilkinson, L., & the Task Force on Statistical Inference. (1999). Statistical methods in psychology journals: Guidelines and explanations. *American Psychologist, 54,* 594–604.

Winer, B. J. (1962). *Statistical principles in experimental design* (2nd ed.). New York: McGraw-Hill.

Wolfe, D. A., Scott, K., Wekerle, C., & Pittman, A. (2001). Child maltreatment: Risk of adjustment problems and dating violence in adolescence. *Journal of the American Academy of Child and Adolescent Psychiatry, 40,* 282–289.

Wood, A., Trainor, G., Rothwell, J. U., Moore, A., & Harrington, R. (2001). Randomized trial of group therapy for repeated deliberate self-harm in adolescents. *Journal of the American Academy of Child and Adolescent Psychiatry, 40,* 1246–1253.

Woodward, J., & Goodstein, D. (1996). Conduct, misconduct and structure of science. *American Scientist, 84,* 479–490.

Zeanah, C. H., Larrieu, J. A., Heller, S. S., Valliere, J., Hinshaw-Fuselier, S., Aoki, Y., & Drilling, M. (2001). Evaluation of a preventive intervention for maltreated infants and toddlers in foster care. *Journal of the American Academy of Child and Adolescent Psychiatry, 40,* 214–221.

Author Index

A

Abikoff, H. B., 209, 210, 211, 212, 241
Agras, W. S., 91
Albano, A. M., 196, 198, 199, 200, 241
Altman, D. G., 281
Altmeier, W. A., 234
Alwell, M., 102
Angold, A., 209, 210, 211, 212, 241
Antes, G., 265
Aoki, Y., 205
Arnold, L., 209, 210, 211, 212, 241

B

Barbosa, G., 252
Barrington, B. L., 75
Barrett, K. C., xiii, 8, 246, 247, 248, 250, 251, 254
Bartko, J. J., 48
Bass, D., 275, 276
Beatty, W. W., 115
Berns, S. B., 272
Bernstein, I. H., 48, 204
Biederman, J., 230, 231, 232, 233, 234, 243
Brockman, L., 8, 56
Brooks, J. O., III, 266

Brown, V. L., 188, 189, 190, 191, 192, 193, 194, 238
Bryant, F. B., 244
Burbules, N. C., 15
Busch-Rossnagel, N. A., 8, 56

C

Campbell, D. T., 6, 83, 86, 93, 113, 114, 116, 117, 118, 129, 131, 133, 135, 136, 137, 285, 286, 287, 295, 297, 303, 309
Carpenter, W. T., 48
Castellan, N. J., 186
Chang, D., 279, 281
Chrisman, A. K., 188, 189, 190, 191, 192, 193, 194, 238
Clarke, G. N., 196, 198, 199, 200, 241
Cobb, B., 102
Cohen, J., 57, 58, 126, 152, 153, 156, 157, 162, 163, 165, 197, 204, 224, 226, 275, 295
Compton, S. N., 188, 189, 190, 191, 192, 193, 194, 238, 241
Connor, D. F., 261, 266, 267, 268, 269, 270, 271
Connors, C. K., 209, 210, 211, 212, 241

Cook, T. D., 6, 83, 86, 93, 113, 114, 116, 118, 129, 131, 135, 136, 137, 285, 286, 287, 295, 297, 309
Cooper, H., 266
Cronbach, L. J., 53, 55

D

Davidoff, F., 281
Dierker, L. J., 196, 198, 199, 200, 241
Dillman, D. A., 64
DiLorenzo, T., 7, 31, 33, 73, 74, 103, 115, 138, 317
Donenberg, G. R., 244
Drilling, M., 205

E

Eckerman, C. O., 136
Egger, M., 267, 281
Eizlrick, M., 252
Elbourne, D., 281
Elliot, G. R., 209, 210, 211, 212, 241
Emanuel, L., 25
Emerson, E., 244
Epstein, D. H., 231
Epstein, J. N., 209, 210, 211, 212, 241

F

Faraone, S. V., 230, 231, 232, 233, 234, 243
Fernandez, M. C., 234
Fishel, P. T., 234
Fowler, F. J., Jr., 125

G

Gaito, J., 36
Gammon, P. J., 188, 189, 190, 191, 192, 193, 194, 238
Gange, J. J., 115
Gardner, G., 266
Glatt, S. J., 261, 266, 267, 268, 269, 270, 271
Glicken, A. D., 31, 35
Gliner, G., 102

Gliner, J. A., ix, xiii, 6, 13, 31, 32, 33, 34, 102, 107, 137, 138, 157, 198, 273, 280, 285, 313
Goodstein, D., 28
Goodwin, L. D., 51, 52, 56
Gotzsche, P. C., 281
Grant, P. J., 188, 189, 190, 191, 192, 193, 194, 238
Gray, J. A., 258
Greenhill, L. L., 209, 210, 211, 212, 241
Grimm, L. B., 229
Grissom, R. J., 161, 273, 274
Guba, E. G., 14, 15, 16

H

Hapler, J., 7, 31, 33, 73, 74, 103, 115, 138, 317
Harlow, L. L., 152, 153
Harmon, R. J., 7, 8, 31, 32, 33, 35, 56, 120, 138, 157, 273, 280, 285, 319
Harrington, R., 215, 216, 217, 218, 219, 220
Hauser-Cram, P., 8, 56
Haynes, R. B., 258, 262
Hechtman, L., 209, 210, 211, 212, 241
Hedges, L. V., 266
Heimberg, R. G., 196, 198, 199, 200, 241
Heller, S. S., 205
Hendricks, B., 75
Herpertz, S. C., 181, 182, 183, 184, 185, 186, 238
Herpertz-Dahlmann, B., 181, 182, 183, 184, 185, 186, 238
Hinshaw, S. P., 209, 210, 211, 212, 241
Hinshaw-Fuselier, S., 205
Holm, M. B., 257, 258
Hoza, B., 209, 210, 211, 212, 241
Huck, S. W., 221

I

Iacono, W. G., 243

J

Jackson, D., 261, 266, 267, 268, 269, 270, 271

Jacob, R. G., 91
Jacobson, N. S., 272
Jeffery, R. W., 91
Jennings, K. D., 8, 56
Jensen, P. S., 209, 210, 211, 212, 241
Johnson, C. L., Jr., 6, 32, 33, 115, 138, 315
Johnson, J. A., 6, 32, 33, 115, 138, 315

K

Kazdin, A., x, 100, 101, 275, 276
Kendall, P. C., 196, 198, 199, 200, 241
Kenny, D. A., 117
Keppel, G., 179
Kerlinger, F. N., 31, 32
Kessler, R., 196, 198, 199, 200, 241
Kim, J., 161, 273, 274
King, C. A., 223, 226, 227, 241
Kirk, R. E., 153 , 272
Klaric, J., 209, 210, 211, 212, 241
Kleinman, S., 230, 231, 232, 233, 234, 243
Kline, R. B., 152, 158, 185
Kraemer, H. C., 36, 91, 126, 157, 209, 210,
    211, 212, 213, 220, 241, 266, 273,
    276, 280, 289
Kratochwill, T., 101
Kuhn, T. S., 14
Kupfer, D. J., 196, 198, 199, 200, 241

L

Lang, T., 281
Larrieu, J. A., 205
Laupacis, A., 279
Law, M., 257, 258
Leech, N. L., xiii, 51, 52, 56, 157, 246, 247,
    248, 250, 251, 254, 273, 280
Lemanek, K. L., 234
Levin, J., 101, 156
Lewinson, P. M., 196, 198, 199, 200, 241
Lincoln, Y. S., 14, 15, 16
Lipsey, M. W., 222, 266, 270, 297
Logan, D. E., 223, 226, 227, 241
Lopez, I. D., 261, 266, 267, 268, 269, 270, 271

M

MacTurk, R. H., 8
March, J. S., 188, 189, 190, 191, 192, 193,
    194, 209, 210, 211, 212, 238, 241

Marmorstein, N. R., 243
Marvel, M. K., 75
Maslin-Cole, C. A., 7, 8, 56
Mastropieri, M. A., 101
McGlinchey, J. B., 272
McMillan, J. H., 286
Medrano, L., 243
Meehl, P., 153
Melloni, R. H., 261, 266, 267, 268, 269,
    270, 271
Melnikov, J., 279, 281
Merikangas, K. R., 196, 198, 199, 200, 241
Mick, E., 230, 231, 232, 233, 234, 243
Moher, D., 281
Moore, A., 215, 216, 217, 218, 219, 220
Morgan, G. A., ix, xiii, 6, 7, 8, 31, 32, 33,
    35, 56, 120, 135, 138, 157, 198, 246,
    247, 248, 250, 251, 254, 273, 280,
    285, 319
Morgens, L. P., 243
Mueller, B., 181, 182, 183, 184, 185, 186,
    238
Mulaik, S. A., 152, 153

N

Nelson, A. H., 241
Neuman, R. J., 252
Newcome, J. H., 209, 210, 211, 212, 241
Newman-Gonchar, B., 102
Nieto-Castanon, A., 243
Nunnally, J. C., 48, 204
Nuovo, J., 279, 281

O

Oaks, M., 155
Offord, D. R., 196, 198, 199, 200, 241
Ottenbacher, K., 10, 99, 100
Oxman, A. D., 265

P

Palham, W. E., 209, 210, 211, 212, 241
Phillips, D. C., 15
Picone, M. A., 7, 31, 33, 73, 74, 103, 115,
    138, 317
Pittman, A., 202, 204, 205, 240

Polanczyk, G., 252
Porter, A. C., 113, 114, 120
Pross, C., 18
Pyrczak, F., 286

Q

Qunaibi, M., 181, 182, 183, 184, 185, 186, 238

R

Rasmussen, E. R., 252
Redding, R. E., 7, 32, 33, 120, 138, 319
Rennie, D., 25
Rheingold, H. L., 136
Ricciuti, H. N., 135
Richardson, W. S., 258, 262
Roberts, L. J., 272
Roberts, R. S., 279
Robinson, D. H., 156
Rohde, L. A., 252
Rosenberg, W., 258, 262
Rosenthal, R., 205, 207
Rosnow, R. L., 207
Rothwell, J. U., 215, 216, 217, 218, 219, 220

S

Sachse-Lee, C., 101
Sackett, D. L., 258, 262, 279
Salant, P., 64
Sample, P., 6, 13, 31, 32, 33, 34, 107, 137, 138, 313
Sass, H., 181, 182, 183, 184, 185, 186, 238
Sayer, J., 230, 231, 232, 233, 234, 243
Schneider, M., 267
Schultz, K. F., 281
Scott, K., 202, 204, 205, 240
Scruggs, T. E., 101
Severe, J. B., 209, 210, 211, 212, 241
Shaddish, W. R., 93, 114, 116, 131, 285
Shavelson, R. J., 200
Shuster, E., 18
Sieber, J. E., 20, 21
Siegel, S., 186

Smith, G. D., 267
Smith, M. L., 9
Spitz, R. A., 135
Stanley, J. C., 133, 136, 137, 285, 303
Steiger, J. H., 152, 153
Stevens, J. P., 220, 221
Stevens, S. S., 36
Stone, W. L., 234
Stube, M. J., 48
Swanson, H. L., 101
Swanson, J. M., 209, 210, 211, 212, 241

T

Thiemann, S., 126
Thompson, B., 163, 228, 249
Tickle-Degnen, L., 258
Todd, R. D., 252
Toppelberg, C. O., 243
Trainor, G., 215, 216, 217, 218, 219, 220
Tukey, J. W., 41, 153, 165

V

Valliere, J., 205
Vaske, J. J., 157, 198, 273, 280
Velleman, P. F., 36
Vitiello, B., 209, 210, 211, 212, 241

W

Wazana, A., 28
Weber-Shifrin, E., 244
Wekerle, C., 202, 204, 205, 240
Wells, K. C., 209, 210, 211, 212, 241
Wenning, B., 181, 182, 183, 184, 185, 186, 238
Wergin, J. F., 286
White, R. W., 13
Wigal, T., 209, 210, 211, 212, 241
Wilkinson, L., 36, 156, 158, 162, 244
Wilson, D. B., 222, 266, 270
Wilson, H., 244
Winer, B. J., 107
Winokur, M., 102
Wolfe, D. A., 202, 204, 205, 240
Wolgemuth, J., 102

Wood, A., 215, 216, 217, 218, 219, 220
Wooward, J., 28

Y

Yank, V., 25

Yarnold, P. R., 229
Yesavage, J. O., 266

Z

Zedeck, S., 179
Zeanah, C. H., 205

Subject Index

A

Accessible population, 123–128, *see also* Population and Sampling

Achievement tests, *see* Standardized instruments

Active independent variable, 3, 69–72, 289, *see also* Experimental approaches

Actual sample, 123–124, 127–128
response rate, 124

Alpha
Cronbach's alpha, 47, 53, 246–248
required for significance, 150, 154, 155

Alternate forms reliability, *see* Parallel forms reliability

Alternating treatment designs, 98–99

Alternative hypothesis, 144

Analysis of covariance, 219–220

Analysis of variance (ANOVA), 176–179, 237–244, *see also* Single factor ANOVA, Two factor ANOVA, Mixed ANOVA

Anonymous, 21

Antecedent variable, *see* Independent variable

Aptitude test, *see also* Standardized instruments
group, 62
Stanford–Binet, 62

Wechsler, 62

Area under the curve (AUC), 273–275, 279–281

Associational inferential statistics, 71, 76–80, ch. 26, 27, 30, 31

Associational research approach, 4–8, 71–74
evaluation of, 319–321

Associational research hypothesis or questions, 76–80
basic questions, 77
complex questions, 79–80

Assumptions, *see* Statistical assumptions

Asymmetrical transfer effects, 92

Attitude scales, 63–64
summated or Likert, 64, 253–254

Attribute independent variable, 3, 72–74, 289, *see also* Research approach

Attrition/mortality, 117, *see also* Threats to internal validity

Authorship, *see* Publication

Axioms, *see also* Constructivist paradigm and Positivist paradigm

B

Basic associational designs and statistics, ch. 26
Cramer's V, 240

357

Basic associational designs and statistics
(cont.)
  linear regression, 223–224, 230
  Pearson product moment correlation
      (*r*), 195–199
  phi coefficient, 204
  Kendall Tau, 195, 199–200
  Spearman rank order correlation (rho),
      195, 199–200
Basic research question, *see* Research ques-
      tions or hypotheses
Behavioral observation, *see* Observation
Benefits of research, *see* Human research
      participants
Between groups design, 103–104, 107–110,
      175, ch. 24, 27, 28
  design classification descriptions,
      107–108
  factorial designs, 107–108, ch. 28
  single factor designs, 175, ch. 24, 27
Bias, *see also* Nonprobability sample, Data
      collection, and Internal validity
Bivariate regression, 223–224, 230
Blind review, *see* Peer review
Bonferroni procedure, 155, 184, 192
Box and whisker plot, 41–43

C

Canonical correlation, 243
Carryover effects, 83, 189–190
Categorical variable, *see* Measurement
Causal-comparative, *see* Comparative re-
      search approach
Cause and effect, 69–74, 113–114, *see also*
      Independent variable
Change over time independent variable,
      106
Chi-square test for independence, 268, ch.
      27
  effect size, 204
Citation, *see* Publication
Clinical significance, xi, 156–157, 160,
      163–166, ch. 36
Cluster random assignment design, 86
Cluster sampling, 125
Cochran Q test, 239
Coefficient of equivalence, *see* Parallel
      forms reliability

Coefficient of stability, *see* Test–retest reli-
      ability
Cohen's *d*, 268
Comparative research approach, 4–8, 70–73
  evaluation of, 317–319
Complex associational analyses (statistics),
      ch. 30, 31, 32
  discriminant analysis, ch. 31
  logistic regression, ch. 31
  multiple regression, 220, ch. 30
Complex research question, *see* Research
      questions or hypotheses
Composite variable, *see* Factor analysis
Concurrent evidence for criterion validity,
      see Measurement validity
Confidence intervals, 153, 160–161, 198
Confidential, 21
Confirmatory factor analysis, 249
Conflict of interest, 26–28
Consent, *see* Institutional review board and
      Voluntary informed consent
Construct validity, *see* Measurement validity
      and Research validity
Constructivist paradigm, 11–12, 14–17, *see
      also* Qualitative research
  causality axiom, 16–17
  generalization axiom, 16
  knower to known axiom, 15–16
  reality axiom, 15
  values axiom, 17
Consumer of research, *see* Research validity
      and Evaluation of
Content evidence for validity, 52–58
Continuous variable, *see* Measurement
Control group, 32
Control of extraneous variables, 116–120,
      see also Internal validity
Convenience sample, *see* Nonprobability
      sampling
Convergent evidence for validity, 55–58
Correlational approach, *see* Associational
      approach
Correlation, ch. 26
  coefficients, 195–196
  confidence interval, 198
  matrix, 198, 224
  Kendall Tau, 195, 199–200
  Pearson, 195–199
  Spearman, 195, 199–200
  statistical significance, 197
Cramer's V, 240

Criterion related evidence for validity, 54–55
  concurrent evidence for criterion validity, 54–55
  predictive evidence of criterion validity, 54–55
Criterion variable, *see also* Dependent variable
Cronbach's alpha, 47, 246–248
Crossover design, 92, 104–105

D

d (effect size index), 161, 185, 222, 267–268, 274–276, 279–281
Data collection techniques, 59–65, 75
Degrees of freedom (*df*), 183–184, 190–191, 196, 202, 205, 210–211
  Chi-square test, 202, 205
  Pearson product–moment correlation, 196
  single factor ANOVA, 183–184
  single factor ANOVA with repeated measures, 191
  t test for independent samples, 183, 190
  t test for paired samples, 190
  two factor ANOVA, 210–211
Dependent variable, *see* Variable
Descriptive research approach, 4, 71–72, 74–75
Descriptive research questions, 76–77, 79
Descriptive statistics, 40–43, 71
  central tendency, 41–43
  variability, 42–43
Design classification, *see* General design classification
Design terminology, *see* General design classification
Dichotomous variable, 36–37, 43, 201
Difference hypothesis or questions, 76–80, 173, 177–178, 239, 242
Difference inferential statistics, 71, 76–80, 219–220, ch. 25, 27, 28, 239
  factorial (complex), 79–80, 219–220, ch. 28, 29
  single factor (basic), 79, ch. 24, 25, 27
Directional hypothesis, *see also* Alternative hypothesis
Direct observation, *see* Observation
Direction of effect, 165, 167–168

Discrete variable, *see* Measurement
Discriminant analysis, 226, ch. 31
Discriminant evidence for validity, 55–58
Dropouts, *see* Attrition and Threats to internal validity
Dummy variable, *see* Dichotomous variable

E

Ecological external validity, *see* External validity
Effect size, x–xi, 57–58, 156–157, 161–164, 267–269, ch. 36
  AUC, 273–275, 279–281
  d family measures, 161–162, 191, 267–268, 274–276, 279–281
    Cohen's *d*, 268
    Glass's Δ, 268
    Hedges' *g*, 185
    eta^2, 185, 192, 211
  interpretation, 57–58, 156–157, ch. 36
  meta-analysis, 267–269
  number needed to treat (NNT), 267, 274–275, 279
  odds ratios (OR), 162, 204–205, 267, 274, 277–278
  phi, 204, 276
  probability of a better outcome, *see* AUC
  r family measures, 161, 267, 274–276
  relative risk, 204, *see* Risk ratio
  relative risk reduction, 162, 274, 278
  risk difference, 162, 204, 274, 278–279
  risk ratio, 162, 267, 274, 278
  risk potency measures, 162, 274, 276–280
Equality of variances, *see* Homogeneity
Equivalence of groups on participant characteristics, 115–118, *see also* Internal validity
eta^2, 185, 192, 211
Ethical issues, 18–28, *see also* Institutional review board
  Belmont report, 19
    beneficence, 19
    justice, 19
    respect for persons, 19
  history of, 18–19
  principles and policies, 19–23, 24–28
  publishing, 24–26
  reviewing, 26–28
  scientific misconduct, 28

Evaluation form, Appendices A & B
Evaluation framework, 285–288
Evaluation of
  example studies, 6–8, ch. 38
  external validity, 133–136, 303–307
  internal validity, 131–133, 298–301
  measurement reliability and statistics,
    296–297
  measurement validity of the constructs,
    301–303
Evidence-based practice, xi, ch. 34
Example studies, 6–8, 13, 137–139, ch. 38
Experimental approaches, 3–7
Exploratory factor analysis, 53, 249–252
External validity, 6, 126–128, 130, 133–139,
    259–260, 303–307
  ecological, 6, 130, 135–136, 138–139
  evaluation of, 133–136, 303–307
  population, 130, 134–135, 138–139
  random selection, 127–128
  single subject designs, 101–102
  testing of participant subgroups, 305–307
Extraneous variable, *see* Variable

F

F statistic (. . . ratio), *see* Analysis of variance
Factor, *see* Independent variable
Factor analysis, 53, 249–252
  confirmatory factor analysis, 249
  exploratory factor analysis, 53, 249–252
  principal axis factor analysis, 249
Factorial ANOVA, *see* Two factor ANOVA
Factorial design, ch. 28
  analysis of, 210–211
  classification of, 175
Factorial evidence for validity, *see* Measurement validity, internal structure *evidence*
Fixed effects model, 270
Frequency distribution, 41–43
Friedman two-way analysis of variance by
    ranks, 193

G

Gain score analysis, 218–219, 221
General design classifications, 103–110,
    175, 292

General linear model (GLM), 178–179,
    244–245
Generalizability theory, 48
Generalize, *see* External validity
Ghost author, *see* Publication
Glass's Δ, 268
Goodness of fit test, 232
Guest author, *see* Publication

H

Hedges' *g*, 185, 222, 268
Hierarchical multiple regression, 226–227
History threat, *see* Threats to internal validity
Homogeneity of variance, assumption of,
    180, 192, 210
Human research participants, 18–23
  Belmont report, *see* Ethical issues
  privacy, 21
  risks and benefits, 22–23
  voluntary informed consent, 19–21
Hypothesis, *see* Research questions or hypotheses
Hypothesis testing
  alternative hypothesis, 144–148, 153
  null hypothesis, 144–148, 152–154

I

Independence, assumption of, 180, 192,
    210
Independent samples, *see* Between groups
    designs
Independent variable, 32–33, 288–289
  active, 32–33, 288–289
  attribute, 33, 288–289
  causal inferences, 33
  factor, 107–110
  levels of, 34, 174–175, 289
  number of, 174–178, 289
Informed consent, *see* Voluntary informed
    consent
Institutional review board (IRB), 19–23
Instrument validity, *see* Measurement validity
Instrumentation threat, *see* Threats to internal validity
Intelligence test, *see* Aptitude test

Interaction effect
  disordinal, 213
  factorial designs, 211, 213–214
  mixed factorial designs, 219
  ordinal, 213
Interitem reliability, *see* Cronbach's alpha
    and Internal consistency reliability
Internal consistency reliability, 47
Internal validity, 113–121, 129–133,
    259–260, 298–301
  associational approach, 114–117, 120
  comparative approach, 114–115, 120
  control of extraneous variables, 116–120,
    130–132
  equivalence of groups on participant
    characteristics, 115–118, 130–133
  evaluation of, 131–133, 298–301, ch. 17
  quasi-experiments, 114–120
  randomized experiments, 114–115
  single subject designs, 101–102
Interrater (interobserver) reliability, 47–48
Interval scale, *see* Measurement
Intervention, *see* Treatment and Active in-
    dependent variable
Interview, 64–65
  face-to-face, 65
  in-depth, 65
  telephone, 65
Intraclass correlation coefficient (ICC), 48
Inverse relationship, *see* Correlation,
    coefficients
Item response theory, 48

K

Kappa statistic, 48
Kendall's Tau, 195, 199–200, 201
Kruskal–Wallis (one-way ANOVA), 186–187,
    221
Kurtosis, *see* Normal curve

L

Least significant difference (LSD) post hoc
    test, 185
Least squares fit, 227
Levels of a variable, 34, 289
Likert scales, 63–64, 253
Linear regression, *see* Bivariate regression

Logical positivist paradigm, *see* Positivist
    paradigm
Logistic regression analysis, 205, 226, 268,
    ch. 31
  classification table, 232
  goodness-of-fit test, 232
  odds ratio, 230–233
  risk ratio, 231
  stepwise logistic regression, 234

M

Main effect, 211–213
Manipulated variable, *see* Active independ-
    ent variable
Mann–Whitney *U* test, 186, 201, 221
  as post hoc test, 187
MANOVA, *see* Multivariate analysis of vari-
    ance
Masked review, *see* Peer review
Matching, 190
Maturation threat, *see* Threat to internal va-
    lidity
McNemar test, 193
Mean (also called arithmetic average), 41,
    see Descriptive statistics, central ten-
    dency
Mean square (MS), 184, 211
Measured variable, *see* Attribute independ-
    ent variable
Measurement, 36–43, 176
Measurement reliability, 44–49, 129–131,
    292–294
  assessment of, 45–48
  definition of, 44–45
  interrater reliability, 47–48
  parallel forms reliability, 46
  test–retest reliability, 45–46
Measurement reliability and statistics, 288,
    296–298
  appropriateness of interpretation, 297
  appropriateness of power, 297
  appropriateness of statistical techniques,
    297
  reliability of measures, 296–297
Measurement scales, *see* Measurement
Measurement validity, 50–58, 129–131, 138,
    292, 294–295
  content evidence, 52, 58
  construct validity, 53

Measurement validity *(cont.)*
  convergent and discriminant evidence, 55–58
  criterion-related evidence, 54–55
  evidence based on consequences, 56–58
  internal structure evidence, 53, 58
  relations to other variables, 53–58
  response process evidence, 52, 58
  validity generalization, 55–56, 58
Measurement validity of the constructs, 288, 301–303
  construct validity of the intervention, 301–303
  construct validity of the outcome, 302–303
Measures of central tendency, 41–43
  mean, 41, 43
  median, 41, 43
  mode, 42–43
Measures of variability, 42–43
  interquartile range, 42–43
  standard deviation, 42–43
Median, 41–43
Meta-analysis, x, 27, ch. 35
  effect sizes, 267–268
  fixed effects model, 270
  random effects model, 270
  weights, 269
Misconduct, *see* Scientific misconduct, Plagiarism, and Ethical issues
Mixed ANOVA, 219
  F values, 219
  interaction effect, 219
  pretest–posttest comparison group design, 219
Mixed designs, 104–110
  describing the design, 107–108
  pretest–posttest design, 107, ch. 29
Mode, 42–43
Multicollinearity, 225
Multiple baseline single subject designs, 97–98
  across behaviors, 97
  across settings, 97
  across participants, 97–98
Multiple regression analysis, 220, ch. 30
  beta weights, 226
  hierarchical multiple regression, 226–227
  least squares fit, 227
  multicollinearity, 225
  simultaneous multiple regression, 227
  stepwise regression, 227–228

Multivariate, *see* Complex associational analyses
Multivariate Analysis of Variance (MANOVA), 243

N

Naturalist paradigm, *see* Constructivist paradigm
Negative relationship, *see* Correlation
Nominal scale or variable, 36–38, 42–43
Nondirectional hypothesis, 144–145
Nonequivalent groups design, *see* Quasi-experimental designs
Nonexperimental, *see* Associational and Comparative research approaches
Nonparametric statistics, 186–187, 192–193, 195, 199–201, 204, 221, 239–240
  Cochran Q test, 239
  Cramer's V, 240
  Friedman two-way analysis of variance by ranks, 193
  Kendall's Tau, 195, 199–200, 201
  Kruskal–Wallis (one-way ANOVA), 186–187, 221
  Mann–Whitney *U* test, 186, 201, 221
  McNemar test, 193
  phi coefficient, 204
  Spearman rank order correlation (rho), 195, 199–200
  Wilcoxon signed ranks matched pairs test, 193
Nonprobability sampling, 125–128
  convenience, 125
  why common, 125–126
Normal curve, 38–43
  areas under, 39–41
  frequency distribution, 41–43
  kurtosis, 40
  shape, 39–43
  skewed, 40–43
  z scores, 39–40
Normal level of measurement, *see* Normally distributed variable
Normality, assumption of, 181, 192, 210
Normally distributed variable, 36–43
Null hypothesis
  significance testing (NHST), 144–148, ch. 21

Number needed to treat (NNT), 267, 274–275, 279

O

Observation, 60–61
  observer as participant, 61
Odds ratio, 162, 204–205, 230–233, 267, 274, 277–278
One group posttest only design, 82, 93
One group pretest–posttest design, 82–83, 93
One-way ANOVA, *see* Single factor ANOVA
Open-ended questions, 64–65
Operational definition, 32
Ordinal scale or level of measurement, 36–38, 41–43
Outcome variable, *see* Variable, dependent
Outliers, 41–42

P

p value, 155–156
Paired samples design, *see* Within subjects design
Paradigms, 11–12, 14–17
  qualitative paradigm, *see* Constructivist paradigm
  quantitative paradigm, *see* Positivist paradigm
Parallel forms reliability, 46
Parametric statistics, 176, 181–185, 190–192, 195–199, 210–214, 223–228, 229–235
  discriminant analysis, 233–234
  factorial ANOVA, 210–214
  bivariate regression, 223–224, 229
  logistic regression, 229–233
  multiple regression, 224–228
  Pearson product moment correlation (*r*), 195–199
  single factor ANOVA, 183–185
  single factor ANOVA with repeated measures, 191–192
  t test of independent samples or groups, 182–183
  t test for correlated or paired samples, 190–191

Participants, *see* Human research participants
Path analysis, 243–244
Pearson product moment correlation (*r*), 161, 195–199, 267, 274–276
  confidence intervals, 198
  effect size, 197–198, 267, 274–276
  r^2, 197
  statistical significance, 197
Peer review, 26–27, 307–308
Percentage agreement methods, 47–48
Personality inventory, *see* Standardized instruments
Phi coefficient, 204, 276
Plagiarism, 24–25
Poor quasi-experimental designs, 82–84, 86, 93
  one-group posttest-only design, 82, 93
  one group pretest–posttest design, 83, 93
  posttest only design with nonequivalent groups, 83–84, 93
Population, 123–128
  accessible, 123–124, 128
  theoretical or target, 123, 128
Population external validity, *see* External validity
Positivist paradigm, 11–12, 14–17
Post-hoc tests, 185, 187, 192–193, 213–214
  Mann–Whitney *U* following Kruskal–Wallis test, 187
  least significant difference (LSD) post hoc test, 185
  Scheffé post hoc test, 185
  Tukey HSD honestly significant difference (HSD) post hoc test, 185
  Wilcoxon following a Friedman two-way ANOVA, 193
Posttest only control group design, 89–90, 93
Posttest only design with nonequivalent groups, *see* Poor quasi-experimental designs
Power (. . . of a statistic)
  appropriateness of power, 297
  evaluating power, 149–150, 154, 297
Practical significance or importance, *see* Clinical significance
Preexperimental designs, *see* Poor quasi-experimental designs
Predictive evidence for validity, 54, 58

Predictor variable, 224, *see also* Independent variable

Pretest–posttest comparison group design, analysis of, ch. 29
  analysis of covariance approach, 219–220
  effect size, 222
  gain score analysis, 218–219, 221
  mixed ANOVA analysis, 219
  multiple linear regression approach, 220
  nonparametric analysis, 221
  recommendations, 220

Pretest–posttest nonequivalent comparison group designs, *see also* Quasi-experimental designs
  analysis, 221
  moderate strength quasi-experimental designs, 85–86
  poor quasi-experimental designs, 82–84, 86
  strong quasi-experimental designs, 85–86
  weak quasi-experimental designs, 84–86

Principle Components Analysis, 249–250, 252–253

Probability of a better outcome, *see* Area under the curve

Probability sampling, 124–128
  cluster, 125
  simple random, 124
  stratified random, 125
  systematic random, 124–125

Publication
  authorship, 26
  multiple, 25
  plagiarism, 24–25

Purposive sampling, *see* Nonprobability sampling

Q

Qualitative research, 11–13
  data analysis, 12
  data and data collection, 12–13, 60–61, 65

Quantitative research, *see* Positivist paradigm

Quasi-experimental approach, 3–7, 70–73, *see also* Quasi-experimental designs

Quasi-experimental designs, 81–88, 93
  evaluation of, 315–317
  poor designs, 82–84, 93

pretest–posttest designs, 84–86, 93
time series designs, 86–88, 93

Questionnaire, 64–65

Quota sampling, *see* Nonprobability sampling

R

r (Pearson product moment correlation coefficient), 161, 195–199, 267, 274–276

r^2, 197, 224

R, 224–226

R^2, 225–226

Random assignment of participants to groups, 89–94

Random assignment of treatments to groups, 85–86

Random selection or sampling, 124–125, 127, *see also* Probability sampling

Random effects model, 270

Randomized experimental designs, 3–7, 70–73, 89–94, 313–315
  crossover design, 92–93
  evaluation of, 313–315
  posttest only control group design, 89–90, 93
  pretest–posttest control group design, 90–91, 93
  randomized experimental design with matching, 91–93
  within subjects randomized design, 92–93

Randomized experimental research approach, *see* Randomized experimental designs

Rating scale, 63–64

Ratio scale, *see* Measurement

Regression threat, *see* Threats to internal validity

Related samples design, *see* Within subjects design

Relative risk, 204, *see also* Risk ratio

Relative risk reduction, 162, 274, 278

Reliability, *see* Measurement reliability

Repeated measures designs, *see* Within subjects designs

Repeated measures independent variable, *see* Within subjects designs

Repeated testing threat, *see* Threats to internal validity

Representative sampling, *see* Sampling
Research
    definition of, 9
    dimensions and dichotomies, 10–13
        laboratory vs. field, 10–11
        qualitative vs. quantitative, 11–12
        self-report vs. observation, 11
        theoretical vs. applied, 10
    purposes of, 9–10
Research approach, 3–5, 69–75, 173–174,
        290
    associational, 4–8, 71–72, 74
    comparative, 4–8, 71–73
    descriptive, 4, 71–72, 74–75
    nonexperimental, 4–8, 71
    quasi-experimental, 3–7, 70–73
    randomized experimental, 3–6, 70–72
Research problem, 31
Research questions or hypotheses, 76–80,
        173–174, 177–178, 236–241, 290
    associational, 76–80, 174, 178
    basic vs. complex, 78–80, 177–178
    descriptive, 76–77, 79
    difference, 76–80, 173, 177–178
Research reliability, 130, *see also* Meta-
        analysis
Research replication, 130, *see also* Meta-
        analysis
Research validity, xi, 6, 129–139, 295–307
    external validity, ch. 18, 133–136, 303–307
    evaluation form, Appendices A & B
    internal validity, ch. 17, 131–133, 298–301
    measurement reliability and statistics,
        296–297
    measurement validity of the constructs,
        301–303
    versus measurement validity, 129–131
Response rate, 124, *see also* Actual sample
Restricted range of scores, 200
Reversal single subject designs, 95–97
    flexibility, 97
Risk, *see* Human research participants
Risk difference, 162, 204, 274, 278–279
Risk potency measures, 162, 274, 276–280
Risk ratio, 162, 231, 267, 274, 278

S

Sample, 122, *see also* Selected sample and
        Actual sample
Sample size, 126

Sample statistic, 143
Sampling, 122–128
    accessible population, 123–128
    actual sample, 123–128
    nonprobability, 125–128
    population external validity, 126–128
    probability sampling, 124–128
    representative sample, 124, 127–128
    sample size, 126
    selected sample, 123–128
    steps in, 123–124
    theoretical or target population, 123–128
Sampling design, 124, *see also* Sampling
Sampling frame, *see* Accessible population
Scales of measurement, *see* Measurement
Scheffé post hoc test, 185
Scientific misconduct, 28
Selected sample, 124–128
Selection of statistics, ch. 23, ch. 32
    basic associational, 178, 240
    basic difference, 177, 239
    complex associational, 178, 242
    complex difference, 178, 242
    descriptive, 40–43
    inferential, 176–178, ch. 32
Selection threat, *see* Threats to internal va-
        lidity
Self assignment or selection, 84
Self-report measures, 59, 64–65
Shared variance, 197, 224
Significance level (alpha level), 150,
        154–155
Significance testing (NHST), x, 144–148,
        ch. 21
    multiple significance tests, 155
Simple main effects, 213–214
Simple random sampling, *see* Random se-
        lection and Probability sampling
Simultaneous multiple regression, 227
Single factor ANOVA, 183–185
    effect size, 185
    interpretation of F value, 185
    mean square between groups, 184
    mean square within subjects, 184
    post-hoc test, 185
    source table, 184
    sums of squares (SS), 184
Single factor ANOVA with repeated meas-
        ures, 191–192
    effect-size, 192
    post-hoc tests, 192

Single factor between groups designs, ch. 24, 27
chi-square test for independence, ch. 27
Kruskal–Wallis (one-way ANOVA), 186–187
nonparametric statistics, 186–187
Mann–Whitney U test, 186
single factor ANOVA, 183–184
t test of independent samples or groups, 182–183
Single factor designs
between groups designs, ch. 24, 27
continuous single factor designs, ch. 26
within subjects designs, ch. 25
Single factor within subjects designs, ch. 25
carryover effects, 189–190
Cochran Q test, 239
degrees of freedom (df), 190
Friedman two-way analysis of variance by ranks, 193
McNemar test, 193
post-hoc test, 192
single factor ANOVA with repeated measures, 191–192
t test for correlated or paired samples, 190–191
Wilcoxon signed ranks matched pairs test, 193
Single subject designs, ch. 15
alternating treatment designs, 98–99
evaluation of validity, 101–102
level, 100
methods of measurement, 99–100
measurement periods, 99–100
multiple baseline designs, 97–98
reversal designs, 95–97
slope, 100
statistical analysis, 100–101
trend, 100
visual analysis, 100
Source table (source of variance table)
single factor ANOVA, 184–185
two factor ANOVA, 210–211
Spearman rank order correlation (rho), 195, 199–200, *see also* Correlation and Pearson product moment correlation
Sphericity, assumption of, 192
Standard deviation, 42–43
Standard normal curve, 38–40
Standardized instruments, 61–64
achievement tests, 62
aptitude tests, 62

attitude scales, 63
Mental Measurements Yearbook, 61
personality inventories, 63
Statistical assumptions, 176, 180–181, 192, 210
Statistical conclusion validity, *see* Measurement reliability and statistics
Statistical regression threat, *see* Threats to internal validity
Statistical significance, 159, 182–183, 197, 273
Stepwise regression, 227–228
Stratified random sampling, 125
Strong quasi-experimental designs, 85–86
Structural equation modeling (SEM), 244
Subjects, *see* Human research participants
Summated rating scale, 63–64, 253–254
Sums of squares (SS), 184, 210–211
Survey population, *see* Accessible population
Survey research, 64–65, *see also* Questionnaire and Interview
Systematic random sampling, 124–125

T

t test for correlated or paired samples, 190–191
effect size, 191
t test for independent samples or groups, 182
degrees of freedom (df), 183
effect size, 183
homogeneity of variance assumption, 180
independence assumption, 180
multiple t tests, 183–184
normality assumption, 181
Testing, 61–64, *see also* Standardized instruments
Testing threat, *see* Threats to internal validity
Test–retest reliability, 45–46
Test validity, *see* Measurement validity
Theoretical or target population, 123–128, 145, *see also* Sampling
Threats to internal validity, 114, 116–120
Time series designs, 86–88, 93
multiple group time-series designs, 87, 93
single group time-series designs, 87–88, 93

Treatment, *see* Active independent variable
True experimental designs, *see* Randomized experimental designs
Tukey honestly significant difference (HSD) post hoc test, 185
Two factor (two-way) ANOVA, 210–214
    effect size, 211–212
    main effect, 211–213
    interaction effect, 211, 213–214
    mean squares (MS), 211
    simple main effects, 213–214
    sums of squares (SS), 210–211
Two by two contingency tables, 206–207
Type I error, 148–149, 228
Type II error, 148–149

U

Unordered variable, *see* Nominal variable
Unrepresentative sample, *see* Nonprobability sample

V

Validity, *see* Measurement validity and Research validity
Values, *see* Variable, levels of
Variable, 3, 5–7, 31–43, 69–75, 288–290
    definition of, 31–32
    dependent, 33–34, 175, 289–290
    extraneous, 34

    independent, 3, 32–33, 174–175, 288–289
    levels of, 34
    measurement of, 36–43
    sets of variables, 35
Variability, 42–43
Voluntary informed consent, 19–21
    comprehension, 20
    information, 20
    voluntariness, 20–21

W

Wait-list comparison group design, 85
Wald statistic, 231
Weak quasi-experimental designs, *see* Pretest–posttest nonequivalent comparison group designs
Weights, 269
Wilcoxon signed ranks matched pairs test, 193
    as post-hoc test, 193
Within subjects designs, 104, 106–110, 175, ch. 25
Within subjects independent variable, *see* Within subjects designs
Within subjects randomized experimental design, 92–93
Within subjects variance, 189

Z

z score, 225